THE POLITICS OF MODERNIZATION

THE POLITICS
OF
MODERNIZATION

DAVID E. APTER

THE UNIVERSITY OF CHICAGO PRESS
CHICAGO AND LONDON

TO MARION J. LEVY, JR.

This book is also available in a clothbound edition from
THE UNIVERSITY OF CHICAGO PRESS

THE UNIVERSITY OF CHICAGO PRESS, CHICAGO 60637
The University of Chicago Press, Ltd., London W.C. 1

FOREWORD, 1967

This reissue of *The Politics of Modernization* presents me with the opportunity to respond to a few of the points raised by critics. The present work, which has stimulated considerable discussion and controversy, is not, of course, intended as a tightly knit treatise, but rather a step towards that end. For this reason it is essential to correct flaws in conceptualization. The next step will be a more precise analytical statement of underlying principles which will take into account objections raised over the analytical looseness of the framework.[1] These include the use of the term modernization, the analytical status of the models — particularly whether they are deductive or ideal types — and finally, the ambiguity of the independent variables. I will comment briefly on each of these points.

The concept of modernization employed here is quite straightforward. What I mean by modernization is the spread of roles which, functionally linked and organized in industrial settings, make their appearance in systems lacking an industrial infrastructure. We can therefore compare societies in terms of degrees of modernization by assessing the spread and proliferation of modernizing roles. The task is to evaluate the political problems posed by their lack of integration. My attempt to describe the political and administrative consequences of such malintegration blurred this emphasis. What was intended as description emerged as definition. This accounts for at least some of the difficulties.

A second criticism deals with the analytical state of the models. The problem does not arise from faulty conceptualization but

[1] At the same time, in collaboration with colleagues on The Politics of Modernization Project of the Institute of International Studies, we are testing these concepts operationally in a comparison of data gathered in West Africa and Latin America on early and late stage modernization.

v

rather from the difference between the explication and the application of a model. The types employed here are propositional, deriving from a generalized theory of choice based on normative, structural, and behavioral dimensions. The first two variables, normative and structural, are independent; behavior is dependent. These normative and structural variables were adapted to fit the case of political systems which embody political choice and thereby determine the range of possible political behaviors. It should be clear then that we are not dealing with an ideal type in the usual sense, that is, empirically based characteristics generalized from a sample of concrete units. However, the model is applied in the manner of an ideal type. Real systems (or concrete units) are compared with the models to identify hypotheses about systems tendencies which can then be investigated empirically.

This general formulation should not be confused with the set of dependent and independent variables used directly in comparison. Although our ultimate question concerns behavior as determined by political systems within the theory of choice, the question which remains is: How do political systems change? To determine this requires a different and more operational set of independent and dependent variables. Without going into the philosophical and empirical problems here, let me simply say that it is the relationship between coercion and information which affects changes from one political systems type to another. If I were writing this book today, the coercion-information hypothesis would occupy a more central place in the analysis. I would reformulate the political system so that coercion and information would be independent variables, with structural variables intervening and behavioral variables dependent.

I have profited greatly from discussions on these and other points with my associates in The Politics of Modernization Project as well as with scholars at universities both here and abroad. Some of my views have changed substantially as a result, and these I intend to discuss more fully in a forthcoming book, *A Structural Theory of Politics.*

D.E.A.

PREFACE

Preoccupation with questions of modernization is not new. It began in Europe in the latter part of the nineteenth century after the consequences of industrialization had become apparent. So altered was the character of Western society that it became a model (or at least a standard) for the comparison of countries elsewhere. Today's emphasis is mainly on the modernization of new nations and their development of national forms of polity, the objects of which are to increase the social product with fair shares for all. Successful models now include Japan and the Soviet Union.

The modernizing polities exhibit such wide differences that attempts to study them require both new methods and fresh ideas. We do not yet have very useful schemes of classification or comparison and therefore cannot make controlled analyses of such complex processes. One form that has recently gained considerable currency — functional method — is somewhat useful because of its two central emphases relating to comparison. The first is concerned with how systems change; the second seeks to find the general meanings in particular modes of activity, regardless of their first appearance of uniqueness.

I want to apply this method (with its emphases) to the comparative study of modernizing countries. To do this, my first object is to present a typology of governmental forms and some theories about how they change, meanwhile demonstrating the relationship between these forms and several functional categories. I regard this as a step toward a more applied form of structural-functional requisite analysis, suitable for political analysis, which follows in a tradition associated first with Talcott Parsons and, more immediately for me, with Marion J. Levy, Jr. A second volume is planned that will present material on several West African countries with which I have been working for the past fifteen years, both alone and in conjunction with colleagues in the West African Comparative Analysis Project. The African materials will deal with countries in the first, or primary, stages of the modernization process, including the change from dependence to independence and the formation of a new polity (having as its object the intensification of modernization efforts). Presently underway is research on several Latin American countries that illustrate the other end of the modernization continuum, that is, old countries that have gone as far as they can toward modernization and now need to industrialize.

It is always particularly interesting to select research examples that represent different stages of such processes as modernization. The questions they raise are rich with variety: Why are some countries able to remain stable in their political forms while changing their social structures? Why do so many other countries need to proclaim that their modernization processes are really revolutionary struggles, when on closer inspection they turn out to be more revolutionary in rhetoric than in practice?

The events are confusing. Our research ideas are similarly untidy. Quite often we are as much imprisoned in our concepts as the political leader is in his rhetoric. Awareness of this has caused some writers to suggest that analysis of contemporary events can rarely be right and often may be harmfully wrong. Scholars assiduously caution one another against overzealous generalization, some even suggesting that our lack of comprehension of the revolutionary life in new nations is so great that present research can add little of value to understanding.[1]

---

[1] For example, in the June, 1961, issue of *Encounter*, one of the most gifted scholars in African studies, Thomas Hodgkin, writes: "Our profound

Misinterpretations and failures to understand the patterns of movement and change are the errors we try to correct through constant research and analysis. Our thoughts about new nations need not be based only on superficial knowledge any more than we need remain ethnocentric in our views. What is required is a new kind of knowledge to describe connections between events different from those to which we are accustomed.

Even if the level of our theorizing remains primitive and lamentably short of our needs and aspirations, there are other reasons to continue studying the modernizing nations. So exciting are they and so genuine are our enthusiasms for them, that to hide our research efforts in a closet would deprive others of highly interesting material. In an earlier day, a scholar feared to put his thoughts on paper until he had perfected them. But our situation is different. The academic community is world wide. It is largely through our writing that we can communicate and exchange our views with colleagues elsewhere. The dialogue is important, if only to curtail ill-formed and meretricious scholarship. To sustain communication between scholars before ideas have hardened and become fixed, is, after all, one of the advantages of the modern world.

My approach is to organize some general questions, formulate hypotheses, locate events for analysis, and gather data where I can find it, in the "field" and in libraries. Rarely is the result a finished product. Material collected in these different ways is so rich and situations so complex that I hesitate to commit myself to a particular set of rigid categories. Any attempt to make ideas consistent, however, involves some effort toward formalization. Inevitably, the result is a constantly evolving set of concepts, and

---

ignorance of African history, our lack of comprehension of African attitudes to the contemporary situation, our remoteness from the ideas of revolutionary democracy, the distortions in thinking produced by our colonial mythology — these, I would suggest, are good reasons for doubting whether we are likely to have any sensible contributions to make to a discussion of the direction of social and political change in post-colonial Africa. Such questions are best left to Africans."

even before the ink is dry on a page, they may have to be refined as more economical ways of working, or more suitable alternatives, present themselves.

Here, then, are theories for burning. By this I do not mean anything very modest but only that a subject as interesting as modernization is bound to be too complex for any theory to remain suitable for long. Those produced at this stage in the development of the social sciences must remain expendable. Contributions made now should be seen only as stepping stones to more scientific theories and more efficient research procedures. It is only in this spirit that one ought to take work of the present kind seriously. To enlarge our sensitivities a little bit, clarify our propositions, and perhaps map a few areas of our ignorance more fully are the tasks at hand.

I will attempt such mapping in three stages. First (since I believe that politics begins with models that are primarily normative and secondarily empirical), I will identify some moral-political problems. The second task is to periodize change in systems, that is, identify the boundaries of a system and demarcate the nature of the subsystems within it. Third, I will abstract basic structural properties of the system and its relevant subsystems. Involved in this task are normative, structural, and behavioral considerations that, when applied to data, will help in the comparative analysis of modernization.

The choice of modernization as a focus of interest is not dictated by reasons of topicality. Rather, modernization allows particular applications of general theories. Asking functional questions about the instruments of government (rather than attempting to discover the significance of a particular institution itself) should allow examination of the differing political modes by which developmental choices are made and political styles are formed. Development we see as a particular form of social change, with modernization a special case of development. Industrialization, the most limited case of all, remains the most significant.[2]

[2] For a definition of modernization, see chapter ii.

Several consequences of modernization ought to be mentioned in advance of our main discussion. Individuals may feel the loss of their moral personalities. Familiar communities are twisted out of shape. The future appears as a sea of adventures, not all of them pleasant. Modernizing societies look for new forms of mastery, a new certainty to replace that which has been lost through change. Even though all modern societies participate in some degree in the dialogue of plans and investment, of entrepreneurship and skills, and of educational and training controls, and in ideologies of engineering and science, individuals themselves are not always ready to relinquish older forms of knowledge for a journey into the unknown, unless they recognize that uncertainty is the price they must pay in the exchange of a past for a future. And this has always been true — ever since those first demands for political participation and equality in India, Ceylon, and Burma and later in Indonesia, the west coast of Africa, and throughout the African continent. Since then the pace of political innovation has accelerated and today is spreading to Latin America.

All modernizing societies are in the process of transition. That is our subject matter. All are in the process of becoming. Becoming "what" is the puzzle. Such transition is from a condition that is not modern to a condition that though modern is not necessarily industrial. Moreover, we can isolate, as a set of abstractions, some qualities that are functionally critical for premodern systems and others that are functionally critical for modern ones; but real systems rarely change by rejecting the one in favor of the other. This lack of a clean break supplies some of the most confusing data that we are obliged to consider.

It is difficult to make comparative studies in systems undergoing rapid transition (because the outlines of each system are changing and their interconnections are therefore hard to grasp). Why is it, then, that so many comparative studies are made on transitional systems? There are certain advantages despite the difficulties. "Promontory situations" that thrust themselves sharply into the mind of the observer when the blandness of stability has been broken overpower the observer by their obviousness. Such obviousness is not to be taken lightly, for there is a danger that the obvious may disguise more important and subtle issues. (I do not see any way around such difficulties.) We can say, though, that such dramatic conditions open new possibilities of choice. This is particularly true in the case of modernization. In its early stages the process may be disorderly; carelessness in the organization of affairs often obtains in an open-ended choice situation. And personalities may count for much. Sometimes one can even trace the origin of a reordering of social relationships to a few individuals. These early stages are periods of maximum social freedom but also of naïveté — the naïveté not of the absurd but of the innocent. Such freedom is an illusion; merely a preface to the difficult and disciplined political periods that follow. But no matter; these times of modernization are also times of experimentation. Exciting and even epic, they have a certain refreshing cheerfulness despite tragic undertones. When cherished institutions are swept away and beliefs come to be regarded as outmoded, a sense of foreboding for some has its counterpart in a sense of adventure for others. Time becomes instrumental. Immortality and the belief in it tends to disappear under the hammer blows of modern thought, perhaps to be replaced by belief in society or, lacking that, in activities whereby individuals aim to realize potentialities of self and personality.

The effect of these conditions during modernization is an exaggerated emphasis on power. Power is both compensation for weakness and disintegration and potentiality leading to fulfilment. The "heroic" leaders of developing countries personify this in their desire to shine even with a brilliance that will someday explode. Here, at last, is consequence! Perhaps most exciting of all, the modernization process produces a powerful urge to individuality, leadership, and ruthlessness at a time when complex industrial societies are wrestling with the problem of the loss of indi-

viduality, with alienation and feelings of individual superfluousness.

For all that, we ought not ignore the negative side. Old forms
of belief and social practices endowed with sanctity are often dismissed with cruelty and carelessness by those in positions of
power. A cheerful confrontation of the future may easily be replaced by deep-rooted despair. For many, modernization is like
hurtling through a tunnel at frightening speed without knowing
what waits at the other end. Fear creates serious political problems. Hence, it is not surprising that in modernizing societies the
mood fluctuates between an exciting sense of new freedom and
hope in the future and a fearful, cynical, or opportunistic view.

But surely political life cannot consist only of heroic periods.
If the situations we describe have a kind of unreality about them, it
is partly because such illusions are important to human society.
These give us the capacity for optimism about what lies ahead,
fraternalism that transcends pettiness, and a feeling for momen-
tary purposes in history. Such periods of illusion are coincidental
with relatively free choice, the consequences of which can restrict and congeal freedom or open up new opportunities for it.
That is why, during the formative modernizing years, men are
given exceptional opportunities to be creative, to exercise their
imaginations in order to find alternatives that will help resolve
their difficulties. And, should it be that men make their own destinies only superficially — in that political leaders are always
hemmed in by practical restrictions — and that times that appear
from a distance to be epic are necessarily ugly and cruel close at
hand, it is all the more pressing to attempt to understand these
events.

Hence, the theme of this book. Despite an emphasis on methods
of comparing governments and studying their political growth and
adaptation, analysis begins with moral content. My contention is
that, in political life, that which is significant (both from the
standpoint of the observer and from that of the participant) can

only be understood in moral terms. In this I hold a point of view similar to the one Naegele ascribes to Durkheim:

> Durkheim dignifies society as a moral phenomenon standing stubbornly beside nature; that must be understood in its impersonal "thereness," much as though it were a collection of related things; and that must also be perceived for what it is not — a coherence of representations coercing individuals by virtue of their ability to fuse what is obligatory with what is desirable, a fusion analogous to the double face of the sacred.[3]

There is a difference between scientific work in the social sciences and in the natural sciences — not a difference of method or technique, since this is rapidly disappearing as the social sciences become more quantitative, but a difference in moral point of view, as related to persons, their obligations, and their desires. This constitutes the uniqueness of social science. Even if we could account for all variables in social conduct, we would still have to deal with the *meaning* of social acts. The consequences of that meaning and the inferences to be drawn from it form the basis of political analysis. Does this mean that beyond science lies moral intuition, that Humpty Dumpty of human experience? I believe the answer is yes. Knowledge of experience requires the total commitment of all our senses.

Thus the overriding purpose of this book is to bring together some general methods and their moral implications. These are extremely difficult factors to integrate and the emphasis on the one or the other will be evident throughout this book. It should be remembered that just as we pull apart reality for some analytical reason, so we put it together again as it suits our needs. Even Toynbee (whom no one could accuse of "scientism") has argued, in the final volume of his massive history, that

> we cannot think about the Universe without assuming that it is articulated; and, at the same time, we cannot defend

---

[3] Kaspar D. Naegele, "Some Observations on the Scope of Sociological Analysis," in *Theories of Society*, ed. Talcott Parsons, Edward Shils, K. D.

the articulations that we find, or make, in it against the charge that these are artificial and arbitrary, that they do not correspond to anything in the structure of Reality, or that, even if they do, they are irrelevant to the particular mental purpose for which we have resorted to them. It can always be shown that they break up something that is indivisible and let slip something that is essential. Yet, without mentally articulating the Universe, we, ourselves, cannot be articulate — cannot, that is, either think or will. And we cannot go on thinking or willing if we regain the unity of the mystical experience. So we have to dissect — and, in dissecting, misrepresent Reality in order to be able to apprehend Reality sufficiently to be able to act and live in the light of the truth as far as we can discern it. Our inability to apprehend Reality completely is, of course, not surprising. It is a paradox that one part of a whole should be able to distinguish itself from the rest and should then be able to achieve even a partial apprehension of the whole, including itself. This feat is miraculous, however imperfect.[4]

An idea is an experiment. It is a way of finding meaning in an experience and relationship in an act. Only a few ideas turn out well. We are still at that stage when, in order to understand error, we experiment with methods of trial. If out of such experiments we get a better understanding of the implications of change, development, modernization, and industrialization, then our efforts are justified.

I owe many of my ideas to the discussions and deliberations of colleagues in three separate groups to which it has been my good fortune to belong over the years, all of which have been generously supported by the Carnegie Foundation. The first, and most continuous, association has been with the West African Comparative Analysis Project. Many of my initial ideas were shaped by our joint work and consultations, which have been enriching and exciting experiences. The members of the project, L. Gray Cowan,

Naegele, and Jesse Pitts (New York: Free Press of Glencoe, Inc., 1961), Vol. I, p. 16.

[4] Arnold Toynbee, *Reconsiderations*, Vol. XII of *A Study of History* (Oxford: Oxford University Press, 1961), pp. 9–10.

Robert Lystad, and most particularly, James S. Coleman, are all collaborators in this work; they not only have kindly consented to my writing it up in this fashion but have provided detailed corrections as well.

Many of the views expressed in this book, particularly those pertaining to ideology and political religion, were first stimulated by the Committee for the Comparative Study of New Nations at the University of Chicago. Three colleagues there — Edward Shils, Clifford Geertz, and Lloyd Fallers — created an environment of such exceptional intellectual discourse that, despite the differences in our disciplines, there prevailed an unusual degree of shared enthusiasm for the comparative study of new nations.

The third group, the Carnegie Group in Comparative Development at the University of California, which contains a scholarly group of rare brilliance and deep interest in the general problems of development, continues to be a constant source of ideas and of criticisms as well. To Reinhard Bendix, Ernst Haas, Harvey Leibenstein, S. M. Lipset, Henry Rosovsky, Neil Smelser, and others, I owe gratitude for research and assistance as well as good collegial discussions.

I am also grateful to Rupert Emerson, Ivan Vallier, José Nun, and Miss Magali Sarfatti, of Harvard, Columbia, the University of Buenos Aires, and the Institute of International Studies at Berkeley, respectively, who have read and commented on the manuscript, and to Hortense Powdermaker, who has made many helpful comments on chapter iii.

I would also like to thank the staffs of the Institutes of International Studies and Industrial Relations and particularly their directors, S. M. Lipset and Lloyd Ulman, for their support in this work. Mrs. Anne Firth Murray has given invaluable editorial assistance. Mrs. Gloria Mims, Miss Judy Cowman, and Mrs. Beatrice Tallent have been unfailingly cheerful in typing innumerable drafts of this manuscript.

DAVID E. APTER

Institute of International Studies
University of California, Berkeley

CONTENTS

LIST OF FIGURES

I

TOWARD A THEORY
OF MODERNIZATION

Camus makes Sisyphus his hero. Sisyphus, returning again and
again to roll his rock up the hill, may appear absurd. Yet on each
occasion he is happy. How odd that seems! And how like our own
times. The work of modernization is the burden of this age. It is
our rock. It is an objective that is not confined to a single place
or region, to a particular country or class, or to a privileged group
of people. Modernization, and the desire for it, reaches around the
world. No matter how difficult the labor, or even, at times, how
fruitless, the rock is shouldered once again, eagerly and with hope.
Perhaps it is the element of hope that allows Camus to conclude
his essay on the Greek myth with the words, "One must imagine
Sisyphus happy." [1]

Modernization is a special kind of hope. Embodied within it are
all the past revolutions of history and all the supreme human
desires. The modernization revolution is epic in its scale and moral
in its significance. Its consequences may be frightening. Any goal
that is so desperately desired creates political power, and this
force may not always be used wisely or well. Whatever direction
it may take, the struggle to modernize is what has given meaning
to our generation. It tests our cherished institutions and our be-

[1] Albert Camus, *The Myth of Sisyphus* (New York: Random House,
Vintage Books, 1955), p. 91.

1

liefs. It puts our country in the marketplace of ideas and ideologies. So compelling a force has it become that we are forced to ask new questions of our own institutions. Each country, whether modernized or modernizing, stands in both judgment and fear of the results. Our own society is no exception. Democratic representative government is clearly an appropriate means by which highly complex and advanced industrial societies have solved serious and perplexing social and moral problems. It has been a dramatic achievement in the West to devise suitable mechanisms for resolving the twin political problems that all governments encounter: orderly change and peaceful succession in office. Much of the study of Western government has been concerned with how to improve these mechanisms. Only recently have social scientists, and more particularly students of politics, directed their attention to similar problems in modernizing societies. Most of such studies, however, have accepted the point of view that representative government, with a few alterations in form and accommodations in spirit, is the most suitable form for all societies.

Events have clearly challenged this assumption. Democratic institutions, as we know them, have undergone such radical transformations in most modernizing societies that it would be sheer blindness on our part not to recognize that they have become something else. Yet how should we regard such countries as Indonesia or Egypt, Ghana or Tanzania? Or, for that matter, India, where the spirit of representative government remains embedded in a Congress party that dwarfs and overwhelms its opposition? There is no comfortable answer. What we are witnessing in the world today is a range of accommodated political systems. Even the toughest of them is weak. Even the most monolithic in form tends to be divided in its practices and diluted in its ideas. Few are totalitarian. Almost all are populist and, in a real sense, mainly *pre*democratic rather than *anti*democratic.

Such systems require both sympathy and understanding. The language of politics needs to be adjusted in part to account for them. All lie somewhere between familiar extreme categories of political forms. To approach such societies as predemocratic allows us to view certain institutions of coercion as perhaps necessary to the organization and integration of a modernizing community. We need to confront the possibility that representative institutions may fail to work in most modernizing societies and therefore be discredited. The preoccupation of political studies with the strengthening of democratic practices has obscured the need for an examination of the role of predemocratic forms of government, which, as a result, has received little attention. The politics of modernization requires us to examine the uses of predemocratic and nondemocratic institutions so that we can make a realistic appraisal of those structural principles likely to lead to representative government.[2]

The dynamic aspect of modernization for the study of politics can be expressed in the general proposition that modernization is a process of increasing complexity in human affairs within which the polity must act. This is why it creates severe political problems. Politics becomes, in large measure, the business of coping with role differentiation while integrating organizational structures. Political actions that arise from such increasing complexity, however, are not pure responses by political leaders outside a

[2] That is the long-range object of the research undertaken here. Indeed, it may even be premature to discuss topics for research or to formulate research strategies about politics in modernizing societies until these broader issues have been made more explicit. In a subsequent volume I plan to offer empirical evidence for the ideas suggested here. The empirical work that will follow this volume will employ data from both West Africa and Latin America, gathered around the following four structural variables, which are not dealt with here:

1. *Equality*: Is there an increase or decrease in equality during modernization in relation to different political forms?

2. *Role distribution*: What is the distribution of modernized roles in the system?

3. *Rates of economic growth*: What are the comparative rates of economic growth, and what are the mechanisms of planning?

4. *Degree of stability*: What is the relationship between stability and growth? How much coercion is required?

These four variables become meaningful for political theory only in the context of very important political issues. It is necessary to examine these larger issues before undertaking research on the variables themselves.

political context. The question is, what is the political context? In the sense in which the phrase is used here, it refers to the particular arrangements by which government exercises authority. As these structures change, so will political responses, and as political responses change, so will structures.

The translation of general approaches in systems theory into an empirical study of modernization is itself a major problem of research. It involves, first, determining the level of reality to be observed and, second, relating the formal system to a set of empirical categories.[3] These are arbitrary decisions, but the research enterprise itself depends on them. Here we will consider "reality" in terms of the ways in which people identify themselves and achieve and express emotional bonds. This is expressed symbolically in the literature and art of a group of people, in their ideology, and in their religious forms of expression. Moreover, such bonds exist in a common-sense world in which everyday events are translatable into abstract forms, for motive and meaning, in much the same way that abstract and geometrical designs may express shared symbolic values in such folk arts as pottery or weaving.

But there are other levels of reality. One common level in the post-Marxian tradition is social stratification. For observers trained in the Western tradition and concerned with problems of modern industrial society, a useful way to order social and political relations for purposes of comparison is through the study of stratification. Not only does this imply sets of positions in a hierarchical arrangement and an examination of the elite-mass relationships that result from such a hierarchy, but it also leads to the differentiation of strata in terms of interests and thus implies a theory of motivation — for example, that people are socially aware and upwardly mobile. Hence, competitive mobility becomes the motive of politics.

[3] See A. Schuetz, "On Multiple Realities," *Philosophy and Phenomenological Research*, V (June, 1945).

This view may serve to exclude an equally valid conception of the community as a reinforcing set of cohesive roles in which the meaning of the self is determined by the collectivity rather than by the hierarchical arrangement of roles. For example, when one examines a Latin American community after studying North American urban society, it makes sense to compare hierarchical relations with a view to discovering how much access and mobility exist. This is a useful comparative approach and a common one. But when one examines a Latin American community after studying African societies, one is inclined to seek some underlying principle of coherence as well. What are the core roles that constitute the meaningful center of the community? How do departures from the meaningful center affirm or deny the central values of the society? This kind of study requires more of an anthropological approach, an abstraction (in the range of reality) from a set of segregated roles, less on the basis of hierarchy than on the basis of meaningfulness (for example, kinship). Such a study can stress aspects of roles that help reveal the stability of a system no matter how much change is under way.

Personal meaning and social meaning; the rhythm and pace of social activity; the roles of the misfit and the innovator; the hierarchy of power and prestige; concern with interpersonal associations, political ideology, religion — each of these implies a different pattern of desire, motive, and choice. Knowledge of these patterns lies between that revealed by structural and behavioral analyses of any given social system. For these meanings and levels of reality we need to screen individuals in their roles, identify congeries of roles in which individuals act, understand the mechanisms by means of which the regulation of roles takes place, and be aware of the symbols by which unities and disunities in roles are articulated.

Perhaps the most important consequence of the study of modernization is that it brings us back to the search for first principles. By this I mean that it requires the unity of moral and analytical modes of thought. Not the study of modernization alone, of course; the rapid-fire developments in social theory and the breakthroughs in the biological sciences, not to speak of the retreat of philosophy into linguistics, have combined to render us philosophically defenseless and muddled. The two most characteristic responses to this state of affairs on the meeting ground between social theory and philosophy have been, first, Marxism, with its insistence on the material plane of reality (which involves the unfolding of historical necessity and the obliteration of the idea of freedom and which can only be genuinely "known" through action), and a second response that does not have a convenient name. The latter involves theories of choice that arise from the analysis of alternative situations in normative, structural, and behavioral terms. This second view depends on a probabilistic rather than a deterministic universe, and its central principle is that there is a relationship between freedom and choosing and that the understanding of this relationship is the object of social analysis. Freedom, in such a view, lies in the critical awareness by the chooser of both the moral and the material consequences of choice.

If the Marxian point of view seems faintly old-fashioned as a philosophy, as an ideology it has force and freshness, especially for those living in developing areas. One reason for this is Marxism's insistence on an evolving material universe that proceeds from a lower to a higher plane. Modernization, in this view, can be understood as a series of altering material relationships out of which a more abundant (and kindlier) world will eventually emerge. Indeed, Sartre speaks of Marxism's appropriateness as a philosophy of scarcity, in the sense that it derives its political relevance from the explanation of scarcity in terms of class conflict and exploitation. He has also dared to challenge contemporary Marxism by adding to it the idea of freedom. Freedom, for Sartre, consists of the ability to understand a relationship between the being of the self and the process of the material world, that is, its functioning. For him work is the means by which the material world and the process of being are co-ordinated. It is in work, and the projects that man sets for himself, that he becomes part of the material world itself and acts upon it. Sartre's position would appear to take him far away from Marxism despite his stated intention to remain within its doctrine.[4]

One important criticism of Marxism is that it cannot present the universe as a contrived reality. Such a criticism may sound surprising. If one accepts the view that there is more than one layer of reality, however, then the idea that there is a single layer, the material, on which items of knowledge may be grafted is unacceptable. From a probabilistic view, the choice of a layer of reality is arbitrary. Selection and definition of appropriate levels are determined by the questions one is asking. Moreover, each level embodies its own theories and contextual rules. A normative plane of reality, for example, demands the use of particular rules for understanding normative evaluations. This type of evaluation is part of the analysis of morals, a separate dialogue in many ways from the analysis of behavior. Separate analyses of structural and behavioral layers of action result in the derivation of different kinds of theories. They can be examined on their own terms, as when the psychologist studies motivational aspects of behavior, and they can be unified into an integrated body of ideas. The latter is what we call a general theory.

If one accepts the notion that there are different layers of meaning relevant to the understanding of choice, one must also take a further step and accept the implicit idea of the observer. By this I mean that the probabilistic approach to reality requires one to occupy the role of observer rather than participant, a passive rather than an active role for the analyst *qua* analyst (as distinct from citizen, revolutionary, reformer, or whatever activist role he may choose to play as an individual rather than as a professional). The probabilistic universe is one in which we are *observers* rather than *workers*.

One difficulty with this approach is that it is better in providing

[4] See Jean-Paul Sartre, *Search for a Method* (New York: Alfred A. Knopf, Inc., 1963), *passim*.

criteria for evaluating what is already consciously known than it is in exploring new layers of consciousness. The latter processes are, at the present state of knowledge, most mysterious ones. Not much is known about how new insights and levels of consciousness are formed. We do know that action can be a way of creating new forms of consciousness. But if this is so, will we not be required to change our role from observer to worker?

One answer is that in practice we move back and forth between these two roles — between observer and worker, between a passive and an active form of observation. Our movement between social philosophies is similar — between some new form of Marxism (stripped of its ideology) and a probabilistic approach to reality. Indeed, one can argue the existence of an interesting dialectic between the two that is a reflection of the movement from the role of observer to that of worker, with the resulting multidimensionality that provides a good basis for viewing both the self in action and the self's action in a wider context. Just as the existentialist wants to locate new layers of meaning between man and his universe through the study of his work, so the probabilist wants to translate these meanings into more rigorous analytical systems that may lead to experimental and operational (contrived) forms of analysis.

Separately, each approach implies different modes of interpretation. The Marxian-existential leads to a single plane of reality, the material. The probabilistic leads to a factoring of truths observed at each layer of reality — a probabilistic consensus (not truth but likelihood). The Marxian-existential, by virtue of its emphasis on "totalization" (synthesis), makes that single reality all-encompassing and therefore too gross to provide answers to questions that lie within it. Is it really useful to study class today, or is it more interesting to study the total situation of choice and the role of class in that situation? Indeed, we need to know more than the ways in which the instruments of competitive conflict reflect material aspects of life — rather, we must see them in the context of our understanding of choice and the precise nature of the relationships involved in choice. This brings me to the concept of choice itself, which I regard as the focal point of the social sciences, uniting normative, structural, and behavioral theory.

MODERNITY AS CHOICE

Some would place the origin of inquiries into modernity in ancient Greece. There, certainly, the distinction between Greek and barbarian comprehended many of the ideas that help us discriminate between the modern and something else, in particular, the idea of the self-conscious pursuit of human ends within a context of critical scrutiny and moral questioning. But can it be said that in this sense the Greeks were any more modern than the ancient Chinese? I doubt it. Indeed, both venerated education, which is an indication that culture was for them a self-conscious concern. Concern with culture in itself, however, is not necessarily modern, even though modern societies are preoccupied with it.

We would perhaps need to look elsewhere for origins of the critical complex of meanings we call modern. One possible view is that modernity began when men gained insight into their economies. With measurable units (money), they found ways to assess preferences, controlling them within a context of a rapidly changing technology. With such concerns, there emerged the desire to make explanations and predictions about social and political life. Certainly, the late mercantilist economists and the early laissez faire theorists, the physiocrats, and above all Adam Smith, abstracted the mechanisms of choice and exchange from the range of activities of which daily life was composed. Thus, modernization as the process leading to the state of modernity, begins when man tries to solve the allocation problem, just as social science was born with the study of choice and preference.

In my view, modernization as a non-economic process originates when a culture embodies an attitude of inquiry and questioning about how men make choices — moral (or normative), social (or structural), and personal (or behavioral). The problem of choice is central for modern man. This is the reason political scientists have so often called Machiavelli the first of the modern political writers and the reason classical and antique civilizations, no matter how noble their conceptions, are nevertheless not modern. To be modern means to see life as alternatives, preferences, and choices.

Self-conscious choice implies rationality. Men will in principle see more than one alternative as plausible. Preferences include the ranking of priorities, and about these reasonable men may differ. Therefore, debate and discussion are characteristics of modernity. In fact, to my mind, they are the critical and minimal conditions of modernity. The Greeks came close, as did the Romans, which is one reason why they fascinate us. But as Fustel de Coulanges shows, the essential features of their cultures were set within the frameworks of religion and kinship, and to impute modernity to them is to forget this.[5]

More important, perhaps, self-conscious concern with choice has led to an attitude of experiment and invention that has changed man's entire outlook. Nature became controllable. Human affairs could be seen as ultimately explicable. The cumulative effect of innovation through industrialization in those parts of the world that became the most dynamic and explosive was to make it clear that modernity was not the property of the few, or of a scientific elite, but rather a fact of culture. Hence, in these times, more than ever before, it is not only interesting but also important to recognize this characteristic of modernity: choice. Societies are now able to choose a direction and means of change. For this reason, theory that can explain how men choose is important. For this reason, too, the normative aspects are critical.

To carry this point of view about choice one step farther: a political system becomes a system of choice for a particular collectivity. Government, which I will define in greater detail later

---

[5] By "culture" I mean the learned symbols and artifacts in a system.

on, is the mechanism for regulating choice. Different political systems will not only embody different ways of choosing but vary in their priorities. Governments will vary in the ways they regulate choice. Thus, there are different systems of choice, and there are choices between systems. One of the characteristics of the modernization process is that it involves both aspects of choice: the improvement of the conditions of choice, and the selection of the most satisfactory mechanisms of choice.

IMPLICATIONS OF CHOICE

The outermost significance of choice is not methodological in any narrow sense but moral. Choices by an individual define his moral personality. Choices by governments comprise the moral aims of society and reflect the ambitions of those within it, thus constituting that measure of satisfaction that will lead ultimately to a stable order. The efforts to find such a moral condition, however, may lead to the most violent and unstable human conditions. The most dramatic of these results from a change in political systems. In such periods the loftiest human purposes may be expressed in violence. Whatever the situation, it is in such times that men make explicit those core values they hope will lead to both a moral community and moral individuals. Perhaps this is the ultimate secret of political life. It is an endless search, sometimes through violence and often in fear of it, for a moral community through which man hopes to realize his individual moral personality. Perhaps, too, it is the ceaselessness of the search itself that gives man his claim to humanity.

Within a general framework that embodies moral "intentionality," we want to know the direction in which society is headed in order to understand the basis on which its authority rests. We seek clues as to whether nations will confound their moral purposes or realize them through modernization, and we generally accept some well-entrenched values as universals, not because

they are embodied in natural law or natural rights, but because
they are sufficiently widespread to seem rooted in common sense —
such values as the respect and dignity accorded to individuals,
and the opportunities provided for each to realize his potentiality.
No modern societies today deny these ideals, although some have
strange ways of attempting to achieve them.

These concerns, although they are important for comparative
studies in general, are particularly interesting when applied to
modernizing and new nations (those that have emerged from
colonial status), which must wrestle directly with problems of
equity and authority as a matter of survival. Countries recently
removed from subject status, only to confront grave problems, may
have little time for moral abstractions. (It is presumed, however,
that when people take their first sturdy steps toward an independence of spirit and mind and an improved political condition they
will do so in the manner that suits them best.)

THE NORMATIVE APPROACH

Perhaps the simplest way to summarize the discussion so far is
to try to translate the distinctions that have been used into types
of legitimacy. We can then show the problems that arise when
legitimacy and political forms are fitted together into a type of
political system.

The Western ideal of government is based on the primacy of
the libertarian principle. The moral purpose of government is to
maximize the condition of freedom. But freedom must lead to
equity. One alternative form, the communist, emphasizes the fulfilment of potentiality. This emphasis, a developmental one, is the
main reason for the moral attractiveness of Marxism to many people in modernizing societies. This is a surprising view of Marxism
since it is far removed from the original analysis of Marx. For him,
it was the libertarian system under capitalism that achieved devel-

opment through revolutionary changes in technique and technology; in fact, for him, this was its main accomplishment.

The developmental objective as a principle of legitimacy is very difficult to evaluate. Some would argue that the most efficient forms of economic growth can be realized by adding the objective of liberty to that of development. Others would argue that the Marxist idea that the potentiality of the citizen is realized only through the actions of the collectivity, is the most significant contemporary means of development.

However we treat these principles of legitimacy, they are clearly related. If the explicit moral rationale for a modernizing society is development, it is ordinarily expressed in terms of realizing potentialities, human and social. I will argue that as such potentialities come within range of achievement, so will the libertarian ideal. At least that is my hope.

The political link between equity and liberty, on the one hand, and equity and potentiality, on the other, has been, historically, the ideal of equality. In modernizing societies it remains a powerful moral force. Since it remains largely unrealized, the management of tensions is often a considerable problem in the new nations. This is one reason they have frequently relied on autocratic and personal rule. When, on the other hand, they have adopted a more democratic approach to government, they have often been plagued by instabilities. One reason for this is that unplanned development results in social inequalities, which can easily harden into more or less permanently organized classes, each with its own subculture, as has occurred in many parts of Latin America. Here, then, are some of the main problems that a normative view of modernization identifies. Can democracy work for modernizing societies? If it fails to work in particular cases, what alternative systems will replace it? In order to answer these questions, we need a better idea of what we mean by different kinds of "systems."

Although it is unfair to judge modernizing societies from the peculiar standpoint of our own political forms, we must neverthe-

less put their efforts in a universal moral cast; otherwise we would
demean their significance. It is no service to the modernizing nations (or ourselves) to judge their policies purely on the basis of
utility. Government is, after all, a reflection of the nobler as well
as the mundane purposes for which people live in society. In this
sense, no government is better than its moral standards, and no
valid moral judgment is premature.[6]

If we accept the view that government actions must be judged
in moral terms here and now (and as the realization of morally
valid goals), what are useful criteria to employ? This is a difficult but crucial question. Asking the moral questions compels us
to find appropriate forms of inquiry. In this sense, it is morality
that impels us to science, not the reverse. In politics we have
some old and still serviceable standards: government should not
be capricious; its politicians should not misuse public power; they
should remain deferential to their trust; and so on. How far is it
possible to extend these questions to matters of political form as
ordinarily conceived? Probably not very far. It is no good evaluating governments on the basis of their organization. A single-
party state, for example, may be meaningfully democratic. A supreme court may not be decisive in developing the rule of law.
Concrete forms of rule have many functional consequences, and
there is no simple relationship between organization, form, and
substance.[7]

---

[6] If we accept this line of reasoning, we must admit that most governments are not very "good" and that some are worse than others. The analysis
of some may suggest possibilities of rapid improvement. For others, where
a moral rhetoric disguises acts of force, violence, intimidation, and deception,
we may simply be compounding these deficiencies if we fail to apply moral
criteria. If we cannot discriminate between governments, it would be a
better alternative to lay aside all judgments in favor of judicious silence.
How comforting to divert our attention to the consideration of purely historical events (and regard contemporary judgments as premature until the
system has already gone through its main evolution and its outlines become
so fixed, its practices so decided, that little further change can be expected).
But this would be to substitute expediency for judgment. See Benedetto
Croce, *Politics and Morals* (London: George Allen & Unwin, Ltd., 1946).

[7] But matters of form are at stake when they embody matters of principle.
We need to suggest types of developing societies, if only to point to the

This point of view lies at the heart of political science, which, as distinct from the other social sciences, begins with the moral aspects of choice. Difficulties arise for comparative study because we have enshrined moral principles in models that have served well in a Western political context. The models we derive from concepts of justice, equity, and the good society may be quite inappropriate for modernizing societies. In our haste for political science to take on the attributes of a science by employing analogies inspired by investigations in the natural sciences, we may confuse form and substance.

Specifically, what I reject are the comfortably formulated descriptive models that are assumed to embody abstract principles of virtue, when, in reality, they embody our preferences and prejudices — for example, the definition of democracy as the operation of a two-party or multiparty system, since "totalitarian" systems exclude more than one party. If we reject descriptive and simplistic models, however, with what can they be replaced?

My analysis will try to answer this kind of question. All around us new moral communities are being established, and the context of moral fulfilment is modernization. Different authority systems modernize by allocating mundane and sacred rewards and promises. Some are more directly devoted to the allocation of the mundane in the hope that individual morality will be encouraged by the satisfaction of mundane wants and that political morality will be reflected in the summation of individual moralities. Others are more interested in seeing an ideal of the moral community realized and mundane satisfactions restricted except as they serve long-run opportunities for achieving the moral community. The one emphasizes the present, and the other the future. If these assumptions are correct we might even say that the way in which man copes with uncertainty is his individual test as a moral personality; and differing political systems offer different solutions

forms of misconduct to which they are heir. How else can we demonstrate their moral potentialities in relation to modernization? Behind any utilitarian judgment of the role of government lies the larger question of moral potentiality.

to the uncertainty of man — the most demanding of contemporary problems.

This moral basis of politics, I suggest, determines the meaning of legitimate authority. "Authority" can be said to be a definition of political morality in a particular setting. In the final analysis it is the problem of the individual or, to use an old-fashioned phrase, a matter of conscience. It is linked to such personal dimensions as immortality, purpose, and meaning. Politics is peculiar insofar as principles of legitimacy are normative first and structural second. Indeed, this relationship of the normative and the structural underlies the theme of analysis employed here as follows. The two normative principles described above, liberty and potentiality, become principles of legitimacy; the first we associate with democracy, and the second has been linked historically with the ideal of the evolution of a community. The forms of government most frequently associated with the types of legitimacy are, in the first instance, constitutional representation, embodying what can be called pyramidal authority and decentralization of power to critical subunits of the system, and, in the second instance, centrally controlled systems, embodying hierarchical authority. (See Figure 1.) These categories will lead us to the development of universalized types of political systems, each of which deals differently with the problem of modernization.

THE STRUCTURAL APPROACH

Structural analysis is concerned with the limits within which particular choices take place.[8] To gain some understanding of these we need to compare units with one another. Hence, the structural aspects of this study begin in comparison and classification, in a search for basic principles around which to cluster

[8] Structural analysis is used here to include all forms of systems analysis that refer to unit change. It includes functional analysis as a method of identifying significant variables in a system.

data. Beginning with a concrete unit of analysis, we ask, What functions must be performed to ensure the survival of that unit and all others of the same type? A structural approach is useful for comparison partly because it avoids the problem of dealing with the unique. For example, we are accustomed to regarding democracy as uniquely related to a multiparty form of competitive politics. If, however, we consider democracy as a system of rule, a function of which includes public checks on arbitrary power, then it is possible to conceive of situations in which a single party, through its internal factions, serves much the same purpose. Structural analysis, then, helps avoid the familiar fallacy that whatever is, is necessary.

Principles of Legitimacy	Form of Government
Equity—"democracy"	Constitutional representation (pyramidal authority)
Potentiality—"community"	Centrally controlled system (hierarchical authority)

Fig. 1. — *Legitimacy and structure.*

As another example, we ordinarily think of government as a specialized instrument of rule. Society X has no such specialized instrument. We then conclude that it functions without a government. But what we really mean is that certain societies are without a formal governmental organization. Because the functions of government can be met in diverse ways, our attention must then logically be directed to other instruments of social life to see if they perform a political role. Government can thus exist where no formal structure exists, and may be found in kinship systems, religious bodies, or other organizations that we are not accustomed to thinking of as government but that, in fact, are carrying out the functions of government.

Still another reason for using a structural method is that, by means of its requisite-analysis form, we may delimit the conditions within which a given system can continue to operate. Structural studies assign significance to activities in such a way as to separate the crucial from the epiphenomenal. Structuralism allows us to apply logical tests (experiments in the mind, as it were) to macro-problems that cannot be neatly controlled in the laboratory.

Structural analysis is itself a comparative method, in a form that directs our attention to an analytical level of thought rather than a descriptive level. The object is to see functional meaning in many diverse activities. Functional equivalences in different actions do not mean, of course, that one action is really like an-other. There is functional uniqueness, just as there is functional similarity. The principle to be followed is an old one. First, we observe many cases in order to find and exhaust functional simi-larities; then we proceed to uniqueness. Structural analysis must therefore be seen in stages: from the general to the particular, from the universal to the unique. At each succeeding stage, what was residual and left in the interstices of the previous stage now becomes central. This descending order of procedure is cumber-some (comparison is not a very efficient method of building theory) but extremely interesting.

What stages of analysis are involved? Three might be demar-cated. The first of these, as we have already suggested, is typo-logical but goes beyond classification to an analytical clustering of characteristics against which concrete systems may be evaluated. This is the basis of "ideal-type" analysis, used so effectively by the late nineteenth-century historical sociologists. Ideal types qual-ify for the appellation "scientific," for they are essentially state-ments of system, that is, an ordered and coherent relationship between parts. Essentially intuitive and non-experimental, they nevertheless engage our attention because they arrange experience in a useful manner. Indeed, Carl G. Hempel has argued that ideal types can be regarded as significant only if they are interpreted as theoretical systems, that is, by (a) specifying a list of character-istics with which the theory is to deal (b) formulating a set of hypotheses in terms of those characteristics, (c) giving those characteristics an empirical interpretation that assigns to the theory a specific domain of application, and (*d*) as a long-range objective, incorporating the theoretical system, as a "special case," into a more comprehensive theory.[9]

This first stage of the analysis requires, at the start, the delineation of boundaries of the units. The selection of units depends on the nature of the problem, but a useful rule of thumb is to look for the largest membership group that meaningfully encompasses the activities we want to examine — in our case, the nation-state.

The second stage of analysis involves us in the problem of meaning. What intrinsic consequences do the activities performed by the unit, arranged in some classification, have for the system? What would happen if some major category of activity was no longer performed? Would the system be able to remain stable, that is, could the boundaries maintain themselves? These questions lead to the form of structural analysis known as requisite analysis, in which the functions that have been delineated are considered as a minimal and irreducible set necessary to the maintenance of the unit. From the functions so selected, the structures are established by a series of logical and empirical exercises. The activities are examined again in order to determine the means by which they deal with the functions. Functions stress meaning in the sense that they indicate the significance of some activities and their equivalences in diverse activities. These functions are the core problems that all systems of a similar type need to handle. Structures are ways to handle the functionally defined problems.[10]

The third stage in structural analysis is the derivation of theories about the data. It is this last aspect of structural analysis that preoccupies us. Our theories will be made explicit, although in this study I make no attempt to marshal supporting data.[11]

[9] See Hempel, "Symposium: Problems of Concept and Theory Formation in the Social Sciences," in *Science, Language and Human Rights* (Philadelphia: University of Pennsylvania Press, for the American Philosophical Association, 1952), p. 84.

[10] See Marion J. Levy, Jr., *The Structure of Society* (Princeton, N.J.: Princeton University Press, 1952), *passim*.

[11] In practice, structural analysis has been largely intuitive and speculative.

Structural analysis, then, is useful for several reasons. It reduces the risk of ethnocentrism. It delineates change in systematic terms and forces the observer to examine meanings on the basis of function. It points up the core problems facing systems. It provides an orderly way of examining large numbers of cases in order to develop comparative theories.

THE BEHAVIORAL APPROACH

Behavioral analysis is concerned with a different level of explanation. Whereas structural analysis is mainly concerned with delimiting the conditions within which social choices are possible, behavioral analysis is concerned with which social choices are made and why. The behavioral looks inside the actors. This method is similar to Weber's category of *Verstehen*. What he regarded as unique to the human sciences, as distinct from the natural sciences, was the capacity of the observer to put himself in the position of someone else and ask questions about motivation. This, however, involves us in a different level of analysis. The structural approach, we have suggested, is an effort to find general properties of systems that limit the range of action open to individuals. This range of action will vary from system to system. The gross behavior delimited is particularly useful for large-scale comparative studies. What is sought is analytical, or qualitative, logical rather than quantitative. In contrast, behavorial analysis, which emphasizes quantitative methods, takes us directly into the study of motivation, symbolic behavior, and, in particular, moral conduct, as these aspects affect individual choice.

Most of the theoretical questions we confront here fall in an area between structural and behavioral theories. There have been many efforts to close this gap; every general theory tries to do so.

This is perhaps as it should be. There is nothing inherent in the nature of this method of analysis that causes this; but when it is applied to macrounits like societies, precision becomes more a matter of logic than data because there is too much material to handle.

In this book I will incorporate several structural and behavioral ideas into a single system for the comparative analysis of political modernization. The analysis can be seen as an inquiry into the conditions that establish and maintain authority during modernization. One approach is to consider the relationship between authority and support. When we consider this set of conditions as analogous to the marketplace, we can observe that individuals maximize benefits by supporting authority. The alternative analogy, the community as an organism — a collectivity with a life of its own — emphasizes the non-empirical ends of supporting authority. The emotional warmth, the sense of creativity, and other "feelings" and states of mind produced by the leader may be sufficient to retain loyalties for a very long time in the absence of concrete benefits. Why? Explanations will in some measure lie in behavioral theories of how loyalties are formed.[12]

It is important to remember that normative aspects of systems are embodied in both structure and behavior. For example, roles are differentiated on the basis of publicly accepted notions of subordinate and superordinate relationships. And the behavior of individuals reflects norms that have become part of the motivational system of individuals. Indeed, many important areas of inquiry, such as the analysis of political socialization, deal with the way norms are absorbed and internalized through the blending of

[12] This general approach incorporates different aspects of the following forms of theory: functional and processual; structural and behavioral. These can be illustrated in the following diagram:

	Functional	Processual
Behavioral	Motivation and perception in systems Examples: Chester Hull; David Easton	Comprehension, meaning, and understanding (sociology and knowledge; ideology) Examples; Karl Mannheim; Harold Lasswell
Structural	Comparative analysis of systems and subsystems and their persistence Examples: Talcott Parsons; Marion Levy; Robert Merton; Gabriel Almond	Comparative analysis of change and innovation according to a dynamic principle Examples; Ralf Dahrendorf; Karl Marx; Max Weber

structural and behavioral principles in concrete instrumentalities (like schools) by concrete individuals.

CHOICES BETWEEN POLITICAL SYSTEMS

The analysis that follows brings together the three approaches by centering on models of government, described in terms of two main criteria; degree of hierarchy and type of values. The first is the measure of stringency of control and is structurally visible in the degree of centralization of authority. The second criterion is the degree to which ultimate ends are employed in action, with ultimate ends understood as "religion" and intermediate ends as "secularity," following Durkheim's distinction between sacred and secular ends. The extremes of these factors combine to form four models, of which two, the secular-libertarian and the sacred-collectivity, are the most interesting. These two normative models are in perpetual conflict and are constantly in danger of being transformed into each other.

Although we insist on the normative characteristics of these models, with all that that implies in terms of types of authority, the distinctions we will use here accord with most of the comparative schemes that have gained currency today that are based on the degree of pluralism. What might be called the "pluralism-monism" continuum has proved to be a better basis for determining types of polities than the "democracy-totalitarianism" continuum because it is somewhat broader and is based on forms of differentiation rather than on the explicit method of government. Competition is another useful criterion. As James S. Coleman has suggested: "Competitiveness is an essential aspect of political modernity, but not all competitive systems are 'modern.' . . ."[13] Edward A. Shils has developed a similar classification, in which the modernization process is described as a progressive sharing

[13] See Gabriel Almond and James S. Coleman, *The Politics of the Developing Areas* (Princeton, N.J.: Princeton University Press, 1960), p. 533.

by the public in an understanding of modern life in such a way that, no longer passive agents acted upon by outside forces, they can utilize their potentialities and their creativity.[14]

These two factors, pluralism and participation, form the basis of almost all the typologies of "political systems" or "polities," and each student adopts some variant of these to suit his particular purposes. Morris Janowitz, for example, in his recent study of the military in the developing countries, notes five types: (1) authoritarian-personal control; (2) authoritarian-mass party; (3) democratic competitive and semicompetitive systems; (4) civil-military coalition; and (5) military oligarchy.[15]

The typology I have used accepts the same principles and to that extent is not different from the others. By stressing values and hierarchy, however, I want to emphasize the way people organize society and feel its pull in terms of durable proprieties, rights and wrongs. This approach will reinforce the point that has recently been made by Gabriel Almond and Sidney Verba in their study of the civic culture. The importance of their book for me lies in its advance from typologies based purely on matters of structural differentiation to a typology based on the forms of cognition and meaning that exist in a particular culture. This leads them to the analysis of "fit" or congruence between the ideals and values of the community and the forms by which it is organized.[16] The problem of congruence, which emerges most clearly in roles, has been the central point of my analysis. Since roles are institutionalized forms of behavior defined by function, both the structural and the behavioral approaches are employed

[14] See Shils, *Political Development in the New States* (The Hague: Mouton, 1962), *passim.* A useful variant of the pluralism-monism continuum is Chalmers Johnson's typology for situations of radical change; see his *Revolution and the Social System* (Stanford, Calif.: Hoover Institution on War, Revolution, and Peace, 1964), No. 3.

[15] See Morris Janowitz, *The Military in the Political Development of New Nations* (Chicago: University of Chicago Press, 1964), p. 5.

[16] See Almond and Verba, *The Civic Culture: Political Attitudes and Democracy in Five Nations* (Princeton, N.J.: Princeton University Press, 1963), chapter i.

in analysis. The structural deals with the organization of roles and their functional relationships. The behavioral deals with the ideas of right conduct embodied in the roles and the consequences of those ideas in the formation of personalities.[17] Any complete analysis necessarily includes both these aspects. As I use the terms, the behavioral approach deals with *which* choices are made by groups or individuals and *why*; the structural approach delineates *what* choices are possible.

To incorporate both structural differentiation and cognitive evaluation in a highly generalized manner is a difficult task. The following approach seems feasible. If we consider the two main variables discussed above, hierarchy and values, we obtain the typology of authority types given in Figure 2.

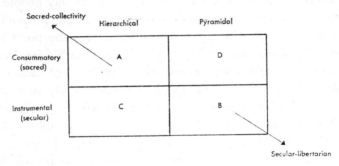

FIG. 2. — *Authority types.*

Types *A* and *B* are derivative of the pure normative models, the sacred-collectivity and the secular-libertarian, and are the polar opposites in this general formulation. As I have already suggested, they are more often than not in conflict with one another. The

[17] The best discussion of the explicitly structural aspect of roles is S. F. Nadel, *The Theory of Social Structure* (Glencoe: Free Press of Glencoe, Ill., 1957). Discussion of the behavioral aspect is to be found in T. M. Newcomb, *Social Psychology* (New York: Dryden Press, 1950), chapter ix. The most important effort to combine these two dimensions of analysis remains Talcott Parson's, *The Social System* (Glencoe: Free Press of Glencoe, Ill., 1951), *passim.*; and T. Parsons, Robert F. Bales, and Edward A. Shils, *Working Papers in the Theory of Action* (Glencoe: Free Press of Glencoe, Ill., 1953).

other two, C and D, may be described as historically significant, and perhaps practical, alternatives to the two major conflicting forms. Type A may be called a mobilization system, and B a reconciliation system. Category C does not have a convenient name. Subtypes might be called modernizing autocracies or neomercantilist societies. Category D is equally difficult to label, but its subtypes may be called theocracies. The last model is most helpful in analyzing traditional societies and will be used explicitly in chapter iii, whereas the other three can be used in the study of most modernizing cases. Type C, for example, would include "Kemalism" and the "Neo-Bismarckian" types now gaining considerable currency in the literature. Type D includes feudal systems.

Each of these types is first a normative system organized around certain structural features and incorporating particular styles of political life and civic action. Most important of all, each of these political systems defines the conditions of choice differently. Three approaches can be used to examine such conditions — normative, structural, and behavioral — each imposing different evaluative criteria. The first consists of the values and priorities that combine in a moral consensus, the second elaborates certain conditions of choice, and the last embodies the conditions under which individuals and groups make particular choices. These three elements, which are present in all political systems, operate within a set of general boundaries — the human and physical resources available at any given time. Inside the boundaries we can see alternative types of political systems that approach the problems of modernization somewhat differently. The extreme model, type B, may, as we have said, be called the secular-libertarian; *it is a perfect information model.* Its opposite, type A, is the sacred-collectivity, *a perfect coercion model.* Between these two extremes the other types have proved to be accommodated or mixed systems of choice.[18]

[18] The best short introduction to the immediate problems of analysis is contained in Karl W. Deutsch's *The Nerves of Government* (New York: Free Press of Glencoe, 1963). See also Wilbert E. Moore, *Social Change* (Englewood Cliffs, N.J.: Prentice-Hall, Inc., 1963). The most important

Let me consider type *B* as a normative system. It can be observed to be analogous to the marketplace. Individual minds within the system become independent units that act upon the external world in order to make it conform to their perception of meaning. Individual minds are, in summation, the means by which the external world is given subjective meaning; yet the objectification of these subjective meanings is the basis of scientific knowledge. Toleration, leading to debate and competition in ideas, is the way to discover truths. Policy is a form of truth for the members of a community. Just as one's person is property and must be safeguarded, so one's mind is sacred and must be free. Ideas are derivations from empirical phenomena and must be tested competitively with other ideas in order to establish truth. And the establishment of truth is the aim of science. Hence, the libertarian model is essentially an extension of the rationalism of the marketplace, with the atomistic, competitive, and free play of ideas controlled only by a legal constitutional mechanism that prevents any group from obtaining a monopoly of power.[19] Its principle of legitimacy is *equity*, and its main emphasis is on allocation.

The limits on this normative type are many. Just as the pure theory of competition in economics does not accurately describe the real world, neither does the secular-libertarian model correspond to an existing political system. Just as, in the first instance, there are monopolies and oligopolies through which a few firms control the market, so, in the case of politics, there are classes and interest groups that wield superior power and give exceptional opportunities to some at the expense of others.

and explicit statement of structural-functional requisite analysis is in Marion J. Levy, Jr., *The Structure of Society* (Princeton, N.J.: Princeton University Press, 1952). See also Juan J. Linz, "An Authoritarian Regime: Spain," in E. Allardt and Y. Littunen (eds.), *Cleavages, Ideologies and Party Systems* (Helsinki: Westermarck Society, 1964), pp 291–301.

[19] The idea of power in this system is the zero-sum approach. There is a given amount of it in the system, and if one group gains more, that of others decreases correspondingly. See Talcott Parsons, "On the Concept of Political Power," *Proceedings of the American Philosophical Society*, CVII (June, 1963).

The structural defect in this normative type in large-scale and complex societies is the ineffectiveness of individual representation. Indeed, the liberal critique of modern society is that modern industrial enterprise has created such conditions of political inequality that individual representation is rendered meaningless. Early Marxism, for example, is essentially an attack on inequalities; it ascribes the failure of the representational system to inequalities arising in the economic sphere. Workers have become subdued to the discipline of the machine, subordinated in political as well as in economic terms, brutalized, and alienated from society. Marx's fame was instantaneous because his critique of the prevailing system was not only drastic but intellectually very powerful. For him, the problem was not merely that the liberal market system did not work in practice; he came to feel it could not work, in either economic or political life. Indeed, even the ethic appeared a vast deception — not scientific but antiscientific. Accordingly, the new science would begin by formulating certain principles of political and social conduct that would serve as universal rules for analyzing the evolutionary aspects of history. The morality of society was to be realized in an evolutionary way when economic groups were deprived of their special privileges, or more specifically, when economic classes disappeared. Indeed, liberal toleration of other systems than the libertarian begins with this critique. Today we can see that there are other problems than the ineffectiveness of the representation system.

In fact, the Marxist critique created a new moral ideology that concedes that some men, having gained a superior insight into themselves and their institutions, both as scientific and moral beings, must realize this superior knowledge in a system of authority. Men of superior intellect who emancipate themselves from the limitations of their own class outlook and the knowledge of their day — by having a scientific understanding of social life — are the ones who must establish the new collectivity. To be scientific is to know these principles and to work for their realization. This is the basis of the modern collectivist community (the sacred-collectivity type): the generation of new power through unity, the unfolding of a moral and scientific personality through the mystique of developing toward a higher plane. Politically, one would not want to represent the people as they are, because "as they are" is debased by the imperfections of the society. Here the principle of legitimacy is *potentiality*, and its main emphasis is on development. It is not surprising, therefore, that many political leaders of modernizing nations are attracted to the Marxian view.

THE SECULAR-LIBERTARIAN MODEL

Underlying Western concepts of democracy is what we have called a secular-libertarian model of polity.

Behaviorally, the secular-libertarian model consists of units that possess two capacities: the ability to reason and the ability to know self-interest. These are the universal behavioral characteristics of human beings according to Locke, for example, who grants them even to individuals in a state of nature. *Structurally*, the system must allow maximum opportunity for the exercise of rationality and the pursuit of self-interest. Hence the emphasis is on a framework that will prevent coercion and provide limited government. The usual realization of this need is a system of representative government with checks and balances designed to prevent tyranny. *Normatively*, such a system takes certain fundamental proprieties as given. Locke, for example, assumes that ultimate ends of conduct will be expressed primarily in terms of religion. Indeed, he suggests that without religion there can be no social contract, which he sees as the foundation of structural constitutionality. Without such constitutionality there can be no political basis for equity.

The secular libertarian model is thus the classic liberal picture of a political community. But we must distinguish between the model and the ideology that stems from it. For example, if the model fails to work because of certain monopolistic practices arising in group political life, or if religion begins to decline and the contract to fail, the result may be the growth of solutions that, although designed to restore the model, appear to attack it. In this sense (and on a purely theoretical level), Marxian theory is designed to create a new rationale for a liberal universe that would be a benign modern equivalent of Locke's state of nature. In practice, however, Marxism as an ideology tends to be employed by systems that at present are opposed to the liberal ideology and the liberal political community.

The more common form of the secular libertarian polity, however, is the liberal utilitarian model. Such a model derives from the classical deist period and emphasizes *mechanical* harmony or equilibrium. The polity is like a vast marketplace. Government represents the sellers, with incumbents and candidates for political office actively engaged in producing policy or in discussing anticipated policy. Citizens are the buyers. The citizens are politically equal, as in the concept of one man, one vote. Power and loyalty are constantly being exchanged for benefits and privileges. The voting mechanism is the equivalent of the market. Preferences are rationally registered by the citizens as choices in the political arena. In this model, the primary value is liberty.

This concept of the polity parallels the pure theory of economic competition and accepts the same values.[20] Citizens registering their preferences act in their political role. In their economic role (as consumers) they register economic preferences in the marketplace. In both, the sum total of private wants emerges as public good. In the political sphere, the attempt of each person to realize his personal benefits on a plane of political equality with others generates power, just as consumer preference manifested by a willingness to spend money in the market generates wealth. Whereas money is the measure and expression of wealth in the market, votes are the measures and expressions of power in the polity.

[20] See Anthony Downs, *An Economic Theory of Democracy*, (New York: Harper & Bros., 1957), *passim*.

There are other similarities between the economic and the political forms of the secular-libertarian model. Information is freely available to voters and officials just as it is to buyers and sellers. On the basis of information, rationality is possible. Hence, political freedom is first a condition of frankness. Knowledge of the product and knowledge of the policy assume an informed public. Knowledge of the public assumes an informed government. The emphasis on education is not solely because of its functional value (that is, to increase our technical skills or for any other utilitarian reason). Rather, education becomes the precondition of information, and information is the basis on which the relationship between public and policy is maintained. Harmony and stability result.

In such a system it is implied that the values of the community are already enshrined in law and custom and that they will maintain the political conditions we have already suggested. Hence, just as in the pure theory of competition there should be no monopoly, so in the secular-libertarian polity there should be no monopoly of power in the political sphere. Power needs to be dispersed, and various systems have been devised to ensure its dispersal. These include the formal checks and balances of our own system and the principle of parliamentary sovereignty in Europe.

How does the secular-libertarian model fail? Interference in its working may come from either side of the polity, citizen or governor. Citizens seeking to maximize their power by organizing into groups can generate special powers, which in extreme cases may render the government helpless. Or the government may seek to minimize the controls exercised over it by various groups. The study of comparative politics of democratic societies concentrates on discovering possible improvements that will prevent both of these occurrences (much as in the economic sphere, government seeks to prevent large-scale combination through antitrust legislation).

Competition between politically equal units is the basis of the system, with competition in ideas reflecting competition of interests, the constellation of which represents the desires of the multitude. Such, briefly, is the ideal of Western libertarian government. It has a high commitment to rules and laws. When the discrepancy between theory and practice is great, individuals become lonely and divorced from the system. If too many withdraw from the political marketplace, a general condition of alienation from the society results. The libertarian model is vastly different when realized in the real world, where there are many special claims to power. Political parties are quite often anxious to limit rather than increase the range of intellectual discourse by focusing on a few issues with symbolic appeal (rather than offering intellectual choice); and we find the same efforts to produce automatic behavior that advertising companies use to encourage our addiction to trade names. Political packaging may produce moral cynicism in the same way that economic activity generated by advertising induces economic skepticism. We can see how, if this should result in alienation, people may draw away from the secular-libertarian model to something else. The theme of alienation runs through the history of secular-libertarian models.[21]

THE SACRED-COLLECTIVITY MODEL

The sacred-collectivity model in its broadest implications contains essentially three elements. *Behaviorally*, it is made up of units whose singular characteristic is potentiality. Individuals, for example, are perceived as nothing more than potentials. *Structurally*, the political community is the means of translating potentiality into some sort of reality. Hence, the society is the key to social life. Moreover, as the primary instrument of socialization, the political community is essentially an educational body. It exists for the improvement of the community itself. The individual is

[21] See Robert Tucker, *Philosophy and Myth in Karl Marx* (Cambridge: Cambridge University Press, 1961). See also the discussion in Philip Selznick, *The Organizational Weapon* (Glencoe: Free Press of Glencoe, Ill., 1960), chapter vii.

merely derivative, a derived personality. *Normatively*, the sacred-collectivity is an ethical or moral unit. Thus, the morality of the individual depends on the morality of the system, which embodies those higher purposes that may be enshrined in kinship, political ideals, and so on. Included under the rubric of this essentially Aristotelian view of the political community would be most traditional societies, theocracies, and certain modernizing ones as well. It is the modernizing societies that are most interesting to us and on which we will concentrate.

Seen as a modernizing force, the sacred-collectivity model stresses the unity of the people, not their diversity. It depends less on the free flow of ideas than on the disciplined concentration upon certain political and economic objectives. It claims a "higher" form of morality than that of the secular-libertarian model, because social life is directed toward the benefit of the collectivity rather than toward that of the self. It is more disciplined because more is concentrated on the priorities of the polity. Equality in the economic sphere is often regarded as a goal to be achieved by the eventual elimination of private property, although not all collectivity systems are socialist. Political inequality exists, but for equalitarian ends.

Operating on very different principles from those of the secular-libertarian model, the sacred-collectivity has its origins in the idea of society organized as a corporation. In the medieval theory of corporations, inequality and status were embodied in legal entities (such as guilds) and classes of individuals (such as noblemen and clergymen).[22] Today the corporation is the state, and the parts of it are functional groupings such as workers and farmers.

The sacred-collectivity model is significant for our purposes because it is an alternative to the secular-libertarian model, which may break down if loyalty to and consensus about the polity are

---

[22] See Otto Gierke, *Natural Law and the Theory of Society*, ed. E. Barker (Cambridge: Cambridge University Press, 1950), *passim*; and O. Gierke, *Political Theories of the Middle Ages*, ed. F. W. Maitland (Cambridge: Cambridge University Press, 1927), *passim*. See also Ewart Lewis, *Medieval Political Ideas* (London: Routledge & Kegan Paul, 1954).

lacking. If, for example, the economy fails to function and mundane satisfactions are unequally distributed, the alienated men who may be produced by these conditions may well look for revolutionary reform under a new moral discipline. This moral discipline will be able to justify inequality and reduce the significance of unequal distribution of mundane satisfactions. We can call this model non-rational because it does not presume a free-flowing pattern of exchange of information between rulers and ruled. The rulers need to be in a position to co-ordinate and discipline the ruled in order to achieve certain objectives, which tend to be highly diffuse, utopian, and spiritual.

This emphasis is particularly strong in hitherto predominantly commercial societies in which inequality is exceedingly great and life-styles range from the most primitive to the most technologically luxurious. To integrate them into a single system is extremely difficult without wholesale alterations in social strata. One means of integration is to introduce socialism in order to restrict social differences. The objective is moral discipline, consensus, and similarity of outlook. Planning, rationality, and progress become associated with the sacred-collectivity model; and individualism, private gain, and the market become little more than other names for egotism and opportunism, and are seen as parochialism and a narrowness of outlook.

A COMPARISON OF THE MODELS

It is necessary to recognize that the two normative models aim at quite different moral ends. The secular-libertarian model essentially accepts society as it is and suggests a framework that will allow modest change over time. It contains a set of presuppositions about the way in which representative government ought to operate: (1) There should not be a monopoly of power any more than there should be a monopoly of corporate enterprise. (2) The same rules apply to all; hence, as legal personalities, all are equal.

(3) Preference can be realized within a framework of law in which those exercising power are checked by legal means — by control over the executive, and so on. Law, the constitution, and the actual mechanisms of government are seen as a seamless web in which the symbol of authority is the social contract (even the term "contract" is taken from law) or a contract between the people that lays out the conditions of government.

The sacred-collectivity model is opposed to conditions as they are. It cannot assume, as can the secular-libertarian model, that an educational system, for example, should create a level of understanding of current problems sufficient to support opposing points of view and that opposing views should be tolerated as long as the problems are shared and communication about them possible. The sacred-collectivity model prefers to cope with such problems politically, through a system of authority that enforces selective communication between people about certain key political problems. If the original aim was to direct people to a common social language, the end result is the establishment of conformity in communication. That is why the political language employed by systems conforming to the sacred-collectivity model is always so important; key terms are continually reinforced and come to define political orthodoxy. It is a system in which consensus cannot be taken for granted but must be built — a directly opposite situation to that obtaining in the secular-libertarian model.

These two models are at opposite ends of a continuum of political systems. What determines the distance between them, however, is not merely their particular forms of government but rather two related components. The first of these components is made up of values and purposes. The secular-libertarian model is rooted in the ideal of individual liberty. The conditions that maximize liberty represent the central purpose. Modern group politics is a step away from the pure type. Pluralism consists not in the number of individual participants (one man, one vote) but rather in groups in competition. These groups (political) try to maximize their power, and individuals give over their loyalties to them. Group-oriented democracy is to the classic libertarian tradition what large-scale enterprise is to the pure theory of economic competition, and in theory has the same relationship to the libertarian model as monopolistic competition has to pure competition.

At the other end of the continuum political groups, not individuals, make up the system. The all-embracing political group is the state, from which subgroups derive their corporate personalities. Individuals exist only as the elementary "particles" of which the corporations are composed. With the emphasis on highly centralized authority, any dispersal of it is seen as dangerous to the whole. Such a system can be based on equality — but equality does not have the same significance it has in the first model, since it does not lead to the realization of individual wants. The secular-libertarian model assumes that equilibrium is produced by means of a policy representing a summation of the wants of its members, carried out within the framework of given values of rationality, freedom, and competition. The sacred-collectivity model assumes that any such policy would be inadequate because of deficiencies of knowledge among the people. Instead, the system must express values of unity, growth, and development. The collectivity type creates authority and carefully allocates it within a community. It can be seen as a community-creating process. The libertarian type caters to an established system of authority, using power within already defined legitimate limits for diverse purposes. It is interesting to note that the secular-libertarian type, awkward in dealing with the problem of establishing authority, resorts to myths of compact such as the social contract to do this.

Historically, we can see a relationship between these two approaches. All libertarian systems have evolved from earlier collective systems, during which authority was established. In this sense, it is possible to consider the two types as concretely interrelated with real systems that first must cater to the problem of authority and then at a later stage can cater to the problem of equity.

Of course, there are problems with this view. Is the secular-libertarian model incapable of establishing authority? This is clearly not the case. But since this model does not set up authority easily, what are the conditions favorable to it, and which conditions favor the alternative form? And if there is a relationship between the two, and the ultimate goal is the secular-libertarian system, is it not perfectly justifiable to favor a militant, organismic, collectivist society if that seems to be the precondition out of which a secular-libertarian model will emerge?

A host of questions arises when the matter is put this way. If a libertarian system is proposed for a new state in which the odds are that it will fail to establish authority, should the attempt be made? Ought nation-builders form the collective variety from the start? The question is not abstract. Since 1945, colonial territories have been provided with libertarian constitutions, many of which disintegrated within a few months of independence. Not one began as a collectivist system. Perhaps this only serves to underline how drastically different the central problems are in these two systems: equity *or* authority.

SUBTYPES

A more empirically useful departure from the pure secular-libertarian model I call a reconciliation system; and a similar departure from the pure state of the sacred-collectivity model I call a mobilization system. In reconciliation systems, given values and purposes generate legitimate authority. Conflicts between individuals and groups trying to realize those accepted values give rise to governmental policy. Policy thus reinforces values. In mobilization systems, new values are being created. This means that political leaders are trying to work out a moral system of authority. In between these types are some interesting combinations. One of these combinations I have called a modernizing autocracy; another is a military oligarchy, and still another a neomercantilist society. These three types are confusing because of the similarity of their basic components. Each of them is a special variant of hierarchical authority and instrumental values. The particular characteristics of each ought now to be made more explicit.

The modernizing autocracy tends to have a traditionalistic ideology associated with a monarch or king who represents the nation. Authority remains at the top, although, in fact, it may be shared through a variety of instrumentalities such as councils, parliaments, party groups, and so on. Examples are Thailand, Morocco, and Ethiopia.

The military oligarchy shares some of these characteristics. It has hierarchical authority and instrumental values, but a military leader (or junta) takes the place of the king. It, too, may decentralize power. The curious problem of the military oligarchy is its inability to deal with politics. Sudan is one testimonial to this failure; Vietnam is another; and Burma is perhaps another.

The neomercantilist society also shares many of these characteristics but is ordinarily headed by a "presidential monarch." In order to support authority it uses a mixture of private and public enterprise in which the critical rationale of economic activities is political. In this it fits the description of mercantilism employed by Eli F. Hecksher. Many mobilization systems turn into neomercantilist societies in practice, particularly when they employ traditionalist ideologies in an attempt to ritualize authority and change charismatic leadership into a more institutional form.[23]

Our analysis will be concerned with specifying the implications of these subtypes and in demonstrating some of their consequences for government. Most modernizing nations are combinations of these types, accepting at least some of the paraphernalia of the reconciliation system (most often a rudimental parliamentary form).

Our concern in the study of a particular nation's efforts to mod-

[23] This usage is derived from the description of mercantilism in the introduction to Heckscher's *Mercantilism* (London: George Allen & Unwin, Ltd., 1955), p. 22. Heckscher describes mercantilism as an "agent of unification."

ernize is not only where the nation may be placed on a continuum but the systemic changes that occur during various phases of modernization. Some countries begin with a framework established by colonial officials who have sought to realize as closely as possible the libertarian ideal. The result is not the ideal but a reconciliation system in which group pluralism soon breaks down into a monopoly of power by one group. It thus becomes a mobilization system — characteristically, a single-party state with a militant leader. At this stage, the mobilization system may change either in the direction of the collectivist model or toward some new synthesis such as a neomercantilist society.

Many theories may be employed as we try to examine the patterns of movement within the modernizing nations. One widespread assumption, however, ought to be made explicit at the beginning, since it is held by many of those who study modernizing nations: The implicit assumptions and values underlying the libertarian model will continue to exist in all the other systems, although in a hidden and disguised way, and will emerge even in the collectivist systems after they have succeeded in building some kind of unity, in developing the material standards of the society, and in providing a sense of identity and worth for individuals. If this is correct, then the long-term prognosis for democracy is hopeful.[24]

STRUCTURAL DYNAMICS

So far our discussion has centered around the problem of choice and its political implications during the modernizing process.

---

[24] Western policy is predicated on the assumption that this is true, just as Soviet policy vis-à-vis the modernizing nations is based upon an opposite viewpoint, namely, that mobilization systems will eventually build up those forms of unity essential to the collectivist society as conceived in Marxian terms. I hold to the first view as an article of faith. But I also hope to show the superior utility of the libertarian system in its handling of complexity. In this sense I believe that modernization ultimately produces libertarian systems.

Policy-making is the process of making choices, and the various elements of the process, which have already been described, are present in every system of choice. Perhaps a diagram will incorporate the various elements more explicitly (see Figure 3).

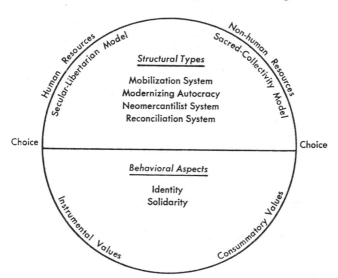

FIG. 3. — *An approach to the analysis of choice (adapted from Marion J. Levy, Jr.,* The Structure of Society *[Princeton, N.J.: Princeton University Press, 1952], p. 11). For definitions of the terms "consummatory" and "instrumental," see chapter iii.*

Two sets of propositions may now be made explicit. The first set deals with the relation of the four types of political system to modernization.

1. Of the four types of operating models, the reconciliation system is the least likely to serve as a satisfactory basis for establishing a new, modernizing polity.

2. Reconciliation systems are likely to attempt to realize modernization through a process of localized initiative and individual entrepreneurship, including private and private-public forms of enterprise. In contrast, mobilization systems are likely to see

modernization as a process of centralized planning and governmental enterprise.

3. Mobilization systems are most successful as "conversion" systems, that is, in (a) establishing a new polity and (b) converting from late modernization to industrialization.

4. Modernizing autocracies and neomercantilist societies are optimal political forms for long-term modernization, in particular, for the conversion from the "early" to the "late" stages of the process.

5. Reconciliation systems are optimal forms when the conversion to early industrialization has been completed, that is, for a modern industrial society.

The second set of propositions restates the first set in somewhat more generalized form. One central functional hypothesis is that *different polities employ different mixtures of coercion and information in trying to maintain authority, achieve stability, and increase efficiency.* I posit, for analytical purposes, an inverse relationship between information and coercion in a system: that is, high coercion systems are low information systems.[25] The political form that achieves an equilibrium between information and coercion will achieve maximum efficiency and authority. Not only will it achieve its goals, but it will produce goals proximate to its economic and social resources. Since political forms have their own dynamics by means of which the relationship between coercion and information is determined, we can treat political form, or polity, as an independent variable, with coercion and information as intervening variables and modernization the dependent variable.[26]

[25] There are many complicating factors in this hypothesis. One of the most interesting is the usefulness of corruption as a political device to increase information without reducing coercion.

[26] Any system of analysis that purports to examine such complex matters needs first of all to be classificatory and then analytical. Radcliffe-Brown has pointed out most persuasively that the "basis of science is systematic classification. It is the first task of social statics to make some attempt to compare forms of social life in order to arrive at classifications. But forms of social life cannot be classified into species and genera in the way we classify forms of organic life; the classification has to be not specific but typological,

If this hypothesis could stand alone, however, proving correct in each case, there would be little reason for governments to engage in coercive practices. In fact, high information systems have a problem of "overloading." [27] That is to say, the decision-makers may receive so much information that they have difficulty acting. Moreover, the information may be preselected and uneven in its sources and emphases. Hence, the difficulty in high information systems is evaluation. This leads to uncertainty. A corresponding hypothesis, then, is that high information systems are uncertainty systems, whereas high coercion systems are deterministic systems. Only if the high information systems have a political framework that can handle probabilities, that is, cope with a probabilistic universe, can they function well. High coercion systems operate with less information. Especially during periods of transition, when uncertainty is frightening, there is a widespread urge for control and a deterministic outlook associated with particular goals.

A third hypothesis combines these two. *Modernizing societies and industrial societies can utilize information only when they possess sound interpretative mechanisms.* Hence, the direction of modernization will be toward a probabilistic universe — and away from a deterministic one — through what I will call a reconciliation system (eventually arriving at representative government), if this is the most satisfactory means of handling and evaluating information. Hence, although one type of political system does

---

and this is a more complicated kind of investigation. It can only be reached by means of the establishing of typologies for features of social life or the complexes of features that are given in partial social systems." He continues, although "typological studies are one important part of social statics, there is another task, that of formulating generalisations about the conditions of existence of social systems, or all forms of social life. . . . The study of social dynamics is concerned with establishing generalisations about how social systems change. It is a corollary of the hypothesis of the systematic connection of features of social life that changes in some features are likely to produce changes in other features." See A. R. Radcliffe-Brown, *Structure and Function in Primitive Society* (Glencoe: Free Press of Glencoe, Ill., 1952), p. 7.

[27] See Wilbur Schramm, *The Process and Effects of Mass Communication* (Urbana: University of Illinois Press, 1955), pp. 16–17.

not change into another in a unilinear or evolutionary fashion, modernization and industrialization do result in a secular tendency toward increasing differentiation and complexity. From this secular tendency, we may infer, on the basis of our hypotheses, a long-run series of political changes leading toward high information and low coercion, that is, to some form of reconciliation system.

CONCLUSION

Predemocratic polities become significant for the study of politics through the analysis of political systems and forms and through the study of legitimacy. Also important are public aspiration and belief. Hence, ideology, motivation, and mobility become critical areas of discussion. The general process of modernization provides a useful setting for revealing these complex political matters.

Modernization may be described in non-industrial societies as the transposition of certain roles — professional, technical, administrative — and the transposition of institutions supporting these roles — hospitals, schools, universities, bureaucracies. Non-industrial modernizing societies, however, lack the powerful integrating thrust found in industrial societies. Social organizations are more chaotic and confused. Politics becomes the mechanism of integration, and authority is the critical problem confronting the leaders.

This conclusion leads to a consideration of the political forms most appropriate to producing and coping with modernization. Indeed, modernization emphasizes certain types of authority. The particular combinations of right that, embodied in authority, we call legitimacy are quite often determined by the goals of the polity. Failure to achieve such goals is thus prejudicial to authority. This means that in many modernizing societies the polity can only be secured by its successes. The efficiency of a regime determines the quality of its authority.

2

SOME
CHARACTERISTICS
OF MODERNIZATION

Modernization first occurred in the West through the twin processes of commercialization and industrialization. The social consequences of these processes can be summed up in the following rather paradigmatic categories: the growth of lending and fiscal devices, the need to support modern armies, the application of technologies in competitive market situations, and the influence of trade and voyages on the scientific spirit — all of which are evidence that modernity in the West attacked religion and superstition, family and church, mercantilism and autocracy. Indeed, we have come to consider science as the antidote for faith, with Galileo as a kind of folk hero of modernization. His triumph is the triumph of reason, and reason as applied to human affairs is the foundation of modernity.[1]

In many non-Western areas modernization has been a result of commercialization and, rather than industrialization, bureaucracy. Some of the same values appropriate to industrial countries have been spread by enterprising men, sometimes in the context of politics and trade and at other times in the context of religion and education. Modernization can thus be seen as something apart

[1] See Giorgio de Santillana, *The Crime of Galileo* (Chicago: University of Chicago Press, 1955), p. 11.

from industrialization — caused by it in the West but causing it in other areas.[2]

Behind these large considerations are smaller ones. Consider what it means to establish a small shop near a traditional market at a time when there is no regularized system of bulk purchasing or wholesale buying, few distributive outlets, and a largely illiterate clientele, many of whom buy on credit. Quite often the Syrian or Lebanese trader in West Africa, or the Indian or Arab in East Africa, or the Moslem in Indonesia represents a crucial prototype for modernization. Suppose our shopkeeper finds that his shop has become a central meeting place, with the more successful customers gathering on the stoop to pass the time of day. Perhaps he will serve drinks and later open a restaurant or a hotel. If he is enterprising he may try to make his shop the local post office. Exchanges of the written word and the cash nexus go hand in hand.

Or the village party organ may establish a reading room and provide literacy classes for adults. A bare office with tattered books comes to mean learning. Clerks in offices formerly represented modernity; but today it may be the uniforms of the youth: Boy Scouts, Young Pioneers, or other local derivatives. Ideologies link the heroes of the country with others, Western and Eastern. Names like Lincoln, Marx, Lenin, Roosevelt, Gandhi, Sukarno, Mao, are all modernizing symbols, linked to particular modes of reform. It is the politicians who are symbols in the developing

[2] The characteristics of modern industrial societies have been usefully summed up in an article by F. X. Sutton as follows:

"1. Predominance of universalistic, specific, and achievement norms.

"2. High degree of social mobility (in a general — not necessarily 'vertical' — sense).

"3. Well developed occupational system, insulated from other social structures.

"4. 'Egalitarian' class system based on generalized patterns of occupational achievement.

"5. Prevalence of 'associations,' i.e., functionally specific, non-ascriptive structures."

See Sutton, "Social Theory and Comparative Politics," reprinted in H. Eckstein and David E. Apter (eds.), *Comparative Politics: A Reader* (New York: Free Press of Glencoe, Inc., 1963), p. 71.

countries and notably not the inventors or craftsmen. Whereas the famous technological inventions changed the nature of "our" society, such innovations are virtually a natural feature of modern society for the people of the developing areas. Indeed, Western society has little meaning apart from its technology for these countries, and its institutions are inextricably linked together — politics and science, inventions and parliaments.

DIVERSE SOURCES OF INNOVATION

Who are the modernizers? A growing literature indicates how curious we are about the personalities who are the agents of modernization. Some argue that they are the marginal men, as in the case of the Chinese in parts of Southeast Asia. Quite often they have been born of marriages between persons from two culturally or ethnically unrelated groups, are at least to some extent multilingual, and are products of an educational system that drew them away from home. Elements of marginality can thus be regarded as a critical factor in the development of modernization skills.[3]

A second factor is the accessibility of innovative roles, a condition that affects youth primarily. In particular, education in the form of either apprenticeship or more formal schooling, has been important in stimulating an interest in the roles of modernity, as have the power and prestige consequences of the roles themselves.

Third, the mass media and, as Lerner has shown, the growth of communications in general have made it possible to conceive of modernity even in the absence of many of its qualities.[4] Nor does it require a large group of those who define themselves as intellectuals, or technicians, to have an enormous "aura effect" in a com-

[3] See Lea A. Williams, *Overseas Chinese Nationalism: The Genesis of the Pan-Chinese Movement in Indonesia, 1900–1916* (Glencoe: Free Press of Glencoe, Ill., 1960), pp. 138–39.
[4] See Daniel Lerner, *The Passing of Traditional Society* (Glencoe: Free Press of Glencoe, Ill., 1958).

munity, because they, in order to make themselves more secure, are the very ones — journalists, writers, teachers, civil servants, engineers, and so on — who need to substantiate themselves with large rural groups and premoderns.

These three factors do not exhaust the conditions that stimulate people to become modern. Quite often it is the organization of traditional society itself, its immobilities and its adaptive qualities, that generates a force for modernization. Often, too, the strength of the motivation depends on the personalities in the society, their creativity and their general buoyancy.[5]

Whatever the quality of the personalities involved, it is clear that modernization creates a catch-up psychology and a sense of being placed at a disadvantage that generate the motivation for change. Any material improvements in a community create a demand for more. As Bernard Lewis has suggested in the case of Turkey, "In the neighborhood of the towns, bus services, piped water, electricity, daily newspapers, and access to urban amenities heralded the dawn of a new age; even in remoter places, a local road, a daily bus, and a few battery-operated wireless sets brought new contacts with the outside world, a new awareness of membership of the larger community, and the beginning of a new process of far-reaching social change."[6] The roles created are those of the bus driver, the wireless repairmen, the reporters, and all the rest whose halo effect is significant. At the same time the conditions of change, the roles of change, and the personalities for

[5] See Kurt W. Back, "The Change-prone Person in Puerto Rico," *Public Opinion Quarterly*, XXII (Fall, 1958). Back points out that for the urbanized and lower economic stratum in which his survey was conducted, personality tests and attitude indices distinguished change-prone from other individuals. "The modernism index had a central place in this complex, showing high relations on the one side to the personality measures and on the other to behavioral indices. This index is made up of two questions, (a) belief in and relation to the new generation, and (b) active planning for improvement of the situation. It shows that the key ingredient in modernism is orientation toward the future. We can conclude that this attitude is based on a somewhat general personality disposition" (p. 340).

[6] Lewis, *The Emergence of Modern Turkey* (London: Oxford University Press, 1961), p. 472.

change need to be fitted together in such a way that their tentative efforts bring results. Otherwise a small degree of modernization may bring despair and bitterness — a knowledge of attempting to be modern but failing at it — as the Banfields show in the case of a southern Italian village.[7]

Quite often it is the main job of government to prevent the population that has tasted modernization but cannot quite cope with it from slipping back. Egypt was plagued with this problem for years. There was more wealth and efforts at modernization in Egypt than in any other Middle Eastern or North African country. Under British administration there had developed large urban areas, a small but significant factory culture, a larger artisan group, and a highly rationalized civil service. The latter, recruited mainly from the urban population (74.2 per cent), were able to go to the university and complete their first degrees (77.1 per cent); most of them were the sons of civil servants, white-collar employees, and landlords (62.4 per cent).[8] Despite the efforts of the civil service, however, it was not until relatively recently that the effects of modernization created that climate of buoyancy and hope that would attract personalities with the capacity for both innovation and self-discipline. This has been one major achievement of the present Egyptian government.

Quite often the first modernizers have been those who realized that if they did not change their roles they would be forever barred from political power. In Africa, for example, some of the earliest modernizers were chiefs whose traditional prescriptions of office clearly delineated a religious rather than a secular role. Yet they could turn their hands to modernization at times, and if not they, then their sons. In almost every major African territory there were schools for the sons of chiefs, and it was to ensure their participation in modern government that they were recruited.

[7] See Edward and L. F. Banfield, *The Moral Basis of a Backward Society* (Glencoe: Free Press of Glencoe, Ill., 1958).

[8] These figures are taken from Morroe Berger, *Bureaucracy and Society in Modern Egypt: A Study of the Higher Civil Service* (Princeton, N.J.: Princeton University Press, 1957), pp. 42–47.

In the case of Ghana, some of the chief-modernizers were treated poorly by the authorities. King Aggery of Cape Coast was first rewarded for his spirit of modernity in prosecuting court cases and public works and later attacked for his political independence and stalwartness, deposed, and deported.[9] Similar treatment was given King Jaja of Opobo in Nigeria. After his recognition as a chief by the British, according to Sir Alan Burns, "Jaja's energy and acumen had full scope. His wealth was considerably increased by trade, and this permitted him to acquire sufficient force to strengthen his position and establish a monopoly in the districts claimed by him." Arbitrator, merchant, shipping agent, and general entrepreneur, Jaja tried to control the trade along the creeks and inlets near Opobo. He, too, was deported.[10]

These examples are cited because, although somewhat unusual, they are quite typical of a certain period in the modernization of a colonial country. More frequently the educated elites were singled out for particular abuse by an ambivalent colonial government, which regarded them, on the one hand, as a product of forward-looking colonial policies in education and, on the other, as a cause of persistent trouble and complaint. The "scholars," as they were often called, were regarded as mischievous, arrogant, and dishonest. Their efforts at modernization were seen as parodying Western institutions and aping the mannerisms and characteristics of their "tutors." Such attitudes can still be found among Europeans in South Africa.[11]

More recently, conflicts between generations have inadvertently produced a similar situation in modern guise. In order to identify

[9] See the description of Aggery in David Kimble, A Political History of Ghana, 1850–1928 (Oxford: Clarendon Press, 1963), pp. 215–20. See also J. E. Flint, Sir George Goldie and the Making of Modern Nigeria (London: Oxford University Press, 1960), passim; P. D. Curtin, The Image of Africa (Madison: University of Wisconsin Press, 1964), chapter xvi; and R. Robinson, J. Gallagher, and A. Denny, Africa and the Victorians (London: Macmillan & Co., 1961), chapter xii.

[10] See Burns, History of Nigeria (London: George Allen & Unwin, Ltd., 1951), pp. 141–42.

[11] See Mary Benson, The African Patriots (London: Faber & Faber, 1963).

comfortable modern roles for themselves, youthful aspirants need to challenge the form and order already established — whether imposed from the outside or not. The clearest example of this is in India, where the Congress party has become so venerable (yet controlling all the main modernization posts) that the youth cast about for party alternatives that will provide them better opportunity to apply their skills and innovative capacities. This is one reason why the Communist party of India continues to recruit young educated Indians despite the conflict with China. (Indeed, for many developing societies, communism has been attractive as a form of modernizing system that will provide stability and control during the difficult period of role search and definition.) Where the obstacles in modernization are great, creative, frustrated, or innovative personalities may seek out the most powerful, drastic, and contrasting system of politics and give it their loyalty. In the Middle East, for example, the disavowal of parliamentary governments that occurred after the 1930's led both to "military socialism," as Laqueur calls it, and to an interest in communism.[12]

In an attempt to summarize the diversity of roles through which modernity spreads, Lucien W. Pye has used a typology that includes several functionally defined types: mediators, transmitters, conveyers, and so on. He has arranged these in terms of tendencies that, although opposite to each other, nevertheless have a modernizing consequence: the *administrator*, who emphasizes rational bureaucratic norms, as opposed to the *agitator*, who awakens dormant demands; the *amalgamate*, who combines both old and new roles in one, in contrast to the *transmitter*, who tends to represent only the new roles; the *ideological propagandist*, who strives to establish a common ideology with the *political broker*, who aggregates special interests.[13]

[12] See Walter Z. Laqueur, *Communism and Nationalism in the Middle East* (London: Routledge & Kegan Paul, 1961), pp. 18–21.
[13] See Pye, "Administrators, Agitators, and Brokers," *Public Opinion Quarterly*, XXII (Fall, 1958). See also D. A. Rustow, *Politics of Westernization in the Near East*, (Princeton, N.J.: Princeton University, Center of International Studies, 1956). For an examination of the problem of the repre-

Whatever the problems with such a typology, it does point up the diversity of modernizing roles with a direct reference to politics, which must be examined in any empirical evaluation of modernization. Of particular significance is the way in which such modernizing roles are linked to those of high status. Role, status, profession, and occupation all need to be examined in order to identify the reinforcing elements of role change and the incompatibilities as well.

Quite often the urge toward modernity is the same as that which produces new forms of art or exotic techniques in painting. Indeed, some of the young Communists in China, for example, mixed poetry with politics in a very explicit way. Even the most sorry demonstration and the most ineffective acts of the party came to arouse the same sense of pride and achievement as a major victory.[14] Both modern nationalism and communism have this much in common; for the youth they represent cultures of modernity, cast in a political mode, through which their supporters seek the liberation of the human spirit.

COLONIALISM AS A MODERNIZING FORCE

Whatever we may think of its practice, colonialism demonstrated the role of commerce and bureaucracy in modernization. By stating this I do not mean to deny the developmental aspects of precolonial systems. Traditional societies were not all subsistence economies — for example, the ancient trade in salt, kola, gold, and

---

sentation of such roles, see the excellent study by Reinhard Bendix, "Public Authority in a Developing Political Community: The Case of India," *European Journal of Sociology*, IV (1963). For a study of role change in the context of local government, see Ursula K. Hicks, *Development from Below* (Oxford: Clarendon Press, 1961); and for a general commentary on "the will to economize," which in many ways represents the beginnings of modernity, see W. Arthur Lewis, *The Theory of Economic Growth*, (London: George Allen & Unwin, Ltd., 1955).

[14] See the interesting discussion of this in T. A. Hsia, *Enigma of the Five Martyrs* (Berkeley: University of California, Institute of International Studies, 1962), pp. 74–75.

slaves between North Africa and West Africa. Various forms of money were in use long before European intervention. Ports and markets were often very elaborate. The traditional Dahomean port of Whydah, for example, was administered by the king of Dahomey, and although Dahomeans did not participate to any great extent in commercial activities, their military requirements were such that they allowed foreigners to operate what became a major entrepôt along the coast.[15] The rise and fall of empires in West Africa — Mali, Ghana, Songhai, Gobir, Bornu, and others — were largely determined by trade and the organization developed to further it, despite large subsistence sectors. Long before the European presence, trading sectors became highly developed, that is, part of the traditional network of trade and commerce, and began to change rapidly. Many of them began to participate in commercial activity in earnest. Once the Europeans set up their trading factories, however, the pace and techniques changed. First came the pioneers and then the trading families. Factories or trading houses were set up in Dakar, Freetown, Monrovia, Accra, and Lagos. Extensive intermarriage took place between the local peoples and the Dutch, Danes, Brandenburgers, French, Corsicans, Italians, Spaniards, and others.[16] Hence it was the direct line between a metropolitan country and an overseas territory that helped to build a set of relationships that were manifested not merely in "old" and "new" roles, or in traditional or modern ones, but in a wide range of intermediate roles.

Because commercial and some industrial enterprises established in the colonial territories had their markets and main source of

[15] See Rosemary Arnold, "A Port of Trade: Whydah on the Guinea Coast," in Karl Polanyi, Conrad Arensberg, and Harry Pearson (eds.), *Trade and Markets in the Early Empires* (Glencoe: Free Press of Glencoe, Ill., 1957). See also Paul Bohannan and George Dalton, *Markets in Africa* (New York: Doubleday Anchor Books, 1965).

[16] There is an interesting literature on West African stratification. See D. Westermann, *Autobiographies d'Africaines* (Paris: Payot, 1943); Jacques Charpy, *La Fondation de Dakar* (Paris: Larose, 1958); M. Banton, *West African City* (London: Oxford University Press, 1957); and Arthur Porter, *Creoledom* (London: Oxford University Press, 1963). Many others could be cited.

investment in the home countries, there is a correlation between the rising economic status of the metropole and the increase in commercialization and modernization of the overseas territory. Overseas development occurred between periods of war or depression. In the period immediately after World War I, for example, investments overseas, capital development projects such as railways, harbors, and schools, and other forms of primary development were characteristic of British territories, where the prevailing philosophy was to place the colonies on a pay-as-you-go basis as quickly as possible and thus end parliamentary subsidies. To some extent the same was true of French colonies, although the overseas investment of France was much smaller.

During the thirties, when overseas funds were unavailable, colonial territories were forced to retrench drastically. This quite often took the form of reduced expatriate staffs, with much more direct administrative control in order to maximize efficiency. Social services were restricted. The growth of local councils, treasuries, and the like was stunted, largely because of their cost, to be renewed once again on a much larger scale after World War II. It is the uneven application of modernizing programs, not the lack of modernization itself, that is the characteristic of different colonial systems. Obviously, different metropolitan powers employed different patterns of modernization; some did remarkably little — the Portuguese in Africa — others did a very great deal. Indeed, with the exception of programs of mass modernization by drastic political methods, colonialism at its best has been one very useful mechanism for modernizing.[17]

[17] Such generalizations are always open to criticism because they are excessively broad. For one thing, there is no colonial "system" except in the very loose sense of the subordination by one country of a non-contiguous territory whose political status is legally defined as inferior to the metropolitan country. In some instances, political reform meant providing greater and greater warrants of autonomy and an enlarged share in political life to the modernized elite within the territory, looking toward the time when representative bodies, which in constitutional practice embody legitimacy, could be established. When a colony could pay its own way and when representative self-government was securely established, then political independence for the territory logically followed.

Political modernization came to have two meanings in colonial systems. First, it meant that there had to be a "Westernized" secular elite that could participate in political life; and second, there had to be "Westernized" forms of government so that the elites could be represented. This was characteristic of the British pattern of political evolution in colonial territories, although there were some profound exceptions to the general rule and the rule itself is of very recent origin.

The desire to foster a brood of Westminster models as a legacy of British rule has been a comparatively recent, even brief and passing, phenomenon in British policy. Exact identity with the British model was neither desired nor demanded: it was repudiated as inconvenient or inhibiting by both rulers and ruled. Imperial and colonial politicians quoted British example or precedent only where it was useful to their case.[18]

It was, of course, useful to the extent that it encouraged the evolution of self-government and independence through conciliar government.

There were numerous variations on the theme of political evolution in the British territories, fewer in the French system, and many fewer in the Belgian, Dutch, and Portuguese systems. France applied a very broad pattern of political evolution throughout large regionally organized groups of territories, such as French West Africa. Within this general pattern, there were very complex adjustments to local conditions.[19]

[18] See Frederick Madden, "Some Origins and Purposes in the Formation of British Colonial Government," in Kenneth Robinson and Frederick Madden (eds.), *Essays in Imperial Government* (Oxford: Basil Blackwell, 1963), p. 2. For an astringent view of colonialism, see Paul A. Baran, *The Political Economy of Growth* (New York: Monthly Review Press, 1962), pp. 163–300.

[19] Even gross distinctions between French and British colonial practice (direct and indirect rule) have turned out to be schoolboy distinctions that are almost useless for analytical purposes. But there are still some important comparisons that can be made. For some time, the French ideal of political evolution overseas was to raise a territory or group of territories to a status similar to that of a department of France, with gradually greater warrants of authority resulting in increased participation in the institutions of French

A description of various colonial systems, however, would divert us from the main purpose at hand. We are concerned here with various colonial systems only as primary instruments of modernization (even though they were transitional political forms). The most general structural variables that may be applied in a comparison of colonial systems over a period of time are, first, whether the colonial government was mainly autocratic or conciliar and, second, whether leadership was personal or impersonal. If we consider various colonial territories — British, French, Belgian, Dutch, and Portuguese — in terms of parallel stages cutting across the usual distinctions between colonial systems, we can see colonialism as a modernization process proceeding through four main stages: the pioneering, bureaucratic, representative, and responsible governmental stages.[20] These need not follow a linear progression. (See the diagram in Figure 4.)

What this diagram emphasizes are the structural changes in colonialism that coincide with policies leading to modernization. Political modernization is a cause of further change. The uniqueness of government as a modernizing instrument can thus be demonstrated by treating it as an independent variable (as a creator of a different environment for itself). Hence, political

---

politics — the National Assembly, the Cabinet, and the like. Some overseas territories were in fact governed as departments. Of course, this pattern was not unambiguous, and such ambiguity can perhaps best be seen in the institutions of the French Union, which would eventually have diverted overseas territories from French metropolitan institutions, which, in turn, would increasingly have become instruments of overseas rather than metropolitan deputies. France did not relish the prospect of becoming a captive of her territories. Still, the emphasis on the metropole, its legal structure, the uniformity of its educational system, the forms of overseas aid, and the fiscal and financial structure (which was more closely linked to the metropole than in the British system) all helped to create quite different attitudes toward politics. The French educational system, for example, helped to spread both Catholic and socialist forms of universalism as political ideologies, whereas the bewildering array of English forms of education — the various mission schools, government schools, and private and public schools — were geared more directly to local political life, local councils, and local problems.

[20] For a detailed discussion of these types in an East African context, see my book, *The Political Kingdom in Uganda* (Princeton, N.J.: Princeton University Press, 1961), pp. 447–59.

modernization is both consequence and cause of modernization, and this is reflected in an appropriately changing governmental system. Some of the colonial systems went through all the various stages leading to independence. Some never really arrived there. The Congo, for example, was in the very first stage of representative government when it became independent; Indonesia was still in the bureaucratic stage; India had had a reasonably long period of representative government; and Ceylon, which was one of the first to do so, had gained responsible government. It should be added that postindependence governments are also subject to the same stages of transition.

	Personal	Impersonal
Autocratic	Pioneering	Bureaucratic
Conciliar	Representative	Responsible

FIG. 4. — *Stages of colonialism.*

Probably the most exciting period in the transition from dependence to independence is the representative stage because, although there are legislative bodies, the responsibility for government remains outside the colony. It becomes an outrageous political condition for many potential politicians, stimulating them to organize followers and to capitalize on grievances. This is the period in which what we will call "Robin Hood" roles are formed — and played by semicharismatic figures who can rally around them the disadvantaged and confused. Lacking the controls of the impersonal but autocratic patterns of government of bureaucratic colonialism, the representative period often coincides with conditions described by Norman Cohn as characteristic of the late medieval period, and with similar results.

There were however many who merely acquired new wants without being able to satisfy them; and in them the spectacle of a wealth undreamt-of in earlier centuries provoked a bitter sense of frustration. In all the over-populated, highly-urbanised and industrialised areas there were multitudes of people living on the margin of society, in a state of chronic insecurity.[21]

So in the period in which personal politics and conciliar forms coincide, a period in which there is widespread unrest and political irresponsibility, the conditions are ripe for nationalist movements, which have as their object the achievement of some new and higher synthesis of modern life, free of the enslavement of race, of subservience, and of inferiority. It is in this context that nationalism emerges with particular sharpness in the colonial societies and attacks government, an alien fortress.

Colonialism is an interesting historical phase. It illustrates a particular sequence of transition, a pattern in which modernization has been universalized and in which some of the important roles of modernity have been acquired. It is replaced in the period of independence by systems that change in response to modernity and that manipulate modernity itself. How each of these responds to the pressure to modernize and how each accomplishes its modernization objectives will be dealt with in succeeding chapters. First, however, it will be useful to discuss modernization more specifically to indicate its relationship to traditionalism, on the one hand, and to industrialization, on the other.

TRADITIONALISM AND DEVELOPMENT

It has been suggested that modernization is the process of consciously directing and controlling the social consequences of increased role differentiation and organizational complexity in a society. The most interesting cases are those in which such differentiation and complexity of organization are not merely prod-

[21] See Cohn, *The Pursuit of the Millennium* (New York: Harper Torchbooks, 1961), p. 28.

ucts of size, or population growth, but rather results of an increase in technologically significant functional roles.[22] Putting the matter this way leads us to speculation on the origins of modernity. We have discussed some of the conditions that led to a change from traditionalism to modernity. Much of our thinking about development, and indeed, the contemporary interest in social change, has been centered on this transition. Nonetheless, attempts to analyze modernity have not handled traditionalism well. The reason is not hard to find. The historical cases are so involved and varied that it is difficult to separate the strands of traditionalism from those of modernity. Even recent attempts to prevent the distinction from becoming blurred by the complexity of the process (by a combination of functional methods and ideal-type analysis) treat traditional societies as composed of a particular set of ingredients, all of which share a certain static quality. Conservatism is thereby linked with traditionality, implying that kind of equilibrium (or delicate balance of social practices and beliefs) that is embalmed within a religious framework and that, by virtue of its sanctity and immemoriality, defies change.

This kind of analysis uses traditionality as an ideal type not to be found empirically in pure form. Problems arise when we examine the traditional society itself. Too often there is a tendency to reify, that is, to take the ideal type as real and static. In practice, traditionality in its various forms and patterns is an essential part of the study of modernization (particularly its political aspects) precisely because it, too, changes. How many of the practical problems of politics, and the more serious challenges to authority, stem from the remaining strongholds of traditionality within the modernizing society?[23] And how often, by challenging tradition-

[22] Less interesting are the cases where complexity occurs as a result of mere population increase, but even in these cases, the effects may be of significance. This is one reason why ancient societies are of interest to us. Moreover, the whole question of the relationship of differentiation and growth to the formation of high cultures, traditional in form, is one that has barely been explored.

[23] See chapter iii.

alism head on, do political leaders cause grave and serious conflicts in their society when they would like to avoid them?

Such issues are not new; many theorists have tried to show differences between traditional and non-traditional societies by citing institutional variations. Maine, for example, emphasizes the peculiar significance of kinship in "primitive societies" by stressing the strategic role of agnatic relationships (as compared with cognitive relationships) in modern society, and links these forms of relationship by means of an evolutionary theory of development. Kinship not only has important effects on status, property, inheritance, and the like, but, as a pattern of relations between men, is "conceptually" different.

> We saw one peculiarity invariably distinguishing the infancy of society. Men are regarded and treated, not as individuals, but always as members of a particular group. Everybody is first a citizen and then, as a citizen, he is a member of his order — of an aristocracy or a democracy, of an order of patricians or plebeians or in those societies which an unhappy fate has afflicted with a special perversion in their course of development, of a caste. Next, he is a member of a gens, house, or clan; and lastly he is a member of his *family*. This last was the narrowest and most personal relation in which he stood; nor, paradoxical as it may seem, was he ever regarded as *himself*, as a distinct individual. His individuality was swallowed up in his family. I repeat the definition of a primitive society given before. It has for its units, not individuals, but groups of men united by the reality or the fiction of blood-relationship.[24]

For Durkheim, too, the differences between primitive and modern societies are very great. As with Maine, the juridical rules of the community indicate the prevailing form of social relationship and, in particular, the basis of solidarity.[25] In primitive society,

---

[24] See Henry Sumner Maine, *Ancient Law* (Boston: Beacon Press, 1963), pp. 177–78.

[25] Durkheim says, "Our method has now been fully outlined. Since law reproduces the principal forms of social solidarity, we have only to classify

which he calls "mechanical," there is a high degree of repressive law, in which similarity of conduct is ensured by the authorities' classification of any significant departures from custom as crimes. These crimes, symbolic acts against community solidarity, exact the most extreme penalties (mainly death). Organic solidarity, that is, "modern" society, on the other hand, is characterized by complex forms of interactions between individuals and groups. Functional interdependence is the key to this solidarity. Repressive law is only a small part of the juridical system. Restitutive law is the main part. Like Maine, Durkheim gives us a concept of evolution of social systems from lower to higher forms. The *deus ex machina* that provides the transition from one to the other is the division of labor.

These distinctions, although powerful, turned "tradition" into a blanket term to cover all forms of social life other than the modern industrial type.[26] They, and others like them, are subject to the criticisms applied by Firth in his analysis of Maine. "His ideas of social development in terms of polar opposites: family to individual, status to contract, penal legislation to civil law, are too arbitrary and naïve by modern standards of analysis."[27] This criticism would also apply to theoreticians like Weber, Sombart, Tönnies, and Durkheim and to some of the more recent ones, like McClelland and Hagen. The latter see in the universalization of modernity an outlook that is necessarily antitraditional (with "traditional" meaning a fundamentally closed, personalistic way of life, relatively fixed and not easily amenable to development).

_____

the different types of law to find therefrom the different types of social solidarity which correspond to it" (Émile Durkheim, *The Division of Labor* [Glencoe: Free Press of Glencoe, Ill., 1949], p. 68).

[26] What all these distinctions, primitive-complex, sacred-secular, folk-urban, mechanical-organic, and *Gemeinschaft-Gesellschaft*, have in common is their implicit notion of development as moving from the simple to the complex — the complex forming an elaborate network of mediating and integrating points in political life, in religion, or in the economy — a notion which I share.

[27] See Raymond Firth's Preface to Henry Sumner Maine, *Ancient Law*, p. xxx.

ROLES AS INDICATORS OF MODERNIZATION

Viewing the change from agrarian to industrial society from a nineteenth-century perspective, the historical sociologists were mainly concerned with the effect of the process on the civic community, with politics seen largely as the evolution of morals. What happens to the family and to the work group when the ties of kin and oath are no longer binding? What forms of normative regulation replace the cross-pressures of the intimate environment? From these questions grew the interest in urbanization, personality, the factory, and culture change and the links these factors have with the regulatory mechanisms of the society.[28]

Today an analysis of society proceeds in terms of professionalization, skill, technology, rationality, and functionality — all terms that we associate with modern society. We identify these abstractions in terms of particular strategic roles in the society, for example, the civil servant, the hydraulic engineer, the community development expert, the university lecturer. How sharp is their contrast to traditional roles — the chief, the priest, the queen-mother, the bearers of the king's patrimony!

Putting the matter in terms of roles, however, only makes us aware how complex the process of modernization is. New roles emerge at every point. In a sense, that is what change really is — the formation of new, adaptive roles in a system. Modernization employs particular roles that have been drawn from various industrial societies (and ordinarily associated with Western industrial society, although modernization can no longer be claimed as peculiarly Western) and that embody choices between life styles and the idea of "career."

[28] Emerging now as a significant form of analysis is the study of the polity as the mechanism of change, with the morality of change embodied in the state itself. Durkheim, in a rather surprising passage, says, "The fundamental duty of the State is laid down in this very fact: it is to persevere in calling the individual to a moral way of life. I say fundamental duty, for civic morals can have no pole-star for a guide except moral causes" (Emile Durkheim, *Professional Ethics and Civic Morals* [Glencoe: Free Press of Glencoe, Ill., 1958], p. 69).

Roles, new or old, modified and adapted, given new meaning by changes, ought to be the beginning point for the analysis of modernization. They provide much of the data for the analysis of politics. They embody new notions of morality. In forming modalities of interaction they illuminate the actual problems that arise in the social sphere, which can be seen as problems of mobility and of direct conflicts in values as well as problems of relationships between people at the work place and at the place of worship. What Banfield describes as "ethos" in the southern Italian village of Montegrano can be translated into "roles." And as S. F. Nadel has suggested, the way roles are put together reveals something of the moral basis of the community and the structure of the society as well. "The advantages of role summation lie in the strengthening of social integration and of social control. For the more roles an individual combines in his person, the more is he linked by relationships with persons in other roles and in diverse areas of social life. Equally, any additional role assumed by an individual ties him more firmly to the norms of his society."[29]

To illustrate these remarks, let us take the proposition that modernization is a slower and less ruthless process than rapid industrialization. In terms of roles this means that during modernization a large number of intermediate roles come into being whose primary functional significance is to mediate between old and new. We can speculate that such roles will in some measure act both to facilitate innovation and to resist it. In the case of industrialization, however, the intermediate roles that have come into being during modernization are swept away, since they have become only obstacles and are no longer of use. For example, commercialization, as an aspect of modernization, may be acceptable to particular groups of individuals who can act as middlemen in an alien community and at the same time resist changing

[29] Nadel, *The Theory of Social Structure* (Glencoe: Free Press of Glencoe, Ill., 1957), p. 71. See also Edward and L. F. Banfield, *The Moral Basis of a Backward Society.*

their family habits and their living arrangements. Retaining a brokerage relationship between town and country, they may rely on familial rather than contractual ties to undertake commerce and may hoard their money (or distribute it in the bazaar to innumerable relatives) rather than invest it for development. Thus, such brokerage roles may at one stage serve as modernization instruments and at another may deter modernization.

There is no such thing as a purely modern role. The lawyer represented modernity in Latin America in 1930. Today it is the economist. Tomorrow it may be the engineer. Certain roles are strategic indicators of modernity at one point in time but not at another. Clearly, then, we must locate meaningful sets of roles that include the most functional careers for a particular level of innovation and that are recognized as most significant by change-oriented members of the community. These may include technical-bureaucratic careers, political careers (when government or party is employed as a modernizing instrument), and so on. How such careers are placed in a society indicates the society's choice of organization and its ways of manipulating organization. A comparative study of modernization begins in the comparison of strategic career profiles in relation to stratification.

THE MANAGEMENT OF ROLES

The complexity of the problem of roles links modernization to politics. The expectation that political leaders will advance their countries from one status to another, as from dependence to independence, is only part of a generally more widespread demand for innovation in the community, including the universal desire to raise living standards. Even raising living standards requires such radically new attitudes of hope and daring and a willingness to tinker and meddle with already established roles that most political leaders are forced to alter the hierarchy of power and prestige and to set their sights on some new corporate image of society in which the modernization roles will fit together, make sense, and work.[30]

Such an environment of changing roles results in a sense of hope as well as grievance. Modernization is often associated with breaking dominance-submission relationships and the repugnant analogies that have been associated with them. Modernization means, from this point of view, the establishment of agencies and instruments of modernity that allow independent rather than dependent relationships. As a result, the development of skills, the awareness of new patterns of time, participation, mastery over nature, and so on, are transformed into a search for personal integrity, worth, and self-respect. These are, of course, well-known observations, but they are worth repeating, since they may somehow help us render more accessible the instruments and institutions of present highly developed countries without being offensive. This is difficult, however, since modernization is linked to a wide range of adjustive emotional attitudes that assert personality, cultural autonomy, and political independence.

[30] Willie Abraham has put the matter as follows: "When one culture borrows some of its industrial technique and institutions from another culture, one can expect that, depending on how central these are in the matrix, they will already be controlled and permeated with other cultural elements, even if these only take the form of tea breaks. It could certainly happen that these borrowed items are in their native setting surrounded by ideals, attitudes, relationships, inter-human habits, which include design of buildings, amenities, types and method of control of labour, relatonships between employees and managers and employers, attitudes of labour to work, and happen to be repeated in their new setting. But even when this is so, the borrowers may still feel considerable pain at their own institutions and techniques having been replaced. This is sometimes due to the mistaken but natural belief that the new institutions cannot be serving the same purpose writ large, or are not informed by the same ideals. But this belief, though sometimes mistaken, has an opportunity of being correct from the very fact that it is natural. Indeed, that this is a distinct possibility is a consequence of the corrosive effect of material culture on the value aspect of culture. The possibility that certain techniques and institutions are already infused with cultural elements of the people from whom they are lifted, may well make it impossible to effect a simple transplantation. It may become necessary to carry out an operation more in the nature of a graft" (*The Mind of Africa* [Chicago: University of Chicago Press, 1962], pp. 33–34). This kind of concern, expressed politically, is one basis for the direct political control of innovation.

In many societies the intensity of belief is not based on blindness and superstition but on a deep-rooted fear that personal identity will be destroyed if religious or political practices are changed. This is why, in the effort to reorganize their societies today, many political leaders rely on the connections they can make with tradition. These connections help to create an inheritance. Israel, for example, in addition to wishing to reinforce her historic claims to the site, is preoccupied with archeology as more than an academic pastime. In Senegal, research by some indigenous scholars is devoted to linking ancient Egypt as a black kingdom with sub-Saharan Africa.[31] In the Convention People's Party headquarters in Accra, there are to be found large murals depicting Africans as the founders of ancient law and medicine. The desire to modernize without losing tradition necessitates a search for a new moral synthesis in which the individual can be related to authority.

Modernity and traditionalism are linked together in fundamental ways, even in the context of modernization. The synthesis between them serves as a primary moral focus. Michael Polanyi's description of science can be applied to the relationship between tradition and modernity. He commented that science, reflecting the modern mind, is in a paradoxical condition. "A new destructive skepticism is linked here to a new passionate social conscience; an utter disbelief in the spirit of man is coupled with extravagant moral demands. We see at work here the form of action which has already dealt so many shattering blows to the modern world: the chisel of skepticism driven by the hammer of social passion."[32]

Both in the modernizing nations and elsewhere men have refined their moral sensibilities along with their skepticism. At no time in history has the world been so sensitive to moral subtleties and more likely to take transgressions seriously. This sensitivity is expressed in the search for new political forms, in the public's

[31] See Cheikh Anta Diop, *Nations Negres et Culture* (Paris: Editions Africaines, 1955).

[32] Polanyi, *The Logic of Liberty* (Chicago: University of Chicago Press, 1958), p. 4.

desire for reform, and in the willingness to apply research and science to human problems. A paradox arises in that the more people desire to ameliorate their ills, the more these crowd in upon them. Each fresh solution only uncovers more problems.[33]

These remarks should also suggest that political development is no mere reciprocal of economic development but rather a complex of factors that results in systemic coherence. This "urge to coherence" may not necessarily materialize successfully. But in the effort to create a more effective integrated system, economic factors will most frequently come to serve political and social needs. The criteria for the economic proposals and programs involved in the development of modernizing nations are first political.[34]

Two related and important concerns that arise from the study of development in general, or economic development, more spe-

[33] This paradox is reflected in attitudes to modern ideologies. None seems able to capture the public imagination for long, either programmatically or morally. In the developing areas, interestingly enough, it is the heroic individual or leader, rather than his ideas, around which the many rally in order to organize themselves. There, leadership and progress can be seen to go together. In the more developed areas, it is more complex than that. Offended morality leads to outrage. We still do not know where outrage will lead.

[34] Perhaps the most consistent efforts to explore the relationship between economic and political development has been in the work of the Social Science Research Council's subcommittee on economic growth. Joseph Spengler, Wilbert Moore, Bert Hoselitz, and others have been trying to establish the conditions surrounding it. There are many others. See Joseph J. Spengler, "Theory, Ideology, Non-Economic Values, and Politico-Economic Development," and Wilbert E. Moore, "The Social Framework of Economic Development," in Ralph J. D. Braibanti and Joseph J. Spengler (eds.), *Tradition, Values and Socio-economic Development* (Durham, N.C.: Duke University Press, 1961); Wilbert E. Moore and Arnold S. Feldman, "Commitment of the Industrial Labor Force," in Moore and Feldman (eds.), *Labor Commitment and Social Change in Developing Areas* (New York: Social Science Research Council, 1960); Wilbert E. Moore, *Industrialization and Labor* (Ithaca: Cornell University Press, 1951). Hoselitz has been more concerned with a historical-economics approach than with a sociological one; see "Main Concepts in the Analysis of the Social Implications of Technical Change," in Bert F. Hoselitz and Wilbert E. Moore (eds.), *Industrialization and Society* (The Hague: Mouton-UNESCO, 1963), and "Theories of Stages of Economic Growth," in Bert F. Hoselitz (ed.), *Theories of Economic Growth* (Glencoe: Free Press of Glencoe, Ill., 1960).

cifically, and that might be added to the factors already mentioned are, first, the problem of how development gets started. That is, what preconditions are essential to initiate development? And second, once begun, does development come to an end? This is an important question, because it involves some examination of retraditionalization, which is another way of suggesting that a new coherence of values, institutions, and organization must be established near the end of a development period and, indeed, that they are part of it. This question is not only important because of the relationship between traditionalism and modernization but also because of the effects of industrialization on both. So dynamic is this latter form of development that we tend to think of it as preventing a new institutionalization of social life, as causing a malintegration in the institutional and organizational spheres (during the conversion from modernization to industrialization), papered over by ideological beliefs that give the appearance of integration without its social reality. Many modernizing societies thus became vulnerable to totalitarian ideologies as they seek to industrialize. Failure to "retraditionalize" poses a continuous political problem in the sphere of basic legitimacy, which no amount of technological achievement can resolve.

Hence, great tension exists in the lives of modernizing men. Schools and universities can hardly be expected to pass on the accumulated values of the community when these are in constant flux. The socialization process becomes a tension-creating system. Moreover, such tension is a key feature of the creative process in modern developing societies. Status conflict, value conflict, marginality — these have all been recognized as having important consequences in producing creative and innovative individuals. In such a condition (when an entire system is regulated by its marginal relationships), the political dimension becomes the focal point of stability, supplying a framework in which conflicts can be worked out. To that extent government becomes the strategic instrument of development, and the result is a high degree of government regulation of social life in order to introduce greater coherence of values and institutions and to cater to creative tension.[35]

OVERLAPPING CHARACTERISTICS OF DEVELOPMENT, MODERNIZATION, AND INDUSTRIALIZATION

Development, modernization, and industrialization, although related phenomena, can be placed in a descending order of generality. Development, the most general, results from the proliferation and integration of functional roles in a community. Modernization is a particular case of development. Modernization implies three conditions — a social system that can constantly innovate without falling apart (and that includes among its essential beliefs the acceptability of change); differentiated, flexible social structures; and a social framework to provide the skills and knowledge necessary for living in a technologically advanced world. Industrialization, a special aspect of modernization, may be defined as the period in a society in which the strategic functional roles are related to manufacturing. It is possible to attempt the modernization of a given country without much industry, but it is not possible to industrialize without modernization.

It is possible for a modernizing country to have a large manufacturing sector and yet fail to develop an industrial infrastructure because its industry is merely an extension of the industrial system of another country. This is a common problem in many Latin American countries. They have a large number of foreign firms involved in processing, assembly, and light industry. These activities build up a local body of workers and technicians, whose operations, however, are integrated with the system of the metropolitan country rather than with their own. This is a normal characteristic of late modernization and represents a classic case of imperialism. Nationalization of such foreign-owned industries

[35] See Frank Barron, *Creativity and Psychological Health* (Princeton, N.J.: D. Van Nostrand Co., 1963).

is therefore an increasingly common feature of the transition from late modernization to industrialization. Recent examples are Yugoslavia, where the rupture in political relations with the U.S.S.R. effectively broke a semicolonial economic relationship, and Cuba, where the same process occurred vis-à-vis the United States.

It is now necessary to link these comments to those made earlier about development. At its broadest, development is the process by which secular norms of conduct are universalized. These secular norms can be thought of in terms of the distinctions introduced by Maine (between status and contract); Durkheim (between mechanical and organic solidarity; sacred and secular beliefs); Weber (between instrumental and consummatory ends; traditional and legal-rational authority); and Tönnies (between *Gemeinschaft* and *Gesellschaft*). They have been elaborated by Parsons in his pattern variables and by Levy in his analytical structures of aspects of relationships (both of which have been modified by Moore by his corrective emphasis on the dynamic properties exhibited by social systems at all stages of the developmental process).[36]

How is modernization, a particular case of development, different from industrialization? Industrialization is that aspect of modernization so powerful in its consequences that it alters dysfunctional social institutions and customs by creating new roles and social instruments, based on the use of the machine. More dynamic than modernization, it is also more narrowly consistent in its processes.

The comparative study of modernization is conceptually more cloudy and in many ways more difficult than the comparative study of industrialization. However, the study of modernization is at present more important to us, especially as a means of identifying

[36] See, in particular, Moore's criticism of the simple model of development that begins with a static notion of preindustrial society, delineates a dynamic transitional period, and ends with the system coming to rest, as it were, in a "developed" but static period once again (Wilbert E. Moore, "Industrialization and Social Change," in Hoselitz and Moore [eds.], *Industrialization and Society,* chapter xv). See also Wilbert E. Moore, *Social Change* (Englewood Cliffs, N.J.: Prentice-Hall, Inc., 1963), p. 42.

those social arrangements that help or hinder industrialization and as a means of observing how changes become adjusted or lead to further change. Clifford Geertz has suggested that "though it may be true that, as an economic process, development is a dramatic revolutionary change, as a broadly social process it fairly clearly is not. What looks like a quantum jump from a specifically economic point of view is, from a generally social one, merely the final expression in economic terms of a process which has been building up gradually over an extended period of time."[37] Included in this judgment is an emphasis on the importance of human or social capital, which seems to be more significant for modernity than material resources. These points appear more obvious after industrialization has become a political objective of government, and decisions and arrangements are made to further it.

ROLE SETS AND GROWTH INDEXES

As I have said, it will be a long time before most of the modernizing nations are in a position to industrialize, even if they continue to modernize strenuously. A modernizing country needs to take part in the international division of labor, so that exogamous industrialization roles may form the support-structure of the country's modernization roles. Modernization roles in Nigeria, for example, depend upon foreign industrial roles. It is not surprising, therefore, that political leaders try to minimize this dependence through the internationalization of dependence, that is, by spreading out international exchanges with a variety of industrialized countries and by efforts at internal industrialization. Efforts to promote the latter may be premature and result in great expense and

[37] Geertz, *Peddlers and Princes* (Chicago: University of Chicago Press, 1963), p. 2. For a case study of this approach in a different setting, see Walter Elkan, *Migrants and Proletarians* (London: Oxford University Press, 1960). See also Claude Tardits, *Porto-Novo: Les nouvelles generations africaines entre leurs traditions et l'occident* (Paris and The Hague: Mouton, 1958).

waste of resources.[38] Modernization, not industrialization, will be the key to development in most new countries for some time to come.

The comparative mode of analysis directs us to those changing forms and values of human institutions that require the patient arts of government. Comparative data available today are rich in examples covering a broad range of political types, races, and cultures.[39] The main guides to modernization that can be compared most easily are the following key sets of modernization roles and growth indexes: career and entrepreneurship roles (numbers and pervasiveness); and technology and per capita income.

Obviously, these four factors vary in degree of explicitness. Administration may be treated as a key form of career, and roles in the civil service, including technical services, may be analyzed. It is more difficult to study entrepreneurs if only because their talent is quite often latent, depending for its appearance on propitious circumstances. Moreover, if we extend the notion of entrepreneurship to include political entrepreneurs, that is, those who

[38] Industrialization, however, will be a symbolic objective and, as such, will be maintained by bringing overseas investment from many different sources into competitive and, therefore, manipulatable circumstances.

[39] Indeed, with respect to the last, one of the nice questions is whether high civilizations modernize more quickly than primitive ones. Quite often it is the highly complex and ancient civilization that shows more resistance to industrialization and the consequences of a machine technology (even when this is held to be a desirable political goal) than the simpler cultures that are embodied in delicate relationships between myth, religion, and social practice. It may prove easier for traditional African societies to become modern than for ancient societies such as India, where the blending of old and new produces great intellectual and social anxieties. One is struck by the disproportionate number of "Western" men in Nigeria and Ghana as compared with India, perhaps not in political beliefs, but in general social conduct and outlook. However, one cannot jump to the conclusion that high cultures resist modernity because of some presumed "anticommercial" virtues or some similar reason. Milton Singer has suggested that Indians can be as commercially minded as any other people (see "Cultural Values in India's Economic Development," *The Annals*, CCV [May, 1956]). I cite this question only to show how wide a sweep there is to the political compass and to show many different areas we must demarcate for research.

organize a following in order to gain access to state resources, then we will have to include a number of political leaders in our figures. An interesting point to be discussed later in this book is the frequent conflict between career roles and entrepreneurial roles, that is, institutionalized modernity versus innovative modernity.

With respect to per capita income, the figures are obtainable, although quite often misleading. Such figures have been used as rough guides for the comparison of countries engaged in economic growth, with or without correction for the special characteristics of each country.

Measurements of technology are less easily obtainable. Efforts have been made to use kilowatt hours as one measure. Probably the energy-employment factor is as useful as any.[40]

What do such indicators show? Rather different things. Career and entrepreneurial roles imply a set of values based on the degree to which rational decision-making — with universal standards of judgment and predictable and standardized rules governing conduct — has become pervasive. As institutions, these roles are more widely comparable; levels of training, skill, and experience are useful measures. Doctors, for example, can be compared across national boundaries on the basis of their performance, knowledge, and standards of ethics, as can civil servants.

Entrepreneurship, as has been suggested, poses some difficulties in analysis. The ability to innovate and challenge accepted forms of practice must be directed toward a desired goal. In both modernizing and industrializing societies, creativity may be evaluated by examining entrepreneurship. Entrepreneurship implies other qualities than mere individual skill. It suggests that in the society there are means of training people who have the potential for imaginative choice, who enjoy exploring alternatives and testing feasibilities.

---

[40] See Karl W. Deutsch's efforts to develop transactional indicators that reflect functional interdependence in *Nationalism and Social Communication* (New York: John Wiley and Sons, Inc., 1953) and "Social Mobilization and Political Development," *American Political Science Review*, LV (September, 1963).

Per capita income also implies certain values. That such figures are available suggests the existence of a previously developed, complex standard of measurement of income and expenditures, investment and consumption. Both gross and net national products have been calculated. The ideas of planning, growth, estimated depreciation on physical plant, and so on, have already become regular items of bookkeeping.

The fourth main factor in modernization, technology, is a measure of the degree to which non-human energy is employed in the conduct of complex tasks. For this reason, it is the most strategic test of modernization, since it implies planning, allocating, and organizing resources around abstract principles that, when applied, will lead to desired results.

THE SPECIAL PROBLEM OF EQUALITY

Modernizing roles, both institutionalized and innovative, are normally associated with very different styles of life from that of the ordinary public. Residential patterns are observably different. (Civil servants, for example, are quite often provided with government estate housing.) A successful entrepreneur may try to show his success by naming an office building after himself, by building a large residence, or by displaying other outward manifestations of success. In countries where modernization problems are severe, these differences in life-styles become points of tension. They distinguish the rich from the poor, the more modern from the more traditional, and the urban from the rural. Here then is an interesting puzzle. Development creates inequality; modernization accentuates it.[41]

This tension between equality of access and extension of the social hierarchy is one stimulus to continual modernization. If

[41] This is one of the reasons why the desire for socialism in many modernizing nations is important — and also why it fails. Socialism, with its emphases on equality and modernity, ends in new forms of inequality.

the stimulus stems from the original assumption that the discrepancies in life-styles and roles characteristic of modernizing societies are temporary, systems able to employ the tension caused by inequity will be able to generate a continuous developmental process. Hence, inequality can be seen both as a cause of modernization and as a result of it. This is particularly the case when government is being used to enlarge the modernized sector. As T. H. Marshall has suggested, inequality in the context of citizenship produces a constant agitation for equality in every sphere. Successful pressure for equality will compress both ends of the scale of income distribution, extend the area of the modernizing culture and experience, and enrich the universal status of citizenship.[42]

Although it is a central feature of the modernization process, the tension imposed by the lack of equality may be extremely awkward to manage. Attempting to manage it provides government with some of its most important work. The adjustment of roles and systems of roles is always difficult, even when inequality is accepted as a norm. How much more difficult it is when modernity and the expectation of equality go hand in hand. Nor do material conditions of equality suffice, for psychic inequalities may remain.[43] The most important point to keep in mind, however, is that such tension contains those principles of legitimacy that I discussed in chapter i, that is, equity and potentiality.

The achievement of equality is an ever spreading moral objective in the modern world. Few modern societies, even if they institutionalize inequality, regard it as a good thing. The desire for equality grows, covering more and more social attributes. Race can no longer serve as a ground for inequality, nor can religion,

[42] Marshall, "Citizenship and Social Class," in *Citizenship and Social Development* (New York: Doubleday & Co., Inc., 1964), p. 116.

[43] "Psychic equality" denotes a condition in which each man feels confident of his worth on the same plane as his neighbor, with all traces of psychological deference or servility in conduct totally removed. Equality of opportunity may exist in objective terms, however, and individuals continue to feel unequal, reflecting a hang-over of older class attitudes and having the effect of crippling individuals, debasing their worth, and making some act and feel lower in the scale of human values than others.

ethnic association, or other attributes. One might say that as secular beliefs associated with the modernization process are universalized there is a corresponding peeling-off of different layers of belief associated with inequality.

The urge to equality is invariably translated into matters of practical political doctrine. Colonialism, which postulated a relationship of inequality in the political sphere, has largely disappeared. No matter how wise an enlightened official may have been, his presence in an alien territory violated egalitarian values. Claims to equal treatment by Negroes in the American South are based on the belief that pigmentation should have no relevance to social hierarchy.[44] Gone, too, is the notion of the lowly but worthy servant or the yeomanlike laborer. There are few countries nowadays where servile positions are regarded as inherently rewarding; nor is a man's worth based entirely on generalized social qualities like self-respect, devotion, thrift, or personal honor.[45]

The "predicament of equality" causes governments to indulge in some rather interesting ideological and structural maneuvers. One advantage in stressing the political condition as the primary expression of egalitarianism (by equating citizenship and equality) is that political hierarchy (and therefore, inequality) may then be defined as an organizational device through which the political elite becomes the instrument of the citizenry. Differences in rewards, both in power and in prestige, can be explained in terms of the need to modernize and, particularly, to attract into the organization individuals most functional to the modernization process, that is, planners, technicians, training officers, community development specialists, and the like. When political hierarchy is defined in functional terms as a corps of technicians, with specific roles and circumscribed spheres of competence, it thus becomes a

[44] See St. Clair Drake, *The American Dream and the Negro*, (Chicago: Roosevelt University, Division of Continuing Education, 1963), pp. 51–64.

[45] Christian doctrine was always ambiguous on this score. On the one hand, the meek were to inherit the earth; on the other, those who became rich and powerful through their own enterprise were the models of the community. Calvinism was never comfortable in the face of meekness.

mechanism to achieve equality — a postponed and somewhat illusory but important norm.

General authority is limited to a few highly diffused, all-purpose roles. By emphasizing change and development, present inequalities may be seen not only as temporary but as necessary for further change. Hence, the public can be led to regard political inequality as a device for gaining equality.

EQUALITY AND THE ROLE OF THE INTELLECTUALS

During the modernization process the intellectuals have a special role to play, for they are most inclined to respect the culture of freedom. At the same time they remain exceedingly vulnerable to an egalitarian-minded public. If they help to make a revolution in the name of the people, they cannot also be expected to be effective in restricting the excesses of the people. In their attempt to identify with the public, intellectuals quite often accuse each other of having inflated egos, of being pompous, and of, in fact, being divorced from the people. In arguing for equality they often downgrade their own enterprises to the point where no one need have any respect for them. People who are denied entry into the clubs of the intelligentsia, for example, are often pleased to take the latter at their own public evaluation.[46]

These tendencies have been particularly evident among intellectuals during revolutionary periods. Shils has discussed the deep politicization of the intellectuals:

> The high degree of political involvement of the intellectual in underdeveloped countries is a complex phenomenon. It has a threefold root. The primary source is a deep preoccupation with authority. Even though he seeks and seems actually to break away from the authority of the powerful traditions in which he was brought up, the intellectual of underdeveloped countries, still more than his confrere in more advanced

[46] See C. Vann Woodward, "The Populist Heritage and the Intellectual," *American Scholar*, XXIX (Winter, 1959–60).

countries, retains the need for incorporation into some self-transcending, authoritative entity. Indeed, the greater his struggle for emancipation from the traditional collectivity, the greater his need for incorporation into a new, alternative collectivity. Intense politicization meets this need. The second source of political involvement is the scarcity of opportunities to acquire an even temporary sense of vocational achievement; there have been few counterattractions to the appeal of charismatic politics. Finally, there has been a deficient tradition of civility in the underdeveloped countries which affects the intellectuals as much as it does the non-intellectuals.[47]

And Lipset has pointed out that the leadership of the intellectuals in new states does not survive the first revolutionary generation.

Three points become clear from these comments. First, the intellectuals are clearly politically engaged. They manipulate the intellectual side of any modernization movement and represent its brains. Second, the postrevolutionary political culture is quite often the creature of the intellectuals; but they are only a precondition of it and not in themselves a sufficient basis for it. Nowhere is this more clearly illustrated than in the American experience, in which a numerous intellectual political leadership created the civic culture that in broad outline has been sustained to the present time.[48] Third, intellectuals are extremely vulnerable to populism and quite often contribute to their own vulnerability in trying to identify with popular groups. Indeed, in countries that take socialism at all seriously, the ambiguity surrounding the role of the intellectual is a good token of the status of political freedom in the country. The most frequently encountered socialist intel-

[47] Edward Shils, "The Intellectuals in Political Development," *World Politics*, XII (April, 1960), reprinted in John H. Kautsky, *Political Change In Underdeveloped Areas* (New York: John Wiley & Sons, 1962), p. 205.

[48] Lipset points out that Philadelphia was the second largest city in the English-speaking world at the time of the American revolution. The educational level of the political leaders was high. Their literary output was very large. Their self-awareness of their role, that is, to establish a style of politics as well as a form of government, was very much in evidence in their statements and published writings (see *The First New Nation* [New York: Basic Books, 1963], pp. 66–74, 90–98).

lectuals are less than brilliant; and if they miss excellence by a wide margin, they are often punitive and resentful. Some overtly compromise with nationalists in order to secure their status, finally losing their moral strength. Others may adopt the "necessities of the revolution" as an article of faith and become willing and faithful cohorts of any regime in power.

Modernization is thus a trying phenomenon for intellectuals; they are bearers of the culture of modernity and at the same time are vulnerable to the forces they help unleash. This is particularly the case in systems in which the ideology is blindly naïve or utopian, as in the Soviet Union directly after the revolution and in many of the developing countries today. Consider a typical statement in the early stages of the Soviet Union:

> But if one then thinks of the schoolmasters of this present day, the absolute unfitness of the bourgeois intellect for the new society, the necessity that this entire generation of intellectuals should disappear in the transitional process of the dictatorship of the proletariat, becomes evident. The annihilation must be definite, for the type cannot be tolerated even in a modified form. It is evident that the very notion of teacher, professor, etc., must be obliterated. The ideal can be approximated only if all co-operate towards "education," considering this as a natural part of their daily work.[49]

There is often a similar emphasis in contemporary modernizing societies. The lowering of educational standards to increase recruitment and to make it more egalitarian can have the effect of weakening the position of the intellectuals and forcing them to the periphery of their society. The emphasis on technical education (to obtain much-needed skilled and trained manpower) may disguise a deeper political objective, namely, a more professionalized and pliable elite, antiseptic in its role and unwilling to engage in the moral issues posed by modernization. This elite, like the civil service, has obedience built into its positions.

[49] S. J. Rutgers, "The Intellectuals and the Russian Revolution," in V. I. Lenin *et al.*, *The New Policies of Soviet Russia* (Chicago: Charles H. Kerr & Co., n.d.), p. 106.

Obviously, the question of the intellectual's role in political modernization is a complex one. It is easy to find fault with the obstinacy and blindness of intellectuals and to root this in the social distance that exists between the educated — the "black Englishman" or "Balliol-Indian" — and the non-educated. But these are hackneyed examples and caricatures. Quite often those who seriously wrestle with the deeper aspects of the politics of modernization (and whose sensitivities are aroused by so ruthless a process) are destroyed by the forces of populism; when this happens, an important part of the yeast of modernization is lacking, and the civic culture is to that extent diminished.

Modernizing revolutions are not mindless; nor are they raw mass movements striking out blindly against injustice. They are complexes of individuals and groups that are seeking solutions to particular problems and see hope in change. But a modernizing revolution, whether bland or bloody, has no subject matter other than that provided by its interpreters and its thinkers, its writers and pamphleteers, its orators and proclaimers. Public meaning is, after all, a political matter and not merely a symposium of private views. In creating this public meaning and identifying the interconnections and directions of change, the intellectuals play a critical role. The regime that can make use of them in this way helps its own cause. When they are alienated, debased, or corrupt, the process of modernization becomes politically more precarious.

One can, of course, overstate the role of the intellectuals. It is important, however, to distinguish them from the elite in general and, more particularly, to separate them as individuals, wrestling with the world as they see it, from their skills or roles.

Most intellectuals have had considerable education and are found in intellectual roles. They are not scattered, like leavening, in all social bodies at all layers of a community. Furthermore, they tend to live adjacent to one another and to intermarry. This reinforces them as a group, on the one hand, but also sets them apart. How the intellectuals are balanced with other groups determines the political form modernization is likely to take and also the state of morality during the process; for ultimately, intellectuals are drawn to the moral implications of political conduct. The role of the intellectual, then, is a key indicator of the nature of the polity during modernization.

YOUTH AND THE INTELLECTUALS

If intellectuals represent one special indicator in modernizing societies, youth represents another. The former may desire equality, but they are in danger of being destroyed by it. Youth wants equality as a right, as a way of succeeding to adulthood. Both groups are dissatisfied, and the one may express the hostilities of the other.

A modernization process depends heavily on youth precisely because the members of this group are ordinarily the most eager to adopt modern roles. They have less to "unlearn," as it were. Modernization is thus a universalizing process among youth that transcends nationality. Youth movements are likely to build fraternal links with one another in many countries just as intellectuals are likely to be known by one another across national boundaries. Congresses and meetings of youth are as much a feature of modern life as are schools and factories. Modernizing youth are deeply politicized, and such politicization is an important part of growing up.

There is a peculiar rhythm to this universalizing process among youth, dependent in large measure, of course, on the shape of politics and the form of authority in a country. We must not forget, however, that youth cannot be considered an undifferentiated group. Some will fill the roles of the modern community and at a senior level. Others may fall by the wayside to become disgruntled and angry young men. Still others may form cadres in the community, which blindly accept an official line. Indeed, once the first political phase of a modernization revolution has passed, succeeding generations of youth may become more rather than less parochial — more wedded to local party cadres than to the wider world, and more provincial than the intellectuals, leaving the latter isolated, at times abused, and rendering them anachronistic and therefore unable to serve the process they helped create. Occasionally, when the youth are cut off from the intellectuals, the resulting process may be modernization by technicians, with the accompanying danger that the less provincial visions of society will disappear. Indeed, the extent to which the youth culture becomes cramped and limited, or turns away from the wider intellectual stream, depends directly on the degree to which the youth and intellectuals become mutually alienated.[50]

[50] How important these interrelations are can be seen in India, where modernization is accepted as a slow process, directed only in part by government and requiring many forms of adaptation and modification. Industrialization is the eventual objective. With a new *Stand* deliberately cultivated by the British, an intelligentsia was built, apart from the pietistic, religious forms that were traditional in Taksasila, Naland, Vallabhi, and other centers of classical learning (where astrology, astronomy, logic, philosophy, history, and law were taught). The modernizing intellectuals were provided with English forms of education to make the Indian officers of government intellectually and morally fit to perform their duties with efficiency and probity, especially in the judicial and revenue branches of the public service where their responsibilities and powers were rapidly growing. What prevented a generational conflict in real and open terms was the continual role of the intellectual in political life and a wider expansion of the intellectual culture into the educational system (see B. B. Misra, *The Indian Middle Classes* [London: Oxford University Press, 1961]). See also Philip Woodruff, *The Men Who Ruled India: The Founders* (London: Jonathan Cape, 1953–54), Vol. I, Introduction.

3

THE ANALYSIS OF
TRADITION

Cultures never give way completely to the new, no matter how ruthless the impact of innovation. The varied responses of tradition to modernization account for many of the differences in political forms among the new nations. Quite often modernizing societies, under some indigenous brand of nationalism or socialism, will disguise a deep connection with traditional practices. In Mali, for example, underneath a rather puritanical brand of Marxism (with its bold claims to a renovated social life under a single political party, the Union Soudanaise), can be seen subtle but significant connections to the centralized politics of the ancient Bambara kingdom. The President of Mali, a descendant of the old Keita royal clans, is a president who walks like a king. The Union Soudanaise accepted Marxism as the overt form within which modernization should occur, meanwhile preserving a link with the past.

Connections between tradition and modernity are rarely simple. Halpern has put the matter exceedingly well in commenting on the role of Islam in the contemporary Middle East.

Today's Middle Eastern revolution is not merely a revolution of rulers or rising expectations. The cumulative growth

81

of ideas, production, and power generated outside the Islamic system has penetrated that system and is tearing apart its repetitive pattern of balanced tensions. A system connecting man, God, and society, is falling apart, and the new forces are still too far out of balance, sometimes even out of touch, with the old and with each other to constitute a stable and resilient new pattern.[1]

Nor are such situations exclusive to non-European systems. In tsarist Russia, the state was confronted with the problem of how to deal with Westernization as a particular form of modernization. The immensely difficult task of adjusting tradition to innovation had to be undertaken so that Western practices and technologies could be adapted to Russia.[2]

General interest in these matters was stimulated in the 1930's by the so-called functionalist schools of British anthropologists associated with Malinowski and Radcliffe-Brown. The social value of their anthropological studies was not only theoretical. Enlightened colonial administrators, puzzling over the question of receptivity to change, helped bring together the theorists of indirect rule and the anthropologists who were concerned with a new, liberal colonial policy (including Lucy Mair, C. K. Meek, R. S. Rattray, M. M. Green, and many others). The anthropologists recognized that traditional factors seem to create immobilities in social structure that abort or minimize innovation. And yet at other times tradition seems to open the door to innovation (the traditionalizing of innovation) by transforming exogenous features of social life partly into endogenous ones and thereby into a living and continuous relationship with the past. Such forms of traditionalism put novelty on trial rather than the people whom novelty is supposed to serve. More frequently, of course, as I have suggested, traditionalism works in the reverse fashion, making in-

---

[1] See Manfred Halpern, *The Politics of Social Change in the Middle East and North Africa* (New York: Rand Corp., 1963), p. 25.

[2] Cyril E. Black, "The Modernization of Russian Society," in Black (ed.), *The Transformation of Russian Society* (Cambridge, Mass.: Harvard University Press, 1960), p. 671.

novation a source of threats and tension both to society and to persons.[3]

TRADITIONALISM AND TYPES OF VALUES

"Traditionalism" (as distinct from "tradition") we will define as validation of current behavior by reference to immemorial prescriptive norms. This is not to say that traditionalist systems do not change but rather that innovation — that is, extrasystemic action — has to be mediated within the social system and linked with antecedent values. Modernity, in contrast, presupposes a much more remote relationship between antecedent values and new goals. Modernizing systems, with their complex and highly differentiated social structures, value change in itself.

These distinctions between modernity and traditionalism leave unanswered the question why some traditional systems accept innovation more easily than others. Answers have been sought in the structural features of traditional societies, while traditionalism has remained a virtually undifferentiated concept. Our discussion in chapter i distinguished between types of values and systems of authority. The analytical scheme applied to modernization can be used to examine tradition. The *normative* and *behavioral* dimensions are represented by values. Values are divided into two types: the first can be called *instrumental*, and the second *consummatory*. From these value types we will derive three systems of authority, which can be called *structural*, instead of the two previously used. Combinations of values and structure help locate the problems that confront the political leaders of traditional systems as they seek to build modern nations. This emphasis on values is designed to draw attention to the belief systems of traditional societies, that is, to the systems of meanings that affect perception. Kinship, for example, is a system that has to be be-

[3] See David E. Apter, *The Political Kingdom in Uganda: A Study in Bureaucratic Nationalism* (Princeton, N.J.: Princeton University Press, 1961).

lieved in, in order to be perceived. Our purpose is to get closer to the motives that orient men's actions without in fact examining those motives in detail. In attempting to do this, I will confine my illustrations to Africa.

It has been suggested in chapter i that one of the classic structural distinctions in social theory is between sacred and secular systems of authority. From the point of view of behavior within a system, what is important is the range of activity endowed with transcendental values. In some societies virtually all activities have a mystical and transcendental side and a special meaning attached to them, whether they are simple actions like washing one's hands or more complex ones like invoking the spirit of one's ancestors. There are real differences in social attitudes that arise from the sacred-secular distinction. The psychic satisfactions derived from the ordinary acts of social life, may be much greater if they are endowed with religious significance. When ritualization, ceremony, and symbolic behavior are intertwined, political as well as social life is affected. The contrast intended here is between those systems that cannot segregate wide areas of social relationship from the religious sphere and those that do not evaluate social conduct in terms of its wider meanings but only in terms of its more narrow and particular ones. This difference is particularly noticeable in the economic sphere of certain cultures where such activities as farming, marketing, and crafts may have been allocated in some measure to special kin groups or to individuals endowed with a ceremonial and ritual office, such as a blacksmith among the Yoruba, a barkcloth-maker among the Baganda, or a weaver among the Baulé (regardless whether the object produced is endowed with some special religious significance).[4]

Embodied in the structural differences between the sacred and the secular, and of interest from a behavioral point of view, are the patterns of gratification peculiar to each. Gratifications un

---

[4] This distinction is somewhat similar to the more familiar intermediate ends–ultimate ends distinction.

follow from the transcendental values associated with an act we will call consummatory, and gratifications that come from the empirical ends realized through an act we will call instrumental. In the comparison of different kinds of traditionalism, it becomes important to distinguish the kinds of gratifications common in a system and the varying and diverse patterns in which they are combined.[5]

As we are using the term, "instrumental systems" are those in which ultimate ends do not color every concrete act. If trade, new agricultural practices, or administrative matters are introduced, the consequences are immediate, fragmentary, and non-cosmological. Such systems can innovate without appearing to alter their social institutions fundamentally. Rather, innovation is made to serve tradition. The characteristic structural expression of instrumental traditionalism is hierarchical authority (a military type of system), with a single king or command figure at the apex.[6] Appointive ranks in the system tend to underwrite the king as

[5] "Instrumental" systems are those characterized by a large sector of intermediate ends separate from and independent of ultimate ends; "consummatory" systems are those characterized by a close relationship between intermediate and ultimate ends. The terms are derived from Parson's categories of "cognitive-instrumental meanings" and "expressive-integrative meanings." See T. Parsons *et al.*, *Working Papers in the Theory of Action* (Glencoe; Free Press of Glencoe, Ill., 1953), p. 105.

The difference between instrumental and consummatory values, for our purposes, can be illustrated by the following example. Consider two traditional systems, one consummatory and the other instrumental in types of values. Both are short hand-hoe cultures, and an effort is made to introduce new agricultural techniques, in particular, the use of tractors. In the consummatory systems, the change from the short hand-hoe system will so disrupt the ritual of hoe-making, the division of men's and women's work, the religious practices associated with both, and the relationship between agricultural rituals and the authority of chiefs that it will be impossible for the leaders to consider a tractor only in terms of increasing agricultural productivity. In the instrumental system, by contrast, the tractor will be viewed simply in terms of its ability to expand agricultural output and will not affect the ultimate ends of the system. In the first instance, such an innovation represents a threat to the system; in the second, it is far likelier to strengthen the system by increasing farm income.

[6] For a discussion of hierarchical authority, see A. Southall, *Alur Society* (Cambridge: W. Heffer & Sons, 1956), especially chap. vi. See also my book, *The Political Kingdom in Uganda*.

the central source of authority. A heavy reliance on performance is a characteristic of office, and the chief who fails to serve his king loyally and well is subject to removal or death. Religion is decidedly secondary in such a system, the primary value of which is service to the king or state. Examples are Morocco, Ethiopia, Buganda, Iran,[7] Afghanistan, and Thailand.

The traditionalism of consummatory systems is much more complex. My view is similar to that expressed by Fustel de Coulanges in deploring the simplistic interpretations of Greece and Rome as prototypes for modern societies; he wrote that examining the institutions of those two systems without knowledge of their religious notions left them "obscure, whimsical, and inexplicable." He went on to say:

> A comparison of beliefs and laws shows that a primitive religion constituted the Greek and Roman family, established marriage and paternal authority, fixed the order of relationship, and consecrated the right of property, and the right of inheritance. This same religion, after having enlarged and extended the family, formed a still larger association, the city, and reigned in that as it had reigned in the family. From it came all the institutions, as well as all the private law, of the ancients. It was from this that the city received all its principles, its rules, its usages and its magistracies.[8]

In this type of system, society, the state, authority, and the like, are all part of an elaborately sustained, high-solidarity structure in which religion is pervasive as a cognitive guide. Such systems have been hostile to innovation. If change comes, it produces fundamental social upheavals, such as migration from ancestral lands to towns and the breakdown of customary relationships. Not only ancient Greece and Rome but many contemporary African societies are examples of this type of system.[9]

[7] See Leonard Binder, *Iran: Political Development in a Changing Society* (Berkeley: University of California Press, 1962), *passim.*

[8] N. D. Fustel de Coulanges, *The Ancient City* (New York: Doubleday Anchor Books, n.d.), p. 13.

[9] Such systems can innovate, however. Indeed, the philosophy expressed by President Senghor in Senegal today is similar to that described by Fustel de

A general hypothesis is that an instrumental-hierarchical system can innovate until the kingship principle is challenged, at which point the entire system joins together to resist change. Such systems are highly resistant to political but not to other forms of modernization.[10] Consummatory ones resist all change.

Consummatory values are most solidly rooted in systems in which the structural expression of authority is pyramidal rather than hierarchical. Pyramidal structure consists of patterns of subordinacy and superordinacy that are limited to such activities as war or legal appeals. For most purposes, a chief or political leader is responsible to his social group, not to a senior chief or official. The chiefs at each level of the pyramid thus have similar powers and are relatively autonomous. This structural form relies heavily on semisegmental kinship relationships. The autonomy of the chief or political leader is thus a reflection of the autonomy of the kinship unit itself.

Of course, societies do not discard traditionalism overnight.[11]

Coulanges; the religious system is to be pervaded by humanistic socialism. Hence, traditional solidarities — the emphasis on family, corporatism in institutions, personalism, and the like — go hand in hand with joint participation in communal economic efforts. By this means, work is to be ennobled and given new meaning in traditional terms. See, for example, the expression of this point of view by M. Mamadou Dia in *L'Economie africaine* (Paris, 1957), and "Economie et culture devant les élites africaines," *Présence africaines*, Nos. 14–15 (June-September, 1957), pp. 58–72.

[10] This hypothesis should hold for both traditional and modernizing systems. The categories of instrumental and consummatory values are universal.

[11] This viewpoint emphasizes social change as changing patterns of accommodation — countless adjustments to changing conditions that periodically become more intensive. Sometimes there is a lack of coherence or "fit" to these patterns, and the political machinery is set in motion to integrate them. (In this sense political activity is a prime motivating force.) The convenient view that traditional society is rigid and opposed to alteration is too narrow. Rarely is traditional society "broken" because of outside influences. It may be true that a poorly integrated system produces marginal individuals with great insecurities, who translate them into creative enterprises crucial to development, but such a theory of development ignores the differences within tradition that deeply affect receptivity to innovation. Hagen argues, for example, that out of traditional society there emerges "a group of individuals, creative, alienated from traditional values, driven by a gnawing, burning drive to prove themselves (to themselves, as well as to their fellows), seeking an area in which to do so, preferably an area in which they can

One sign of transition is ideological confusion. Some traditional societies are theocracies, in which religion and politics are merely two aspects of the same phenomenon, and certain beliefs are sacrosanct. To illustrate these remarks I will describe several traditional societies (or more properly, societies with a high commitment to traditional values) and show how certain structural features of their social life and certain behavioral consequences of their values have combined to produce different adaptive responses to colonialism, a force for modernization. I draw my examples from my own research experience in Africa.

Consider African traditional societies that predate European trade, commerce, or colonial hegemony. Assume that the political hierarchies of some of these societies were structurally highly differentiated, whereas others were less so. Also assume that some African societies were differentiated in cognitive rather than structural terms, with the result that in some, religious values and beliefs were pervasive throughout the full range of social acts, whereas in others there was a wider toleration of secular conduct.

Hierarchical structure in Africa was particularly noticeable in such societies as Dahomey, the Moslem emirates of northern Nigeria, the Mossi, the Bambara, the Zulu, the Barotse, and the Baganda. There is a large literature dealing with these kingdom states — or centralized states, as they were sometimes called — as

---

gain power, and preferably also one in which, in some symbolic way, they can vent their rage at the elites who have caused their troubles. Moreover, their (perhaps unconscious) rage at the group disparaging them will cause them to turn against some of the values of the group disparaging them." But it should be pointed out that traditional societies have always known how to control the emotionally enraged. Moreover, it does not always follow that the creative innovator with an urge to power is always alienated from traditional values. One would have to know more precisely which traditional values and what kind of "rage" the innovator shows. Heroic and exceptional leaders are also innovators (that is why they stand out in their communities). To some extent, modernization in its early stages is dependent on exceptional individuals no matter what the sources of their energy and purposefulness. See E. E. Hagen, "How Economic Growth Begins: A Theory of Social Change," in Manning Nash and Robert Chin (special editors), *Journal of Social Issues*, XIV (January, 1963), 33; and Hagen, *On the Theory of Social Change* (Homewood, Ill.: Dorsey Press, Inc., 1962).

they attracted a great deal of interest on the part of Europeans, some of whom professed to see in them a recapitulation of European history. Quite often, for example, their hierarchical societies were regarded as African forms of "feudalism" (a point of view now largely restricted to Soviet writing on Africa).[12]

However, African traditional societies were not all elaborate hierarchies. There were systems that showed very little political division of labor and that noticeably lacked the notions of territoriality and tribal identity. One of the most powerful ethnic groups in Nigeria, the Ibo, for example, had virtually no concept of "Ibo-ness," living as they did in small autonomous communities with only a rudimentary political hierarchy. Similar cases were the Kikuyu, the Nuer, the Tallensi, and the Tiv. Such societies were based mainly on one form or other of the segmental lineage system. The differences between the hierarchical and segmental systems were made the subject of special study by M. Fortes and E. E. Evans-Pritchard in their pioneering work, *African Political Systems*. They characterized these two groups along the following structural lines. The more hierarchical were those having "centralized authority, administrative machinery, and judicial institutions — in short, a government — and in which cleavages of wealth, privilege, and status correspond to the distribution of power and authority." These they regarded as "primitive states." [13] What they called "stateless societies" were not defined residually to the primitive states, although such societies were without government in terms of their definition. Such stateless societies, however, had as their principal form of organization some variant of the segmental lineage system. Subsequent studies have shown the utility of this distinction. John Middleton and David Tait have

---

[12] It is perhaps even more restricted to I. Potekhin and his followers. For a good survey of Soviet writing on Africa, see S. Abramova, *Études Africaines en USSR* (Moscow: Academy of Sciences of the U.S.S.R., African Institute, 1962). See also *Les Africanistes Russes parlent del'Afrique* (Paris: Présence Africaine, 1960), and Edwin M. Loeb, *In Feudal Africa* (The Hague: Mouton, 1962), *passim*.

[13] Fortes and Evans-Pritchard (eds.), *African Political Systems* (London: Oxford University Press, 1940), p. 5.

been able to make further structural differentiations of the segmental lineage type.[14]

More recently, L. A. Fallers has described segmental systems in
the following terms.

> It is important to stress here the point that the genealogical
> framework that unites the several local communities in such
> societies is a *cultural* system, a system of *ideas* — in fact a
> kind of *political theory* — which may have rather little to do
> with "biological reality." It is a way of thinking and talking
> about community and trans-community political relations
> in the idiom of kinship and in terms of the idiom persons of
> the most diverse biological origins may, by means of "legal
> fictions," be treated for political purposes as if they were
> members of a single unilineal descent group.[15]

The political consequences of these "fictions" about kinship are
very important.

> A problem requiring decision may arise, for example, in the
> form of a dispute between communities, or between individ-
> ual members of different communities, concerning the pos-
> session of territory for grazing or agriculture. In such situa-
> tions, since there is no chief or council to exercise continu-
> ous, society-wide authority, decisions must be arrived at by
> *ad hoc* gatherings of representatives of the groups concerned
> or through arbitration by neutral parties. Such conciliation
> or arbitration is usually successful, however, only when the
> groups concerned are roughly equivalent in size and when
> they are in a position of what Fortes has called "comple-
> mentary opposition" in the genealogical scheme; since there
> is no superordinate authority able to impose a solution, an
> effective decision must represent a high degree of consensus
> and must be supported by substantial balance of power.
> Groups related to those immediately concerned tend to be
> drawn into the dispute until larger groups of equivalent

[14] Middleton and Tait (eds.), *Tribes without Rulers* (London: Routledge
& Kegan Paul, Ltd., 1958), *passim.*

[15] Fallers, "Political Sociology and the Anthropological Study of African
Politics," *European Journal of Sociology*, IV (1963), 314.

scale and complementary genealogical positions are engaged, at which point accommodation becomes possible.[16]

It will be readily observed that the two forms of traditional
authority described here, the hierarchical and the segmental, are
parallel to the modern forms described in chapter i.

An elaboration of this dichotomy has been attempted by Aidan
Southall, who has distinguished a group midway between the
hierarchical, or primitive, state system and the stateless, or segmental lineage, system. Such societies he calls "pyramidal systems." Pyramidal systems are combinations of the two types
described by Fortes and Evans-Pritchard and might be called
"segmental states." Southall suggests that it is useful to distinguish
the pyramidal from the hierarchical form as follows:

> In the pyramidal structure of segmentary societies there
> is surely a vertical distribution of power, though this may be
> largely in an upward rather than a downward direction.
> For example, this may result from conflict between segments
> of the lowest order, leading to joint action between segments
> of an ever higher order until an equilibrium is reached. The
> important point about the powers exercised in this way is
> that they are virtually of the same type at the several differ-
> ent levels of the pyramidal segmentary structure.
> On the other hand, the power structure of the fully devel-
> oped state may be described as hierarchical rather than
> pyramidal, because similar powers are not repeated at all
> levels, but certain powers are reserved at the top of the struc-
> ture, and lesser powers distributed to the lower levels of it.
> Furthermore, in the case of even the lesser powers, exer-
> cised at the lower levels of a hierarchical power structure,
> there is the recognition that such powers are delegated from
> the top of the structure where, in theory, political power is
> monopolized.[17]

[15] *Ibid.*, pp. 314–15.
[17] Southall, *Alur Society* (Cambridge: W. Heffer & Sons, 1956), pp. 250–
51. Southall goes on to say that the pyramidal form is a "distinct type, though
there is considerable variation within it. In the segmentary lineage system
there is a degree of definition of powers at the lower levels of the system

Whatever the defects of this kind of structural differentiation among political systems, it is useful to talk about these three different types of authority as a way of classifying traditional societies.

Pyramidal systems of authority are to be found in Africa among the Ashanti, the Yoruba, and many other ethnic groups. This type of system is not confined to Africa, of course, but is a universal type. The simplest form of pyramidal system is illustrated in Figure 5.

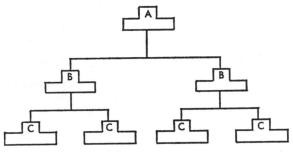

FIG. 5. — *Pyramidal authority.*

In the African cases, each of the levels represents particular segmental groupings organized on the basis of kinship. Segments may conflict with one another, ally with one another, and share in common activities, depending upon the rules and tasks at hand. Migration of segments or absorption of one segment by another is common. Most important, however, for each segment the powers of the chief or the equivalent are more or less identical; the levels of the pyramid are based upon historical seniority, which may, under certain circumstances, allow or require intervention of a senior segment into the affairs of a junior. Rules of combination of segments are fairly precise.

In a sense, the "family" image is the one that prevails. Linked to his clan by lineage, the chief is normally a descendant of a

---

which fades at the upper levels into violence regulated only by the balance of power between opposing segments."

mythical ancestor from whom legitimacy is derived. Systems of
the pyramidal type are normally extensively consultative.

The hierarchical system is patterned along bureaucratic or
military lines. At the top is a central command figure, paramount
chief, king, military commander, dictator, or the like. He combines in his role symbolic, integrational, ethnic, and sanctional
functions. Subordinates have power at the leader's pleasure. The
simplest form of hierarchical authority is illustrated in Figure 6.

FIG. 6. — *Hierarchical authority.*

Such systems are based upon a distribution of authority in which
power rigidly inheres at the top, to be distributed at the discretion of the leader. No subordinate units as such have rights or
claims on this power.

The third kind of authority is segmental. Writing of the Nuer,
an example of this type, Evans-Pritchard says:

> The lack of governmental organs among the Nuer, the ab-
> sence of legal institutions, of developed leadership, and,
> generally, of organized political life is remarkable. Their
> state is an acephalous kinship state and it is only by a study
> of the kinship system that it can be well understood how or-
> der is maintained and social relations over wide areas are
> established and kept up. The ordered anarchy in which they
> live accords well with their character, for it is impossible to
> live among Nuer and conceive of rulers ruling over them.[18]

Perhaps the best illustration of segmental authority is contained in the diagram first developed by Godfrey Lienhardt for

[18] E. E. Evans-Pritchard, *The Nuer* (Oxford: Clarendon Press, 1940), p.
181.

the Nuer, although other possible kinship relationships than the simple agnatic lineage need to be incorporated (see Figure 7).

In this diagram, four segments (A, B, C, D) converge at a central point O. Each segment, represented by a heavy main-lineage line, is coequal and, generationally, more or less coeval. The lighter lines represent sublineages. Such systems are sometimes ruled by particular elders in age-grade systems or by councils appointed from the lineage representatives.

As we shall see, these types of authority have implications far beyond the traditional societies being discussed at present.[19]

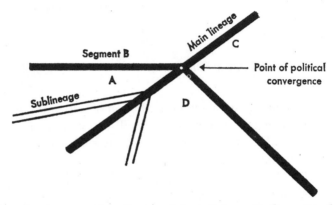

FIG. 7. — *Segmental authority. Adapted from Godfrey Lienhardt, "The Western Dinka," in John Middleton and David Tait (eds.),* Tribes without Rulers *(London: Routledge & Kegan Paul, Ltd., 1958), p. 127. See also L. A. Fallers, "Political Sociology and Anthropological Study of African Policies,"* European Journal of Sociology, *IV (1963).*

SOME ILLUSTRATIVE EXAMPLES

Combining the two main dimensions of our analysis of traditionalism — the three types of authority and the two types of values —

[19] In particular, hierarchical forms are characteristic of mobilization systems, and pyramidal authority is characteristic of reconciliation systems — two developmental types that we will rely on heavily in our subsequent analysis. Segmentary authority is the basis of the international state system.

with examples of African societies, we obtain the table given in Figure 8.

We shall describe further two of these systems — Baganda and Ashanti — noting some of the relevant characteristics of the Ibo as well. The classification of the three systems not examined in detail will have to be very tentative; however, a few comments about them are in order. Although all of them are theocracies, much in the same way that ancient Greece and Rome were the-

Value Type	Authority Type		
	Hierarchical	Pyramidal	Segmental
Instrumental	Baganda	Fulani-Hausa	Ibo
Consummatory	Dahomey (Fon)	Ashanti	Nuer

FIG. 8. — *Comparative traditional systems.*

ocracies, some are less all-encompassing than others. Both the Baganda and the Fon, for example, were military kingdoms, the king in the latter instance being a representative of the deity.

The identity of the divine and human patterns of organization is seen again in their hierarchical and specialized character. The continued existence of the world and of society is maintained in accordance with the same principles. Herskovits rightly observes: "Dahomean culture is based on control by an officialdom, which, under the monarch, was of an essentially hierarchical character similar to that ascribed to the gods. . . ."[20]

The aggressive character of Dahomean traditional society did not serve instrumental ends or immediate and practical benefits;

[20] Quoted in P. Mercier, "The Fon of Dahomey," in Daryll Forde (ed.), *African Worlds* (London: Oxford University Press, 1954), p. 233. Mercier also points out that there is a "remarkable correspondence between the government of the universe and that of human society, between the structure of the world of the gods and that of the world of men. These two essential aspects of the cosmogony are complementary and comparative; the king who sustains society is naturally compared with the divinities who sustain the world" (p. 233).

it was more a reflection on the incumbent trustees of ancestral prescriptions. Lesser, appointive chiefs reflected the same obligations and were bound to observe the king's strictures because of his near deification. An elaborate range of cosmological and religious beliefs pervaded all aspects of social life.

The Fulani-Hausa system is an interesting contrast because, although it has centralized authority, its structure is pyramidal rather than hierarchical. There are exceptions to this general rule, and superficially the system might appear to represent a model hierarchical system. But the Fulani-Hausa blends an organizational structure based on pre-Moslem indigenous lineage and the military-religious hierarchy of the conquering Fulani, with the result that there are many variations among the separate kingdoms. Zaria, for example, has officials appointed by the Emir, with titles and ranks that are not hereditary. But Zaria is an exception. In most of the Fulani-Hausa kingdoms, government is decentralized through replicable political offices that are recruited on the basis of hereditary lineage.[21]

These powerful Fulani-Hausa states were also Moslem. The Fulani, having established their hegemony over the Hausa and other pagan groups during the *jihad* (holy war) conducted by Uthman dan Fodio at the beginning of the nineteenth century, established markets and an elaborate tradition of scholarship with remarkable results.[22] Paradoxically, the spread of Islam resulted in a widening of the area of instrumental behavior and social conduct, including the sphere of politics.

[21] The Zaria system would fall into the same category as Baganda, that is, hierarchical authority and instrumental values. M. G. Smith says that "unlike vassal chieftains, officials of Fulani Zaria were appointed, promoted, transferred, and dismissed at the king's pleasure, and without any formal restrictions, hereditary or otherwise, limiting the ruler's freedom of action" (*Government in Zazzau* [London: Oxford University Press, 1960], p. 9).

[22] The great Fulani conquerers were quite often considerable scholars in their own right. Uthman dan Fodio is supposed to have written eighty-five works in Arabic, his brother Abdullah, seventy-five, and his son, Muhammad Bello, ninety-three. Cited in Thomas Hodgkin, *Nigerian Perspectives* (London: Oxford University Press, 1960), p. 42.

The third group, the Nuer, is a predominantly segmental society whose social life consists of highly ritualized observances in
which religious elements are continuously reinforced. Structurally,
there is virtually no political differentiation. Evans-Pritchard, as
we have seen, suggests that the Nuer have no government and
live in a state of "ordered anarchy." Internal tension is given to
the system by the "feud."

> The feud is a political institution, being an approved and
> regulated mode of behaviour between communities within
> a tribe. The balanced opposition between tribal segments
> and their complementary tendencies towards fission and
> fusion, which we have seen to be a structural principle, is
> evident in the institution of the feud which, on the one hand,
> gives expression to the hostility by occasional and violent
> action that serves to keep the sections apart, and, on the
> other hand, by the means provided for settlement, prevents
> opposition developing into complete fission.[23]

There are, of course, mediating roles that repair breaches between the segments. One such figure is the "leopard-skin chief,"
who, however, has little authority and derives what influence he
has from his sacred association with the earth and a residual power
to bless or curse — a power that Evans-Pritchard suggests is very
rarely, if ever, used.[24]

The ordinary life of the Nuer centers on cattle. Ghosts and
spirits are contacted through cattle, and ritual observances are
mainly associated with them. Evans-Pritchard suggests that "he
who lives among the Nuer and wishes to understand their social
life must first master a vocabulary referring to cattle and to the
life of the herds."[25] From our point of view, this combination of a
segmental social structure and what might be called a cattle
cosmology has rather curious consequences. It produces a wide
range of acts that, in purely instrumental terms, have marginal

[23] E. E. Evans-Pritchard, *The Nuer*, p. 161.
[24] *Ibid.*, pp. 172–77.
[25] *Ibid.*, p. 19.

consequence and whose primary value is consummatory. This is particularly the case with the feud. The feud is a troublesome form of behavior to comprehend because, on instrumental grounds, it seems to be so pointless. Indeed, its primary function seems to be that it reinforces emotional ties and obligations between kinsmen, thus reinforcing, as Max Gluckman has pointed out, the pattern of social life in the society as a whole. Conflict preserves the vitality of the group. A wide range of emotional relations serves as the primary satisfaction and, as a by-product, the work of the tribe gets done. Gluckman suggests that "at every point each man is pulled into relations with different men as allies or enemies according to the context of situation. A man needs help in herding his cattle: therefore he must be friends with neighbours with whom he may well quarrel over other matters — or indeed over the herding of cattle." Such behavior results in a network of taboos and discriminations that constitutes the social order.[26]

What is lacking is a primary emphasis on a functional division of labor. For the Nuer, functional roles and instrumental behaviors are based on kinship and the ritual observances that reinforce it. Hence, in this society, consummatory values are determinant.

What inferences can be drawn from these three examples? First, we can expect in the latter case that structural flexibility will preserve the consummatory belief system. The Nuer will probably be able to resist innovation and development less by attacking it than by ignoring it. We would expect that each segment, by reproducing the cosmology of the entire tribe, will show a sticking power of great strength. For that reason, the Nuer will be able to resist modernization without fighting it. It simply will not have much effect on them.

The Fulani-Hausa have a very different pattern. Here, pyramidal authority provides resiliency while instrumental values allow carefully considered and controlled portions of change.

[26] Gluckman, *Custom and Conflict in Africa* (Glencoe: Free Press of Glencoe, Ill., 1955), p. 17.

Islam provides a wide range of combinations between authority and instrumental practices and at the same time emphasizes the community aspect of political and social life. I suspect that the blend of instrumental values, ritual prohibitions, and the emphasis on a generalized community that is inherent in Islam (as well as the elaborate mixture of lineage and clientele political arrangements) is the reason the northern emirs in Nigeria have been able to organize themselves so successfully for modern political life, in fact, to the point of dominating nearly all of Nigeria. At the same time, they are able to control and digest the aspects of development that appeal to them, rejecting those that they find threatening. Such a system is adaptive while remaining conservative. Given to compromise and negotiation, and with a clear notion of secular interests, the Fulani-Hausa nevertheless do not become easily engaged in massive development or imbued with ideas of change and progress.

In our first case, the Fon of Dahomey, hierarchical authority based on kingship was so intertwined with the religious beliefs of the whole society that the system could not survive French hegemony. Shortly after the French established their control around Porto Novo (one of the tributary areas of Behanzin, the Dahomean king), they were attacked. Behanzin's attack was unsuccessful; he was deported, and the kingdom of Abomey was virtually eliminated. Those chiefs (bureaucratic appointees) who were subordinate to the king were able to remain in their positions. Thus, the subordinate units of the system maintained the formal structure, although the belief system had failed with the elimination of the central figure. Its authority structure and value type were so closely linked that when the keystone of the first disappeared, so did the second. The result was a large influx of individuals to schools, Western churches, and the like. It is a startling fact that Dahomey, one of the poorest of the African countries, has been the most receptive to development. "Dahomey, the smallest territory of the Federation [former French West Africa] and the last to come under French control, is also the poorest in natural re-

sources. But it holds a great trump card in the abilities and intelligence of its people, especially the Fons, and no other territory
has so high a percentage of children in school." [27] The elite have
migrated all over French-speaking Africa, they have become successful civil servants and have adapted themselves to mission
schooling and Christianity.

Here, then, a combination of rigidities — hierarchical authority
and consummatory values — produced the most complete break
with the past. The three systems we have just described can be
ranked for receptivity to development in the reverse order of
their presentation here.

BUGANDA AND ASHANTI

Buganda is today a part of Uganda, one of the new African
states. Uganda, working hesitantly towards a federation with
Kenya and Tanganyika, is led by a militant prime minister, Milton
Obote. Only a few years ago the issue of federation was sufficient
to cause major turmoil in the country. The reasons were varied
and complex, and most of them are not valid today since federation
no longer means domination by Europeans. But other issues center
around the parochialism of the Baganda, the people of Buganda.

As one of the most important kingdom states in the lake area
of Eastern Africa, Buganda was regarded very favorably by the
Europeans who first came upon the country in the latter half of
the nineteenth century. First Arabs and then British and French
missionaries were welcomed by the king, or *Kabaka*. Kabaka
Mutesa I encouraged competitive religious observances by the
three main groups, Moslem, Protestant and Catholic, although he
died a pagan.

For the Baganda, Christianity came to denote a superior technological and educational status. The older religious system,
which was associated with the institution of clanship, gradually

    [27] See V. M. Thompson and R. Adloff, *French West Africa* (Stanford,
Calif.: Stanford University Press, 1958), p. 142.

gave way to a hierarchical chieftaincy system and finally disappeared without producing much internal strain. Christianity
aided the Baganda in maintaining their society. Their only point
of concern was the missionaries, who, in gaining adherents, tended
to usurp the functions of chiefs. Since the latter remained responsible to the *Kabaka*, whereas the missionaries were not, a disturbing element was introduced into the political system.

The competition among religions resulted in religious wars,
which were eventually resolved by allocating fixed numbers of
chieftaincies to Catholics, Protestants, and Moslems. The religious
factions became tantamount to political parties within Buganda.

The missionaries themselves commented on how quickly the
Baganda took to education and became ardent religionists.[28] After
British intervention and the establishment of a protectorate over
Uganda, Catholic and Protestant school systems were established.
The chiefs were the best educated group in the population. Catho-
lic chiefs were products of Kisubi, and Protestant chiefs were prod-
ucts of King's College, Budo. Both were modeled after British
public schools.

Freehold land tenure was also introduced by the British and
eight thousand square miles were distributed among one thousand
chiefs and notables, who thereby became a kind of squirearchy.
The recipients of the land were mainly Catholics and Protestants.

Whatever the innovation — civil-service chieftaincy, a parliament and council of ministers, modern education, or freehold tenure — the system was strengthened. The instrumental quality of
hierarchical kingship was never displaced. The innovations that
were most easily accepted were those that strengthened the Buganda government and also facilitated the individual's efficiency
within it. As a result, the organization of political life, which had
always been the crucial social structure in Buganda, was regarded
as continuing from the past, with each innovation simply perfect-
ing and strengthening an established system. All novelty came to

[28] See R. P. Ashe, *Chronicles of Uganda* (London, 1894); and A. R. Tucker.
Eighteen Years in Uganda and East Africa (London, 1908).

be regarded as a device for strengthening tradition. As we shall indicate below, the main structure of authority that emerges from a study of the Baganda is that of a modernizing autocracy in which the government of the *Kabaka* and the *Kabaka* himself represent effective nationalism.

In Ashanti, on the other hand, responses to innovation were relatively complicated. Chieftaincy, despite its tiers of relatively autonomous units of government, was nevertheless hemmed in by restrictions. The office faced inward to the people, to whom, by lineage and totem, the chief or headman was related. Instead of the individual atomism of the Baganda, which was sustained by regard for the *Kabaka* and the external force of hierarchical authority, an elaborate system of religiously sanctioned self-restraints on behavior was the basis of the Ashanti chiefs' authority. When alienation from the land began to occur in undue measure, chieftaincy was affected and the stable confines of the social system were undermined. The introduction of Christianity helped to weaken the traditions of chieftaincy and removed the control exercised by the dead ancestors over the living. The result was excesses by the chiefs, who turned to the British authorities for support. When education was introduced, the chiefs had to be ordered to send their children to school. Although they could not disobey the orders of district officers, they often sent the children of their slave lineages rather than those of royal blood. The succeeding generations of chiefs were thus by no means the best educated in their societies. The support required to maintain their authority violated customary restraints on behavior; and their excesses soon came to be regarded as perversions of traditional society, from which younger and better educated elements began to disaffiliate. Christianity helped ease the process of disaffiliation, and there developed, along with an increase in urbanization and the growth of villages, the phenomenon of town-Christian and village-pagan. An important indication of the inability of the Ashanti to absorb the innovating effects of colonial rule (basically the same in both Buganda and Ashanti) was a series of wars between them and the British. In the end, the *Asantehene*, or king of Ashanti, had to be exiled. Indeed, from 1901 to 1935, the Ashanti Confederacy did not exist as such.[29]

In the sense in which "traditionalism" is understood in this study, both the Ashanti and the Baganda had traditionalist systems: both required validation of current behavior by appeal to immemoriality, and both had myths of origin involving a powerful figure who was associated with the formation of the society and from whom the king claimed descent. In the case of the Ashanti, the powers of origin were embodied in the Golden Stool rather than descended through persons. In Buganda, descent was reckoned through the line of kings, or *Kabakas*. That the preservation of power and continuity should reside in an object, as in the case of Ashanti, as distinct from a person, as in Buganda, is not without significance. For in Ashanti, those in power serve the present by serving the past. The visible repository of authority is a symbol of ancestral concern. In Buganda the king was, as both John Roscoe and L. A. Fallers have called him, despotic.[30] Although pomp and ceremony surrounded, and still surround, the king, he was not regarded as a descendant of a line of royal ancestors. He was rather the punishing, aggressive, and virile representative of a dynamic people expanding their military hegemony in the Lake Victoria region. Hence, the essentially religious and theocratic nature of the Ashanti state, and the more secular and military character of Buganda.

Other important differences existed between these societies. In Ashanti, the prototype of political organization was the extended family, which included up to one hundred members, who were held together by strong solidary affiliations. Families lived together in villages, and it was unusual for an Ashanti to live apart with only his immediate family. The Ashanti also had an elaborate lineage system whereby recruitment to office and the allocation

[29] J. N. Matson, *Warrington's Notes on Ashanti Custom* (2d ed.; Cape Coast, Gold Coast: Prospect Printing Press, 1941).

[30] See, in particular, John Roscoe, *The Baganda* (London, 1911), p. 232.

of rights and duties were organized. The core political unit was the village; the largest unit was the division, over which a paramount chief presided; and the divisions were joined in a confederacy. The center of the confederacy was the division Kumasi, which had established a compact with the other Ashanti divisions in a historical episode veiled in mystery and magic. An elaborate balance of checks and controls on authority extended from the village to the division, including restrictions on the exercise of power by the *Asantahene*, or king of the Ashanti Confederacy.

The system in Buganda was much simpler in one respect and much more complex in others. Unlike the chief in Ashanti, who was a religious and a lineage figure and, moreover, elected to office, the chief in Buganda was appointed by the king, or *Kabaka*, and was responsible to him. The chief was subject to summary dismissal at the pleasure of the *Kabaka*. (Much closer to the Ashanti pattern was an earlier, pre-*Kabaka*, clan system, which continued to play a part in subsequent periods.) The king was both *Sabataka* (head of all the clans) and *Kabaka*.

Every Muganda (the singular form of "Baganda") was a member of a clan, and membership was hereditary. The elders of clans had responsibilities over the family, the social conduct of individuals, and inheritance. Appointed chiefs reflected the powers of the *Kabaka*. Clan elders, who were elected from eligible lineages, reflected religious and immemorial powers. These two bases of authority were in constant conflict. Increasingly, performance in serving the *Kabaka*, and thereby the state, became the basis of chieftaincy. Performance and service were readily observable, since Buganda, as a military system, was in the process of expanding at the expense of her neighbors.

The acceptance of hierarchical authority was thus associated with successful national aggrandizement, and the pure authority of the *Kabaka* was not mitigated by any other countervailing principle. Tension within the system was produced by conflicts between clanship and chieftaincy. The *Kabaka*, however, represented the central authority in both systems, that is, *Sabataka*, or head of all the clans, and *Kabaka*, or head of all the chiefs.

There were two immediate consequences of the twin systems of organization in Buganda. First, since clans were scattered throughout the country, an individual on the move could find a clansman in all areas and receive certain benefits from him. This not only facilitated mobility but also ensured considerable uniformity of custom and behavior throughout the system.

Second, the chiefs, who were territorial governors for the king, were military leaders as well. Their followers were loyal to them because they reflected the *Kabaka's* authority. This military-administrative system of organization included a massive radial network of military roads converging upon the center or capital. The capital itself was often moved, however, so that there was no "center" and "hinterland."

The result was a "suburban" pattern of daily life in which clanship counterpoised chieftaincy but in which each man looked to the king. In time of war, which was often, the military-administrative system required almost no modification. The necessary mobilization took place under the chiefs. Food continued to be produced, and family life managed to go on quite satisfactorily. The Ashanti, in contrast, had to shift to a quite different formation in time of war, returning to their pyramidal organization when peace was restored.[31]

What were some of the innovations that the Buganda system was unable to absorb? The most characteristic was the inability to adjust to any permanent limitation on the power of the *Kabaka*. Whether chief or peasant, educated or not, the Baganda maintained the same unabashed veneration for the office of the *Kabaka*.

---

[31] The Ashanti had a complex hierarchy of chiefs. At the pinnacle of the hierarchy was the *omanhene*, or divisional chief. Independent in his sphere of authority, he was nevertheless hedged about with restrictions. His was a religious role symbolizing lineage relationships to ancestors; only members of a founder's, or royal, lineage were eligible to be elected to the chieftaincy. The same held true for village chiefs and headmen. During war, a division chief and others would take a position in the army, and a hierarchical rather than pyramidal system of authority would come to prevail. See E.

Or, to put the matter another way, the principle of national aggrandizement was never lost, and the *Kabaka* was its symbol. Each
of the major conflicts that aroused the Baganda and posed serious
problems for the protectorate government centered on possible
dangers to the autonomy of Buganda or diminutions in the authority of the *Kabaka*. The Baganda, then, in contrast to the Ashanti,
have instrumental values: their ends are relatively well defined
and essentially patriotic.

Both Baganda and Ashanti developed their own forms of tribal
parochialism. The former were adept in retaining considerable
political autonomy, and the Uganda Agreement of 1900, which
stipulated the relations between the Baganda and the British,
became a legal bulwark of ethnic nationalism and political parochialism. In Ashanti, where no such constitutional relationship
existed, internal conflict created instabilities that eventually led
to mass nationalism.

In more contemporary terms, in Buganda, nationalist politicians
have so far been able to make little headway and are regarded
by the Buganda government as malcontents and ne'er-do-wells.
This makes for an unusual situation, since, before independence,
the British authorities were anxious to see country-wide nationalist
political parties develop as the solution to building a modern
state.[32] In Ghana (Ashanti), the party nationalists have become
tantamount to the state itself, regarding chiefs unenthusiastically,
to say the least. Not only have they taken active steps to break the
chief's power, but the paramount chief of Ashanti, the *Asantehene*,
has been their particular target. In the last encounter between
the *Asantehene* and the party government, the former had to admit
defeat. The quasi-religious character of traditional society in
Ghana has been replaced by the quasi-religious character of
modern nationalism. These developments will be analyzed more
closely below.

Meyerowits, *The Sacred State of the Akan* (London: Faber & Faber, 1951),
especially chap. x.

[32] See *Report of the Constitutional Committee, 1959* ("Wild Report") (Entebbe: Government Printer 1959), pp. 33–35.

CONTRASTING CONSEQUENCES OF POLITICAL MODERNIZATION

Uganda and Ghana are in the process of modernization. Practically, this has meant establishing parliamentary institutions by which to govern the whole country. Ghana has developed more rapidly. Per capita national income is double that in Uganda. More effective internal transport and trade facilities are to be found in Ghana, and Africans participate actively in all aspects of technical and commercial life. In Uganda, until recently expatriates monopolized the more important sectors of the economy and were the predominant racial groups in the civil service. Africanization of the civil service in Ghana is virtually complete, with only a few technical services still performed by Europeans, and these mostly on contract.

Ghana is economically well off for an African country.[33] Since 1951, 80 per cent of its internal savings has been based upon a single cash crop, cocoa. Other sources of income are gold, bauxite, manganese, industrial diamonds, and timber. It has advanced economically under a series of development plans, the first of which was primarily concerned with expanding basic transportation facilities. Railways were extended and a deep-water port built at Takoradi. The principle of a reserve fund for economic contingencies was established early. The first ten-year development plan was launched at the end of the First World War, and except during the period of the world depression, Ghana has been development-conscious. Both under the later stages of colonialism and under her present nationalist government, she has been a social welfare state.

What has been the effect of innovation in Ghana? Traditional

[33] A population of approximately five million in an area of over 90,000 square miles is divided into several main tribal groups. The northern peoples are mainly pagan. The central group is the seat of the once-powerful Ashanti Confederacy. The southern groups — Fante, Ga, Ewe, and others — have had the longest contact with Western commerce and education. There are old families inhabiting the former "factories" of early traders who intermarried with the local people and established their own family dynasties. See J. Boyon, *Le Ghana* (Paris: Armand Colin, 1958), pp. 7–10.

chieftaincy and social organization increasingly became a focus
for internal resentments. Bitter conflict over land developed. The
pattern of self-restraints on behavior was upset. Land alienation
in the form of concessions was common. Considerable friction
developed between chiefs who took seats in legislative and other
conciliar bodies set up by the government as well as in traditional
councils and the urban, educated elites that emerged with the
spread of modern commerce. Each emerging group thought itself
destined to inherit political power. These conflicts prepared the
ground for mass nationalism in Ghana after the Second World
War. The chiefs, failing to consider the sources of mass nationalism, regarded it simply as one episode in a long and stable cultural tradition that would help to restore chieftaincy to its proper
role.

The Western-educated elites regarded the nationalists as
usurpers of their roles, and the British viewed them as dangerous
malcontents, subversive to public peace and good order. Such
rejections gave fervor to the nationalists, who joined together in
the Convention People's Party (CPP), seeing in adherence to a
party a new meaning for Ghana as a national society. The party
brought about a closer integration of the different peoples making
up the territory, and it made economic and political institutions
African, rather than foreign, by using them to work toward self-
government. Politics had already tended to become polarized between traditional and modern authorities during the last stages
of the colonial period; and after World War II the fundamental
issues of traditionalism and modernity became wrapped up in
the more complex conflicts over democracy.

The major achievement of the CPP in Ghana was the organization and maintenance of an effective mass political organization.
Centers of communication were established in the towns and
villages, which required members to co-ordinate the activities of
others. The CPP was a social group as well, a fraternity of the
disadvantaged, and as such encouraged its members to better their
position by means of national political institutions and political

freedom. A widely diverse membership was provided with a feeling of confidence in the future. New opportunities would result from the goal of self-government. A vision of a new society that was as vague as it was powerful was the moral claim of the CPP. Yet in creating a mass political organization devoted to achieving independence, the CPP incorporated elements that had no long-run natural inclinations toward one another. More particularly, traditional groupings formed centers of opposition to the leader of the party and president of Ghana, Kwame Nkrumah, both inside and outside the party. The main source of opposition was Ashanti. The *Asantehene* and his council helped plan the organization of an opposition, the National Liberation Movement (NLM), which renewed an old alliance between intellectuals and traditional authorities.[34]

With opposition demands for a federal system of government, the situation rapidly grew dangerous. One cabinet minister, a leading CPP figure from Ashanti, was ambushed outside his house and his sister killed. For almost two years government leaders did not dare go to Ashanti. Moreover, the appearance of successful traditionalism in Ashanti encouraged other opposition groups. In Accra, Nkrumah's own constituency, an Accra people's movement, essentially parochial and anti-Nkrumah, was formed. Throughout the country traditionalism and the natural organization of the ethnic and tribal group seemed the only possible alternatives to party rule by the Convention People's Party.

In attacking traditionalism, movements like the CPP assume the characteristics of infallibility, a tendency to brand splinter groups and the opposition as playing into the hands of the "feudal" elements in society. This in fact has now become official doctrine in Ghana, which in 1964 adopted the one-party political pattern. In this conflict between traditionalism and modernity, there is a

---

[34] In 1957 the NLM joined with other tribal parties like the Ga Shifimo Kpee to become the United Party. The former leader of the opposition and NLM official, K. A. Busia, became Ghana's first political exile, to be followed by others, including K. A. Gbedemah, the former CPP minister of finance.

continuous affiliation to and disaffiliation from powerful social groupings, with each making a total claim to the allegiance and support of its members. Traditionalism, which serves the opposition as an effective rallying ground for popular support, is branded as subversive.[35]

What, then, has political modernization meant in Ghana? The party of solidarity, in attacking tradition, has jostled the public into functionally useful roles for the pursuit of modernization. The basic goals of those who have inherited the mantle of British power are to hold on to that power and to modernize as rapidly as possible. Modernization has come to require many individual attitudes and forms of social organization antithetical to traditional behavior and has therefore attacked head-on traditional ways of believing and acting.

Thus, for a time, the Ghana government was unable to make use of traditionalism to support innovation. The past became a dead weight on the government, which by inducements (and by kicks and blows as well) sought to drive people toward a new way of life. Because of the government's loss of support in the traditional sectors of society, the burdens of modernization on Ghana were intense and resulted in a relatively autocratic system.[36]

Let us turn once again to Uganda. Although the Baganda did not suffer national defeats as did the Ashanti, religious wars in the latter part of the nineteenth century resulted in the deposition and restoration of the *Kabaka* by Europeans on two occasions.

[35] Indeed, at the Accra African People's Conference in December, 1958, tribalism and religious separatism were defined as evil practices by Africa's leading nationalists. It was resolved that "those African traditional institutions whether political, social, or economic which have clearly shown their reactionary character and their sordid support for colonialism be condemned" (All-African People's Conference, "Resolution on Tribalism, Religious Separatism, and Traditional Institutions," *Conference Resolutions*, Vol. 1., No. 4 [Accra: Conference Secretariat, 1958]).

[36] This situation has been altered to some extent today, and traditional features have become a part of the present system of authority; see the discussion of the new modernizing autocracy in chapters x and xi. See also my chapter on Ghana in James S. Coleman and Carl Rosberg, *Political Integration in Tropical Africa* (Berkeley: University of California Press, 1964).

The Baganda have never forgotten this. Given the special position of the *Kabaka* in the structure of Buganda society, their cavalier treatment on the part of Europeans deeply wounded and aggrieved the Baganda. Even during the period of their closest collaboration with the British (roughly from 1900 to 1926), such grievances were nursed. A singular touchiness thus characterized relations between the British and the Baganda. Unlike the typical governmental district, Buganda stoutly resisted changes in political organization if they originated with the protectorate government. The *Kabaka* as a symbol of modern nationalism has been continuously strengthened. [37]

When the Uganda Agreement of 1900 was signed, the *Lukiko,* or African parliament, which was dominated by the chiefs, was empowered to distribute land on a freehold basis to the most important people in Buganda. The three most powerful ministers received the largest estates (with the exception of the *Kabaka* himself); other chiefs were given land according to their rank or general status.[38] Few pagans received any land.

Since chieftaincies, and therefore also family wealth and position, were allotted on the basis of religion, both Protestants and Catholics came to have considerable stake in the modified system. Both groups had some wealthy families in possession of land and in important positions in the community. The Moslems received the least of all the religious groups, and paganism quickly disappeared.

Those in the clan system who were traditionally entitled to certain burial estates or clan lands and who lost those lands during the parceling-out of freehold became the first political force in Buganda. The clan system thus formed the "natural" opposition to the government of chiefs. Considerable internal dissension re-

[37] The *Kabaka,* in addition to holding the kabakaship in Buganda, has become the first president of Uganda.
[38] Uganda Agreement of 1900, Para. 15 (see *Laws of the Uganda Protectorate, Native Agreements and Buganda Native Laws* [London, 1936], pp. 1380–81.

sulted, and gradually, the *bataka*, or clan groups, came to represent the *bakopi*, or peasantry. Landholding became almost synonymous with prestige and social position.[39] Indeed, it appeared for a time that the system would be based on dynastic landholding families rather than on the traditional principle of easy access to political office through performance. Yet other innovations helped to prevent this. The expanded educational system, for example, which was enthusiastically supported by the Baganda, was not limited to the children of chiefs but included peasant children. Education was regarded as a major basis for entry into the political hierarchy (which remained the only major social organization throughout Buganda).

The instrumental values of the Baganda, colliding with a threatened monopoly of political roles by the families of the senior chiefs who had received land, or by important Protestant and Catholic leaders, prevailed over both elites without altering the autocratic principle of hierarchical kingship. This allowed progressive modification of the *Lukiko* and greater opportunities for the public as a whole. Unlike the consummatory system of Ashanti, where individuals had virtually to withdraw from the traditional system in order to seek new careers and opportunities in a different kind of society, the Buganda system was modified in practice and at the same time posed few contradictions in principle.

Although the Buganda government was often in conflict with the peasantry, it was the conflict of a government and its loyal opposition. The British, through a Resident, built up the influence of the chiefs and the ministers of the Buganda government, whom they regarded as modern because of the ease and alacrity with

[39] Important in preventing such dissension from assuming proportions of "class conflict" was the fact that peasants could, and did, buy freehold land. Moreover, no landless peasantry was created since everyone could get a leasehold property at a nominal and fixed rental. Migration to towns was deterred, and no urban-rural cleavage developed. Buganda remains a rural "suburbia." See A. W. Southall and P. C. W. Gutkind, *Townsmen in the Making* ("East African Studies," No. 9 [Kampala: East African Institute of Social Research, 1956]), *passim*.

which they learned to collect taxes, adapted themselves to methods of bookkeeping, and were able to control the public. Thus the autocratic principle has prevailed in Buganda until the present. Innovations are believed to have come not from an alien source but through the Buganda government itself. The country's leaders are able to maintain social discipline, because to act against the *Kabaka* is to act irresponsibly, and a sense of awe and formality in social relations has helped retain public support.

As a result, the Baganda have regarded themselves as exceedingly blessed in a state of political autonomy. Until 1962, the Buganda government was the most successful nationalist "party" in the country. Success in the economic field as well, particularly with the cotton and coffee crops, brought the Baganda considerable wealth as compared with the rest of the protectorate. Such visible indicators of a high standard of living as tin roofs on their houses, number of bicycles, number of hired laborers from elsewhere on their land, and number of educated people added to their complacency. They have been able to absorb new forms of income and to accept standards of education, knowledge, skill, and training as requirements for jobs such as chieftaincies, while retaining the essential character of their political system.

The freehold system, the chieftaincy system, the methods of recruitment and standards of selection for the political hierarchy, and the acceptance of the idea of cash crops all helped to make Buganda extremely modern in many ways. *But the prerequisite for accepting any innovation on the political level was to find some real or mythical traditional counterpart.* Hence, if the *Lukiko* was now a regular council with minutes, committees, and a budget, it was also regarded as an age-old institution. If chiefs were now almost invariably large landowners or related to the original holders of freehold, in custom they were found to be the equivalent to those who had formerly been responsible for controlling "heads," that is, families and soldiers.

In 1955 several important measures were passed. The District Councils Ordinance gave the district governments both executive and legislative powers, enabling them to make bylaws on a wide range of subjects.[40] In Buganda, after the deportation of the *Kabaka* for refusing to co-operate with the protectorate government (part of his effort to retain autonomy for Buganda), a new agreement was signed that enhanced the powers of the *Lukiko*, made the *Kabaka* in effect a constitutional monarch, and gave the Baganda three new ministries —(health, education, and natural resources) in addition to the three they already had (prime minister, chief justice, and treasurer).[41] These reforms gave to Buganda and to the district governments substantive warrants of authority and responsibility to attend to most of the economic and social schemes that were regarded as necessary to modernization. In Buganda the autocratic nature of the system has now come under attack — but the attack is still exceedingly mild. Elsewhere, in the districts, the effort to achieve local autonomy is regarded as the essence of political modernity.

What the system in Buganda cannot absorb are challenges to the principle of autocratic or hierarchical kingship.[42] As a result,

[40] See *District Councils Ordinance, 1955* (Entebbe: Government Printer, 1955).

[41] See *Buganda Agreement of 1955* (Entebbe: Government Printer, 1955).

[42] Resisting the first direct elections to be held in Buganda in 1958, the Baganda saw themselves threatened by devolution of authority to an African national government. Opposed to the nationalism of political parties, they regard representative government on an all-Uganda basis as tantamount to the destruction of their society. In a pamphlet justifying the position of Buganda, the *Katikiro*, or prime minister, pointed out that the "peaceful growth of Western democracy in Buganda has been possible because the Baganda's customs and traditions are adaptable to new ideas which do not seek to uproot their fundamental political conceptions. . . ." Yet, he warned, "The Baganda cannot exist as a people unless the *Kabaka* is the head of the political structure in his Kingdom. Therefore, any constitution which envisages placing any other ruler or any foreign monarch in the position of the *Kabaka* of Buganda has no other intention but to cause the Baganda to cease to be a nation." More important, he concluded, was the fact that "from time immemorial the Baganda have known no other ruler above their Kabaka in his Kingdom, and still they do not recognize any other person whose authority does not derive from the Kabaka and is exercised on his behalf." M. Kintu, *Buganda's Position*, Information Department, Kabaka's Government (Kampala: Uganda Printing and Publishing Co., 1960), pp. 1–2.

it was the protectorate government and British officials who tried to build a modern national state in Uganda. How difficult it was is well illustrated by the fact that in the first direct elections in 1958 Buganda refused to participate, as did several other districts.[43] Uganda became independent in October, 1962. An awareness has now emerged among many Baganda that the absorptive capacity of the traditional system and its instrumental values has been reached. Younger groups are anxious to build a larger national society, a united Uganda. An uneasy coalition exists between the political traditionalists in a Buganda party, *Kabaka Yekka*, and the governing United People's Congress. But Uganda still has a "Buganda problem."

In both Ghana and Uganda tribal or ethnic parochialism has persisted with widely varying results. Buganda parochialism has itself been a form of modernity. Civil service chieftaincy and bureaucratic norms have bolstered the kingdom. Indeed, the Buganda government is widely regarded as the most progressive force in the country. Hence, for the Baganda, to be modern is to be parochial.

In Ashanti, modernism clashed directly with traditionalism. The religious aspect of the traditional political and social structure was the source of a network of restraints on behavior. When the traditional structures were disrupted by innovations in commercial enterprise and colonialism, traditional authority was quickly undermined. Yet, because traditional authority was so much a

[43] Subsequently, a constitutional committee recommended the establishment of responsible government at the center, with a legislature possessing seventy-two elected seats. (See the *Report of the Constitutional Committee, 1959* ["Wild Report"], which anxiously notes the need for political parties in order to create effective central government.) The Buganda government voiced its bitter opposition, but other districts saw in it the possibility of a political society not dominated by Buganda. With the Baganda anxious to secede from Uganda entirely if that was necessary to maintain the position of the *Kabaka* and the Buganda kingdom, bitter conflict developed between the Buganda government, on the one hand, and party politicians allied to British authorities, on the other. Party politics has won, but the struggle was bitter.

part of daily life and custom, those who broke with the past found themselves in drastic need of new and powerful social affilia- tions — for to break with tradition was to break with family, lin- eage, and ancestral fidelity.

In contrast to Ashanti, Buganda has remained the most power- ful solidary association possible. It is still possible for all those who belong to the kingdom to achieve social satisfactions within Buganda and its government. In Ashanti the formation of a new political party itself created new and powerful symbolic attach- ments. The Ashanti members of the CPP became fiercely devoted to the organization. The messianic role of the leader was based on the aim of the party to develop a new morality to supplant the old. Hence, deep cleavages in society remained after self-govern- ment had been obtained, posing the problem of nation-building after independence rather than before it.

The Baganda are particularly interesting because they represent the extreme case of controlled and selective adaptation — they traditionalized innovation when they chose and rejected those aspects of it that would have produced too much to digest. This was not an entirely smooth and harmonious process, of course, but it worked amazingly well for the most part. With respect to values, the Baganda endowed far fewer ordinary acts with ulti- mate ends than did the Ashanti.

THE IBO

At the other end of our structural paradigm are the Ibo of eastern Nigeria. The Ibo number close to four million and repre- sent one of the most significant ethnic groupings in Nigera. Their grouping is based on similarities in language and custom rather than a sense of territorial or national identity. In the past social life was organized around patrilineages clustered in hamlets and villages, a group of which was the most general form of political unit.

Authority inhered in the male head of the household and the

senior elders of the lineage. The lineage elders formed a council
that decided among disputants, allocated land, and so on. The
council did not consist entirely of lineage elders, however; distinguished or rich men in the community were able to purchase
titles, and those with high titles became members of the council.
In addition to lineage relationships, there were age-grade relationships, which were divided into sets. These sets provided funds
for mutual assistance and control and, among the men, served in
war as police units and in other regulative capacities.

Some of the Ibo groups were engaged extensively in trade, including the trade in slaves. Among them, the Cross River Ibo and,
in particular, the Aro were heavily involved. The famous Aro
"Long Juju," an oracle that accumulated individuals for slave-
trading while purporting to decide disputes, was one of the more
notorious outgrowths of the Ibo propensity for trade. There were
other such trading oracles, but the Aro-Chuku was the most
powerful. Its use of belief for highly instrumental purposes is
worth some discussion. Dike describes it as follows. The Aro-
Chuku oracle was

> universally respected and feared throughout Iboland, and in
> fact, by every tribe in eastern Nigeria. This Oracle was sup-
> posed to reside in the territory of the Aros, a section of the
> Ibo tribe. In 1854 Baikie wrote of the "noted City of Aro
> where there is the celebrated shrine of Tshuku [God], to
> which pilgrimages are made, not only from all parts of Igbo
> proper, but from Old Calabar, and from the tribes along the
> coast, and from Oru and Nembe. . . ."
>   Aro people . . . exploited this belief in their Oracle in
> many ways, principally in order to dominate the life of the
> region economically, and they made themselves the sole
> middlemen of the hinterland trade. This they did by estab-
> lishing Aro colonies along the trade routes of the interior —
> like the Greeks, the course of whose colonizing expeditions
> was largely directed by the priests of the Delphic Oracle.
> In its wake they organized a trading system which had its
> ramifications throughout practically the whole of the coun-
> try between the Niger and the Eastern side of the Cross

River. Every quarter of Aro Town had its "sphere of influence" in matters of trade. "For instance the country between
Aro-Chuku and Awka belonged to the quarters of Utari,
Amove and Ndizioggu." Acting as mediators between God
and the clans and assuming themselves to be the spokes-
men of the Almighty, they held a' privileged position
throughout the land, erecting what amounted to a theocratic
state over eastern Nigeria. Aro colonies became the divinely
ordained trade centres in the interior; Aro middlemen the
economic dictators of the hinterland . . . and with wealth
came great political influence.[44]

It was not only in the slave trade that consummatory values
were manipulated for instrumental ends, with corresponding institutional changes in the system. Palm oil was vital to the "city-
states" that began to grow up in response to trade and commerce.
Elaborate networks for its transport between the coastal city-states
and the hinterland developed, and with them the demand for education, particularly in the form of clerical training. The household
and village units rapidly adapted to the increase in commerce;
when segments of the community moved to new places, they
easily maintained their core structure. So modest in scale was
the core that it easily adapted to new functions. The lineage structure was reinforced by the age set. Success was rewarded traditionally through the title system. The rewards for material success
had always been recognized; the combination of solidary cohesive-
ness and individual reward of local tribal associations was easily
translated into local commercial lending and other trade associations. In other parts of Nigeria, as well as among the Kikuyu of
Kenya, groups with a decentralized and segmental system of organization and instrumental values also show these characteristics.
Other examples could no doubt be given. Dike says that perhaps
"the overriding genius of the Ibos, Ibibios, Ijaws, Ekoi, and
Efiks and their political institutions, lay in their extraordinary
powers of adaptability — powers which they displayed time and

   [44] K. Onwuka Dike, *Trade and Politics in the Niger Delta, 1830–1885*
(Oxford: Clarendon Press, 1956), pp. 37–38.

again in the nineteenth century and throughout the period of the Atlantic trade in face of the constantly changing economic needs of Europe. No less was their genius for trade." [45] It was not only in the trading sphere that this talent for adaptation and innovation made its appearance. The Ibo were also active in politics and were the main force in building a mass nationalist political organization in Nigeria. They willingly adjusted their local organizations and communities to modernization but at the same time resisted active administration by the British. When, for purposes of organized administration and local government, taxes were imposed, native treasuries established, and warrant chiefs appointed in areas to which chieftaincy was alien, the reactions ranged from subtle to overtly violent. But the latter was rare; the Aba riots were perhaps the most outstanding example. [46]

There were also nativistic movements among the Ibo. These, with predominantly consummatory values, were facilitated by the community and age-grade emphases within Ibo life, which in turn were reinforced by the movements. The range of consummatory values was limited enough to support rather than eliminate instrumental values. It is not without significance that the first nationalist movements in Nigeria among the Ibo were based on accommodated organizations such as the Ibo State Union and its

[45] *Ibid.*, pp. 45–46. Dike quotes Talbot as follows: " 'They are a people of great interest and intelligence,' declared Dr. Talbot, 'hard-headed, keen-witted, and born traders. Indeed one of the principal agents here, a [European] of world-wide experience, stated that, in his opinion, the Kalabari [a Delta people] could compete on equal terms with Jew or Chinaman.' "

[46] James S. Coleman describes the riots as follows: "The rumor that women were to be taxed, and dissatisfaction over the abuses of native court members and warrant chiefs, precipitated a women's movement that spread like wildfire through two of the most densely populated provinces of the Eastern Region at the end of 1929. Chiefs and Europeans were attacked indiscriminately and there was widespread destruction of property and goods, belonging mainly to trading firms. The riot was not quelled until the police, in an overwhelming show of force, killed fifty women and injured an equal number. An unusual feature was that the women, all illiterate, not only initiated but also were the only participants in the uprising" (*Nigeria: Background to Nationalism* [Berkeley: University of California Press, 1958], p. 174).

various branches, separatist church movements, and farmer and traders' associations, which were quite often assisted by councils of elders, age-grade sets, and the like. Zikism had strong mystical bonds. The National Council of Nigeria and the Cameroons (NCNC) was a strong blend of all these elements and had its own church, the National Church of Nigeria and the Cameroons. For the Ibo instrumentalism in both the economic and the political spheres could be integrated with consummatory values, and structural flexibility allowed both kinds of values to maintain themselves side by side. Another way of describing this emphasis on instrumentalism has been suggested by M. M. Green.

> In this densely populated country where the land is over-farmed and it is hard work to get a living, it is perhaps not surprising that there is an almost hypertrophied sense of property. Theft is execrated as one of the worst and most shameful of offences, and is considered as deserving extreme penalties.
>
> Money, the economic symbol, bulks large in the minds of these people, inveterate traders as they are, with a skill in market transactions that amounts almost to genius. There is a song of which the burden is that children are better than money. On the other hand, the women sing of their husbands as being money makers. . . .[47]

Europeans always found it hard to understand the Ibo, as, indeed, do other people in Nigeria, who often fear them. More than any other single ethnic group they arouse hostility. In the north, where they are employed as lorry drivers, road or gang foremen, clerks, and so on, they are bitterly disliked. As a result the NCNC has never been able to develop a satisfactory non-ethnic base, although it has gone much farther in this direction than any other political party in Nigeria.

Here, then, we have a pattern of development different from those of the Baganda and Ashanti. With localized and often individualized responses to innovation and without a central traditional authority — relying instead on local associations — the Ibo

[47] Green, *Ibo Village Affairs* (London: Sedgwick & Jackson, 1947), p. 88.

adapted to commercial life and transposed the localism of the community into the individualism of the trading society. The politics of the Ibo are above all practical and economic, not ideological and dogmatic. Zikism did not last very long, and there is no Ibo-sponsored form of African socialism except in the most broadly defined terms.

What general guides to modernization and adaptation to development can we draw from these illustrations? Certain types of traditional systems are highly resistant to all forms of innovation, whether endogenous or exogenous. The extreme case among our examples would be the Nuer (segmental-consummatory). Other systems, such as the Fon (hierarchical-consummatory), are capable of endogenous development but resist exogenous development fiercely, with virtually no capacity to adjust. Still other systems actively utilize exogenous innovation and modernization in order to strengthen their systems and increase their flexibility, for example, the Baganda (hierarchical-instrumental). The Fulani-Hausa, on the other hand, were able to preserve their system only by blunting modernization and selecting those bureaucratic aspects of it most designed to appeal to the British and most capable of segregating modernization values that might offend tradition. Highly manipulated and selected innovation was the rule (pyramidal-instrumental). The Ibo readily took to exogenous innovations in the economic sphere and resisted them in the political sphere; at the same time their localized institutions were capable of withstanding considerable pressure (segmental-instrumental).

In general, then, we can say that consummatory values make it more difficult for systems to absorb exogenous change and modernization. The most brittle and unadaptive form makes the least accommodation and, in fact, allows its system to be reversed; for example, the transition among the Fon has been from one extreme to the other, from powerful traditionalism to accommodated anti-traditionalism. For the least brittle but also least adaptive, the effect is virtually complete apathy and disinterest. Two systems,

the Baganda and the Fulani-Hausa, were able to traditionalize innovation and therefore survive the process of modernization
intact, the Baganda in a "progressive" manner and the Fulani-
Hausa in a "conservative" manner. One system became preoccupied with egalitarian political forms and created the first mass,
but non-ideological, party in Africa, the National Council of Nigeria and the Cameroons.

These comments are designed to indicate some of the variations
that are to be found among traditional systems in the face of
modernization. We can now indicate the political forms of their
responses and can examine the growth of modernizing political
groups.

4

CHANGING PATTERNS
OF STRATIFICATION

The most direct impact of modernization on traditional societies is in the formation of new roles associated with the modernizing process. Some of the new roles, however, may be only partially new, that is, accommodationist in nature. Tribal unions, for example, may become thrift and lending societies, employing clerks and minor accountants who facilitate a smooth and ready transition to certain aspects of modernization, such as commerce, but not to others. Other roles may be entirely new and outside the context of either accommodationist or traditional roles. As modernization proceeds the hierarchy of power and prestige must be broad enough to encompass traditional, accommodationist, and new roles or a new hierarchy will replace it.

In practice, the substance of modernizing politics is in large measure the result of incompatibilities between these three types of roles. The effort to adjust and modify them is particularly difficult in the absence of an impersonal dynamic mechanism such as exists in industrial countries. The modification and rearrangement of such roles, the selection of role priorities, and the use of restratification to provide possible solutions to the problems of role incompatibilities are all strategically important aspects of political policy-making. The claims put forward by competing political groups, each representing some portion of the total stratification system, are the means by which role malintegration is transformed into political conflict.

One way to illustrate the structural relationships in a society is to rank its roles hierarchically on the basis of power and prestige. A role is a functionally defined position in a social system. It embodies norms of conduct and expectations of action. Roles represent the structural order. Congeries of roles make up organizations. The normative aspects of roles make up institutions. The values of a community, for example, represent a summation of the normative aspects of its various roles.

Another way to indicate structural relationship is through the use of stratification categories. Caste refers to a highly compartmentalized social or ethnic group having ritualized boundaries. Class we define as a multibonded group that is the product of converging dimensions such as occupation, income, and education. Status implies a continuous scale of invidiously valued positions.[1]

In modernizing societies the three types of roles indicated above — traditional, accommodationist, and new — are to be found in three types of stratification systems — caste, class, and status [2] — which often exist side by side. Modernization affects the first by breaking down ritualized role relationships between members of different castes, whether these are racial-cultural, as between Europeans, Asians, and Africans in East Africa, or religious, as in India. Class stratification is usually poorly articulated [3] in the earlier stages of modernization. It is reflected in differences in residential patterns, life styles, education, and social outlook (not to mention wealth). Status competition, which is found in industrial societies as well as modernizing ones, often exists within the senior elite or modernizing "class" itself. Indeed, class distinc-

[1] See Ralf Dahrendorf, *Class and Class Conflict in an Industrial Society* (London: Routledge & Kegan Paul, Ltd., 1959), p. 302.

[2] See the excellent discussion "Class Stratification and Stratification Indicators," in Bernard Barber, *Social Stratification* (New York: Harcourt, Brace & Co., 1957), pp. 73–185.

[3] See S. N. Eisenstadt, "Social Change: Differentiation and Evolution," *American Sociological Review*, XXIX (June, 1964).

tions are easily confused with status competition, particularly since both can be found within the modernized sector. One difference between them should be noted. Whereas class tends to promote solidarity among its members, status tends to drive individuals apart and to isolate them in an infinitely extended system of small-scale differentiae that become the basis of competition.

In a society that is modernizing, the combination of role type and stratification type produces a situation in which the innovators in the system are (1) status conscious, that is, aware of their position in the social system *vis-à-vis* others and, in addition, aware of the advantages and disadvantages of a given status position; (2) engaged in role-testing, even if only vicariously, that is, exploring the legitimate limits of their roles and experimenting to the point where they can expect sanctions of one kind or another to be initiated; and (3) future-oriented, in the sense that they expect changes in their life-chances and will attempt to produce the conditions that will lead to their securing what they desire.

The first characteristic concerns how roles are defined and ranked to form a hierarchy. Two important questions about this characteristic involve the values that underlie hierarchy itself — what beliefs do people hold about the ranking of roles, and how fixed is the behavior demarcated by a role? (The values of rank may change, causing roles to alter. The actual behavior of individuals may be so consistently at variance with ideal prescriptions that the role itself may begin to change. These general attributes of roles in changing societies are extremely important.)[4]

The second characteristic involves the institutionalized criteria of stratification. That is, what are germane criteria for entry into roles and performance by incumbents? Institutionalized criteria are economic, religious, political, generational, and the like.[5] Here the difficulty is not so much defining the institutional criteria as accounting for the differences that may exist between the-

[4] Marion J. Levy, Jr., *The Structure of Society* (Princeton, N.J.: Princeton University Press, 1952), pp. 159–64.
[5] See Kingsley Davis and Wilbert E. Moore, "Some Principles of Stratification," *American Sociological Review*, X (1945), reprinted in S. M. Lip-

ory and practice. All the members of the senior civil service in a modernizing country, for example, may be the most highly qualified in terms of educational criteria. They may also all be members of a set of old families. Quite often apparently germane institutionalized criteria disguise other criteria that are less so.[6]

The third characteristic is essentially a continuation of the second, and concerns how the conflicts in roles and position in the hierarchy induce an interest in the future. Perhaps separate spheres of social life are involved. Traditional societies with segmental authority and consummatory values can, for example, duplicate their small universe and ignore the change taking place all around them. If, at some point, the eldest sons find work in a town and acquire a desire for tin roofs, schools, and medical facilities, then conflicts in role and hierarchy become intense.[7] Moreover, we may be dealing with two or more stratification systems, the first composed of those in the modernization system and the other of those who have no wish to join it.[8]

The combination of role sets and types of stratification produces some interesting problems for government. The possible combinations can be seen in Figure 9. Although it is not necessary to explore all the analytical possibilities, we will mention two as indicative of the problems posed in the stratification sphere. Conflicts may occur between role types within a single stratification category; for example, innovators within a caste may conflict with

set and N. J. Smelser, *Sociology: The Progress of a Decade* (Englewood Cliffs, N. J.: Prentice-Hall, Inc., 1961), pp. 469–72.

[6] Another problem in this regard is that the institutional criteria may be in fundamental disequilibrium with one another. By that I mean that the traditional criterion for power and prestige may be age, with age considered as synonymous with wisdom, whereas those considered eligible for power and prestige roles in the modernization sector are almost certain to be young, having recently finished their education. Here the problem becomes extremely sensitive because legitimacy of power and prestige is questioned and roles are defined differently.

[7] See Lloyd A. Fallers, "A Note on the 'Trickle Effect,'" *Public Opinion Quarterly*, XVIII (1945), 314–21.

[8] See Audrey Wipper's discussion, "A Comparative Study of Nascent Unionism in French West Africa and the Philippines," *Economic Development and Cultural Change*, XII (October, 1964).

accommodationists or traditionalists. In Senegal, the traditionalists, the chiefs (A1), joined forces with the accommodationists
(A2), who were members of various Moslem brotherhoods, in
order to prevent innovation by those willing to accept colonial

Role Type	Stratification Type		
	Caste (A)	Class (B)	Status (C)
Traditionalist (1)	A 1	B 1	C 1
Accommodationist (2)	A 2	B 2	C 2
Innovative (3)	A 3	B 3	C 3

FIG. 9. — *The relationship between role and stratification.*

reform (A3). Conflicts may also occur between caste, class, and
status groups (that is, between stratification categories), as in
India.

As an approach to the analysis of modernization, stratification
has its difficulties, however, because it is, in effect, a reflection of
the evaluation by members of a system of roles in terms of power
and prestige. We will examine the various aspects of stratification
in two major stages. In this chapter we will be concerned with the
many possible forms of conflict between roles and types of stratification, paying particular attention to sharpening the relationship between status and class. The latter relationship will be
considered in the context of induced change from above by an
elite. In the next chapter we will concern ourselves with conflicts
that arise within an elite, that is, within the status system, which
will be treated as a competition of different types of innovative
roles within the status system (category C3 in Figure 9).

Changes in the ranking system and in the definitions of power
and prestige roles in each of the cells of the diagram in Figure
9 express conflicting values: open or closed recruitment,

achievement-based or ascription-based eligibility, and the changing functional definitions of the roles themselves.

A generous and well-defined sense of grievance is one result of these conflicts. Never a purely technical-economic problem, the relationship between roles and stratification becomes sharpened by the growth of public expectations, which are a political matter.[9]

The more complex and intense such conflicts, the more likely there is to be a polarization of solutions in terms of the two opposite political systems discussed in chapter i, the mobilization system and the reconciliation system. The mobilization system tries to resolve many of these difficulties by eliminating them. The reconciliation system allows them to compete. In the first instance, a highly generalized normative ideology is likely to result, whereas in the second, explicit ideological statements are highly unlikely. Among Marxists, the relationship between grievance and class consciousness is the critical link in their theory of social change. Such consciousness is not automatic, especially for the "lower classes," but requires a vanguard instrument, the militant Communist party. As Bernard Barber suggests,

> An essential component of the Marxian analysis of class consciousness is the problem of recognition of class interests. Marx felt that the stratification system was essentially a mechanism for unjustly distributing economic goods and other social rewards among the different social classes. If this unjust mechanism was to be changed — and Marx wanted it not only changed but eradicated — then people must become aware of their class interests, that is, of their

[9] At first, expectations may be low, and therefore relative satisfaction is readily achieved by simple benefits that surprise and delight people. When they come to take these for granted, they may easily lose the capacity for surprise and gratification. Once the people of a poor country become fully aware of the conditions of life in a rich one, their own modest increments seem paltry by comparison. People do not compare their present greatly improved situation with a previous period of poverty but rather try to blot out that previous period from their memories. Instead, they compare their conditions of life with those in other countries and find themselves perpetually dissatisfied.

differential rights in and access to these goods and rewards. Class consciousness with regard to interests, Marx hoped, would make people not only see the inherent injustice of a stratification system, but want to eliminate it, by force if necessary. But Marx knew that even broad social classes were not always conscious of their interests. A class that existed objectively but was not aware either of its own existence or of its interests, Marx called a class *an sich*. When such a class did become aware of its existence and interests, it became what Marx called a class *für sich*. Marx felt that the upper or "ruling classes," as he called them, were conscious of their own interests and deliberately organized themselves to pursue these interests by means of political and other social agencies, in which, he assumed, they had the predominant influence. The lower or "exploited classes," as Marx called them, were not on the whole conscious of their interests. This lack of class consciousness was one source of their exploitation. Hence, Marx decided it was to be a primary task of the socialist vanguard of the lower classes to teach their fellow-sufferers about their class interests not only directly but by stirring up the class conflict that would make differences of class interest apparent to everyone.[10]

Marxian views on stratification turn our attention to the relationship of property or ownership to stratification. However, they fail to deal with political solutions to role-stratification conflicts. In our terms, they are as follows: (1) mobilization systems that try to change the power and prestige hierarchy entirely — that go beyond the mere circulation of elites to alter the hierarchy in some substantial manner — and are propelled toward socialism as an ideology; (2) reconciliation systems that maintain the basic hierarchy intact, enlarge the area of mobility within it, and add new roles without destroying old ones; (3) modernizing autocracies that try to accommodate new roles to tradition and to widen the sphere of competence and expertise of old ones and are therefore politically more conservative. How government itself works as a mechanism of stratification can be observed by examining political recruit-

[10] Barber, *Social Stratification*, p. 219.

ment. The various structures of government, which will be discussed in detail in chapter vi, supply the categories to be used in an evaluation of social stratification. Here we need suggest only briefly how governments deal with stratification problems.

The process of decision-making is a description of the crucial and concrete power relationships of the unit. Accountability represents the degree to which power is a symmetrical process, that is, the degree of responsibility with which power is shared among those who provide an informational check on the decision-makers. An evaluation of allocation should show how government tries (a) to alter stratification, (b) to increase mobility, and (c) to regulate non-political sources of power. The boundaries of enforcement and punishment are determined by the degree to which stratification — in the sense of the defined limits of roles in the hierarchy — is flexible.[11] Recruitment into government is a particularly important means of mobility. In modernizing countries the political route to power and prestige usually brings with it other forms of wealth. Indeed, in mobilization systems, the "socialism" of many of the leaders represents little more than an effort to control economic resources.[12] For them, accountability remains very limited. Decision-making is restricted to a small circle of men capable of organizing specific goals and willing to allocate roles, discipline the performance of role occupants, and recruit for these roles in terms of goal achievement.

[11] When a high degree of repressive law is associated with hierarchy, the system will be relatively inflexible and less adaptable by non-political means. (In such a system changes in stratification can occur only through direct government action.)

[12] Without too much adaptation, the argument of M. Djilas would apply to most mobilization systems. "The movement of the new class toward power comes as a result of the efforts of the proletariat and the poor . . . only to the extent necessary for developing production and for maintaining in subjugation the most aggressive and rebellious social forces" (Djilas, The New Class [New York: Frederick A. Praeger, 1957], p. 42). A similar comment was made more forcefully by Leon Trotsky in 1937; see The Revolution Betrayed (New York: Doubleday Doran and Co., 1937), pp. 86–143. The best treatment of these matters is in Ralf Dahrendorf, Class and Class Conflict in an Industrial Society (London: Routledge & Kegan Paul, Ltd., 1959), pp. 117–54.

What this brief discussion is designed to indicate is the reciprocal relationship between government and stratification. Problems of political modernization appear sharply as ideological conflicts over roles. Roles need to be fitted and adjusted in terms of rank. Government policy must make the adjustments. How well it does so will depend on the type of political system. The hope that all modernizing societies share is that restratification will achieve greater equity for all. In practice, however, most political leaders would settle for what S. M. Lipset called "collective mobility." As he defines it, this is the increase in social bargaining power of a given stratum of "skilled workers, or those possessing a certain level of education . . . as a result of the commitment by a society to industrialize rapidly." [13] This is particularly the case for those occupying professional and technical roles that symbolize modernity.

POLITICAL TYPES AND ROLE LINKAGE

The complexity of role conflicts indicated in Figure 9 creates the central problems of authority during modernization because the various roles that make up the stratification system represent functional positions in the society, and, at the same time, are the means by which individuals identify themselves, create their "self-images," and define their work and their satisfactions. [14]

Industrial societies have a wide set of interlinkages (as Durkheim suggested). Modernizing societies are just beginning to build these interlinkages and quite often are doing so through the mechanisms of a political party. Under such circumstances the

[13] Lipset, "Research Problems in the Comparative Analysis of Mobility and Development," *International Social Science Journal*, XVI (1964), 36–37.
[14] The period of role search is always a period of ambiguity even in highly stable societies, and this is one reason why the youth culture is always a disturbing one. If role search becomes fundamentally disorderly and there is no way to link roles effectively to one another, because of the absence of organizational units such as the factory system or other sets of institutions that are articulated throughout the community, then the power and prestige system must find some other basis of support.

mutually reinforcing aspects of roles do not generate a stable pattern of authority but the reverse.[15]

The most obvious way for a government to deal with political problems that originate in the malintegration of modernization roles is to restratify their society. This, however, as my earlier discussion of the various aspects of stratification should have implied, is not so easily accomplished. Only the most militant of modernizing societies make the attempt. Where such an effort is made, power and prestige become highly centralized, with the result that local decision-making becomes inconsequential. The work load increases at the top. Nothing operates smoothly. All aspects of social life are politicized.

As centralization occurs, conflicts between groups decline in number and increase in intensity. In particular, new accountability structures produce clashes of interest between party politicians and technical experts. The division of labor in mobilization systems — in which political entrepreneurs cater to the organization of the society and technical entrepreneurs cater to their specialties — very quickly breaks down in practice. Mobilization systems are normally compromises between these two competing accountability groups. Professional politicians confront professional technicians.

STRATIFICATION POLICY IN A MOBILIZATION SYSTEM

In mobilization systems, as compared with other forms of political system, this conflict is intensified because the likelihood is great that property will be either nationalized or control over it

[15] One can observe this in very diverse situations. In India, for example, the consequences of caste-fixed urban relationships, residential patterns, and factory or work place (even today) interfere with functional roles. This causes unrest, managerial uncertainty, and lowered efficiency. The situation becomes a direct political problem, as well, when caste groups like the Scheduled Castes Federation take on qualities of a trade union, a caste, and a political party challenging the Congress Party. See the interesting discussion by Arthur Niehoff, in "Caste and Industrial Organization in North India," *Administrative Science Quarterly*, March, 1959.

directly organized by the state. Allocation of resources will be dictated by the two accountability groups on the basis of feasibility and modernization goals.

Political recruitment is based on functional or political professionalization. This consideration determines germane criteria for entry into the hierarchy.

In practice, few mobilization systems restratify to any great extent.[16] Roles are peculiarly persistent and do not change easily. To the extent that a system does restratify, it can be regarded as radical, that is, the transformation of power and prestige in a system is a radical policy. However, the more radical the mobilization system — that is, the more successful in restratification — the more conservative it will become. This is one reason why many mobilization systems tend to become neomercantilist systems.

STRATIFICATION POLICY IN OTHER HIERARCHICAL SYSTEMS

It will be remembered that the modernizing autocracy modernizes by traditionalizing innovation. This means that the prevailing hierarchy will not be altered very much. The neomercantilist society is likely to deal with modernization in the same way, although only after a period of restratification has already occurred. Modernization roles are either grafted on to prevailing ones or are stabilized by becoming institutionalized. Decision-making in these systems remains concentrated in form, and in this respect it is close to the mobilization system (although there is likely to be a much wider diversity of accountability groups).

Perhaps the most important feature of both the modernizing autocracy and the neomercantilist system is their ability to integrate the two competing and antagonistic groups: the political elite and the technical, managerial, and intellectual modernizing group. In the mobilization system, such a conflict often exists

---

[16] If we discount the radical rhetoric of most mobilization systems and look at their practices, we find that few of them change stratification as much as they claim. The main exceptions to this include China, Cuba, and Algeria.

in the form of antagonism between the political party and the civil service; in the modernizing autocracy, either a division of labor is worked out or the older elite roles are simply expanded and broadened to include new expertise. In addition, these two systems can incorporate traditional roles or roles recently traditionalized with innovative ones.

That these are not trivial matters becomes clear if one contrasts Japan and Latin America. In the former, the modernizing autocracy successfully integrated new roles and traditional ones. In the latter, especially in reconciliation systems such as Peru and Mexico, the landowning aristocracy, the church, and the military became dominant after 1825, with mainly disastrous results.[17]

The sensitivity of the modernizing autocracy to change depends mainly on widening access to the political hierarchy by the acceptance of new standards for recruitment that accord with other values in the system and by holding more or less constant the other requisite and contingent structures of the system. The modernizing autocracy normally does this by extending instrumental values on the basis of functional expertise and by disallowing new roles that might affect the society's critical consummatory values. In other words, the modernizing autocracy rejects those aspects of modernization that it cannot easily accept and, as a system, maintains a considerable degree of selectivity.

[17] See the interesting discussion in John J. Johnson, *Political Change in Latin America* (Stanford, Calif.: Stanford University Press, 1958). Johnson writes: "The middle sectors were unable to take advantage of the differences that arose among the ruling elements. The elites were agreed on the major economic issues. The Church was encouraged to continue as the interpreter of the social value system. Consequently the issues that drove the elites into different camps were essentially political ones: centralism *vs.* federalism; executive *vs.* legislative and judicial power; civilian control *vs.* militarism; the relationship of Church and State. The disputes over those issues often led to political disorderliness and to fratricidal wars that left material devastation and moral degradation in their wake. The disputes were, however, of such a nature that the contending groups could fight for political advantage without involving the great mass of the population except as it served their purposes. Hence the struggles never created a power vacuum into which the lower or middle sectors of society could rush. Also, once the issues were defined, all other differences receded into insignificance, with the result that little room was left for new parties to prosper" (p. 20).

New political roles, in particular, are disallowed by the modernizing autocracy, which restricts access to power and prestige by virtue of role change. Coercion is applied against those who seek to create such roles.

The most interesting possibility for stratification policy in the modernizing autocracy is the reliance on bureaucratic and military organizations to maintain the stratification system. If new political roles cannot be prevented, the normal policy of the modernizing autocracy is to (a) increase political recruitment through the military and the bureaucracy, (b) allocate resources and the disposal of resources to the military, and (c) employ the military organization as a coercive instrument. All of these policies can be effective in a modernizing autocracy partly because the military is the one organization that is usually traditionalist in its political values but instrumentalist in all others, that is, it takes the goals of the state as given. However, if the military should become the primary accountability group in the system as well as part of the government, and thereby become engaged in authoritative decision-making, then the system has changed to the type referred to here as the military oligarchy.[18]

All three of these hierarchical instrumental systems tend to rely on private ownership of property, although they may clearly control the allocation of resources directly, applying priorities that might be different in mobilization systems. But there is an amaz-

[18] Despite the fact that military oligarchies appear to have modernizing values, and indeed, the nature of a military organization, with its command, planning, and technological biases, appears almost the prototype of modernity, they rarely serve as successful modernizers. The army may take peasants and make them into modern men, but it cannot rule effectively. Nor is it able to generalize its values into society. Perhaps the one exception to this has been the army in Israel. A whole generation has grown up for whom military training, a perpetual state of emergency, and a quasi-military situation for all able-bodied men are inextricably linked with modernity. Moreover, since it is a citizen army, the effect on stratification is egalitarian. Everyone must serve, whether European or Oriental, religious or non-religious. It would be interesting to study the degree to which militarism now affects decision-making and accountability in Israel, despite the obvious success of its democratic form of reconciliation system.

ing degree of similarity in the actual programs for development in both systems. With the alternatives for development so limited, modernization programs depend more on how far along the system already is than on differences in type.[19]

STRATIFICATION POLICY IN A RECONCILIATION SYSTEM

Reconciliation systems attempt to expand the modern sector of the stratification system by allocating resources on the basis of competitive bargaining between diverse groups. The result is that overlapping caste, class, and status conflicts persist, with traditionalist, accommodationist, and innovative forces forming the basis of diversity. Such self-perpetuating conflicts lead to stagnation and political instability. Only if the modern sector in a reconciliation system can drastically expand educational and economic opportunities can it prevent power from being fractionalized among many competing accountability groups. Rarely can the reconciliation system prevent stagnation by diverting resources to the modernized sectors in order to provide sufficient and diverse opportunities through multiple patterns of recruitment to public and private roles. Not only is this a most uncommon situation in the reconciliation system, but in addition, recruitment to the modernized sectors is likely to be less than open. Decision-makers, in the reconciliation system, trying to prevent the fractionalization of power, recruit their friends and followers to the modernizing roles. Coercion is applied to those opponents who might upset the system, not by central government policy but indirectly through family, local government, or local party organs. The private economic sector, clubs, trade unions, and the like, may be instruments of localized coercion.

The system of stratification in the reconciliation system is, as in the modernizing autocracy and the military oligarchy, a system of

[19] But it would be most misleading to examine the Ghana Seven-Year Plan and the Nigerian Five-Year Plan, for example, and conclude that they have much the same objectives and impact.

control. However, such controls are likely to be unofficial and private rather than official and public. Since stratification depends on the absorption of values establishing superordinate and subordinate relations, modernization policy, and changes in stratification, is effected by indirect means. Allocation of resources, then, is more important than coercion. Political recruitment is more important than either; stagnation and corruption can therefore easily be the result.

If we contrast the stratification policies of the types under discussion, the most striking differences are between the mobilization system and the others. The mobilization system, by restratifying, has problems of legitimacy. Radical in the way it handles its modernization objectives, it must reflect in its ideology legitimizing values as well as modernity. The military oligarchies are profoundly conservative, even though their actual achievements in modernization may be as great or greater than those of mobilization systems. For them, however, the key problem is adaptation, not legitimacy. Reconciliation systems tend to be moderate in their policies, making stratification adjustments only in response to competitive pressures from various groups in the system.

To carry out the kind of analysis suggested, we must ask the following questions: (1) What is the effect of government policy on the power and prestige hierarchy in terms of roles?[20] (2) How are the germane criteria for power and prestige roles altered by government actions? (3) How responsive is the government to demands for social mobility? (4) How coherent is the hierarchy in terms of its ideology?

[20] The most systematic effort to develop stratification profiles is at present underway at the DiTella Institute in Buenos Aires. Work in progress under the direction of Torcuato S. DiTella includes the use of stratification variables programed on computors to test hypotheses. See DiTella, "Political Effects of Intra-country Country Discontinuities" (paper presented to the International Social Science Council, Buenos Aires, September, 1964).

MODERNIZATION THROUGH AN ELITE

In each of the political systems that have been mentioned, modernization creates a sharp discrepancy between those who represent extreme modernity, the status-elites, and those who represent the public in caste or class sectors of the stratification system. Elite-mass conflicts in each political system provide some of the dynamic points of social intersection that produce political action.

When traditionalism begins to disintegrate we think of older groups giving way to new, salaried, urbanized, and educated groups that are gaining new status in the hierarchy. The grievances over losses of status-identity and the sense of hopelessness that may be forced on those at the bottom of the scale may give rise to explosive situations. However, it is impossible to link anxiety and anger directly to changes of status and role because too many possibilities arise in the modernization process. Urbanization may cause traditional institutions to decay. But it may also bring them into the cities, not only into the quarters where kinsmen live together (retaining many older practices and customs), but even into factories and offices. In Middle Eastern countries it is not uncommon to recruit labor by notifying the head man in a shop that more employees are needed; the head man in turn recruits his kinsmen. The town does not inevitably cause a decline of traditional status but may only modify it. It may change the nature of the hierarchy, the command over resources that is permitted individuals, and the identification of those who control the hierarchy itself.[21]

Examining modernization through the elite allows us to distinguish between modernization "from above" and modernization "from below." Modernization from above is the most common form today because of the pressure for planned change that exists in almost all modernizing societies. Modernization from above involves the reorganization of the country and the rearrangement

---

[21] See Barber, *Social Stratification*, chap. xvii.

of its power and prestige hierarchy on the basis of the functional significance of roles and organizations in the modernization process. Ordinarily, this involves the specific application of plans, rules, and orders that become identified as the graded steps and sequences (usually set at five- or seven-year intervals) of a development plan. Modernization from above requires hierarchical authority organized by a modernizing elite. Sometimes this elite is expatriate, as in the colonial period. At other times it is domestic. The pattern of modernization through an expatriate elite is an extremely complex one. The following quotation, concerning India, will indicate some of the advantages as well as the disadvantages of this form of modernization.

For many years now, the Political Service had been recruited two-thirds from the Indian Army and one-third from the Indian Civil Service. They were picked men, picked from picked men. The Service presented the possibility of a career which, as Lord Curzon had said, might be as fascinating as any the history of the world could offer. . . . The Resident did not administer; he was in the State to guide, to advise, to suggest. The less directly he interfered the better. He needed rare qualities; he must not let leisure degenerate into idleness nor forbearance into indifference. There were many great men among the Residents, men who wisely and gently guided the rulers of the States to which they were accredited. But theirs was not a training to prepare men for revolution.[22]

The peak of the stratification pyramid was occupied by men who represented a secular vision and instrumental values. They created roles that caused the Indians to live like them and to repudiate them at the same time. Even Nehru showed this ambivalence in his partial rejection and partial acceptance of the guardian role. He remained, in many ways, a secular intellectual even while seeking to affirm tradition.

The Indian case was not unique. Commenting on Egypt during

[22] Philip Woodruff, *The Men Who Ruled India: The Guardians* (London: Jonathan Cape, 1953–54), Vol. II, p. 270.

the period of Dual Control, Cromer remarked, "Lastly, the employment of a number of honourable and capable British officials has probably done more than anything else to check corruption. Their mere example has counted for much. The Egyptians pay an unconscious compliment to English integrity by very rarely offering bribes to British officials." [23]

Wherever modernization occurs from above, the result is more or less the same: status (but not necessarily power) is given to elites who personify the values of modernity, that is, functional skills and knowledge. Hierarchical authority is necessary because pyramidal systems cannot contain or control the consequences of induced change. This is particularly true if the latter form of modernization is used in a reconciliation system. A reconciliation elite, with its emphasis on instrumental values, is threatened by a system in which equality has become a consummatory end. This has been understood for a long time. Indeed, it was Aristotle who suggested that no person should be advanced by the state out of all proportion to others.[24] Mill pointed out other possible difficulties when he suggested that

> in a really equal democracy, every or any section would be represented, not disproportionately, but proportionately. A majority of the electors would always have a majority of the representatives; but a minority of the electors would always have a minority of the representatives. Man for man they would be as fully represented as the majority. Unless they are, there is not equal government, but a government of inequality and privilege: one part of the people rule over the rest: there is a part whose fair and equal share of influ-

[23] Earl of Cromer, *Modern Egypt* (London: Macmillan & Co., Ltd., 1908), Vol. II, p. 424. There are many other modern examples of the effect of *Stand* on values for modernization. See, for example, Robert Delavignette, *Freedom and Authority in French West Africa* (London: Oxford University Press, 1950), for a good statement of the French position. The idea originated with Max Weber and formed the basis of his inquiries into the role of the mandarin in the Chinese bureaucratic system, the Brahman in India, and the priests in Israel.

[24] Ernest Barker (ed.), *The Politics of Aristotle* (Oxford: Clarendon Press, 1948), Book V, "Causes of Revolution and Constitutional Change," pp 203–4.

ence in the representation is withheld from them; contrary to all just government, but, above all, contrary to the principle of democracy, which professes equality as its very root and foundation.[25]

In reconciliation systems, however, *inequality* and development go together.[26] The result may be to prepare the way for a potentially revolutionary force; witness, for example, the Indian state of Andhra Pradesh. The state was formed in 1956 out of nine Telengana districts of the old Hyderabad state, together with eleven Andhra districts (four Rayalseema and seven Circars). In the legislative assembly of the state there are 301 seats, of which 300 are elected on universal adult franchise. The area is an interesting mixture of wealth and poverty, with an overall literacy rate of the electors of 6.2 per cent.[27] In the general election of 1962 the Communists gained, as did the independents and some local parties, at the expense of the Congress party.

Communication in the district is poor. Only 2 per cent of the population cultivate land they own, entirely or in part, "and it is from this two percent that nearly all the district's politicians come." [28] The Congress party relied on its local authorities, including landlords, caste elders, and village officers, to bring in the vote. The Communist party organizers played on the theme

[25] J. S. Mill, *On Liberty, and Considerations on Representative Government,* ed. R. B. McCallum (Oxford: Basil Blackwell, 1948), p. 190.

[26] Socialists attempt to minimize hierarchy in housing, education, and other key aspects that affect the aspirations, modes of conduct, and manners of the citizens but create a rigid hierarchy in the political sphere, that is, the "command system." By emphasizing the commonality of people, differences between them (residence, education, religion, and so on) are eliminated by an enforced solidarity in which all people are equal because they are identified as equal. This also removes the necessity of reflecting the different interests of groups in government, since their overriding interests are held to be identical, centered on particular goals in society. Hence, the need for representation disappears, at least in theory. In such a system there is democracy by definition rather than substance.

[27] The all-India level of literacy is 16.5 per cent. The material on Andhra Pradesh is taken from Hugh Gray, "The 1962 Indian General Election in a Community Stronghold of Andhra Pradesh," *Journal of Commonwealth Political Studies,* I (May, 1963), 296–311.

[28] *Ibid.,* p. 297.

of common struggle, working on emotional attachments that derived from a local peasant uprising led by the Communists some years before. In other words, an earlier pattern of strikes and struggles led by Communists was used to make more concrete the theme of common suffering and identity with the people of the area. In addition, the Communists did much more direct campaigning and began much earlier than the Congress politicians. Gray quotes the Congress canvassers as saying that "when they went to villages, some people said 'We haven't seen you since the last election, why should we vote for you? . . . We see the Communists regularly, not only when they want something.'" Gray mentions some other very interesting differences in approach:

> Congress speakers stressed the material benefits derived and expected from a Congress government, that the Congress party was the party of the victors of the Independence struggle, Nehru and Gandhi, and they gave particular promises — electricity, roads, school buildings, etc. — to particular villages. The Communists talked about the rule and oppression of the landlords, emphasized that their party stood for economic and social equality, and denounced the alleged corruption and greed of all Congress politicians.[29]

The Communists — as a modernizing political elite — attacked the system. Their electoral success indicated the degree of alienation from the system by large parts of the community. They were even able to run popular candidates who were themselves landlords but who were also well-known Communists. Their theme of puritanism derived from the attack against Congress party corruption. Working on the local level, they established what Gray calls a "new unitary equilibrium," creating "party villages" with "a concentration of authority in the party instead of a leading local family. . . . These, together with a continuing and relatively efficient party organization, were able to keep alive the myth of solidarity and violence."[30]

The Indian case is interesting because it illustrates a character-

[29] *Ibid.*, p. 307.   [30] *Ibid.*, p. 310.

istic of the reconciliation system that most disturbs Western observers, namely, its vulnerability in modernizing countries to communism. Movement in the other direction, in which a professionalized elite or even a military elite comes to power, may produce slightly better results. A military oligarchy is frequently, however, an unstable form of polity. This is so even when instrumental values legitimize an officer caste that exercises power responsibly. In this situation, unless the officer caste separates from the army and becomes part of a professional or political status elite, the result is likely to be political instability. Such a separation has occurred in Egypt. Much earlier the same situation occurred in Turkey. After the Turkish revolution, the army leadership ruled the state. Eventually, the military elite became separated from the army and frankly political. Of course, there are many instances where military bureaucracies are unable to cope with politics and resort to corruption, abuses of power, and reliance on coercion. One has only to cite the cases of Vietnam and South Korea.

An elite is also created by the political group or political party that serves as a primary modernization instrument. The claim of the political party is that it can do exactly what the military or the civil service groups cannot, that is, provide equality merely through membership. Modernization through roles in a political party may occur from "below" and "above" simultaneously. This is particularly the case where modernization represents a populist and egalitarian revolution.

It is one of the advantages of the mobilization system that it may allow elite control of the consequences of induced change by segregating inequality within a strategic political instrumentality, such as a "vanguard" within a populist party. All other forms of inequality become suspect, at least in theory. In ideologies of reform, this vanguard is linked with the mass. Party leaders see themselves as social reformers. They have sought to legitimize their roles by making modernity into an ideology. One of the reformers in the period just before the Chinese Revolution of 1911

(Liang Ch'i-Ch'ao), for example, followed the pattern of German social reform.

> Liang defined himself as a social reformer, and clearly, most of his ideas on this subject were derived from the German "social policy" school of economists and politicians. He often proclaimed the advantages of reformist policies in Germany and Japan, identifying himself with these movements. To him, social reformism was practical socialism, or, as one of his followers put it, "broad socialism." It involved an intensive program of social legislation and a mixed economy. . . .[31]

Modernizing societies may also have to deal with dying elites, which retain great reservoirs of power that may be stirred if they are sufficiently aggravated. The great fear among African political leaders is that tribalism, or some form of uncontrolled traditionalism, will be an effective counterforce to their objectives and desires. Ethnic or other traditional parochialism can hardly halt modernization efforts. Nevertheless, in the conflicts between old elites and new, and between new elites and counterelites, so many intermediate roles may arise, part modern, part traditional, that modernization may be impeded.[32]

[31] R. A. Scalapino and Harold Schiffin, "Early Socialist Currents in the Chinese Revolutionary Movement," *Journal of Asian Studies*, XVII (May, 1959), 341.

[32] See the extremely interesting discussion of the "new middle class" in the Middle East and North Africa in M. Halpern, *The Politics of Social Change in the Middle East and North Africa* (Princeton, N. J.: Princeton University Press, 1963). Halpern points out that "the thrust toward revolutionary action on the part of the new middle class is overwhelming. It is itself the product of an unfinished and uncontrolled revolutionary transformation of society. It intends therefore to organize social change rather than become its victim. Even those who do not possess this broader vision, but who nevertheless would like to live in the same style as the average man in the more conservative industrialized nations, will have to upset the status quo much further before they can hope to enjoy the benefits of a stable new status quo. Unlike the great majority of the Western salaried middle class, this new class cannot afford to perpetuate the traditional norms and laws of society even though it is already being threatened by the confusion of standards and the growth of extremism in its own ranks" (p. 75).

EDUCATION AND THE POLITICAL SOCIALIZATION OF THE ELITE

The command over resources embodied in a hierarchy of power and prestige roles is an expression of the legitimacy of differentials in rank. Or, to put the matter somewhat differently, roles, hierarchically ranked, are statements of differential rewards, and insofar as these differences are regarded as legitimate, they represent values in the community and, as well, reinforce authority. In this respect, the study of stratification is also a study of motives and interests, out of which subordinacy and superordinacy may be established.[33]

In a modernizing society education has such critical importance for both the forms of stratification and their consequences that roles will differ in form and political functions, depending upon how educational policy is formulated. This is so for two reasons. The first is that political socialization of the elite occurs mainly

[33] Almost all contemporary studies since Marx begin with some analysis of stratification. Indeed, if we are asked to draw a quick picture of a society, we almost invariably begin by describing class relations. Whether we begin at the "top," that is, with those in the most highly regarded power and prestige positions, or at the "bottom," we try to sketch in the key ranks and show their significance. If we also speak in terms of classes, this implies that upward and downward mobility will be a critical concept for evaluating political life, as will participation, interest, and the norms of access to the hierarchy.

This is a very important and clearly valid approach. However, it is also peculiarly Western. It is the sort of emphasis that arises out of our own understanding of society, intertwined as it is with the history of Western politics. There is, of course, another dimension that ideology helps us to understand (if we do not treat it as merely a reflection of class interest). This other approach is not an alternative to the study of stratification. It merely points to a different level of social reality. Anyone who has worked extensively with African societies will understand the approach being suggested, namely, the perception of roles in terms other than hierarchy. What this means is that people who might be regarded as highly ranked, and who receive deference according to that rank, may also be seen as reinforcing elements of the social structure in terms of kinship, religious, or other emotional bonds that obscure the matter of rank itself. Under such circumstances, for example, hierarchy may not serve as a system of motivation, and aspirations may occur along quite other lines.

in the educational system. This means that the educational system is used to transmit civic values. The second is that the qualifications for modernized roles include understanding of the norms associated with rational choice and knowledge. These are necessary (but not sufficient) conditions of eligibility in the modernized sector.[34]

These functions of education are not novel, of course; consider the following quotation on the thirtieth anniversary in 1913 of the founding of Waseda University:

> The true aims of education of Waseda University are the realization of the independence of study, the practical application of study and the cultivation of model citizens. As Waseda University considers independence of study its true aim, it has emphasized freedom of investigation and originality of research with the hope that it might contribute to the world's scholarship. As a practical application of study is also one of Waseda University's aims, it has taught, along with the study of theory for its own sake, ways to apply theory and practice. It hopes thereby to contribute to progress. As the making of model citizens is also an aim of Waseda University, it expects to cultivate good, loyal subjects of our constitutional empire who will be self-respecting, promote the welfare of their own families, prove useful to state and society, and who will participate widely in world affairs.

> This requires an explanation. The civilization of the world never remains stationary. It progresses from day to day. All the ideas and sentiments and all the social conditions of the world are undergoing change from day to day and month to month. To build a state and to form a society at such a time, or to establish university education for the betterment of the state and society there must be a great ideal. Japan today stands at the point of contact between the civilizations of the

[34] In industrial societies the key to stratification is occupational structure. Both education and occupational structure are crucial indicators of stratification in modernizing societies. I merely wish to stress the research advantages of treating education as strategic for modernization. See Coleman's discussion of the political aspects of education in James S. Coleman (ed.), *Education and Political Development* (Princeton, N.J.: Princeton University Press, 1965), pp. 3–32.

East and the West. Our great ideal lies in the harmony of
affecting these civilizations and in raising the civilization
of the Orient to the high level of that of the Occident so
that the two might co-exist in harmony.[35]

One could not ask for a more explicit formulation. It suggests why
education, related as it is to civic training, on the one hand, and
functional skills for particular occupations, on the other, is perhaps the most sensitive indicator of the structure of a society in
terms of the hierarchy of power and prestige.[36]

Examination of the educational system helps to explain the
formation of elites, the changes in outlook between generations,
the style of civility, and the values that a society embodies in
its important roles. The effects of popular or mass education differ
obviously from more elite forms. Some countries, such as Japan,
have combined both, with the result that there has developed a
very high degree of homogeneity of outlook and social values.[37]
Some societies use education as the basis of restructuring roles,
establishing a new hierarchy, and linking political incumbents
with the newest political generations to become eligible for important roles.[38]

Stratification based on various institutional factors (such as
economics, politics, religion, generation) can be represented by a
pyramid or by the forms of strategic roles and the number of role

[35] William Theodore deBary et al., Sources of Japanese Tradition (New
York: Columbia University Press, 1958), p. 697.
[36] See Mary Jean Bowman and C. Arnold Anderson, "Concerning the Role
of Education in Development," in Clifford Geertz (ed.), Old Societies and
New States (New York: Free Press of Glencoe, Inc., 1963), pp. 247–79. See
also Peter F. Drucker, "The Educational Revolution," in Amitai and Eva
Etzioni (eds.), Social Change (New York: Basic Books, 1964), pp. 236–42.
Drucker points out that forty years ago "schools still assumed that education
was for non-work." This is clearly not the case in modernizing societies,
where the value placed on education virtually pre-empts all others.
[37] See Robert Ulich, The Education of Nations (Cambridge, Mass.: Harvard University Press, 1961), chapter x.
[38] Of course, not all modernizing societies alter roles drastically. I shall
suggest below that one distinction between reconciliation systems and modernizing autocracies, on the one hand, and mobilization systems, on the
other, lies in just this area.

incumbents. Educational rankings have been suggested for this. If we wished to compare modernization in French-speaking West Africa from 1930 to 1958, for example, with that in Ghana or Nigeria, we would begin with the educational hierarchies. The span at the top, relatively small in the case of French-speaking West Africa, is larger in Ghana and Nigeria. At the secondary level, the difference between the two areas is even greater. The proportion of illiterates is much higher in French-speaking West Africa. The differences in modernization between these countries can be traced to other indicators, but education works well. Of course, this aspect is only a small part of a very complex picture; however, the educational hierarchy is closely parallel to the occupational one, with relatively fewer high power and prestige positions open to Africans in the French territory as compared with the former British colonies, although some of those that were open in French West Africa were at the highest levels. The small numbers in an occupational and educational elite are themselves significant. It is possible for them to know one another and to meet frequently. The universities and schools they have attended are much the same, and their careers and life histories closely parallel one another. The patterns of intimacy and hostility, political organization and tactics, all follow in some measure from the relative position of peers in the power and prestige hierarchy. Not a few of the political differences between the forms of nationalism in the former French and British areas can be explained in some part by the differences in education manifested in the stratification systems.

CAREERS AS PROTOTYPICAL MODERNIZATION ROLES

The analysis of modernization roles is different from the general analysis of stratification, although the former analysis will also direct our attention to wider problems of hierarchy, access, and mobility. We need to determine more precisely the critical set of modernization roles in any given system. We may expect that the critical cluster will show significant variations depending on the type of political system.

In my view, the critical set of modernization roles in any system is composed of roles that are recognized as "careers." By this I mean something broader than "profession" (in fact, it may encompass several professions) and narrower than "occupation." Indeed, we can distinguish roles in terms of these three operating criteria, namely, occupation, career, and profession, ranked in a descending order of generality. Whereas "occupation" is the most widely used category for identifying roles, particularly in modern society (with education as a predictive but subordinate criterion of occupation), "profession" is the most significant criterion of modernity because it implies standards, expertise, and a calling, all characteristics associated with the manipulation of choice through control of certain rules. Examples are the lawyer (rules of the system), the doctor (rules of health), and the civil servant (rules based on technical or management skills.) Important as the category "profession" is for determining modernization, however, it by no means exhausts the roles significant for the modernization process. Nor does "occupation," as a category, limit the range in any significant fashion. For these reasons, the concept of "career," which includes only some occupations but all professions, becomes useful.

A career can be distinguished from an occupation in terms of the following characteristics:

1. It has a "life span." There is a "rounded" quality to it, with a publicly perceived beginning and an end; it is different from being employed or unemployed in an occupation. One can speak of the career of a politician or a businessman without much difficulty. It is harder to speak of the career of a mechanic. Workers do not have careers. A policeman may be described as having a career, as may a midwife, but these roles are at the boundaries of the career concept.

2. There are well-defined canons of reward. The rewards of a

career are built into the career itself; money, power, and service.

3. Entry into a career requires preparation, which may be elaborate, as in the case of the professions, or which may involve suitable experience. The career of a businessman, for example, may require a record of experience in a variety of previous occupations.

4. Within a career, there is a line that establishes criteria of performance and success.

These four factors, span, reward, preparation, and performance are intrinsic to the concept of career and are intimately related to the publicly held ideas about the outlines of a particular career. In other words, public expectations about a career are based on those four criteria. An examination of careers, then, should bracket the critical modernization roles in a system, and a comparison of career roles should help us determine how choice works and, in addition, how differential rates of modernization proceed.

What is required for this type of comparative study, in addition to manpower data, educational information, and general census data, is a survey of careers from the following points of view. Given a sample population, what careers are recognized as such and how well are they understood in terms of the criteria listed above? Second, how accessible are the means of entry? Third, what is the wastage rate either from people dropping out of careers or from emigration (as with the "brain drain" from Britain to North America)? Fourth, what are the career ratios between systems? Fifth, what discrepancies exist between careers and supporting infrastructures? (In many modernizing countries, careers exist only precariously because the infrastructure is weak.)

We can use the concept of career as a useful operational tool for comparing modernization in different settings. In addition to comparing modern careers with traditional and therefore non-career roles, we may ask which are the prevailing sets of careers in countries that have been modernizing for a long period of time. Only then can we evaluate the information we have collected in terms of stratification, that is, in terms of access, mobility, education, training, and the like, as well as from the point of view of general modernization norms such as universalism, functional specificity, and competence. It is the analysis of career in the context of stratification, moreover, that makes it possible to understand various ideological expressions of discontent and the relationship between modernization and legitimacy.

5

INNOVATION, PROFESSIONALISM, AND THE FORMATION OF CAREERS

Only a few generations ago, countries that sought to modernize turned to the West, where the industrializing process had achieved remarkable prominence. At that time the measure of modernization was not economic but political and was demonstrated in the freedom of action engendered by parliamentary democracy. In Latin America, for example, the first political act of most of the various governments newly liberated from Spain was the establishment of constitutional forms modeled on the Western and, quite often, the United States pattern. Having made the necessary institutional arrangements of representative government, they assumed that the economic benefits of freedom would follow from the political form. The result has been an unfortunate history.

In Turkey, a more successful example, modernization came in the nineteenth century through various dissident groups in the bureaucracy of the Ottoman Empire (the Porte), the employment of foreign teachers (mainly French), the study of engineering and philosophy in Paris by young wealthy Turks, the identification of bureaucracy with innovation and modernity, the widespread use of foreign languages, and an appreciation of Western art (and more particularly, Western letters). A core of modern careers was established that helped identify modernization with liberalization. Nevertheless, the introduction of political ideas did not lead to parliamentary government.[1] The result was, instead, a military oligarchy and "Kemalism."

The Turkish case is cited because it raises an important question. How direct is the relationship between stratification and modernization? Implicit in the description of the origins of modernization in Turkey is the idea that it was an elite, trained in Western ways, that set off a "modernization revolution." When a new elite is grafted to the existing hierarchy of power and prestige, the effect is likely to be explosive. This view conforms to most of the elite theories of change and innovation. Edward Shils, for example, in restricting his inquiries to the role of intellectuals,

[1] "Many of the Turkish diplomats of the Tanzimat era supplemented the training given to the young employees attached to them by encouraging them, as well as the members of their own families, to increase their knowledge of Western languages. It is under such circumstances that Ali Pasa was able to master French and Munif Pasa learned German. When, toward the turn of the nineteenth century, the American educator, George Washburn, displayed surprise at Vefik Pasa's knowledge of Western thought, Vefik Pasa answered that while in France, he had had the occasion to become a neighbor of Ernest Renan and that they had often discussed questions relating to religion. The following remarks by a secretary of the British embassy in Istanbul in the thirties gives an inkling of the level at which conversation could be carried on with the more brilliant products of this drive to learn languages of up-and-coming young bureaucrats: 'We read together the best English classics — amongst them the works of Gibbon, Robertson and Hume — and studied political economy in those of Adam Smith and Ricardo. My friend Longworth had strong Protectionist views. I was an ardent free-trader. We spent many an hour in fierce argument in which the effendi [Ahmed Vefik] joined in great vigour and spirit. . . . He was a perfect store of information on all manner of subjects . . . and . . . a smattering of scientific knowledge, which he afterwards considerably extended.'" The passage and the quotation are taken from Serif Mardin, The Genesis of Young Ottoman Thought. (Princeton: Princeton University Press, 1962), pp. 209–10. Nor has this pattern disappeared. See the discussion by Herbert H. Hyman, Arif Payaslioglu, and Frederick W. Frey, "The Values of Turkish College Youth," Public Opinion Quarterly, XXII (Fall, 1958).

accepts the view that it is this particular group within the elite that represents the cultural and moral basis of a modernized community. The intellectuals are the critical mediators between traditionality and modernity. In the Weberian sense, they are the upholders of civic virtue.[2]

Doubtless the intellectuals are significant for modernization. Moreover, it is difficult not to regard the elite as a modernizing force, generating new norms of functional relevance to innovation and in general serving to create patterns of motivation that were not present in traditionally oriented societies. However, such a view is most useful in the earliest stages of change — in the period of transition from a clearly traditional system to a modern one. During such a period, it is possible for a few key individuals, occupying roles of great power or prominence (the implications of which cannot be ignored by a prevailing hierarchy of power and prestige), to have great impact. In a later stage of the process, it is not so clear what the effects of the intellectuals, or for that matter, any other particular group, may be. Leonard Binder, recognizing this difficulty in his assessment of the role of the elite in national integration, points out that modernization creates great gaps in social communication without necessarily developing a new pattern of integration; he argues that it is the "middle level" elites that hold the key to a new integration.[3]

This opens up a promising new line of inquiry, although not very much work has been done on "middle-level" elites. There is one interesting study of five privately owned factories in Poona, India, which employs stratification criteria relating to caste and class. A particularly useful finding of this study is that middle-level elites in the factory system tend to reflect the traditional caste hierarchy. For example, only a very low percentage of production and maintenance employees in the five factories were from the Brahman caste. Members of this caste were instead con-

[2] See Edward Shils, *Political Development in the New States* (The Hague: Mouton & Co., 1962), *passim*.

[3] Binder, "National Integration and Political Development," *American Political Science Review*, LVIII (September, 1964), 630–31.

centrated in supervisory tasks, a situation reinforced by the fact that educational attainment tended to follow caste lines. Thus traditional class and caste stratification was maintained rather than modified in the local factory system.[4]

One of the problems of relating stratification data directly to politics is that the general conflicts occurring within the hierarchy of power and prestige and the particular and strategic functions of the elite have never been successfully meshed on an analytical level. It is not difficult to point to patterns of estrangement between new elites and traditional ones. But it is difficult to go much further with this concept than, for example, S. N. Eisenstadt has by pointing to the "flexibility" of the traditional setting and the "system of values" as the critical set of interacting variables for a study of elites. "Sufficient flexibility makes it possible for such questions as Westernization versus traditionalism to constitute a continuous focus of discussion without giving rise to mutually exclusive solutions — either in terms of the traditional values or of modern secularism."[5] Interesting though this may be, it is much too general a statement for analytical use.

The study of social stratification in general and the separate studies of occupations, education, professionalization and the like, have not successfully employed the concept of the modernizing elite. Such a concept, useful as it is for analyzing certain stages of modernization, requires a more selective application. In our discussion we shall attempt to indicate a more narrowly significant

[4] Richard D. Lambert, *Workers, Factories and Social Change in India* (Princeton: Princeton University Press, 1963), *passim*. Lambert points out that in the newer factories the proportion of Brahmans employed was much higher than in older ones. "In general, the high proportion of Brahmans in the three newer factories seems to be a function of their demand for higher educational levels in their work force . . . rather than any specific caste selection, although what role, if any, is played by the fact that the three newer factories are owned and directly supervised by Brahman owners has not been determined" (p. 50).

[5] Eisenstadt, *Essays on Sociological Aspects of Political and Economic Development* (The Hague: Mouton & Co., 1961), p. 50; see also the general discussion, "Development of Elites, Patterns of Value and Political Transition," pp. 49–53.

cluster of modernization roles that are instrumental in implementing the process of modernization. These roles fall within the category of "career roles." Career roles are likely to become directly engaged with other roles that are significant in the politics of modernization. Through the relationships between these two types of roles, the broader consequences of the modernizing elite can be evaluated.

In order to employ this approach, it is first necessary to define a career role and specify its significance. Second, we will suggest the reason modernizing elites have important functional-political significance during modernization. Third, we will attempt to indicate patterns of role conflict within the modernizing elite in the different types of political systems that have already been delineated. We will also be able to discuss the rise of a critical new set of careers whose growing functional significance derives from their technical expertise and whose source of power is the general desire for modernity itself. These new careers have exceptionally dynamic consequences, not unconnected with the fact that in many cases, they are part of an international network of professionalized roles. This network becomes a status group, not a class, with the power to universalize itself. Corresponding careers in more highly developed countries would be the new technocrats in France, the military planners in research institutes in the United States, and the social engineers in the Soviet Union. Their counterparts in modernizing societies are the government statisticians, community developers, collective farm managers, party cadres of trade unions, office workers, and so on. The modernizing elite derives its importance from these careers, although the particular emphasis in modernizing societies is on the development of managers and civil servants, technicians and political organizers.[6]

[6] Modernization is always associated with particular groups that cluster around some institution — a university or school, a government ministry, a church, a corporation. It is common to find those occupying modernizing roles living alongside non-modernizers without substantial effect on either

THE ORGANIZATION OF CAREERS

Industrialization is a consequence of modernization — not an inevitable one, to be sure, but possible, given the right combination of opportunities and the proper conditions of choice. Today the degree to which countries have accomplished modernization and industrialization objectives may be measured by the spread of career roles. Some countries, most notably in Asia and Africa, are in the early stages of modernization. For them, careers are mostly associated with the professions and the civil service. Other countries — Spain, Argentina, Brazil, Chile, and Cuba, for example — are in the later stages of modernization. With their real prospects in major industrialization, they exhibit a widely differentiated network of careers. Still others, like Yugoslavia, Poland, and Romania, are in the primary stages of industrialization and make virtually all skilled occupations into careers.[7]

Unfortunately, the concept of career is not very explicitly defined in the literature. In one common usage it is synonymous with occupation and profession, with the addition of the notion of job stability. I have in mind a more limited use in which "career" and "career pattern" are combined "as a series of adjustments made to the institutions, formal organizations, and informal social relationships involved in the occupation, or sequence of occupations, which make up the work history of a person or group of

group. Insofar as the modernizers converse in the language and thought of the non-modernizers, they can maintain a dialogue.

The modernizers tend to admire science. Modernity may mean technological advance and gadgets — the accumulation of technological property and complicated machines. These modern instruments give special groups of moderns great influence. Demographers, statisticians, and, above all, economists begin to replace those in the so-called liberal professions. Their influence takes time to be felt, becoming manifest when the modernizing groups perform the functions discussed above.

[7] An inadequate career structure makes it difficult for modernization and industrialization to go on side by side. Industrialization cannot today be the agent of modernization. Long before industrialization is possible, a well-equipped body of modernizing men must occupy roles of both functional and political importance, as in both tsarist Russia and pre-Communist China.

persons." [8] In particular, what I call a career — in terms of modernization — should reflect institutionalized change rather than innovative change.

In effect I wish to segregate patterns of occupational roles, or some sequence of them, that have considerable job stability and distinguish them from the intermediate roles that incorporate traditional and modern elements. The assumption here is that many occupations in modernizing societies embody several diverse functions. A fishermen's society in Lagos might be ethnic and traditional in its organization, co-operative in the way it shares the proceeds of the catch, commercial in the way it markets its fish, and virtually a business organization in the way it disciplines its members. Religion and magic, commerce and investment, may all be involved. Libations may be offered to the gods of the sea, certain days may be forbidden for fishing, and at the same time the purchase of boats, nets, and modern fishing equipment may be possible precisely because of the pooling of resources that membership involves. But the fishermen's organization may remain outside the political community in any meaningful sense. It may facilitate modernization, but it may also resist planning, the resettlement of families, the abolition of slum areas, removals from burial grounds, and the like.

Hence, we can readily admit that although the immediate effect of such a wide range of functions can be viewed as modernizing, the latent consequences may actually retard modernization. This variable effect can produce important cultural and social discontinuities where they are least expected. Increasing the complexity of the system is, therefore, not necessarily accompanied by increasing cultural coherence.

One means of locating the areas of maximum coherence in a modernizing system is to isolate and compare profiles of identifiable career patterns. The professional role, on the one hand, that is, the teacher, the lawyer, the doctor, and so on, requires a long

---

[8] Julius Gould and William L. Kolb, *A Dictionary of the Social Sciences* (London: UNESCO, Tavistock Publications, 1964), p. 73.

training period during which intellectual skills and relevant expert knowledge are acquired. This knowledge, moreover, is embodied in a corpus with a particular objective, for example, curing the sick, administering and protecting equity, or teaching. There is a standard of ethics connected with the professional role, and the profession takes steps against violators of this standard. Moreover, a profession, by virtue of its special knowledge of the rules of its subject, regards itself as best able to interpret the rules for others. Hence, professions normally exhibit a high degree of autonomy. When this breaks down the consequences are sharply felt, as when doctors go on strike.

A career pattern, on the other hand, is broader and includes multiple occupational roles. A doctor may have a career as a politician, in which case his professional role does not occupy much of his attention. In the United States the multiple roles of lawyers are complementary. Careers may also be segregated from the intermediate modernization roles mentioned above. They are not roles with fluctuating significance for modernity. Career roles may be delineated in terms of two distinguishing characteristics: occupation, or cluster of occupations, and professionality. In the first place, careers are those occupations that control the rules of a system or a significant subsystem.[9] In the second, as control occupations, they must be based on stable and reasonably differentiated spheres of competence. Because of these characteristics it can be said that a career is more general than a profession and less general than an occupation.

It should be clear from the discussion of career at the end of

[9] Everett Hughes once characterized the special "license" provided to the occupants of career roles as the authorization to possess "guilty knowledge." They know the relevant secrets of their craft and also its countersecrets. "The lawyer, the policeman, the physician, the reporter, the scientist, the scholar, the diplomat, the private secretary, all of them must have license to get — and, in some degree, to keep secret — some order of guilty knowledge" (Hughes, "The Study of Occupations" in R. Merton, L. Broom, and L. S. Cottrell, Jr. (eds.), *Sociology Today* (New York: Harper Torchbooks, 1965), Vol. II, p. 448. Of course, career roles involve more than guilty knowledge — that is, discretionary authority over rules.

chapter iv that I am using the term to denote the result of a process, namely, the extension of the norms of professionalization to non-professional roles. Indeed, if it were not such a barbarism we might speak of the "careerization" of certain occupations, particularly those of a technical and managerial nature. The extension of the norms of professionalization does not, however, transform an occupation into a profession.

Perhaps the most important difference between a career and a profession is illustrated by the positions of the incumbents of both kinds of role. The concomitant of a role with norms of service and commitment, that is, a professional role, is socially awarded autonomy and freedom to act beyond the technical limits of the role itself. This freedom is implied in the idea of a "calling," as Weber pointed out, and is symbolized by the "tradition of the robe." The robe is worn on public and ceremonial occasions by the minister, the judge, and the professor. This underscores a wider responsibility than sheer competence would justify. Other examples come readily to mind. The family doctor was expected to give advice on all sorts of problems encountered by his patients beyond his medical knowledge. The lawyer becomes the counselor and the politician. Broad knowledge is assumed for those occupying the "liberal professions," as is personal authority and discretion. Included in this assumption of discretion is the feeling by people that privacy will be maintained and that confidences will not be violated. Nothing, from this point of view, is more shocking than the lawyer who violates confidence or the priest who violates the secrecy of the confession.

Careers, on the other hand, embody competence based on expertise. Any wider authority for the occupant of a career role depends on the functional significance of the career itself and the exceptional performance of the occupant. The measure of such success is a change in status.

Moreover, careers produce competitiveness between individuals. The consequences of such competitiveness are many. On a behavioral level, it may produce extreme anxiety and aggressiveness.

On a structural level, it tends to intensify the urge toward professionalization. There are thus two opposite forces at work. The liberal professions are increasingly transformed into careers. This process becomes more and more rapid as organization *qua* organization in highly industrialized systems undermines the autonomy of the professional role.

An example of this process is afforded by the academic profession. As universities grow in size, with larger faculties and greater numbers of students, they become more and more like other forms of large-scale corporate enterprise. A common complaint on the part of professors is that they are becoming "employees," so subject are they to regulations and restrictions. It is not the bureaucratic restrictions, however, that are important in and of themselves. Rather, it is the withdrawal of the academic from his generalized sense of commitment toward a definition of his sphere of competence in terms of his specialty that is most significant. Within these narrower limits he feels more secure in his competence and functional importance.

But there is a great loss implied in his withdrawal. The larger idea of a calling and the norms of service and commitment are reduced and with them the obligation to maintain the profession as a whole. There is less interest in protecting the norm of academic freedom. That norm is built into the autonomy of the professional role of the professor but not into the professorial career role. Indeed, the diminution of the professional role reduces the right of the professor to speak on issues beyond his competence. Academic freedom becomes instead an institutional norm of the university rather than a professional norm of the academic. Yet universities, like other large institutions, are not really in a good position to defend this norm, since they are inextricably linked to all the major social institutions of the society. The effect is a danger to the entire concept of responsible knowledge and the norms of free intellect. Moreover, professors contribute to this situation. They are engaged in the same status competition that exists in other large enterprises, and frequently more directly. Power becomes the basis of autonomy rather than the other way around — that is, in an earlier time, professional autonomy was the basis of power.

Careers include the technical and managerial roles of officials in commercial and industrial firms, members of the higher civil services, top political roles, and the like. But such roles are not inevitably careers. An occupation regarded as a career in one setting may not be so considered in another. Administrative roles in a spoils system would be difficult to consider as careers. The term "career civil service" implies a stable system, competitive entry on the basis of examinations, competence, promotion, and other norms of administration. When these elements are present, it becomes possible to think of careers in administration. Today, for example, a career in administration is possible in private as well as public organizations. The same could be said for the role of politician. In some countries it is clearly possible to speak of a political career, whereas in others it is possible to move from a career into politics and out again. Of course, in many cases both are possible.

As a general rule, careers in politics are more likely in mobilization systems than in any other since in the former the political mode is the key to all other modes of social organization. Certainly, the degree of organization in a system helps to lock careers into a set of patterns. It can be argued that the more bureaucratic a society, the more its careers are likely to extend into politics.

Career patterns are different in different systems for at least two reasons. The first is that the degree of modernization varies. The second is that, whatever the degree of modernization, variations in the organization of political life will be reflected in variations in career roles.

Further, the degree to which careers are perceived as such in a system determines the extent of public orientation towards modernity. Hence, unlike the intermediate roles in the modernization process, which disguise traditionalistic orientations, careers are a purely modern idea, embodying the values of modernity in the eyes of the public. The profile of careers in a country ought, therefore, to be a useful indication of its degree of modernization. We should also be able to identify a set of demands that registers the desire to professionalize an occupation into a career. The idea of career pattern or career role thus has important consequences for both structural and behavioral aspects of choice. On the structural side, modernization may be defined as a progressive translation of as many occupations as possible into careers. This translation, moreover, is one of the ways in which social mobility is achieved (apart from individual movement within a given hierarchy), that is, through the increased status of an occupation in terms of its characteristics as a career. For this reason, an increase in the number practicing a career helps to develop solidarity in the system.

In terms of behavior, careers provide aspirations. Since these aspirations are directed toward the modern sector or the most rapidly modernizing sectors of a system, the career is an important motivational impetus toward particular types of training. Individuals anticipate the direction in which to channel their energies in order to achieve a particular career. Their lives become less unpredictable and their choices therefore more meaningful. The pursuit of a career also helps to satisfy the identity function and becomes an important feature of modernizing societies, as we will indicate later on.

As suggested earlier, different types of political system produce different career patterns. In a reconciliation system, the pattern depends largely on the degree of modernization already achieved. The establishment of career lines thus varies with development. In a mobilization system, there is a tendency to transform all occupations into careers; identity is located in the work place and solidarity in the social unit, and intermediate affiliations comprise the society as a whole. Non-careers include mainly non-organized roles, that is, those outside the administration of a political or industrial unit. Hence, the independent small shop-keeper is not likely to have a career in a mobilization system, although he is considered to have an occupation. Perhaps some examples will make these points clearer. In the United States the transformation of the civil service system to a "career system" was an important change in the role of civil servant. What happened in the civil service is now underway in a variety of other areas of life. One indication of this is the use of euphemistic occupational titles, such as "inspector," "engineer," or "administrative assistant," when what is meant is various kinds of workers or clerks. Such titles are not merely appeals to vanity. They carry with them the token of professionality or at least the recognition of skill and perhaps authority. The fact that such titles are also recruitment inducements in a tight labor market merely underscores some of the pressures to make careers out of occupations.

In the U.S.S.R., for example, labor itself becomes a career. The concept of worker (or peasant, for that matter) provides a sense of organizational discipline in a collective — industrial, farm, or administrative. Under such a system, there are other less desirable behavioral consequences, such as "careerism," or an excessive preoccupation with the stratification ranks of a prestige role rather than its substance. When a mobilization system arises as part of a revolution or an independence movement and at the very early stages of modernization, as in many of the African countries, career possibilities are limited to a few professional-technical roles. Careers cannot be spread over a very wide range of occupations without considerable prior development. This does not mean, however, that mobilization systems that lack such development (that is, which are in the early stages of modernization) will not attempt to create a stable career system for major clusters of occupations. The process of creating careers is one way of strengthening solidarity and identity.

THE FUNCTIONAL SIGNIFICANCE OF AN ELITE

In chapter iv we attempted to conceptualize the uneven patterning of roles in their relation to stratification. Now we need to relate careers directly to the politically relevant modernizing elite. Three functions of this elite can be specified as follows: the goal specification function, the institutional coherence function, and the central control function.

1. *The goal specification function* involves the organization of resources around a defined set of objects. The choice of a set of objects may result from entrepreneurial activity. It may also result from professional expertise. In the first instance, it is possible to speak of political as well as economic entrepreneurs. In the second, administrative roles in a civil service might be considered careers. A question that arises immediately is, Which roles carry out the goal specification function with respect to modernization?

2. *The institutional coherence function* involves the linkage of diverse roles into a community. For example, the antimodern effects of those intermediate groupings, part accommodationist and part resistant in nature, that arise in the interstices of traditional and modern roles must be minimized. One way this may be done is through their effective linkage to more clearly modern roles, by which process they are pulled in a modern rather than a traditional direction. Such links may be effected by the establishment of career patterns, which, when they have become widely identifiable in the community, will represent a means of mobility. Another, and more common, way in which links may be established is to employ political brokers who will negotiate between the intermediate and modern groups.

3. *The central control function* involves the mechanism of coercion in a society. Such central control may be more or less concentrated in amateur or professional groups. The most significant group, in the latter instance, is the civil service.

These three functions are handled by elite roles. The more important the elite role, the more strategic its functional significance. It should be possible to identify empirically the roles that handle these three functions during a period of modernization.

Here we will indicate only some of the most commonly recognized roles, although there are certainly many others.

Perhaps the most important elite modernization roles are the technical and civil services of a country. These groups possess many of the characteristics of professionality including lengthy periods of education and training, a guildlike organization, a standard of performance, and a sphere of competence. Career aspects, lifespan of the role and a normally predictable course, are extremely well defined.[10] We can see that such careers represent a coherent pattern. The incumbents of such roles represent institutionalized change.

COMPETITION BETWEEN SIGNIFICANT ELITES

Not all elite roles are careers, and not all careers fall within the significant body of elites. When the functional significance of both career and non-career elite roles is large, one can expect a direct confrontation between these two groups and a struggle for power. It is this struggle for power which generates conflict in the elite sector and gives special importance to those elites that are politically significant.

In the preceding chapters of this book, I have indicated that one of the important differences between modernizing and industrializing countries is that in the former, roles are integrated by political means whereas in the latter, roles are integrated by the workings of the industrial system itself. In modernizing societies the problem of regulation becomes particularly great for those career roles that come to be regarded as prototypes of

[10] Another set of elite roles includes the professions, such as law, medicine, education, and the like. One would expect these roles to be as important as the technical and civil service roles. In certain situations, however, some of the professional roles, such as that of lawyer, may be reduced in functional significance as careers to the point that the careers themselves disappear. For example, if "people assessor," or some such title, replaces "judge" and individuals plead their own cases or choose any person they wish to represent them, the career of lawyer may well become insignificant.

modernity. Thus, the problem of role conflict is not an abstract one but is in fact the competition of claims to maintain or gain critical control over the exercise of various functions. In many modernizing societies, such conflicts exist between civil servants, politicians, managers, and the like.

Different systems will allocate functional significance in the modernizing process to different sets of careers. These different sets may be regarded as profiles of modernization in the particular societies. We can discuss these profiles in terms of four modernization roles, the civil servant, manager, political entrepreneur, and political broker. The first two are prototype modernizing careers. The last two are the least oriented toward careers and, moreover, represent innovative change rather than institutionalized change.

1. CIVIL SERVANT

Civil servants, through their expertise and their modes of organization, comprise the single most important group for the translation of government policy into social practice. But they are a difficult group for political leaders to deal with or assimilate because, on the one hand, they are generally better educated than the politicians, with a subtler awareness of their own position, and on the other, they have a greater security of tenure, which creates a totally different outlook.

Civil servants tend to live in a relatively sophisticated world, with power deriving from that sophistication. They identify modernity with themselves. They may read Camus or Sartre or the *New Statesman*. They retain links with the world of the university. A few see their ideal counterpart as the United Nations civil servant. A set of theories and a literature, both German and American, are there for them to turn to for reassurance. Schools, or institutes, of public administration help support their roles.

Because of their functional significance, they come into direct contact with politicians and managers. Often the result is competition over the allocation of functional occupations. This competition becomes exceptionally important in the last stages of modernization and the primary stages of industrialization.

2. MANAGERS

Managers generally represent a high level of skill in their occupations. They are usually at the beginning point of a career and are not very high on the scale.[11]

3. POLITICAL ORGANIZERS: THE ENTREPRENEUR AND THE BROKER

Posed against the civil servants and the managers are two types of political organizers. The first is the political entrepreneur, who organizes individuals for particular purposes: party rallies, voluntary labor, mass literacy campaigns, backyard blast furnaces, and so on. Particularly in societies where there are many institutions of a mixed traditional and modern nature that contain traditional, accommodationist, and innovative roles — such as churches, separatist movements, charitable and social organizations, clubs, and fiscal and burial societies — the political organizers are likely to embody roles that spread the values of modernity by focusing on particular instrumental ends. On the other hand, they are also potential centers of separatism, parochialism, and the perpetuation of non-modern values. In order to attain modernization without parochialism, the society must infuse its intermediate groupings with a sense of corporate responsibility by means of an ideology of modernism. Typically, this is the work of the political entrepreneur.

The second type of political organizer is the political broker, who, although at the non-career end of the scale, represents a modernizing role. Brokers are the individuals who act as negotiators between intermediate groupings. All modernizing societies

[11] The manager is usually a man from the shop and is close to his origins with the people. He is the factory equivalent of the political broker (but he tends to be much more honest and humorless). Confused by the superior manners (and mannerisms) of the civil servants, he is concerned only about practical efficiency and in rough and ready terms.

require a large number of such brokers. Both of the political organizer roles tend toward the non-career end of the range of modernizing roles, but some political entrepreneurs may develop political careers.

If we consider the criteria already discussed, the degree of career specificity and the functional significance of a particular elite role, we will have a rough guide to the kinds of conflicts likely to arise between roles. If political entrepreneurs, for example, attempt to acquire all three elite functions for themselves at the expense of the civil servants, we may expect constant conflict between the two groups. (See Figure 10 for a diagram of this situation.)

Degree of Functional Significance	Degree of Career Specificity	
	High	Low
High	Civil servant	Political entrepreneur
Low	Manager	Political broker

FIG. 10. — *Role conflict in modernizing careers. In any given system, the roles that appear in the different quadrants will be in conflict with one another. Civil servants have the strongest claims to professional status and rank highest on the career specificity scale.*

SOME NORMATIVE ORIENTATIONS OF ROLES

We have specified the functions of careers and their political significance and have identified some critical modernizing careers. We have also identified some critical non-career modernization roles. The first two were the civil servant and the manager; the second two, the political entrepreneur and political broker. These roles may be mutually compatible but are more likely to be mutually antagonistic. There are behavioral reasons for this. One reason is that these roles tend to follow different norms. The civil servant is likely to be a *theorist*. He wants to use his knowledge to effect highly generalized actions according to a particular set of principles. The political entrepreneur, in contrast, is an *ideologist*. He exhorts people to action. The manager tends to be a *pragmatist*. He works out practical solutions to problems on the basis of his immediate experience and expertise. The political broker tends to be a *compromiser*. Moreover, the theorist and the pragmatist have built-in tendencies toward careers. This is not necessarily the case for the ideologist and the compromiser, although the former is likely to be interested in a career if he stops being an ideologist and becomes a theorist. A civil servant, on the other hand, will no longer have a career when he ceases to be a theorist and becomes an ideologist.

As the norms of roles change, their functions will also change. In mobilization systems, for example, we may find two different patterns of careers, depending on the degree of modernization or industrialization already achieved.

Norms	Functions					
	Goal Specification		Institutional Coherence		Central Control	
Theorist						
Ideologist	X	Political entrepreneur				
Pragmatist					X	Manager
Compromiser			X	Political broker		

FIG. 11a. — *Modernization profile of Mobilization System I.*

We can now bring together some of the structural and behavioral implications of these remarks in the form of possible profiles of modernization. These profiles are, of course, speculative in character and should be regarded as hypotheses. At the point of conversion from modernization to industrialization, the typical pattern in a mobilization system might be that in Figure 11a.

At a later stage in development, however, the mobilization system pattern is likely to be that in Figure 11b.

Norms	Functions					
	Goal Specification		Institutional Coherence		Central Control	
Theorist	✕	Civil servant				
Ideologist			✕	Political entrepreneur		
Pragmatist			✕	Manager		
Compromiser					✕	Political broker

FIG. 11b. — *Modernization profile of Mobilization System II.*

In contrast, in a reconciliation system during modernization, we would expect to find the combination of roles in Figure 11c. By manipulating the functions of careers, these modernization roles help to create and shape them.

A question that arises, if an earlier hypothesis about modernization is correct, is whether the organization of careers lies predominantly in the hands of ideologists (the political entrepreneurs)? A second question concerns certain role consequences of industrialization. Does the role of the civil servant assume greater functional significance in a period of industrialization? The civil servant helps to organize career roles. His activities may have the effect of raising theory to a new functional significance when vulgar ideologies give way in the face of it. Moreover, theory requires knowledge. The informational role and the career organized

Norms	Functions					
	Goal Specification		Institutional Coherence		Central Control	
Theorist					✕	Civil servant
Ideologist						
Pragmatist			✕	Manager		
Compromiser	✕	Political broker				

FIG. 11c. — *Modernization profile of a reconciliation system.*

around the absorption and use of information should become increasingly significant. These are only a few of the many possible speculations about the patterns of career roles. Other illustrations than those in Figures 11a, b, and c might be suggested. The modernizing autocracy is likely to use the civil servant for goal specification, the political entrepreneur for institutional coherence, and the political broker for centralized control. The neomercantilist society is likely to use the political entrepreneur for goal specification, the civil servant for institutional coherence, and the manager for centralized control. In each case, the combination of roles helps to determine the pattern of careers in a system, which in turn determines the character and stamp of the pattern of modernization.

THE CAREER AND ITS MODERNIZING CONSEQUENCES

Because of the uneven pattern of modernization and the peculiar mixtures of modernizing roles, the ideologies of modernization may be blurred, the groups mixed, and the objectives highly generalized. Moreover, the occupants of modernizing roles do not necessarily remain in a particular role. Political entrepreneurs may rise from the military. The bureaucracy may become politicized. Political brokers may become prominent leaders. Ideologies reflect the resulting confusion and, despite various emphases, try to blend nationalism, socialism, and traditionalism. These blends obscure the very important systems-processes that we have been describing throughout this book, but it would be most unwise to discount them. Our contention has been that fundamental modernization processes, despite the appearance of confusion and mixing, tend toward a peculiar kind of confrontation, which is reflected and located in the organization of career roles in the various modernizing systems. At its widest limits, the modernization process is the confrontation of the ideologue and the scientist, not because their respective ethics are antagonistic but because of the changes that occur in the modernization process itself.

The three functions of modernizing roles are actually different aspects of the same general process, that is, the conscious manipulation of change. Professionalism and the career roles expand dramatically. Politics becomes the preserve of the career expert, who is himself a technician. The old amateur and non-career characteristics of the political entrepreneur are replaced by the scientific planner and the expert in attitude surveys. Formation of government policy on critical issues tends more and more to resemble a scientific enterprise. On the other hand, these changes indicate the decline of politics as we are accustomed to think of it. Politics declines as it becomes the property of a technical career role. At the same time, of course, the technical career role becomes political.

In this way many fundamental aspects of choice in social life become increasingly politicized as modernization advances, and, as we have said, politics in the usual sense undergoes a drastic decline. This development is intensified by a condition of war and semiwar among the major industrial nations, which serves as a continual stimulus. The necessity of controlling national destinies and planning for the future (not to speak of survival) becomes the central focus of the choice mechanism. In this sense modernization in industrial nations continues to have a technological paradigm to follow in the evolution of the career role. The politicization of technical roles for planning and the allocation of resources coincides with a virtual revolution in technique. The result is exceptional opportunities for scientists, social scientists, and technicians. These professions come to dominate in the military, the bureaucracy, and in other bodies such as educational institutions. They originate in the universities and the technical institutes, of course, rather than in government and gain power because of their functional expertise.

If we recall that some modernizing societies are proportionately farther behind the most advanced industrial countries than they were thirty years ago — and the objective of catching up is very explicitly formulated in the ideology of modernizing societies (as a claim to legitimacy as well as a desirable goal) — these technical tools become even more significant. Their prestige increases with their command over new techniques. Applied knowledge takes on dignity (whereas in the past it was discounted). The political significance of the teacher and the technician rises as the modernizing governments engage in research, take a more accurate census, test opinion, conduct manpower surveys, allocate funds for education, and study geographical mobility, migration and so on. Modernizing societies are thus *trend conscious*, and it is the *trend-testers* who suddenly become significant, especially in the absence of active public opinion or an informed opposition.

Schools and institutes in modernizing societies increasingly emphasize mathematics. Soon sampling techniques and computer programming will probably be added to their programs. The result of the catch-up attitude has been the formation of a scientific elite around which a more general "class" of moderns could be organized, with the canons of science becoming functionally relevant. Overseas universities, polling and survey centers, and United Nations technical bodies all help to reinforce the scientific career role. Overseas aid now involves a revolution in technique that is far more significant in shaping ideas, changing power relations, and spreading the values of science than in gaining the nominal objectives of a program or project.

Moreover, the growing reliance on science has consequences in the personal as well as the social sphere. For the occupants of these careers identity is based on the ideology of social engineering. An enduring contribution to modernization is defined as immortality. Meaning is derived from the evolutionary objectives inherent in the modernization idea, and purpose from professional expertise. The emphasis is on creativity and initiative and a real need for freedom.

No matter how the modernizing roles are arranged in each

system, they need to *create* information in order to carry out their functions. That is the primary activity that unites them, despite their differences. Technical competence is acquired in order to provide political leaders with sufficient information so that they may act. This information is not for the public but for specialized groups and for special purposes. It is in the manufacturing and utilizing of information that the latent functions of the modernizing elites become manifest.

One indicator of these latent functions is ideology. Ultimately, the modernizing elites must accept an ideology of science (whether or not they accept nationalism or socialism at the same time). This type of ideology is based on the need for information, verification, experimentation, and empiricism. Modernizing elites must also accept rules of eligibility based on technical expertise. During modernization, exceptional opportunities arise for technical and managerial personnel, agronomists, statisticians, marine biologists, economists,[12] public administration experts, fiscal and banking specialists, psychologists, and others, to become political entrepreneurs, brokers, civil servants, and managers. In order to attack the most pressing problems that affect the internal political life of the modernizing country, these roles need to become identified with those of the scientist and the social scientist, with both sets taking on new dimensions as a result. Scientific roles are usually accompanied by a certain modesty, a knowledge of the limits of authority, and a sense of the limits of competence. This would appear to obligate scientists to accept whatever political system they find in their societies. But the obligation is less strong when they are simultaneously civil servants or political brokers. Since their real need is for information, they will demand more and more in order to get on with their jobs. It is not a big step from a demand for free access to information to a demand for liberty as a right. In most cases, moreover, the scientists in mod-

---

[12] In Latin America today, the economist has displaced the lawyer as the key figure of modernity.

ernizing roles are supported by the universities, and universities in modernizing countries are often the focal points of liberty.

The implications of these comments need to be made very clear. Scientists play politics and share the roles of the modernizing elites. These dual roles require the intellectual and professional "space" that will allow the incumbents to exercise their expertise. They need freedom to think and work as well as to direct action. Because of these needs, modernizing elites may become the carriers of freedom itself.

They may not prefer, or even observe, the forms of representative or democratic government. But if their activities have the effect of checking the power of arbitrary government, the scientists within the modernizing elite may well become a powerful accountability group (and possibly even a consent group), entrusted with the allocation of resources according to technical priorities. They may recruit on the basis of training and expertise and share in decision-making in critically important sectors; and as this decision-making role grows, so will its political significance. But even if the scientists represent a steady force in favor of a reconciliation system, *they will not necessarily be a force for democratic government as we know it.* Quite the contrary, the libertarian values of most of the scientific technicians fall far short of a belief in representative institutions, if only because that form would make them subject to the mercies of an uninformed electorate and its political representatives.[13]

What the foregoing analysis suggests in terms of our analytical

[13] In this connection, Alfred North Whitehead quotes Shaw's *John Bull's Other Island* as follows: "In my dreams it is a country where the state is the Church and the Church the people: three in one and one in three. It is a commonwealth in which work is play and play is life: three in one and one in three. It is a temple in which the priest is the worshipper and the worshipper the worshipped: three in one and one in three. It is a god-head in which all life is human and all humanity divine: three in one and one in three. It is, in short, the dream of a madman." Whitehead is particularly interested in the theme of work as play and play as work, which is fundamental to the ethic of mobilization systems with their technocratic bias; see Whitehead, *The Aims of Education* (New York: Mentor Books, 1963), p. 51.

diagram is the following: highly developed and industrialized societies emphasize the career of the scientist (see Figure 11*d*). This career increasingly includes that of the social scientist as well. The role of the scientist is not only important functionally; it is also related to the growth of bureaucracy. Science helps to rationalize social life. Bureaucracy spreads. Theory becomes an ideology. As this happens, the civil servant becomes the ideologist of science.

We have discussed the significance of careers in terms of three functions: goal specification, institutional coherence, and central control. These three functions determine the power of a career. We have suggested that conflicts arise between modernizing roles that are highly specific careers and those that are not. Civil servants and managers were identified in the first group and political entrepreneurs and brokers in the second. It has also been suggested that each of these has a particular dominant normative orientation. The civil servant is oriented toward theory, the manager toward pragmatism, the broker toward compromise, and the political entrepreneur toward ideology.

Norms	Functions					
	Goal Specification		Institutional Coherence		Central Control	
Theorist	✕	Scientist				
Ideologist					✕	Civil servant
Pragmatist			✕	Manager		
Compromiser			✕	Political broker		

FIG. 11*d*. — *Modernization profile of a highly industrialized society.*

The combination of variables employed here, when placed against the general pattern of stratification, will help us identify some of the specific conflicts and tendencies that arise and the way each type of system handles these conflicts.

Consider three different types of stratification: caste, class, and status. Each may characterize a system. Or all three may be present in one system. As we have pointed out, modernizing societies tend to contain all three. If we are to see the effects of a particular pattern of functionally significant careers upon political modernization, we will need to observe the changes in stratification.

What happens, for example, when a member of a caste in a caste system comes into contact with the ideologically oriented political entrepreneur, the pragmatic broker, or the theoretically oriented civil servant? In the first instance, we would expect a dramatic confrontation, with possibilities of conversion from one type of total belief system to another. In the second, we would expect a partial weakening of belief in caste prescriptions on the part of the caste member and a tentative exploration of actions normally excluded as legitimate behavior. In the third, we would expect a pattern of deference and the acceptance of a kind of authority based on the civil servant's claim to superior knowledge.

Many other relationships or tendencies are possible. Each of the modernizing roles has a different impact on each segment of the stratification system. For the status hierarchy, for example, the civil servant represents professionalism. The manager represents the impact of adaptive technique on efficiency. The political broker emphasizes accommodation of alternatives. The political entrepreneur imposes an orientational discipline on the status hierarchy.

Without going any farther in the hypothetical list of impacts, it is clear that, insofar as there is competition between entrepreneurs and careers, there will be competing normative pulls on each type of stratification. In this way political conflict is generated through efforts to modernize and results in political action.

6

THE POLITICAL PARTY AS A MODERNIZING INSTRUMENT

We have suggested various indicators of modernization (such as per capita income and education) and certain roles that are necessary to the modernization process (such as civil servants, merchants, intellectuals, and students). These indicators and roles are associated with modernization as a total phenomenon, embracing all aspects of social life including the political. We then identified some of the problems of elite-mass relationships and pointed out certain conflicts between career roles representing institutionalized change and political roles representing innovation. In the area of political modernization, no single role is of greater importance than that of party politician. This is because political parties are themselves historically so closely associated with the modernization of Western societies and, in various forms (reformist, revolutionary, nationalist), have become the instruments of modernization in the developing areas. The political party is such a critical force for modernization in all contemporary societies that the particular pattern of modernization adopted by each is quite often determined by its parties.

TOWARD A DEFINITION OF POLITICAL PARTY

In surveying the political and social life of the Maghrib, Nevill Barbour remarked,

> The political life of contemporary Morocco has original and complex characteristics which cannot be fitted into any of the existing categories of twentieth-century political science. Morocco cannot be called a democracy, since all power is legally concentrated in the hands of the King. But neither is it an absolute monarchy since political parties play a significant role. It is not a dictatorship if there is more than one party. Presumably one-party regimes are dictatorships, and countries where political parties are not significant we would find absolute monarchies.[1]

This statement, though somewhat unclear, does throw into relief the difficulties that are inherent in defining the scope of political parties in developing societies. Clement Moore spells out the difficulty in characterizing the Neo-Destour in Tunisia.

> . . . Though a well-organized political party with a mass following, the Neo-Destour is neither a constitutional mass nor a totalitarian party. The categories of Western political scientists . . . cannot adequately explain Tunisia's dominant party. The Neo-Destour resembles the Congress Party of India, the CPP of Ghana, and various territorial offshoots of the RDA in French-speaking Black Africa more than it resembles European political parties. Political scientists have not yet devised a generally accepted model to characterize these newer but highly structured parties. However, they may be called "national" parties, and they have a number of traits in common. They all originated as elite and then as mass parties in reaction to a colonial situation. Their leaders assimilated the political culture of the colonial power, which to a greater or lesser extent constituted the ground rules of the conflict between the two.[2]

[1] Barbour, *The Politics of Maghrib* (London: Oxford University Press, 1959), pp. 109–10.
[2] Moore, "The Neo-Destour Party of Tunisia," *World Politics*, XIV (April, 1962), 463.

Sigmund Neumann, in trying to segregate crucial elements of political parties, suggests the following:

> A definition of "party" might as well begin with its simple word derivation. To become a "party" to something always means identification with one group and differentiation from another. Every party in its very essence signifies *partnership* in a particular organization and *separation* from others by a specific program.
>
> Such an initial description, to be sure, indicates that the very definition of party presupposes a democratic climate and hence makes it a misnomer in every dictatorship. A one-party system (*le parti unique*) is a contradiction in itself.[3]

There are good reasons why political parties are so hard to define. Their genesis is difficult to disentangle from the evolution of the modern society and state; the role of a party often changes substantially as political conditions in a country change (particularly in modernizing societies, where various political developments may bring about an elaborate and complex polity from a rudimentary one); and in developing countries, a peculiar relationship exists between state and society — they are linked together by party solidarity. It is this last aspect more than any other that establishes the general basis of agreement on the rules of the polity.

In terms of one set of relationships, a primary function of parties is to organize public opinion and test attitudes and to transmit these to government officials and leaders so that the ruled and rulers, public and government, are in reasonably close accord. The entire representative principle of government rests on this relationship. From this point of view, we may see parties, first, as intervening variables between the public and the government.

A second significant characteristic of political parties is that their form is determined by the entire sociopolitical framework of the society. They depend upon the degree of modernization in a society for their pluralism and diversity; they require a constitu-

[3] Neumann, *Modern Political Parties* (Chicago: University of Chicago Press, 1956), p. 395.

tional framework or political regime congenial to their functioning (no matter which type they are); and they depend upon the groupings in the society for their membership. In this sense, political parties are dependent variables, with society and governmental organization, election or co-optation procedures, and the like, the independent variables.

A third significant aspect of political parties is their obvious importance as subgroups in the system with their own means of generating power. In terms of this aspect, which is most critical in the new nations, where the party is often the microcosm of the future society, the party can be identified as an independent variable. Society and government become dependent on party organization, the decisions of party leaders, and the framework the party imposes on society.

If the observer does not sort out the three aspects of political parties — as intervening, dependent, or independent variable — the political situation in a country will seem confused and baffling.

THE MODERNIZING IMPACT

As political parties become organized in a modernizing society, they engage in a variety of activities, not all of which are familiar to Western observers. In order to arouse political interest (sometimes for the first time), they make use of technologically advanced artifacts. Political action means loudspeakers, mobile propaganda vans, and business suits. The briefcase becomes as much the mark of the politician as of the civil servant.[4]

[4] Speaking of Africa, Thomas Hodgkin emphasizes the special significance of improved transportation. "A modern political party must be able to deploy, with reasonable ease and speed, its leaders and organisers. It must ensure a reasonable degree of central or regional control over local branches and groups. It is highly desirable (and, in the political context of French Africa, essential) to enjoy means of rapid communication between the colonial territory and the metropolitan capital. These technical preconditions of effective party organisation, propaganda, and pressure, have been largely satisfied in post-war colonial Africa. It would be hard to exaggerate the revolu-

The relationship between party and modernization, whether modernization in technology or organization, appears clearly in the campaigns and manifestoes of the various political parties, As a goal, modernization is particularly effective since the desire for education is widespread throughout the developing areas. The employment of all the mass media during political campaigns, the use of journalists, cartoonists, poster-makers, and pamphleteers, also helps to identify political action with modernity and to stress the instrumental role of party activity in change and innovation. Similarly, the registration of voters, compilation of lists, and appointment of polling officers, voting papers and ballot boxes, the use of school children as messengers and of schools as meeting halls, and even the organization of a country into voting constituencies, districts, and wards, all encourage the identification of the mechanics of politics with a modern culture.[5]

Because political activities bring the parties into direct contact with the population, they, more than the civil service, army, or even the government itself, have the most immediate impact in developing communities. The other primary carriers of modernization — schools, Christianity, Islam, business firms and commer-

---

tionary political consequences of the creation of an efficient internal and international air net work. In practice, this means that M. Mamadou Konaté [now deceased], deputy for the French Sudan [now independent Mali] can attend a meeting of his party executive in Bamako in the morning; take part in a session of the *Grand Conseil* at Dakar in the late afternoon; and speak in the National Assembly in Paris next day. Dr. Nkrumah, Mr. Awolowo and Isma'il al-Azhari can combine their party, parliamentary and ministerial duties in the same way. At a less exalted level, the improvement in road communications has made it possible for the middle-rank leadership of parties — national officials, regional and district secretaries and agents — to penetrate into obscure villages in lorries, private cars, party vans, or even on bicycles. Thus party propaganda and slogans can be widely diffused, local branches established, and local grievances ventilated. The gospel is preached; new converts are won; the faithful are confirmed — even in the remoter bush" (Hodgkin, *Nationalism in Colonial Africa* [London: Frederick Miller, Ltd., 1956], p. 143).

[5] See the fascinating account of the elections of May, 1956, and March, 1957, in Nigeria by Philip Whitaker (Western Region) and J. H. Price (Eastern Region), in W. J. M. Mackenzie and Kenneth E. Robinson (eds.), *Five Elections in Africa* (Oxford: Clarendon Press, 1960).

cial enterprises, the market, a cash economy, and so on — are all utilized (and in a widespread manner) by the contemporary nationalist political party. The party needs money and keeps books. It develops a press and printing establishments. The techniques of management are employed to hold followers and to regularize authority and leadership. The party penetrates churches and mosques. Intense movement, from country to city, and from rural hut to modern, air-conditioned offices, characterizes the activities of party leaders and, more important, their followers. Outside the party headquarters of virtually all nationalist parties congregations of people can be found who are hoping for a handout or benefit, buttonholing a politician in order to complain about something, or basking in the aura of modernity. Simply to be there, talking and chatting with others about politics and personalities, is exciting and cosmopolitan.

And what a strange combination of organizations fall under the general rubric "political party." Sometimes they are simply coalitions of different organizations, some directly political, others not. The Burmese (AFPFL) Anti-Fascist People's Freedom League, for example, was a coalition that included socialists and Marxists in the Socialist Party of Burma, the All-Burma Peasants Organizations, the Federation of Trade Organizations, the Trade Union Congress, the Women's Freedom League, Burma Muslim Congress, Kachin National Congress, the Union Karen League, Chin's Congress, the United Hill People's Congress, the All-Burma Fire Brigade, the All-Burma Teacher's Organization, and the St. John's Ambulance Brigade. In the national elections of 1956 it won 148 out of a total of 250 seats, after which it began to break apart because of internal corruption and conflicts in personalities and ideologies.[6]

In contrast to the loose structure of coalitions such as the Burma AFPFL are the strongly "articulated," to use Maurice Duverger's

[6] See the description by Lucian Pye, in Robert E. Ward and Roy C. Macridis (eds.), *Modern Political Systems: Asia* (Englewood Cliffs, N.J.: Prentice-Hall, Inc., 1963), p. 336.

phrase, or militant parties. An example is the Parti Démocratique of Guinea, a militant party dedicated to "permanent revolution." It is based on democratic centralism, with an elaborate local structure composed of 7,000 village and ward committees, 163 sections, assemblies, congresses, and auxiliaries under tight control of the party. It has a youthful membership (with a mean age of thirty-seven) and without doubt is the pre-eminent organization in that society. Government is its dependency and the public its raw material.[7]

In Guinea, as in some other African states like Mali and Ghana, the political party has become more than a substitute for the colonial power. It organizes power from "below," where government might otherwise have no independent validity or vitality of its own. In a sense, we can say that the party actually generates power, shapes it, and applies it to government, which, one step removed, translates it into its various decisions and acts.

To a certain extent a party in a modernizing nation does not need to commit itself to a particular schedule of benefits on which it is periodically judged (as in the West). It has the advantage of being a window to a wider world for many in the villages, linking immediate effort with a wider purpose. The individual suddenly sees that he is more than a unit in a kinship structure. He may be elected as a representative of his fellows or be given a post. He may feel the flood of self-esteem that comes with authority. The diffusion of generalized power provides a *feeling* of participation, beyond that gained in regularly scheduled elections and periodic and rather formal referendums, that is immediate, local, and enjoyable.

Shared responsibility through the political party is most effective in single-party countries in which the major issues of state

[7] The best description of the PDG is Bernard Charles's "Un Parti Politique Africain, Le Parti Démocratique de Guinee," *Revue Française de Science Politique*, XII (June, 1962). See also L. Gray Cowan's useful discussion in Gwendolen M. Carter, *African One-Party States* (Ithaca, N.Y.: Cornell University Press, 1962). The best review of political parties in Africa is Thomas Hodgkin's *African Political Parties* (London: Penguin Books, 1961).

are excluded from public discussion. In such countries the local variations in policy bite most deeply into people's lives and become the focal points for experiment and heated debate. Quite often political trivia are the substance of developmental politics, with the wider issues of politics remaining remote from the individual and impossible for him to comprehend.

Under such conditions, the party attracts more of our attention than government. Leaders are almost always leaders of parties first and government officials second. There are powerful exceptions to this generalization. But the exceptions are made more interesting by the general rule. In Morocco, for example, it is surprising that El Mehdi ben Barka is in exile and Hassan is on the throne. In most such cases it would be the other way around. The kings and colonials depart, and the party leaders remain. Clearly then, modernizing political parties can go much further than their Western counterparts because they, in effect, serve as microcosms of the new societies. Even when the parties are monopolistic (that is, when the party's ideology is the foundation of legitimate authority in the state), their structures incorporate such diversity that the real instruments of bargaining and debate in the country — the "legislatures" — are the party congresses, the presidium, or the national party executive rather than the formal governmental organization.

In modernizing systems, then, it is obvious that parties are rarely limited to the more or less passive role of transmitting private wants to the makers of public policies. Nor are they aggregative devices, collecting varying expressions of want, belief, and outlook in some faithful manner. Quite the contrary, the political parties of a modernizing society play an active entrepreneurial role in the formation of new ideas, in the establishment of a network of communication for those ideas, and in the linking of the public and the leadership in such a way that power is generated, mobilized, and directed.

Hodgkin has pointed out for Africa what is clearly also the case elsewhere. There "mass parties" have developed a multiplicity of functions of a "judicial, administrative, police, educational, and social welfare type" in addition to their "conventional electoral and parliamentary functions. In the case of parties in opposition to a colonial regime, this is liable to mean that the party becomes, in effect, a parallel state. In the case of parties in power it may mean a blurring of the distinction between the functions and responsibilities of the party on the one hand and those of the government and administration-on the other." [8]

THE PARTY AND INTERMEDIATE POLITICAL ROLES

We have suggested that a distinct feature of modernization is the proliferation of roles in the areas between traditional and modern life. Political parties and their auxiliaries serve as the framework in which these intermediate or accommodationist groups are interrelated. This is an extremely important task if we consider how difficult it is, even in Western societies, for different functional groupings to have a common political language. If, as C. P. Snow has said, the technician and the intellectual are inarticulate in each other's presence, how much greater are the barriers to communication in a modernizing community between farmers and civil servants, laborers, lorry drivers, and intellectuals who have only some aspects of tradition in common.[9]

Modernization brings people together into different social clusters based on occupation and work, education, foreign travel, and

[8] Hodgkin, *African Political Parties*, p. 167.

[9] So different are the traditions in many cases, however, that a recounting of them may drive the community apart, particularly when the traditions are ethnically based. Thus, in Ghana, political conflict arose in the form of ethnic antagonisms between 1954 and 1957. The most extreme form of ethnic conflict occurred in the Congo and served to focus modern conflicts, for example, between rural and urban groups, ethnically advantaged and ethnically disadvantaged, socialist and Catholic. Older ethnic issues helped to concentrate newer forms of antagonism so that the lines of cleavage on all issues were similar. Modern political parties, particularly of the type that emphasizes solidarity by monopolizing loyalties, try to bridge these "primordial" sentiments.

religion. They may live together in residential areas or blocks of flats reserved for, say, civil servants or technicians. Primordial attachments to linguistic groups or particular ethnic associations give way in the more generalized modern complex of relationships. On the other hand, new tensions and conflicts leading to mutual antagonisms that are just as intense and divisive as any of those in the past may arise, as was suggested in the previous chapter, from the separation of the highly educated from the uneducated, the urban from the rural, and all those who come to represent the modern establishment from the general population. Moreover, these modern divisions may be linked with traditional ones, as, to some extent, occurred in the Congo, with disastrous results.

The differentiation brought about by modernity can thus drive wedges between peoples as well as link them. This is why the elite-mass relationship is so important. Men may join together to turn out a machine product or to build a road, but their mutual understanding may remain limited to matters connected with the machine or the road. Otherwise, their life styles, housing, kin relationships, and general intellectual orientation may diverge even more than before. In most traditional societies, after all, everyone understood what roles were available. The chief or king did not live so differently from the farmer, only a bit more elaborately. Not so today, when cultural differentiation follows economic differentiation and sets up barriers to an effective set of intermediate groupings.

It is the political party that links the various functional bodies together. Party groups may be organized in factories, schools, churches, clans, extended families, and co-operatives, which will then be linked together by their connection with the party. No matter how reluctant he may be, the civil servant with the overseas degree may be forced to communicate with a rural party official or with a taxi driver who may have an important position in the party. To this extent, channels of communication are opened up between otherwise hostile or non-communicating groups, bringing them into sets of relationships out of which the state is built. This, more than any other factor, is the basis of the success of the single-party state. Its monolithic structure helps create many intermediate groupings in the society and binds them together, even those parts that are likely to be hostile to each other. Hence the political party derives its significance in terms quite opposite to those of the elite.

Where such a function is not limited to political parties, as in the cases of the army in the Sudan and the civil service in Ethiopia, it may be possible to maintain the continuity of tradition into modernity or alter it to conform to a new perspective. Such political groups often become "government." [10] But their success is very rare in the absence of an effective mass party.

In the West, political parties are thought of primarily as representative instruments, a means of insuring peaceful and regular alternation of governments through the succession of leaders to public office. The democracy practiced by a multiparty government is one of the few systems in which succession in public office is a regular and healthy feature of political life. Without bitter purges and internecine warfare between oligarchs (as occurred, for example, after the deaths of both Lenin and Stalin in the Soviet Union) or conflicts over leadership (as in countries as diverse as Turkey, Vietnam, South Korea, and the Dominican Republic), stable multiparty democracy has solved the problem of peaceful succession in public office.

Whatever the form parties are important not only in the "circulation of elites," to employ Pareto's phrase, but also as an instrument of political education and socialization that shapes the habits and attitudes of a people toward government. Parties, for example,

[10] In Western societies, the situation is very different. The presence of several competing political parties distinguishes the democratic from the autocratic modes of government. Competition for votes is widely regarded as the best method of insuring accountability by the political leaders to those who elect them. Political virtue is maintained through periodic elections at which the government and opposition parties present themselves to the electorate for popular approval.

extract certain policy modalities, which can be understood by voters, from the discontinuous and chaotic practices of government. By distinguishing the important from that which is not and by identifying current and historical issues with popular figures, parties arouse interests and passions in the political process. Parties help people, from childhood on, assimilate values about government and the form of the political process.[11] This is particularly important in modernizing nations, where generational differences and political socialization often vary. By defining permissible forms of political behavior, the socialization function of political parties determines the nature of political tolerance in society and the orientation of leaders and followers.

Representation, peaceful succession in office, and the socialization of values intrinsic to democracy are the functions of parties in societies that are approaching the secular-libertarian model; but they are all means to an end. This end is the constant scrutiny and re-evaluation by citizens of the problems they face and the solutions they pose. As Karl Jaspers puts it, "The democratic idea requires justice for human variety and for the scale of rank among men, which can never be objectively determined. In the democratic ethos of equality no one is either despised or idolized. The greater and more solid carry weight; self-restraint is practiced for the love of quality, yet no one demands recognition of his own superior quality." [12] Multiparty democracy helps to institutionalize and continually reinforce the qualities stressed by Jaspers. It is fickle with heroes and hard on villains. In the restless search

[11] In many of the new states, the parties make particular efforts to attract youth and to influence their early training and education. Herbert Hyman has shown that in democratic societies even children adopt political prejudices and preferences very early in life, largely as a result of the influence of the family. In a sense, the political modernization process in which political parties engage in the developing areas begins with the transfer of political socialization from the family to youth auxiliaries or other bodies. During colonial periods, the same functions were performed by the Boy Scouts, as in our own society. See Hyman, *Political Socialization* (Glencoe: Free Press of Glencoe, Ill., 1959), chapter iii.

[12] Jaspers, *The Future of Mankind* (Chicago: University of Chicago Press, 1958), pp. 310–11.

for issues and grievances, political parties do more than find a response that will propel them to public office; they also probe for weaknesses in persons in power and in policies and subject them to the spotlight of publicity. This itself is a humbling experience. It helps to maintain the attitudes of fraternalism and individualism that are fundamental to the democratic way of life.

In the sacred-collectivity model, on the other hand, those functions disappear and the parties become devices for mobilizing and disciplining the population. Public offices become sinecures and autocratic regimes alternate with purges, revolts, and other forms of instability. These qualities make orderly change difficult and may intensify contempt for law and constitutionality. Instead of socializing values of compromise and accommodation, the moral imperative of the state becomes all-important, to the point that it saps the individuality of the citizen by denying him his moral and political personality.

These, then, are some of the functions and influences of political parties and elections. More important than their class basis, or their ideological structures, or even the quality of the leadership they train, are their capacities to represent the people, effect peaceful transition, and make men into sober political beings capable of accepting responsibility.

THE ROLE OF AN OPPOSITION

The varied significance of political parties in different societies explains our difficulty in dealing with them under a single general heading. Many features of parties in developing societies are clearly different from the Western pattern. On the other hand, they are ordinarily different from certain prototypes with which they are sometimes compared, such as the Communist party. Indeed, in almost all the new nations, political parties typically show elements of both; in particular, they are organized around characteristics of both.

Single-party regimes are the clearest cases of this. Some of them explicitly employ democratic centralism, Marxian ideology, and the organization of cadres subject to an elaborate discipline. Yet, in ideology, they may be quite similar to more right-wing parties although they may not make of party a spiritual instrument. One has only to contrast the Ivory Coast with Guinea to see organizational similarities but ideological differences. In commenting on the Ivory Coast, for example, Aristide R. Zolberg remarks that the Parti Démocratique de Côte d'Ivoire became between 1952 and 1957 a

> successful electoral machine through the skillful use of various techniques, including cooptation, patronage, and economic pressures. This might have been sufficient if the party had operated within a well-established constitutional framework whose legitimacy was firmly institutionalized. Under such conditions, relatively low participation might even be considered politically advantageous. But the P.D.C.I. was not merely a machine. It claimed to be also an all-encompassing movement that based its legitimacy on overwhelming support from all strata of the population.[13]

The presence or absence of an opposition party is for Westerners the crucial factor in determining the nature of the role of a political party and its activities. And there is no doubt that this is critical. No amount of emphasis on traditional forms of decision-making or traditional democracy can disguise the fact that, as a concrete structural characteristic of modern society, two or more parties competing for political power within the rules of a particular constitutional framework create a different kind of polity than the single-party regime.[14] The question is how different are multiparty governments and for how long? Many of the single-party regimes represent compromises between prevailing groups

[13] Zolberg, *One-Party Government in the Ivory Coast* (Princeton, N.J.: Princeton University Press, 1964), p. 215.

[14] See the excellent discussions of the problem of multiparty government in K. W. J. Post, *The Nigerian Federal Election of 1959* (Oxford: Oxford University Press, 1963); and Richard L. Sklar, *Nigerian Political Parties* (Princeton, N.J.: Princeton University Press, 1963).

and a militant "vanguard" party; the dialogue between them
serves as an instrument of modernization and communication by
generating grievances in which genuine issues are reflected. Indeed, out of such compromises a stable pattern may be created.
Immediately after independence, however, single-party regimes
are concerned to create authority. This is why the role of a political opposition has proved ambiguous in most newly independent
nations. New governments rarely see the necessity for a regular
opposition party, nor do they always accept the idea that opposition is a normal and desirable feature of government. Most modernizing nations have developed after a prolonged period of
struggle with colonial authorities, during which nationalist leaders
have come to monopolize loyalties. In addition, opposition groups,
having themselves been associated with nationalism at some stage
of their existence, often have the antigovernment reflex common
to those who have been dedicated to changing the fundamental
character of a country rather than working for reform within
well-established rules of political action. Indeed, many opposition
leaders in modernizing nations regard the new government much
as they did its colonial predecessors, that is, as illegitimate.[15]

Fear that opposition will produce factionalism, corruption, and
separatism is pervasive in modernizing nations. The opposition
parties are often blamed for producing a situation that in fact is

[15] Hence, when we look at many of the nations that attained independence
since World War II, the outlook for the opposition appears bleak. In Burma,
charges of party corruption and selfishness led to an army takeover. It was
the army rather than the politicians who swept the squatters from the cities
and distributed food to the hungry. In its zeal and efficiency, the army made
the politicians look like foolish men, more proficient at scrutinizing monastic
texts than at dealing with the problems of the day. Facing similar problems,
Indonesia was riddled with factionalism. Political party conflict was found
in every organized sector of life: the army, the trade unions, the civil service,
and even clan and village organizations. The country was so divided by party
conflict that even "guided democracy" was impossible to achieve. Government was a coalition of oppositions. See Herbert Feith, *The Wilopo Cabinet,
1952–53: A Turning Point in Post-Revolutionary Indonesia* (Ithaca, N.Y.:
Modern Indonesia Project, 1958), pp. 165–93. In the Sudan, the independence of the nation was challenged by political groups retaining strong ties
with Egypt. The army took over in part to safeguard newly won autonomy.

inherent in the postindependence period of the new nations. When the cement of nationalism is weakened, a new basis for social solidarity must be found. Independence is an act of parliament or a stroke of the pen; then the real difficulties begin. Power is left to the nationalists like gold dumped in the streets, and many are bruised in the hectic scramble to gather it up again into the strongbox of the nation.

Rare, indeed, is the responsible opposition that can prosper in such a climate. Rare, too, is responsible opposition. Modernizing nations therefore tend to have either a great many parties or a single dominant party that outlaws opposition or only nominally tolerates it, as in some of the French-speaking African countries using the list system of elections (in which the list obtaining a plurality of votes wins all the seats).[16] In some nations in which there are a great many parties, such as the Sudan, the army has taken over in order to preserve independence (the two main parties were so fundamentally divided over the issues of closer union with Egypt, Islam, ethnic parochialism, and a host of other matters that government had become a shaky coalition between one large and several small parties).

Few examples of a successful postindependence multiparty system can be found among the new nations except Israel and Nigeria. In the latter, recent events in the Western Region would indicate that in the multiparty system there is a coalition based on necessity rather than principle. In most other new nations unity is seen to lie in the personality of a strong man, powerful and pure, who will lead the nation to harmony and achievement. The prototype of this pattern of modernization is Kemalism and the Republican Party in Turkey.[17]

[16] This system at least has the virtue of embodying in principle what it denies in practice, that is, the multiparty system.

[17] See Kemal H. Karpat, *Turkey's Politics: The Transition to a Multi-Party System* (Princeton, N.J.: Princeton University Press, 1959). Karpat shows how "reforms were to be carried out by coercion and force, and the degree of force was determined by the number and the variety of the reforms needed. Such a view implied that the reforms were decided and carried out by an 'elite' which acted on behalf of the people. The elite praised the 'new'

Of course, bringing all political claimants together under one roof does not necessarily result in a monolithic party. Thomas Hodgkin's remarks about the mass party are generally instructive.

The regional leadership of a mass party, while it usually includes representatives of the younger *militants* — brought up in the party and giving it their undivided loyalty — may also have to find room for the leaders of what in Senegal are called *clans*, dominant local personalities and their followings. Indeed, in seeking to draw into the leadership of its *fédérations*, or *sections*, or constituency executives those whose "ties with the locality are strong," the mass party may find itself obliged to seek local alliances with the heads of powerful *clans* — whose basis may be regional, ethnic, religious, economic, ideological, or any combination of these. In the elite parties, this raises no special problems, since such parties are essentially confederations of *clans* [in Senegal]. But in the mass parties — which normally regard themselves as disciplined, centralized, monolithic expressions of the popular will — the clan should, in theory, have no place.[18]

But they have a place, as do the chiefs in regional organizations of the Convention People's Party in Ghana and the *ejidos* of rural Mexico in the Partido Revolucionario Institucional.[19]

Indonesia is another example. Clifford Geertz describes the situation in a small town in Java, Modjokuto, in the disorganized period following Japanese occupation; he suggests that, to a certain extent, the need for new patterns of organization

has been met in the years since Independence by the greatly increased importance of the institutional paraphernalia of Indonesian nationalism, although in general terms Mod-

and despised ignorance. They also could not avoid despising the 'ignorant,' that is, the people who had not succeeded in getting a formal education or acquiring 'modern' manners.

"It is in this atmosphere of force and coercion that the Republican Party gradually identified itself with the state and the nation. Placing itself above any control, and encouraged in part by the success of strong governments in Europe, it continued to expand its domination" (pp. 72–73).

[18] Hodgkin, *African Political Parties*, p. 90.

[19] See Nathan L. Whetten, *Rural Mexico* (Chicago: University of Chicago Press, 1958), chapte· for a discussion of the *ejido* system.

jokuto still suffers quite severely from a lack of effective
social forms around which to organize its life. This institutional paraphernalia consists in the main of four major all-
Indonesia political parties — the *Partai Nasional Indonesia*
(PNI), or Nationalist; the *Masjumi*, or Modernist Moslem;
the *Nahdatul Ulama* (NU), or Orthodox Moslem; and the
Partai Komunis Indonesia (PKI), or Communist — plus a
whole set of organizational appendages. As well as its political organization proper, each party has connected with it,
formally or informally, women's clubs, youth and student
groups, labor unions, peasant organizations, charitable associations, private schools, religious or philosophical societies,
veterans' organizations, savings clubs, and so forth, which
serve to bind it to the local social system. Each party with
its aggregation of specialized associations provides, therefore, a general framework within which a wide range of social activities can be organized, as well as an over-all ideological rationale to give those activities point and direction.
The resultant complex, as much a social movement as a
political party proper, is usually referred to as an *aliran*, the
Indonesian term for a stream or current; and it is the *alirans*
which today form, inadequately and incompletely, the core
of Modjokuto social structure, replacing the traditional status
groups of the prewar period.

Each *aliran* is headed in Modjokuto by a party directorate,
composed in the main, of the leaders of the various auxiliary
organizations within its ideological camp. To a steadily increasing degree, the members of the directorates — less than
a hundred men in all — form the town's "new men of power,"
an as yet heterogeneous and unconsolidated local elite.[20]

The fact that this multiplicity of organizations, each having
some functional role to play in the community, is joined in some
fashion within a political party underscores an important function
— linkage — of political parties in modernizing areas. The union
of the various societies, organizations, and auxiliaries brings the
highly complex but often discontinuous features of life into some
kind of organizational harmony and control. Indeed, the effort to
ensure harmony has a strong effect on the party's ideological defini-

[20] Geertz, *Peddlers and Princes*, pp. 14–15.

tion of what society ought to look like at some future date. If these characteristics are, in turn, coupled with tighter control by the party over all its rivals and auxiliaries, a type emerges that we will call the "party of solidarity," in which the party organization determines the critical relationships of society.

The reasons for the rise of the party of solidarity are, of course, complex. But one cause of such a pattern of development is the existence in the society of conflicting organizations that mirror primordial lines of cleavage, such as those between tribes, languages, or religions. In such a society, the fundamental differences that separate its members will be extended into the modern political party structure, which will exploit these differences and conflicts with all its technological and organizational skill.

There are, of course, still other reasons why new nations have tended to adopt the party of solidarity. It may have grown out of an earlier political movement in which the diverse groups and associations were held together by a unifying ideal, such as independence, personified in the figure of a heroic leader. This is, after all, the age of heroic leadership in developing areas, and the Garibaldis, Washingtons, and, we might add, Cromwells of the new nations are the Nehrus, Tourés, Sukarnos, and so on. Once their accomplishments have come to be accepted as routine they are reduced in stature and take on more normal proportions. What, then, is to hold movements together after heroic leadership begins to dissolve? It is the party of solidarity, with its institutionalization of leadership, ideology of authority, and organization of structural relationships along strongly articulated lines.

Indonesia is again a good example, for the situation described by Geertz has changed. The party of solidarity has replaced the parties of representation. Faced with rebellion in Sumatra and a diversity of political parties, both ethnic and religious, Sukarno established his doctrine of "guided democracy." In 1959 the constitution of 1950 was suspended, a new political manifesto was enunciated, and a political slogan, USDEK (from the Indonesian terms for "constitution," "Indonesian socialism," "guided democracy," "guided economy," and "Indonesian national character"), was adopted. Manipol-USDEK became the main coalition in the state, with the others either abolished or left to wither on the vine.[21]

Thus it is that a single well-organized group can appeal to a diverse population and limit political fragmentation while retaining popular support. In fact, a single well-organized group can be preferred by the people to several political parties. This is particularly so when bitter rivalry between parties has divided a country. The greater the rivalry, the stronger the wish of people with passionate political attachments for an end to party conflict. Of course, they are not enthusiastic about accepting the dominance of any other party than their own. Hence, they may look to an outside force (army, civil service) to save them from themselves. Excessive fear of tyranny thus may produce oligarchy.

In societies where there is a dominant party of the congress type and a nominal opposition, factionalism and intraparty intrigue are the prevailing political style. Politics comes to resemble that in a bureaucracy, in that each party official builds up support for himself inside the party and seeks to outmaneuver the others. To avoid this, the leaders of mass parties attempt to impose discipline in the guise of fraternalism. Effectively organized, the single mass-party system can become a weapon for change and discipline in a society. Conflict occurs within the ranks, but the party presents a united front to outsiders. In this way, conflict and difference do not appear to challenge the unity of the party; and loyalty to the party becomes loyalty to the state.

Quite often, political leaders in single mass-party governments discover that political opposition has not disappeared but is latent

[21] See Michael Brecher, "Political Instability in the New States of Asia," in Harry Eckstein and David E. Apter (eds.), *Comparative Politics: A Reader* (New York: Free Press of Glencoe, Inc., 1963), pp. 617–35. See also Lucian Pye, "The Politics of Southeast Asia," in Gabriel Almond and James S. Coleman (eds.), *The Politics of the Developing Areas* (Princeton, N.J.: Princeton University Press, 1960); and Herbert Feith, *The Wilopo Cabinet, 1952–53: A Turning Point in Post-Revolutionary Indonesia.*

and underground. If, in order to permanently destroy opposition, government tries to control information, public opinion, voluntary associations, and the like, the definition of democracy is likely to be changed. From a pluralistic mass-party system based on representation, however nominal, of geographic constituencies with relatively heterogeneous populations, it may become a single-party system based on the functional roles in the modernization process, for example, civil servants, military men, trade unionists, plant managers, and technicians. In this sense, there remains latent in the "national socialism" of some of the single-party mobilization systems a tendency toward a corporate "democracy" that is both populist and autocratic in practice. But it will be the party that determines the character of the state.

A MORPHOLOGY OF POLITICAL PARTY DEVELOPMENT

The foregoing remarks may be clarified by the paradigm in Figure 12. How do these groups of characteristics arise and why are they so powerful? In particular, they arise after a certain period of time has elapsed, during which factions composed of moderniz-

Social Units	Representational Parties	Solidarity Parties
Party	*Pluralistic:* competes with other parties.	*Monopolistic:* seeks to eliminate other parties.
Community	*Representative:* seeks to incorporate divergent views in order to win widest following.	*Directive:* seeks to amalgamate grievances in order to overthrow existing order or, when in power, to bend the community toward the goals laid down by the party.
Government . . .	*Constitutional:* limits party action by constitution, convention, and electoral rules.	*Extraconstitutional:* accepts legal order only when forced to. When in control, the party bends the government and constitution to its own ends; it makes the state subservient to itself.

Fig. 12. — *Party relationships and characteristics.*

ing elites and coalitions composed of groups of factions have begun to gain public support and build up a widespread sense of grievance and dissatisfaction, not merely against social conditions, but against alien rule, that is, the authority of the state. From this stand, there is no turning back. Parties of representation demand substitution of the representative principle for alien rule. Parties of solidarity specify a future state of affairs (and manipulate popular support) as the basis of government.

Factions begin as ethnic, syncretistic clubs, such as tribal associations, which put forward grievances for redress. Coalitions are formed from factions in order to maximize their effectiveness by showing widespread support. These coalitions become institutionalized as political parties for the purpose of gaining access to government; at this stage, they identify modernity with political representation. Seeking even broader support, the parties form national political movements that aim to change the basis of political legitimacy and cut across premodern forms of association. Before long, a militant group arises that poses a choice between a continuation of parties of representation (in competition with one another or in a coalition) and a party of solidarity that denies the right of any party other than itself. If the latter is chosen, a new factionalism develops, often like a court around a king, in which bureaucratic party politicians and individuals compete for political favor.

Thus, our morphology of political parties in the modernizing societies begins in faction and may also end in it. In between, parties of representation and/or parties of solidarity are formed. The pattern in modernizing societies is in this sense not typologically different from that in the West. The old boys' associations and political clubs that began in India in the late nineteenth century, and also in West Africa and parts of Latin America, were different in style and circumstance from the Reform or Carleton clubs in England or the Jacobin clubs in France, but in all cases this type of association initiated a cycle of political modernization and evolution toward more or less universal modes of modern politics. Some groups turned into political movements that found expression in revolution. Others broke into competing parties of representation, operating within a legal framework of constitutional government and reinforcing it by the need to compromise. Other movements became parties of solidarity, militant and ideological, that sought to universalize their own values by transforming the society and political framework, that is, the modernization system.

Examples of political clubs can be found in most of the developing countries. Generally, these clubs begin as student organizations, that is, as modernizing instruments, or at least as organizations that deliberately attempt to embody some mixture of tradition and modernity. One example from Western Nigeria is the Egbe Omo Oduduwa, the Society of the Descendants of Oduduwa, the mythical founder of the Yoruba peoples. This organization was started in 1945 in London by Yoruba students, one of its founding members being Obafaemi Awolowo, leader of the "Action Group" and formerly premier of the Western Region and leader of the opposition in Nigeria.[22] In 1948, Egbe was set up in Lagos as well, when the chiefs became concerned over political attitudes among the youth and the effects of political activity by the National Council of Nigerian Citizens Party. The chiefs decided to emphasize the following: cultivation of Yoruba language, culture, and history; provision of scholarships for Yoruba boys and girls to obtain secondary and university education; promotion of a strong Yoruba state within Nigeria and "generally [to] create and actively foster the idea of a single nationalism throughout Yorubaland"; protection of the chiefs; and co-operation in the achievement of an independent federal Nigeria.[23]

Out of this came the Action Group, a curiously ambivalent organization, which directed its nationalism increasingly outward to encompass all Nigeria, in 1959 contesting the general election even

[22] Chief Awolowo has since been convicted of sedition and sentenced to ten years in jail.
[23] See the excellent discussion in James S. Coleman, *Nigeria: Background to Nationalism* (Berkeley: University of California Press, 1958), pp. 344–45.

though dependent on Yoruba nationalism for its strength.[24] In order to contest the elections in non-Yoruba areas, the Action Group joined forces with minor and local parties so that it could say fairly that it was a national party representing a large and fragile coalition rather than an integrated and strongly articulated organization.

We could cite many other instances of the growth of political clubs and their role in political organization. Sometimes they begin as ethnic cultural associations or old boys' groups. At other times they will be parliamentary organizations or perhaps Marxist discussion circles, as in former French West Africa.[25]

POLITICAL COALITIONS

The prototype of political coalitions, though they vary widely, is perhaps India's Congress party, particularly in its founding period. Like other political parties, the Congress party began as a club for the small "Westernized" middle class of university-educated Indians who had demanded entry into various civil service and professional posts. Widely differing groups, having in common only their participation in the modernized sector of the system, were brought together over the years to press for electoral reforms (such as the Morley-Minto reforms of 1909) that would extend the elective principle in the Indian councils, expand education, recognize the role of Islam, and the like. The extension of the electoral principle brought about coalitions of quite diverse interests until 1920, when the party became more strongly artic-

[24] See K. W. J. Post, *The Nigerian Federal Election of 1959* (London: Oxford University Press, 1963), for a detailed analysis of the role of political parties in Nigeria.

[25] Speaking of such parliamentary clubs, Hodgkin writes of the Northern People's Congress, "The NPC has some of the characteristics of a club for parliamentarians from Moslem areas of Northern Nigeria" (Hodgkin, *African Political Parties*, p. 156).

ulated and disciplined under Gandhi — and in our terms, a party of representation.[26] As Myron Weiner points out:

> Until the 1920's the urban, professional intelligentsia which dominated the Indian National Congress had little communication with the masses of the country. The nationalist movement itself arose first in those areas where the Western impact was greatest: Bengal, Madras, the Punjab, and Maharashtra. The early Congress conferences were held in urban centers: Poona, Calcutta, Bombay, Karachi, Delhi, and Madras. British influence, wittingly or unwittingly, provided the impetus for a truly national nationalist movement. The unification of India by the British had facilitated the growth of a feeling of being "Indian." British higher education not only introduced Western liberal ideas and led to the emergence of professional classes, but also provided the language — English — whereby the educated elites of various parts of the county could communicate with one another.[27]

Much the same could be said of the effects elsewhere of alien rule, language, and education in the formation of clubs that coalesced into congresses, "fronts," associations, and the like. In Ghana there were such groups as the Ratepayers Associations, the Aborigines' Rights Protection Society, and, on a territory level, the National Congress of British West Africa, which had its own "Ladies Section."[28] In Senegal and other parts of French West Africa, trade unions and professional organizations became proto-parties during the "Popular Front," before political organizations could be established. In East Africa and the Congo, coalitions

---

[26] See the brief discussion in Rupert Emerson, *From Empire to Nation* (Cambridge, Mass.: Harvard University Press, 1960), p. 342.

[27] Weiner, "Party Politics in India," quoted in Eckstein and Apter (eds.), *Comparative Politics*, p. 708.

[28] The best discussion of coalitions in Ghana is in David Kimble, *A Political History of Ghana, 1850–1928* (Oxford: Clarendon Press, 1963); for Nigeria, Coleman, *Nigeria: Background to Nationalism*; and for Africa in general, Hodgkin, *African Political Parties*, and I. Wallerstein, *Africa — the Politics of Independence* (New York: Vintage Books, 1961). For the Middle East, see Manfred Halpern, *The Politics of Social Change in the Middle East and North Africa* (Princeton, N.J.: Princeton University Press, 1963).

were often formed on the basis of separatist church movements, independent schools, and local farmers' and business associations.

Whatever the form, the coalition stage in the development of political parties is particularly interesting for three reasons. First, it is the basis of political linkage; political leaders come to be identified in terms of adjacent and relevant associations rather than political clubs per se and become aware of the commonality of interests with non-educated people. Second, it is the means of bridging diverse primordial loyalties that might otherwise prevent the formation of any effective and mobilized political pressures. Third, it provides experience in developing specific programs and reforms, ranging from moderate to radical, including the drafting of proposals, constitutional engineering, and the building of programmatic ideologies. Such coalition parties provide the necessary background without which movements, parties of representation, and parties of solidarity would be impossible. As Ruth Schachter Morgenthau has pointed out, parties are "among the oldest national political institutions in West Africa, wholly Africanized long before the governments or the civil services. . . . Hence parties give better guidelines to African politics than those formal institutions of government which were set up by French and British colonizers at least in part as a condition for their recent political withdrawal. . . ." [29]

POLITICAL MOVEMENTS

When the political coalition suddenly gains a mass following around a particular ideology or heroic leadership, it acquires the special characteristic of modernizing nationalism. In the resulting nationalist movements we find a curious combination of spontaneity and organization. The spontaneity derives from the joyful

[29] Morgenthau, "Single-Party Systems in West Africa," *American Political Science Review* (June, 1961), reprinted in Eckstein and Apter (eds.), *Comparative Politics*, pp. 693–705. See also Morgenthau, *Political Parties in French-Speaking Africa* (Oxford: Clarendon Press, 1964).

and sometimes completely emotional identification by people, even if only for a short time, with an image of the future and particular leaders. Sometimes the movements are inspired by religious motives, as in the case of the Moslem brotherhoods; however, there are also the large political movements of the Middle East and the commercial or mercantile ones of the Tidjiania in West Africa and North Africa. Sometimes they are based on a common status or color, as in the populist and fraternal interterritorial organizations, such as the Rassemblement Démocratique Africaine until 1958, in which the branches, regional associations, and congresses cut across territorial boundaries. And sometimes they are strongly local and traditional, like the Bataka movement in Uganda right after World War II. The central characteristics of the movements, whatever their forms, are their spontaneous and populist qualities — the direct relationship between the leadership and the people, the high degree of emotional appeal of their programs, and the simplicity of their aims. Movements form around some highly diffused and general goal, the accomplishment of which, it is believed, will resolve all major problems. This goal is the "political kingdom" for Nkrumah or national independence, both economic and political, for virtually all political leaders.

Because it widens the base of the coalition party by including otherwise contradictory and conflicting social groupings, the movement represents a profound change from the coalition in at least one important respect — the amount of non-rational excitement it can produce. Political movements are directly akin to religious ones. They allow people to feel purified and personally better organized by virtue of membership. And membership itself is an informal matter. It is a matter of feelings more than party cards, loyalty rather than organization. Because of the weak organization of the movement, it tends to be very fragile, breaking up when some of its primary objectives have been accomplished. It is in the transformation of the movement into a party, either of representation or of solidarity, that the constitutional future of a country and the nature of its polity are quite often determined. This is

the ultimate result of the efforts of the political leaders in movements to transform the restless sweep of public energy, liberated
by and flooding through the political sector of social life, into
something more stable and permanent — in other words, to institutionalize loyalty and authority.

PARTIES OF REPRESENTATION

Parties of representation operate within the framework of the
reconciliation system and have highly institutionalized leadership
roles. The party of representation accepts the reconciliation system
but also requires electoral rules and the determination of policy
by a party caucus, which takes the form of national conferences.
The resulting program usually concentrates on material welfare
and promises of specific benefits to particular groups. Reform is a
characteristic and permanent ideology.

Parties of representation rarely derive from political movements
but rather from political coalitions. They widen the coalitional
base, including as many possible interests and voluntary groupings, such as trade unions, women's organizations, and the like,
while allowing these organizations considerable autonomy and
freedom. Their main function is to ensure a fairly large turnout
of voters during election time. Hence, the auxiliaries are not disciplined components of the party; they are incorporated, but independent, elements (of youth, women, workers, and so on),
much as in the case of the Labour party in Britain, with its trade
union, constituency party, and co-operative society members. In
addition, the party of representation has a large direct membership.

The party of representation is not the central fact in the social
and personal life of the individual. Quite to the contrary, party
membership shares his interest with other organizations — church,
club, and the like — becoming stronger at times, particularly during campaigns. It is not the all-encompassing central focus of ex-

istence. Its youth wing may serve some of the purposes of a fraternal organization, keeping alive old friendships of days abroad. It may help to deal with particular problems resulting from government activity. In Nigeria, for example, the two main political parties, the Action Group and the NCNC, competed with one another to handle local grievances that arose from an urban redevelopment scheme in Lagos, in which just compensation to displaced owners of businesses and residents was most difficult to determine. Party "lawyers" were available in every block to represent persons with problems of this kind. They organized residents' associations, meetings, and occasionally a disturbance; they also mediated conflicts of interest, partly in the hope of gaining new adherents and partly as a means of establishing their political branches in newly settled areas.[30]

Parties of representation have a characteristic style. In additior to handling grievances, they also provide considerable entertain· ment and recreation. Quite often, in modernizing countries, the parties run lending and thrift societies, hold dances, and sponsoi or help to sponsor charitable functions. In many ways they act much as voluntary associations in Western countries. Churches, discussion groups, and youth and children's organizations are quite often either directly sponsored by the party or assisted by local party organizations. Party schools often give courses of instruction in subjects ranging from Marxism to sewing. What distinguishes these activities of the party of representation is the looseness of their organization and their autonomy, as we have already suggested. The party auxiliaries tend to be locally based around a church, school, or other institutional center in a village or town; their relationship with the central party is therefore not vertical but horizontal. In other words, the local branches of the party are related to local and semi-autonomous voluntary associations in such a way that membership in the one does not automatically produce membership in the other.

[30] See Peter Marris, *Family and Social Change in an African City* (London: Routledge & Kegan Paul, Ltd., 1961), especially chapter vii.

The party of representation normally faces in political opposition either another party of representation or a party of solidarity. In most of the modernizing nations, when a party of representation confronts a party of solidarity, the latter usually wins. Restricted by lack of organization, the former cannot take actions that would alter its diffuse character. Even when the party of representation is the sole party in the country, each of its autonomous or semi-autonomous parts tends to become the focal point of corruption and competition. The party of representation does not function efficiently as a single party.

Perhaps the most striking illustration of this is Liberia. There the True Whig Party has remained in power since 1883. As J. Gus Liebenow points out, "The period from 1869 to 1883 represents the only period of intensive interparty competition in Liberia during which the opposition had more than merely a theoretical chance of unseating the ruling party." [31] Without internal discipline and militancy based on ideology and effective control within the whole organization, a party requires rewards, patronage, and corruption to keep its members together. In Liberia, according to Liebenow, the

> mechanisms whereby the True Whig Party has maintained its dominant position for more than eighty years have been fairly well developed. Patronage is the keystone in the arch. Inasmuch as there is only one elected executive in a highly centralized unitary state, the party that captures the presidency enjoys a monopoly over the distribution of patronage in its various forms. The opposition can make promises but only the ruling party can actually deliver the rewards to the faithful. In the face of repeated failure at the ballot box and of the constant seduction of the opposition by the True Whig Party, it is difficult for a second party to hold its following together from one defeat to the next. The opposition must rely on the voluntary contributions of the faithful. The True Whig Party, on the other hand, levies a yearly "tax" upon every public employee to the extent of one

[31] Liebenow, "Liberia," in Gwendolen Carter (ed.), *African One-Party States*, p. 359.

month of his salary over a two-month period, and there is no
public accounting of the party treasury.[32]

Parties of representation evolve slowly, their growth linked to
the development of centralized political institutions. Even when
they originate with nationalist or socialist ideologies (for example,
the Wafd in Egypt or the Baath in Syria), their tendency is to
reduce their ideology to slogans and to allow the entire system
to rest on personal bargaining. This often results in political in-
activity and *immobilisme*, as in Sudan, Pakistan, and Burma; an
outside force may easily displace the party of representation, as
the army did in these states. Or, faced with such problems as
immobilisme, the party of representation may introduce elements
of the party of solidarity, as did the Tanganyika African National
Union (TANU). Even when successful, the parties of representation have failed to capture the popular imagination. The NCNC in
Nigeria, the Congress party in India, and the Union Progressiste
Sénégalaise in Senegal, for example, have been extremely successful in politics, but they have certainly not been very dramatic.
Their leadership tends to be stable and elderly. The UPS, for example, has its own youth movement (Mouvement des Jeunes de
l'UPS), with, however, none of the militancy of the JRDA in
Guinea or the Young Pioneers in Ghana.[33]

Parties of representation do not need to differ much in structural terms from parties of solidarity. That is to say, their formal
organizations may outwardly look quite similar. Much more important for the strength of the party is the role of local party
officials and the relationship between party employees and local
units of the party. Normally, there are local branches or committees based on locality rather than function. These are grouped

[32] *Ibid.*
[33] The best analysis of the political party pattern in Senegal is by William
Foltz, in James S. Coleman and Carl Rosberg (eds.), *Political Parties and
National Integration in Tropical Africa* (Berkeley: University of California
Press, 1964). See also Michael Crowder, *Senegal: A Study in French Assim-
ilation Policy* (London: Oxford University Press, 1962); and Ernest Milcent,
"Senegal," in Gwendolen Carter (ed.), *African One-Party States*.

into regional or district groups. Coordinating bodies link the two levels. On the highest level is a party congress or conference with a national secretariat or executive bureau to handle the daily affairs of the party. Party decision-making is consultative, relatively informal, and not very binding. The caucus tries to sound out the views of the various subordinate organizational bodies. The relationships are loosely structured.

PARTIES OF SOLIDARITY

Parties of solidarity originate from the desire to change the community, to restructure social relationships, and to develop a different form of consciousness and morality and therefore are usually found in mobilization systems. The party of solidarity seeks through human investment in mass action the derivation of capital with which to undertake certain basic development projects. Party life has a monolithic quality, in which the claim upon members is total allegiance. The party becomes the central force in the life of the individual around which his intellectual perspective, occupation, and service to the community revolve; even his marriage, his house, and the way he lives are affected by his party affiliation.

Unlike the party of representation, which stresses the wisdom of an aging leadership, the parties of solidarity, although bureaucratic and hard to displace, go through periodic purges and skip a generation between party leaders and new recruits, on the grounds that the middle generation is basically unreliable and opportunistic. Hence, the militant nationalist at the top of the party leadership tends to identify with the very youngest in the party, which flatters the latter without encouraging any expectation of his displacing the former. The result is a sense of youthfulness and vigor that, refreshed each generation, keeps the parties of solidarity young.

Characteristically, the parties of solidarity began in political movements. The various parts are held together by a considerable degree of ideological manipulation. Revolutionary slogans and the desire for rapid change help to reinforce the mutual dependence of the parts of the organization. These parts, in which membership is usually mandatory, include youth organizations, women's associations, and trade unions. They not only have an explicitly party character but are instruments of political socialization and control as well. Quite often in the colonial period, the party of solidarity had to function as if it were a party of representation; for example, it had to contest elections. And for that purpose it built up constituency organizations based on geographical area. After independence the organization based on function became more significant, with the territorial unit merely the locale for party administration by officials of the various party auxiliaries.

Discipline is constantly stressed in the party of solidarity, as is unity. Each of the parts contributes to the monolithic quality of the party rather than to pluralism. Being expelled from the party is almost as bad as losing citizenship in the state, and joining is virtually a rite. Indeed, the atmosphere is not dissimilar to that described by Maurice Duverger as the personalization of power. One betrays the leader by not following the party's dogma. The leaders are the prophets, the supermen, or the kindly but stern fathers who created independence and will lead their followers on to modernization and development.

The party of solidarity has in various ways been described many times and there is no need to enlarge on it here.[34] It is perhaps important, however, to point out that the parties of solidarity appeal particularly to youth and employ the language of revolution and dramatic change. They have an inherent tendency to oligarchy, as Robert Michels pointed out, and also a tendency to what might be called revolutions in rhetoric and resolutions in practice. Indeed, in the modernizing nations, over time, there is a

---

[34] For an explicit and more detailed analysis of the party of solidarity, how it developed, and its organization and internal problems in Ghana, see my article, "Ghana," in Coleman and Rosberg (eds.), *Political Parties and National Integration in Tropical Africa.*

tendency for the parties of representation and the parties of solidarity to resemble each other more than do their counterparts elsewhere. The youth are the hope of the parties of solidarity. Hence, in all the mobilization systems, one finds Young Pioneer groups, vigilance brigades, and the like. Their education is ideological, because through ideology new values are identified and simplified.

PARTY AND GOVERNMENT

A central distinction in the morphology of political parties is based on the way a particular type of political party helps to shape the pattern of future modernization and the nature of authority in the system. Parties of representation operating within a constitutional, representative government normally fulfil at least three main functions. These are (1) control over the executive, (2) representation of interests, and (3) recruitment to office. Control over the executive requires some kind of conciliar machinery through which checks on arbitrary and capricious power can be effective and regular. This mechanism of control becomes part of the institutionalized system of values and as such intertwined with public sanction and legitimacy. This is the reason parties are regarded in democratic societies as intrinsic to the political process. Similarly regarded as essential to democracy are the other two functions.

These functions receive a different emphasis in parties of solidarity, whose main purpose is in inducing solidarity and in giving direction to the public. They are the "vanguard" instruments of the state, and they are designed to maintain a relationship between legitimacy, goals of the state, and public support. For them the problems of relative scarcity and inequality are threatening; they normally identify their goals as industrialization and the elimination of all forms of inequality save the political. This accounts to some extent for the appeal of socialism in modernizing countries run by parties of solidarity. It segregates (or tries to) inequality to the political sphere, justifying it on organizational grounds — organizational means to achieve moral ends. This is the reason modern political parties of solidarity acquire a role in determining legitimacy. Parties of solidarity normally attempt to transform the entire stratification hierarchy, whereas parties of representation seek to widen, modify, or preserve the existing one. To attempt the former adds a compelling moral and symbolic aspect to party politics. Normally associated with the attempt is a prophetic or charismatic leader who challenges the prevailing hierarchy in the name of a higher morality. Hence, there is an affinity between parties of solidarity and highly personalized leadership.

The special role of political parties in modernizing systems derives from their unique ability to confer or withdraw legitimacy. This is particularly true for the party of solidarity, but less so for the party of representation. For the latter, the relationship is reversed; the party of representation derives its legitimacy from the legal government.[35]

Parties of both the solidarity and representational types try to maximize their support *less in terms of electoral victories than in terms of increasing their veto power over legitimacy* (1) by promoting mobility (in fact, serving as instruments of mobility themselves), (2) by providing an overarching system of social interrelationships that cuts across different and otherwise conflicting hierarchies, and (3) by pressing for particular objectives in government, which they have cast in an ideological framework. These three aspects of the role of party deserve particular consideration.

How do parties promote legitimacy? One common way is simply

---

[35] This is the usual case. It is by no means clear, however, where legitimacy rests in a country like Nigeria, for example. The basis of the constitutional order is less beliefs about it than the mutual checkmate of political groups, all of which need the legal framework in order to perpetuate their own existence. There is, then, at best, an ambiguous loyalty to the constitutional order exhibited by the political parties, which are motivated less by proprieties and norms of politics than by manipulative statecraft. The Northern Region government, for example, can hardly be accused of democracy.

to demonstrate the mass support that is available for party leaders to manipulate. This technique is more pronounced in the party of solidarity than in the party of representation; but many systems, in practice, combine the two, for example, the coalitional or list system, in which the most powerful list in elections gains all of the seats in a legislature. In this type of system the principles of representational parties, as well as many of their organizational features, are maintained together with the sense of power provided by the party of solidarity. This legitimizes a reconciliation system in theory and to a lesser extent in practice.

Such types claim to represent legitimacy through the representation of the interests of the coalition and diverse sources of support. Parties of solidarity, on the other hand, extend legitimacy by virtue of an ideal to which the popular membership serves as a testimonial of agreement. Those who are excluded from either the coalition or the party of solidarity are regarded as politically irrelevant; those who are within are an elect that anyone who demonstrates loyalty can join. Hence, the political public — that is, the relevant party membership to which the government is "legitimately" responsive — includes not the entire community but only those portions of it within the party orbit.

Another way to promote legitimacy is through the ritualization of charisma. Sometimes the ritualization process breaks down, and the institutionalized leadership role becomes instead a bureaucratic one. Whether this happens depends, in part, on the character of the leader himself. For example, S. M. Lipset shows how a near-charismatic figure, George Washington, eliminated that quality of the role by personal self-effacement, causing bureaucratic and institutional supports to emerge.[36] Quite often the ritual establishment of the political party leader occurs simultaneously within the party of solidarity and the state, for example, in the emergence of presidential monarchies. This development is accompanied by purges within the party of solidarity and the

[36] See Lipset, *The First New Nation* (New York: Basic Books, 1963).

elimination of opponents in government, in the name of the goals of modifying stratification and achieving modernization.

Both of the party types — for all their similarities and differences — have one very sharp area of disagreement, although it is rarely articulated. Words may be the same or similar, the language as flamboyant, and the party structures virtually identical. But the ultimate difference between the party of solidarity and the party of representation will remain, based on widely divergent conceptions of politics. The first emphasizes an organic society, communalist perhaps, evolving and growing, unfolding its potentialities. These potentialities are believed to be inherent either in the nature of man's personality, and the personality of the society in question, or in the unfolding of a set of superior ideas. The present, then, exists to serve the future. Life is ultimately purposeful and must be made so. In this respect the party of solidarity helps define the character of a mobilization system. The other, the party of representation, views politics as an elaborate system of bargaining for support. It is based on compromise. It corrupts ideologies by not taking them too seriously. It can stand competition and, indeed, requires it. It defines the character of the reconciliation system.

One common consequence of both types of party is a further sharpening of role conflict. As we mentioned earlier there are conflicts between career roles and entrepreneurial roles and also between entrepreneurial roles. The entrepreneurial roles that derive from parties of solidarity tend to be monopolistic, with the party leaders driving out all competitors who represent alternative types of parties. The political entrepreneurs that derive from reconciliation system, on the contrary, are not monopolistic but instead are likely to welcome competition as a principle of recruitment to entrepreneurial roles. No matter how monopolistic the practices of the political entrepreneurs from the parties of solidarity, however, and no matter how successful they are in driving out their counterparts in the parties of representation, they still have to cope with the representatives of career roles. The political entrepreneurs must compete with the occupants of careers. Hence, we will consider political parties from the point of view of such conflicts and in the context of voluntary associations other than political parties.

OTHER POLITICAL GROUPS

Not all of the most important political groups take the form of parties. Religious bodies and other voluntary associations, for example, may be equally important — at times more important than political parties themselves.[37] (Our analysis must touch on them, but space does not allow a full discussion of many.) Included as other political groups are professional and veterans' associations, church bodies, trade unions, farmers' associations, and the like. These groups may take on a special significance in developing areas when functional (in terms of modernization) rather than geographical bases of representation are adopted. The idea of the corporate state as a modernization system is based on the effectiveness of functional political groups.

A large literature is now devoted to the role of the voluntary association and other forms of political groups in the modernizing process. At times these groups can blend contrary traditions very effectively. Halpern comments on an example involving Islam and Marxism.

> To Moslems previously accustomed to a monistic view of life, Marxism therefore appears not as a materialistic approach rejecting spiritual values but rather as a new monistic philosophy projecting spiritual values upon a materialist base. Once Mohammed, they say, had to overcome the ties of kinship and an ancient polytheism in order to establish the community of believers. Now only Marxism seems radical

---

[37] By political groups I mean to include all groups acting to place their representatives in significant decision-making positions, that is, interest groups, pressure groups, and political bodies.

enough to organize the community to deal with widespread
want, toil and injustice in the face of the first genuine historical opportunity to overcome them.[38]

Indeed, the socialism of many of the extremist political groups
that occupy the shadow world between functional association
and political party is particularly interesting. They emphasize use
of the state in development but without a consistent philosophy.
Whether we consider the Egyptian Moslem Brotherhood or the
Jama'at-i'Islami movement in Pakistan, the League of Ghana Patriots in Ghana or the Stern group in Israel, we can see that political groups that accommodate only by setting a standard for extremism — and by that standard arbitrarily setting new valuations
on tradition and modernity — are significant, although short-lived,
generating authority and political orthodoxy during the modernizing period.

There are, of course, many kinds of political groups, some that
act politically only part of the time and others that have a more
permanent political quality. In the first category are a number of
different kinds of organization ranging from armies to literary
associations to old boys' associations. In the second are party
wings, auxiliaries, youth movements, and the like. It will be obvious that the consequences of an army's engaging in political activities are ordinarily much greater than a literary society's.

Quite often the attempt is made to employ armies as an equivalent of political parties. Social life is rigidly segregated from politics and the normal modes of political expression are curbed.
Armies represent an interesting combination of tradition and instrumental values. They can come to represent a form of authority
involving unquestioned obedience within a command system and
in this respect can be employed by modernizing autocracies. The
technical education, the emphasis on efficiency, the color and
flamboyance of military life, parades, drills, and the sense of

[38] Halpern, *The Politics of Social Change in the Middle East and North
Africa*, p. 161.

accumulated power in massed manpower and weaponry, all help to make the army into a critical political device and, in some instances, the substitute for a party. Where the party and army coexist, the relationship is almost invariably uneasy. Guy Pauker has recently described the ambiguous career of the military in Indonesia, for example, suggesting that, despite rising militarism, the officer corps does not use its capabilities for reform and progress. "It accepts the role of partners or even instruments of a group of emotional, radical nationalists, and shares in the benefits of power without serving, as far as can be seen, the interests of the people of Indonesia." [39] The army has become an instrument of repression rather than control and is deeply divided internally. In Burma the substitution of army for party worked better, with the army serving much as a civil service, or, more particularly, as the British colonial service. The great weakness of the army is its inability to handle political conflict smoothly.[40] On the whole, armies are not very useful substitutes for political parties of either the solidarity or representative types.

Much the same could be said for bureaucracies. They are, by their nature, limited in scope and support. They can manipulate power but cannot generate it. The rules of their craft and the built-in service regulations in almost every successful civil service delineate roles that are functionally specific and not general enough to allow the monopolization of power.

POLITICAL PARTIES AND AUTHORITY

The modernization roles that can be most easily transposed from one setting to another are those associated with education, including teachers, civil servants, and technical experts. It is not surprising, for example, that during the early stages of colonialism

[39] Pauker, "The Role of the Military in Indonesia," in John J. Johnson (ed.), *The Role of the Military in Underdeveloped Countries* (Princeton, N.J.: Princeton University Press, 1962), p. 222.
[40] See Pye, "The Army in Burmese Politics," in *ibid.*

such roles generally emerged relatively quickly and claimed particular significance and recognition. Early nationalists were frequently journalists, lawyers, teachers, and doctors or medical practitioners. Indeed, the modernity of their role was one qualification for leading the public in a direction of modernization.

Bearing in mind the discussion of the conflict between career roles and entrepreneurial roles, we might expect that with the increase of modernization roles political authority would be shared primarily among those who occupy careers. But such has rarely proved the case. Instead, the opening-up of the political hierarchy because of the increase in modernization roles has quickly produced competition between non-technical "moderns." The result is a curious and inverse process of role definition and authority: namely, the more functionally diffuse the political role, the greater the claim to authority; and the more functionally precise, the more effectively subordinated. There seems to be a basic antagonism between the first-stage professional elite, which, through nationalism, opens up the political area or social stratification to the public, and those who push the professional elite out of the way in the name of democracy. At the top of the hierarchy are all-purpose roles, whether of the charismatic or entrepreneurial type, which possess a high symbolic content. Many of the party elites are regarded as low in the power and prestige scale in all except the political area. The spread of modernization creates conditions that limit and downgrade the authority of the professional modernizing elite. This means that within any given modernization period the entrepreneurs have an immediate advantage over those in career roles.

There is something special, then, about politics as a mobility mechanism that produces competition between specialist and generalist roles, between the technician and the political entrepreneur. What I have in mind is the broader question of the relationship of the specialist to authority. The early nationalist claims to authority — for the greater participation in politics of local (as distinct from indigenous) people — were made by professionals who demanded equal treatment for all qualified men. Technical training was thus a point of entry into the power and prestige hierarchy at a time when the superordinate roles were monopolized by expatriates operating under a colonial mandate. Later on, however, claims to entry based on expertise could be met by the acceptance of local professionals in subordinate and technical positions. Nationalists who claim to run a country are usually rather anxious to avoid this and seek the more general forms of education rather than the technical.[41]

By and large the professionals and technicians who were the first to form political clubs and old boys' associations — in effect, to become politically socialized — were by-passed by the development of political parties, whether of the representational or solidarity type. In British territories, this trend was exaggerated by the restrictions placed on civil servants' engaging in politics.

In modernization politics the professional and the technicians form themselves into two types of associations. One represents elite clubs; the other civil service associations. Civil service norms render the members of its associations subordinate to the political leaders. Their professional skills and functionally specific roles render them manageable, and they are cut off from the broader mass of the public. Their prestige is great, but their power is circumscribed, except of course, in the area of specific functional competence.

Two common exceptions to the pattern of political authority in which career roles are subordinate to entrepreneurial roles are the military and the engineers. Both have the capacity to build general positions of authority into their technical roles that are easily converted to all-purpose symbolic roles. Particularly clear examples of this are the armies and military bureaucracies of the modernizing nations, which have great prestige and virtually as much power as they take the trouble to exercise. More-

[41] There were many reasons for this. The prejudice against technical education common in many developing areas is a recognition that technical roles are subordinate to non-technical ones.

over, they are not, with very few exceptions, engaged in actual military operations. Indeed, few officers of the armies of new nations have experienced military action at all. Theirs is a particularly political profession.[42]

Three types of political leadership roles thus make their appearance in modernizing societies. Each can claim, in the name of modernity, to be a residuary legatee of legitimacy: the professional and technical career roles organized in elite parties or professional associations; the political entrepreneurs who lead parties of either the solidarity or representative type; and the military-civil service bureaucracies (without whose support authority rapidly changes hands). Each group represents a modernization thrust of a different kind. The first and third utilize skills, training, and education rather than political competition to gain support.

Conflicts between these three types of modernization roles are common after a modernizing country has become independent. Each tries to avoid claims to authority by the others. Each tries to manipulate and control the others. Political leaders seek to manipulate their civil servants, military officers, and leading professionals in order to prevent them from exercising a potential veto over legitimacy. Friction and intense conflict are the ordinary conditions of political life between representatives of party bureaucracy, military bureaucracy. and civil service.

This conflict between elites takes place within all modernizing societies. But where the political party is strong and the society weak, it creates exceptional problems. This is one reason for the need for a party of solidarity — the special relationship between party and government in what is commonly called the single-party state. Government defines its relevant public in terms of solidarity parties, each of which exerts private control over significant segments of the population.

Thus, the role of political parties in modernizing societies differs

[42] Burma is perhaps an interesting exception to this generalization. See Moshe Lissak, "Social Change, Mobilization, and Exchange of Services between the Military Establishment and the Civil Society: The Burmese Case," *Economic Development and Cultural Change*, XIII (October, 1964).

fundamentally from their roles in more developed and industrial ones. As an instrument of representation, the party cannot faithfully reflect grievances in the community without weakening the conditions of authority. It requires mass support. Diversity is absorbed in the context of party discipline. The party has its own bureaucracy. Its leaders contend with one another for factional support. Perhaps most important of all, however, political parties in modernizing societies must supply psychic satisfactions, no matter how much patronage or other rewards and punishments they have at their disposal. This gives them a millennial quality. They cannot simply be go-betweens in the dialogue between ruler and ruled. Rather, the party creates a political hierarchy of power and prestige, which, in turn, is translated into party membership and position.

From the several roles they play in society, political parties derive varying significance. By generating or reflecting grievances, articulating issues, and establishing programmatic aims, they represent a segment of the total community. But, although subject to the authority of government, as are all other subunits of the system, such as trade unions, they also help allocate power through the distribution of offices. In the first capacity they *control* government. Their members acquire a dual allegiance. Mobilization systems, in particular, exploit this dual allegiance and assert the primacy of the party in the name of the state. The role of party in a mobilization system is thus quite different from its role in any other type of system.

It should be clear, then, that parties are not merely the passive transmitters of opinions from the individual to the marketplace of the collectivity. They represent a set of subgroup variables, especially in the case of parties of solidarity, that drastically affect social stratification, while giving concrete expression to grievances and relative scarcity as particular issues. Hence, in modernization, political parties play a critical role by building a system around themselves, by becoming a modernizing device manipulated by political entrepreneurs.

7

THE REQUISITES
OF GOVERNMENT

So far my object has been to provide the context for analyzing the problem of modernization. I have suggested that it is important to consider the political rather than the economic variable as independent in modernizing societies because the ensemble of modernization roles is not integrated by a dynamic subsystem based on rational allocation, as is the case in industrial societies. Instead the subsystem is usually the political party or some other political group such as the army or bureaucracy (or in some instances, a religious body).

The strategic instrument of the political variable is government, which I have defined as a concrete structure. As used here, it will mean, in addition, a particular collection of individuals that has defined responsibility for the maintenance and/or adaptation of the system of which it is a part. Carrying out this responsibility by making choices that are binding upon the members of the system is the main activity of government.

How broadly or narrowly these choices are conceived constitutes one basis of differences between governments. Some governments will cater to the needs of only a part of the community (and use that part to discipline the rest). This is characteristic of oligarchies representing a particular class or caste. Today, however, most governments operate in a climate of populism and mass participation. How such populism is controlled and shaped, as well as the degree of responsiveness by government to the demands of the public, constitutes the characteristic problem of government, especially in modernizing societies.

Indeed, so widely discredited is the view that government should ally itself with privilege in order to maintain the system that no government today uses this principle as a norm of legitimacy. Where such an alliance does in fact exist, it is disguised as a transitional phenomenon. Modernization is thus associated with the breaking down of norms of government based on privilege. Modernized societies are most often characterized by an openness and fraternalism that reflects a deference to the public and a recognition of human potentialities. Because of these qualities, government might be assumed to be a mere reciprocal of society. This, however, is not the case. Under circumstances such as those produced by modernization, government is a characteristically active agent rather than a passive one that faithfully reflects society as it is. Government in most modernizing communities helps to shape society according to differing norms of participation, with the underlying purpose of realizing potentialities of human and social resources. Its decisions (the exercise of its responsibility to choose) determine the moral character of the society. Government in modernizing societies tries to optimize satisfactions for a plurality of its members in order to generate the power to modernize, which is limited in turn by the need to maintain loyalty and to legitimize actions.

Given this role, it can readily be seen that not only is government the key instrument of politics but it strikes a sensitive balance between what society is and what it should become. The balance varies in each type of government. Five governmental authority types have been introduced in earlier chapters: the reconciliation system, the modernizing autocracy, the neomercantilist society, the military oligarchy, and the mobilization system.

The middle three are variations of the same type, namely, the combination of hierarchical authority and instrumental values. Each represents a particular relationship between morality and efficiency. Morality, expressed in norms of legitimacy — potentiality or equity — represents one set of boundaries delimiting each of these types.

THE BOUNDARIES OF GOVERNMENT

It is not surprising that different approaches to government result in different conceptions of the modernization process. In systems tending toward the secular-libertarian model, modernization is the by-product of the individual and group action stimulated by the visions of political and economic entrepreneurs. This means that the primary emphasis is on life styles associated with modernization, the education necessary to obtain those life styles, and the maximization of social distance between those in the modernization sector and those outside it. A kind of *Stand* is created that others can emulate so long as the government continues to invest in education and training to assure the equality of opportunity. Social mobility is partly a result of the activities of the entrepreneurs; the task of government is to see to it that opportunities do not congeal or become restricted through the monopolistic political practices of any particular group. A "good" government, in that sense, creates greater opportunities while regulating the activities of members, or, in other words, maintains the rules of the system while simultaneously providing for growth. Such a libertarian system maintains a hierarchy of power and prestige while enlarging its span. The entire process is regulated by the voting mechanism as employed in representative government.[1] The key to success in the system is a constantly widening flow of benefits and, more important,

---

[1] This view simply extends Max Weber's distinction between *Wertrationalität* and *Zweckrationalität* into the political sphere; see *Theory of Social and Economic Organization* (Glencoe: Free Press of Glencoe, Ill., 1957).

access to power and prestige roles. Hence, the problem of equity.

The libertarian model tends to break down when the inequalities produced by modernization cause large groups in the population to withdraw from the system. The "market" fails to work not only because the voting mechanism is too insensitive to register the order of preferences in the community; it also fails when government holds back consumption of the entire social product and invests a part of it to ensure a larger total at a future date. Moreover, many of the issues that divide people during the modernization process are nursed as private grievances and are not registered in their full significance in representative bodies. Hostility, anxiety, and conflict may become chronic as a result. Instead of the one-to-one correspondence between individual demand and government response implicit in the pure theory of the libertarian model, government may become increasingly divorced from the public interest (as distinct from special interests). An ever present possibility is that government's interest in equity in the context of growth may change to an interest in authority in the context of control.

These comments explain why so many new nations in the process of modernization choose the single-party, heroic-leadership pattern of government that tends toward the sacred-collectivity model. The primary problem of the sacred-collectivity model is to maintain authority while transforming power and prestige through the establishment of new values. If equity is the key problem in the type of system that may be described in terms of a market, authority is the key problem that confronts the sacred-collectivity model. The first is based on a distributive concept in which justice is the abstract way of expressing individual and group claims in the system. The second is based on a development concept in which equity must be postponed until a substantial increase in community wealth has been achieved. This is why I suggested in chapter i that the sacred-collectivity model ultimately links efficiency with authority, or rather authority with efficiency.

Both these models of government, however, share one feature.

They issue two sets of decisions. The first is a set of stratification decisions; the second, a set of ideological decisions. By stratification decisions I mean those through which governments make constant efforts to create conditions of greater social mobility, either within the prevailing rank or by some modification of the ranking system itself. Through the set of ideological decisions, governments generate greater authority than might be necessary to satisfy mobility needs. Since they need to satisfy psychic and aesthetic needs, they manipulate morality. The first set of decisions, concerning power and prestige (stratification), can be regarded as the rationalistic aspect of governmental decision-making. The second set of decisions (ideological) goes beyond the rational to a non-rational level. Any stable polity requires both.[2]

If government is defined as the critically strategic unit of a system, then failures of government will imply failures of the entire system. To the extent that this relationship is valid, governments may fail if their decisions to change stratification are insufficient to maintain public loyalty to the regime or if the non-rational aspects of their authority are no longer perceived. The first kind of failure results from a denial of equity. The second results from political cynicism. These, then, are the political difficulties to which each model type we have described is subject.

There is a more general way of studying the conditions that must prevail for government to maintain itself in its setting, that is, in the larger unit of which it is a part and to which it is linked

[2] Some of a society's problems can be satisfied by the readjustment of resources through reallocation roles, thus providing surcease from grievances as they appear. Whatever the range of problems, however, the first activity of stable government is the adjustment of goals to needs. By this means, a policy for meeting the problems of modernization is organized.

Such political efforts, however, are rarely sufficient, particularly when the problems are of so deeply moral and cultural a nature that they strike at the personal identity of individuals. This is what makes the innovative process so complex. It is not novelty per se that is the problem. One finds the theme again and again, sometimes expressed sentimentally, sometimes aggressively. The modernizing man asks, "Who am I?" "What is my identity?" And how elusive the answer is. Quite often a man's identity depends on someone else's definition.

in terms of morality and potentiality. To analyze how well government works we must specify the conditions under which equity or authority may fail. To do this I will put forward a theory of government based on two functional requisites of government and four contingent functions, and another theory based on two structural requisites and four contingent structures. The functional and structural requisites are the critical concepts for the general analysis of governments and the ways in which they change, whereas the contingent functions and structures are designed to elicit more particular (but still comparable) knowledge of societies and governments. These functions and structures should allow us to find our way to a general comparative analysis of modernization and changes in systems and a deep probing of the uniqueness of each system being compared. First, however, some comments on how requisite analysis works might be useful.[3]

THE ANALYSIS OF GOVERNMENTAL CHANGE

Before going on to a discussion of the functional requisites of government, I will restate the definition of government: In a system, government is the most generalized membership unit possessing defined responsibility for the maintenance and/or adaptation of the system of which it is a part. It is very difficult to obtain such functional requisites for analytical rather than concrete units. This has been one of the difficulties encountered by both David Easton and Gabriel Almond, for example.[4] Analyzing systems of politics or authority by function is a way of seeing many concrete units in interaction, but it does not adequately select, or sample, the strategic concrete units on which actual empirical observation

    [3] They will also be, by implication, an attempt to refute the arguments that this form of analysis is static and conservative and uninterested in change.
    [4] See Easton, "An Approach to the Analysis of Political Systems," *World Politics*, IX (1957), 383–400; and Almond, "A Functional Approach to Comparative Politics," in Gabriel A. Almond and James S. Coleman, *The Politics of the Developing Areas* (Princeton, N.J.: Princeton University Press, 1960).

must be made. Hence, the definition of government cannot be so broad that it encompasses too general a range of phenomena, like Easton's "authoritative allocation of values"; nor so narrow that it obscures the diversity in government's exercise of power, like the legal definitions that tend to concentrate on the more formal exercises of power. On the basis of our definition of government, if the system is a society, then the national government of that society is most likely to be the concrete unit of government. Similarly, if the system is a local community or a province or a district, then the local government of that area is likely to be the concrete unit.

The same conditions apply if the system is a trade union, a church organization, or a political party. That is, it is also possible to speak of their respective governments. Each of these governments can be observed separately in relation to its system, and they can be observed together as parts of government on a larger scale, within which functional requisites are shared. Hence, in the first instance, it is possible to examine how the government of a system works in the context of the system. In the second, it is possible to see how the different levels of government, public and private, local and national, share the functional requisites of government, or, if the functional requisites are not maintained, how the system changes from one type to another.

What gives government its special quality is its role in a larger system. I suggested earlier that the most important problem for social science is the analysis of choice. That means that the most important human activity is choosing. Individuals make choices and so do groups. *The difference between choices of government and choices of all other groups is that the choices of government have implications for all members of the system of which government is a part and are binding upon the members.* Unless this point is clearly understood, much of the discussion that follows will remain obscure.

There is then a peculiarly intimate set of relationships between governments, their equity and authority problems, the effectiveness of their decisions, and the evaluation of such efforts on the basis of the persistence or alteration of their systems. This intimate set of relations can be seen in terms of the functional requisites of government, that is, the functions that all governments must perform if they and the systems of which they are a part are to survive.[5]

To rephrase what has been said earlier, the crucial concerns of government are those that threaten the existence of the unit of which it is a part. With its practical monopoly of coercive powers, government has an indivisible responsibility for protecting the system. This responsibility can be seen in terms of two strategic activities of particular significance in modernizing societies, where cultural strain manifests itself both in the changing stratification system and in the formation of political groups as well as in the policies enacted in pursuit of modernization: first, as we have suggested, adaptation and integration of roles and role sets, including the institutionalization of values associated with roles; and second, the encouragement of loyalty and support, out of which legitimacy is created, focused, and applied to government. We have already suggested that in modernizing societies the second function is often performed very badly by government and political groups may come to assert a veto power over legitimacy. If this situation becomes extreme, then government is reduced to a formally established bureaucratic office with little power. Real power lies with the political bureau or other agency of the party. Governments

[5] One other point needs to be stressed before going on to a consideration of the qualities, structures, and politics of government. It follows from our definition that government is a concrete structural requisite for any social system. That is, in all social systems there will be some identifiable group with the qualities described above. Such a group may be highly elaborate and well defined, legally as well as functionally, or it may be extremely loose and subtle, embedded in groups with ostensibly other purposes. Even in the most segmental kinship system, however, there is a government according to our definition, as there is also in highly elaborated political organizations. Our definition also implies that, although any substructure of a society (or other social system) has a relationship to the maintenance of society, government is the most strategic substructure. We are not saying that if you set up a government you automatically create a society. Rather, the minimal requirements for the maintenance of government must allow for society in such a way that both can exist.

always have their own subgroup dynamics that have consequences for the entire community, whereas the dynamics of other political subgroups may or may not have consequences for the entire community. In other words, political groups can be defined as intervening variables between stratification and government and as independent variables acting on both. Government must be seen as an intervening variable between one stratification period and another, or one systems period and another, and as an independent variable acting on stratification. This is what makes political analysis so complex; one needs to be able to see that, in concrete applications of authority, the instrument of authority turns into an independent variable. Without such a view, political analysis is simply residual to some other form.

VIABILITY AND THE FUNCTIONAL ANALYSIS OF CHANGE

Several recent attempts have been made to establish functional categories. Talcott Parsons has produced the best general set, which he has organized into four central functional problems with respect to the maintenance of control; namely, pattern-maintenance, goal attainment, adaptation, and integration. Marion Levy has also established a set of functional and structural requisites for any society, from which government can be seen as the strategic concrete unit for handling crises in solidarity, economic allocation, political allocation, role differentiation, and integration and expression. (I have, in the past, considered it useful to regard the structural requisites of any society, as worked out by Levy, as the functional requisites of government.)

Both Parsons and Levy would, however, require us to make a systematic study of an entire society, from its work habits to its leisure activities, from its kinship groups to the ideas held by competing subgroups, before they would permit us to make an effective analysis of politics. Perhaps there is no escape from this, but I am inclined to the view that a more narrowly limited set of inquiries can treat even the larger functional problems by more indirect means, namely, the study of government.[6]

Almond has inclined to much the same position in his functional categories related to the political system (which is itself, in his view, a conversion mechanism for translating functional inputs of political socialization and recruitment, interest articulation, interest aggregation, and political communication into output structures of rule-making, rule application, and rule adjudication).[7] As I have already suggested, difficulties in this kind of analysis stem from the lack of a firm definition of "political system," with the result that it is virtually impossible to separate the political from other kinds of systems. It is not exactly clear, therefore, how the functions and structures are derived and how they relate to each other. More important, their requisite status remains unspecified.

Perhaps the most important deficiency of the functional approach is that it cannot be tested except in the most extreme conditions. Since large-scale units like societies show considerable adaptive flexibility and their leaders great skill in supplying alternative instruments and modes of operation in order to prevent social breakdown, the viability test — or what Amitai Etzioni calls the survival model on which functionalism is based — may be applied in research only when it is already quite apparent that a society or other unit has become unviable and a system change is in order. In other words, it may only serve as an explication of the painfully obvious. Such criticism, if valid, would suggest that functional analysis would be more useful for historical studies than for prediction, even though its purpose is to delineate theoretically the conditions for system change. On the whole, this criticism must be accepted as valid.

The majority of functionalists work with survival models. This has left them open to the criticism that although so-

---

[6] This is not an attempt to assert the significance of my discipline, which will stand or fall on its merits rather than on claims to subject matter.

[7] See Almond and Coleman, *The Politics of the Developing Areas*, pp. 3–64.

cieties or other social units have changed considerably, the functionalists still see them as the same unit. Very rarely does a society, for example, lose its ability to fulfill the "basic" (i.e., survival) functional prerequisites. This is one of the reasons why it has been claimed that the functional model does not alert the researcher to the dynamics of existing social units.[8]

Whether or not the viability test in functional analysis is scientifically useful is, of course, a matter of the purpose of the analysis. We must ask, however, Is it a good basis for testing the truth or falsehood of propositions? Despite the grave operational weaknesses in this approach (and even if the sole test of science were its operational statements and positivistic explanations), it has the logical advantages of rigorous deductive analyses. Hence, it can maximize the use of logically related facts and thereby eliminate descriptive propositions that are based on faulty conceptualization. But even pure operationalism and inductive methods provide no answer.[9]

Operationalism defines as meaningful that for which empirical tests of meaning are technically precise. This definition admits only one dimension of reality as an acceptable subject matter, however, which is one reason why operationalists are so often charged with triviality. What may be discarded in the interests of precision, and because the investigators' techniques were not sufficiently subtle, may turn out to be the critical variables.

Abraham Kaplan suggests further problems with the "operational" test of entities.

There is also a difficulty of quite another sort. Most scientific concepts, especially the theoretical ones, relate to experience

---

[8] Amitai Etzioni, A Comparative Analysis of Complex Organizations (New York: Free Press of Glencoe, Inc., 1961), pp. 78–79.

[9] As Abraham Kaplan has remarked, "If intelligence is defined only by the tests, how shall we explain why the tests were constructed in just that way, or even why they were constructed at all?" (The Conduct of Inquiry [San Francisco: Chandler Publishing Co., 1964], p. 40). Kaplan also points out that this is not a real shortcoming of operationalism that it is dependent on theories but that it is not a theory itself.

only indirectly. Their empirical meaning depends on their relations to other concepts as fixed by their place in the theory, and it is only these others that have a sufficiently direct application to experience to allow for specifying operations. We do not measure how high is the morale of a group or how deep is the repression of a memory by the manipulation of physical objects in any way at all comparable to the manipulation involved in measuring the temperature of a gas or the hardness of a mineral (both of which are also "intensive" magnitudes like the first two). Operations are used, but the interpretation of their outcome depends on the meanings of an open set of other terms.[10]

The complex and symbolic aspects of politics with which we have been dealing cannot be identified as operations in a narrow and strict sense. That being the case, what utility do they have? The answer is that they provide the theoretical framework from which those variables that organize meaning may be selected. To quote Kaplan again (in a discussion of Peirce), "Meaning is purpose abstracted and generalized so as to fit any occasion. Every meaningful statement, Peirce suggested, may be regarded as determining a correlation between desire and action." [11] What we may say is that meaning is a plan of action, and policy is a statement of plan. Policy becomes the empirical phenomena we attribute to government, and the analysis of policy leads us to the study of desire, the conditions of which are to be found in both consummatory and instrumental values.

The value of functional analysis in general, then, is that it helps us to understand the purposes and meanings of actions. Cognitive mapping is the task that it undertakes. The viability approach merely sharpens the focus, restricting the analysis of purpose to the survival of the unit and a set of meanings based on that purpose. This helps us to understand the properties and widely differing activities of certain systems and leads to the exploration of different levels of meaning, latent and manifest, cognitive

[10] *Ibid.*, pp. 41–42.
[11] *Ibid.*, p. 43.

and emotive. In this sense functionalism relies first on semantic empiricism and only second on operational empiricism; that is, it is pragmatic before it is operational.

How then do such considerations relate to the study of modernization and government's role in it? A range of problems is imposed by modernization. The particular empirical groupings through which the problems are resolved translate these problems into issues adopted by concrete political groups. Government is the strategic concrete group that handles the problems of modernization. It now becomes necessary to identify the implications of government action both in relation to its own survival and in relation to the larger unit of which it is a part. To do this requires an examination of the conditions of viability for government, since alteration in government type will have empirical consequences.

On the one hand, viability may mean the ability of the unit to be maintained in its setting, in which case the requirements of viability must fit all cases of the general type under consideration. On the other hand, it may refer to a change in the setting itself. Such a change, for example, would be transition from a modernizing to an industrializing society.

The transformation from modernization to industrialization involves changes in the economic infrastructure of society such that the main coherence of values, both instrumental and consummatory, is associated with industrial development and the new or accommodated roles are defined accordingly. Industrial enterprises and their adjunctive bodies are the main source of social dynamism. Consummatory values not inclined toward industrialization and the industrial process are departures from the norm.[12]

---

[12] Countries approaching the point of change from modernization to industrialization include Argentina, Chile, Brazil, and Venezuela. Paradoxically, as the transition occurs, political factors become more rather than less pronounced. Governments are less stable and quite often more autocratic. Choices are uncertain, and uncertainty leads to non-rational acts of decision-making. These are the troubles that plague many Latin American countries and that make them so complex and interesting to study. But they are also

Under such circumstances, the independent variable in the over-
all pattern of system change is predominantly economic and no
longer predominantly political. The nature of legitimacy has therefore been altered, since legitimacy is dependent on the moral
sector, the consummatory values of the society (which government must adapt and protect), rather than the efficiency sector,
which embodies instrumental values. These two types of values
are the behavioral boundaries around types of government.
Among modernizing societies, various types of systems represent
different proportions of instrumental and consummatory values.
Changes in this proportion are important only when they are reflected in a new coercion-information balance within the system.
This is an important point since, clearly, changes in incumbents of
political offices do not ordinarily reflect a change in legitimacy.[13]

Legitimacy, we have said, is derived from the two types of
values, consummatory and instrumental. Consummatory values
are based on a particular set of moralities. These may be expressed
in a political ideology, an integrated set of cultural norms that
are widely dispersed in the population, or contradictory sets held
by mutually antagonistic groups. In the case of modernizing
societies, the last situation is encountered most frequently. As a
result of the pre-eminence of political values in modernizing societies, political leaders claim for their views a coherence with
all other values. This is the reason modernizing societies so often
politicize all social life and minimize the sphere of private action.

---

the reason their "revolutions" are suddenly becoming serious ones, not
epiphenomena.

[13] A particular form of government is institutionalized only when it becomes morally valid. Hence, legitimacy is related to a set of conceptions
held by significant members of the polity about the rightness of a political
pattern, which, in turn, provides the pattern with a set of proprieties. Legitimacy is thus a behavioral term referring to a set of limits on governmental
action. It is with reference to legitimacy that right conduct in office is defined. When legitimacy is withdrawn (or dissipated among excessively diverse and competing groups), government is weakened. In this respect, a
general functional test of viability is a description of the basis of legitimacy
in a government.

Morality is thus part of the viability test of government. It is represented by consummatory political values.

A second viability test of government involves its instrumental values. The adequacy of these can be judged on the basis of efficiency. When government is regarded as inefficient or powerless to deal with problems and unable to make provision for the future of the society, support is withdrawn.

The two aspects of legitimacy, consummatory legitimacy and instrumental legitimacy, set the conditions of a government's viability. Efforts of other groups to prevent either one from being maintained provide the "motivation" of government and stimulate governmental policies. If it is correct that both types of legitimacy provide the limits within which government must operate, then the effort to reinforce them, or at least prevent their decline, represents the ultimate political objective.

The achievement of goals by government depends, therefore, on government's making choices adequate to sustain legitimacy, that is, ultimately acceptable in terms of morality and efficiency. In order to make such choices, governments first use information. Knowledge of the object of choice and of the advantages and disadvantages of the various alternatives is required because alternatives embody both consummatory and instrumental values.[14]

THE FUNCTIONAL REQUISITES OF GOVERNMENT

To preserve legitimacy is a necessary object of government. Hence, government requires appropriate information in order to settle problems that arise. The above discussion should make it clear that information includes knowledge of the values involved in a choice situation, both consummatory and instrumental. *In-*

[14] Quite often the two kinds of values impose quite different criteria, as when the instrumentally most advantageous decision would result in an offense to the consummatory values of the community.

formation, then, is one functional requisite of government without which it cannot maintain itself in its setting.

Included in the concept of information is knowledge of the limits within which the public will support action. Beyond such limits, public solidarity will break down, and the need for drastic and coercive action arise, affecting the relationship between consummatory values and instrumental ones. This relationship, always complex, is particularly delicate with governments that are concerned with equity, for example, and that value the individual highly. They are, therefore, restricted in the direct means of coercion open to them. Systems that value the total community and its potentiality to the point that the achievement of community goals is itself a supreme consummatory value, and all other values are subordinate to it, are able to use a high degree of coercion when necessary to achieve such goals. The latter type of system normally requires a practical monopoly of *coercive* functions to carry out its responsibility for reinforcing legitimacy. A second functional requisite of government is thus *coercion.*

There is an important dynamic relationship between these two functional requisites; namely, that the ratio of coercion and information varies inversely. High coercion results in low information, and high information exists where there is low coercion.[15] If the objectives of government are to make effective choices and to find an acceptable balance of the moral and the efficient, the consummatory and the instrumental, the way government goes about this will be reflected in its use of information and coercion.[16]

How is information obtained? One source is the various groups

[15] Coercion leads to poor information, which, in turn, results in a completely chaotic and capricious pattern of political life. Jacob Burckhardt gives a good example of this from the fourteenth and fifteenth centuries in Italy. He points out that at that time the capricious rule and personal despotism of Italian states and principalities made virtually all government illegitimate. Espionage, violence, the purchase and sale of loyalties, were all so widespread that even the family of a ruler was contorted by vindictive purposes. And, as in more modern despotisms, astrology became a substitute for knowledge, and religious bigotry a substitute for morality. See Part I of *The Civilization of the Renaissance in Italy* (New York: Harper Torchbooks, 1958).

[16] The relationship may not always be direct. For example, corruption may be a means of obtaining information during a high-coercion period.

in the society to which government regards itself as accountable. Information presumes communication between government and these groupings. Another source is what might be called the feedback of decision, that is, knowledge of the consequences of actions taken. If an industry is established in a particular area and bottlenecks appear in production, for example, the interruption of the productive process will provide information.[17]

Coercion becomes necessary in the absence of knowledge, when leaders wish to prevent information, or when knowledge from

[17] It is often the case that high-coercion systems are unable to make use of the information that is available. In the Soviet Union there is a difficult predicament. "Committed as servitors to the Central Committee, the social scientists find themselves, sometimes reluctantly, compelled to fulfill the role of ideologists rather than scientists." The result is that even when they engage in operational research on labor efficiency, religion, and a number of other interesting problems, they are barred from following up their findings by asking more theoretical questions. For example, it was discovered that "dissatisfaction in one's job could reduce productivity from 10 to 20 per cent, while satisfaction in work could raise it from 10 to 15 per cent. Their most unusual finding, however, was that the chief cause for dissatisfaction with one's job was (what they called) 'the poor organization of industry.' A workingman, for example, would report in the morning at his factory, but the necessary raw materials would not be on hand for manufacturing to begin. The workingman would then receive his basic daily wage, but through no fault of his own, he would earn no production premia. This situation was wholly unlike the experience of American workers, for whom managerial inefficiency is not a primary factor in job discontent. The Leningrad sociologists are clearly, however, circumscribed in the use they can make of their findings. They do not ask: to what factors in the functioning of the Soviet economy do the workingmen attribute the poor organization of industry? To what extent do they regard such malfunctioning as inherent in planned economy? To what extent do they regard it as arising from remediable bureaucratic abuses, malpractices, and inefficiencies? The poor organization of industry, it was found, was the chief reason for the high labor turnover, for the wandering from job to job. Why have the unions failed to express the workers' discontent? Is there a repressed longing to express their dissatisfaction in political terms?" See Lewis S. Feuer, "Problems and Unproblems in Soviet Social Theory," *Slavic Review, XXIII* (March, 1964), 119, 121. Feuer then points out that even surveys and questionnaires are highly suspect in their findings. "Would a young worker jeopardize his bread by articulating honestly and fully the dissatisfaction he feels when he knows that all he says can be made available to the government? In a totalitarian society, there is an indeterminate margin of error in all interviewing and questionnaires, but the study of that margin of error and the degree of its indeterminacy is the most significant unproblem in the methodology of Soviet social science."

previous decisions has been ignored. It also occurs as punishment. All governments employ some coercion. Their proportions of coercion and information vary. The differences in the mixtures of these two factors are the basis for differentiating the types of authority that I have employed.

Because consummatory and instrumental values are so often in direct conflict with one another (for example, the "old" versus the "new"), coercion is required to restrict such conflicts and information is needed to avoid them. Quite often it becomes a primary aspect of government activity to create new consummatory values and thereby establish, as much as possible, different solidarities and identities. Characteristically, mobilization systems do this by elevating ideology to the level of a religion. I shall discuss this in greater detail in a later chapter.[18]

The mixture of coercion and information that a government employs has an effect on the type of system, because if the proportions are substantially altered the structural relations of government will also be altered.

THE CONTINGENT FUNCTIONS OF GOVERNMENT

The contingent functions of government are indicators of government viability in the sense that they serve to evaluate legitimacy in terms of consummatory values. These functions were derived during the period of my first field work in what was then the Gold Coast. I was struck with the similarity in behavior be-

---

[18] Problems for government involving consummatory values arise in two areas: first, the building of a community, a nation, and a society; second, the formation of characters and personalities suitable to a modern society. The first consummatory value can be called *solidarity*, and by this I mean the shared feelings that give the members of a group a sense of mutual responsibility. The second consummatory value can be called *identity*, and by this I mean individuals' defined sense of worth and insight into the character of their relations with one another. The consummatory values embodied in modernization, then, are solidarity and identity; and the functional requisites of government, that is, coercion and information, operate with these as moral limits or boundaries.

tween individuals who followed their chiefs in the rural areas and those who followed the prime minister in the towns. Closer analysis of the roles of chieftaincy and the particular charismatic leadership of Kwame Nkrumah showed an amazing number of parallels. In both instances the occupants of the roles grew beyond ordinary proportions, taking on certain sacred, or sacred-appearing characteristics. These characteristics were more significant for the maintenance of authority than their actual concrete achievements.

Struck with the similarity between chieftaincy and charismatic leadership as functional equivalents, I realized afterward that the reason for this functional equivalency was that both chieftaincy and charismatic authority were specific subtypes of government. Insofar as the functions of chieftaincy and charisma were similar, it was because both were forms of government. Hence, the functions would apply to all government, including constitutional government. In other words, it seemed to me that in examining the functions of a particular government in the Gold Coast, I had uncovered a universal set of functions for government. These were (1) sanctional source, that is, the source of social norms;[19] (2) symbolic referent, that is, the symbolic link between past and future that joins people together (one might call this the "immortality" function, which will be discussed later on); (3) integrational integer, that is, the responsibility of government for the orderly arrangement and performance of the roles in the system, including governmental roles; (4) ethnic or subethnic definition, that is, the definition of membership in society on the basis of race, nation-state, or the like.[20]

In the case of the Gold Coast, the performers of these functions

[19] David Easton has regarded this function as so central that he has, in effect, based his definition of a political system around it — the authoritative allocation of values. See *The Political System* (New York: Alfred A. Knopf, 1953).

[20] See my book, *Ghana in Transition* (rev. ed.; New York: Atheneum, 1963), p. 305. Here these functional requisites were directly employed in the context of a modernizing society. See also chapter xv for their application to the problem of retraditionalization around the role of a presidential monarch.

had changed from the government of a particular ethnic group by a chief and his council to the government of a national society through charismatic authority employed by a prime minister and his cabinet. Further analysis showed that although these functions were important they were less highly generalized than coercion and information and were contingent upon the way government handled the latter. Nevertheless, the impact of changes in the coercion-information balance, insofar as it affected legitimacy, could be observed in these "contingent" functions, and thus they could be used to help explain in substantive terms how systems changes occur.

The contingent functions, for example, are of great help in answering questions about charisma. What are its ingredients? What happens if charismatic authority changes to another kind, as it would if a system change occurred because the mixture of coercion and information had changed (and the relationship between decision-making and accountability had changed)? Or, to take another example, violations of legitimacy may demonstrate themselves first in the contingent functions. It may be that available information indicates that the problems of a society are so difficult that coercion ought to be employed in order to change the immediate limits of the situation. This, if legitimacy is not to be destroyed, will involve manipulation of consummatory values. The mobilization system or the modernizing autocracy may be a better way to solve the problems and initiate modernization than a reconciliation system. If the manipulation of values is unsuccessful, then coercion will have violated legitimacy and government will change to another type. The violation of legitimacy will have been revealed when government no longer served as a sanctional source, a symbolic referent, an integrational integer, and a source of ethnic or subethnic definition, that is, when it failed to perform its contingent functions.

Government may appear to violate the more devoutly held proprieties, with the result that it can no longer be accepted as a sanctional source. It may become so intensely disliked by the public that as a symbolic referent it has negative rather than positive associations. As an integrational integer, people may try to by-pass it and therefore reduce its central significance. Finally, people may decide to leave the country and adopt another ethnic definition or citizenship. Any of these occurrences would reflect a serious condition in society with respect to the legitimacy of government. The contingent functions are ultimately a means of describing identity and solidarity in a community. Failures in either of the two functional requisites (information and coercion) are registered first in the contingent functions and account for changes from one type of system to the other.

Can the pressures on government be studied in such general terms? Can such categories impose a standard of evaluation for the performance of the functional requisites? I think so, but we require more analytic categories for the purpose. Actions by government to handle the problem load form a pattern that can be divided into structural requisites and contingent structures. These structural requisites and contingent structures may be used to study the outputs, or activities, of government. Outputs represent decisions designed to affect loyalty through social mobility (that is, decisions that affect the social stratification of the system as a whole) as well as decisions designed to manipulate values, the non-rational component of political manipulation.

THE STRUCTURAL REQUISITES OF GOVERNMENT

The structural requisites of government are, at minimum, two. All governments require a *structure of authoritative decision-making* and a *structure of accountability*. By authoritative decision-making, I mean a pattern for making decisions that the members of the unit regard as legitimate. By accountability, I mean that government, as a decision-maker, must be answerable to a group other than itself.

Different types of systems mix the proportions of decision-

making and accountability differently in response to the proportions of coercion and information. Mobilization systems tend to
have low accountability, whereas reconciliation systems tend to
have high accountability. Changes in the mixture or proportions
will induce changes in the type of system. Hence, if greater accountability should develop in a mobilization system, according
to this theory, more information would be produced and the
government would move in the direction of a reconciliation
system. The more hierarchical the structure of authoritative
decision-making, the less accountability in the system, and the
more accountability, the less hierarchical the structure. Not only
are the two structural and functional requisites thus dynamically
interrelated, but it can be seen that hierarchy plays the same role
in modernizing societies as it did in traditional ones, and with the
same consequences.

As in traditional societies, authoritative decision-making in
modernizing ones can be *hierarchical, pyramidal,* or *segmental.*
Command or military systems are an example of the first type,
federal systems of the second, and regional systems and the international system of the third (in the sense of coalitions between
equal members forming or breaking up according to the nature of
a particular conflict). Those that have been called unitary systems
would fall between the hierarchical and pyramidal forms.

The structural requisite of accountability is indicated by the
degree of *influence* and *control* exerted over government by non-
governmental or quasi-governmental bodies, such as statutory
bodies, trade unions, political parties, and the like, and the patterns of consent through legislatures or other representative
groupings — in other words, the degree of control that is manifested over the executive. A high coercion situation will show itself
in hierarchical authority and low accountability. A high information situation will show itself in high accountability and pyramidal
or segmental authority.[21] The functions depend on the structures

[21] I have deliberately avoided terms like totalitarianism and democracy because they are customarily associated with particular forms of government

as follows: Government obtains information through the groups to which it is, in varying degree, accountable. Government exercises coercion through the decisions it takes and their enforcement. Changes in the relationship between coercion and information result from changes in the relationship between decision-making and accountability. The functional and structural requisites are thus in dynamic relationship to one another, with alterations in the one automatically registering alterations in the other; such alterations indicate a change in the system of authority that each government represents.

I will return to the analysis of these relationships in succeeding chapters. Now, however, I want to discuss the contingent structures of government that are of particular relevance to modernizing societies.

CONTINGENT STRUCTURES

At this point I would like to emphasize that the structural requisites and their contingent structures lead us to the analysis of policy and its consequences just as the functional requisites and their contingent structures lead us to the analysis of authority. The contingent structures are important because they link the viability of government to efficiency, that is ,to its ability to realize instrumental values. Policy is the mechanism whereby problems of the system are actually handled. Policies result from the operation of structural requisites, that is, the structure of authoritative decision-making and the structure of accountability. The actual units involved may include highly organized and differentiated instruments, such as a cabinet government or Politburo, as well as localized and fragmental ones. The structure of accountability reveals

---

and practices. It is quite possible to have a high information system in which there is, nevertheless, very little democracy as we understand it in the West. It is true, I think, that, in the long run, high information systems will become democratic in terms understandable in the West, and I will comment on this in subsequent chapters.

the responsiveness of the system to various reference groups in the community. Some may be, in effect, veto groups (as in the case of a legislature); others may be interest and influence groups, such as trade unions, business organizations, or professional bodies. The two structures, authoritative decision-making and accountability, may be viewed as two different aspects of policy-making. Like production and consumption, they can best be studied by taking a sample of policy decisions over a period of time and by asking about the criteria used to define the particular decisional problem, the projected outcome and its effects, and the various bodies that serve as reference groups for the decision-makers. Essentially, the relationship between the decision-makers and the groups to which they are accountable is a reference-group question of a special sort. The reference groups are themselves part of the system of authority. What we call contingent structures are, in effect, an elaboration of the structural requisites and represent analytical substructures of government. These are, first, the substructure of political recruitment, which is the mechanism whereby people are brought into government, whether by elections, co-optation, appointment, or other means, and the effects this structure has on (a) stratification, because it represents a mobility factor within the political hierarchy, and (b) political groups, since they are directly involved in the recruitment process as a means of gaining their objectives. The second substructure, that of enforcement and punishment, involves the mechanisms whereby the limits of roles are defined as well as the violations and amendments in roles and the degrees of tolerance for discrepancies between ideal and actual role behavior. In systems where there is very little tolerance, or where every violation is taken as somehow symbolic of a violation of the society (what Durkheim meant by repressive law), one expects to find a very different kind of justice from that in systems where law is nonsymbolic and justice is defined as individual rather than social. The third substructure, resource determination and allocation, consists of the instruments by which resources in the community are deployed by government, which may or may not own and/or operate them. The fourth substructure is a consent group, from which assent to a decision is required before it becomes binding. Such a consent group may be official, like a parliament; semi-official, like a Politburo or central committee in a Communist society; or unofficial but required, as in countries where interest groups have special powers.

Whereas the functional requisites and contingent functions, when taken together, give some indication of the nature of ideology and loyalty in a society and of the symbolic presence of government, the structural requisites and contingent structures provide a basis for evaluating the consequences of government for the society. This last can best be observed in restratification and also in ideological manipulation by government.

These comments complete our sketch of the main variables that will be used for analysis. At its most general level, it has consisted of four main parts, with the relationships between the parts constituting a system. The parts are themselves composed of variables that, again at the most general level of analysis, form their own subsystems. The four main parts are as follows: (1) parameters: consummatory and instrumental values; (2) independent variables: coercion and information; (3) dependent variables: authoritative decision-making and accountability; (4) intervening variables: developmental types (authority systems). The concrete units are political groups, including voluntary associations, political parties, interest groups, and the like, which are the carriers of values, and government.

The study of the functional and structural requisites does not require a drastic reformulation of tried and true questions. We still ask questions about the nature of leadership in government, the way in which government works, and whether or not decision-making is highly centralized or segmented, capricious and immune to responsibilities or highly responsible to claims and consent groups. Perhaps we may be able to attach a wider meaning to the conventional distinctions between competitive and pluralistic systems, which will involve political groups and wide segments from the stratification system, and the narrower and more exclusive forms. These are key questions in political science and remain so here. My usage links them to the problem of system change and allows wide comparisons to be made. Hypotheses about change and resistance to change, for example, that I have applied to traditional societies can also be applied to modernizing ones. Examining the ways in which the functional requisites operate will indicate the values of the system. The structural requisites and contingent structures indicate the responsiveness of government policies to the problems posed. An analysis of policy will also show how government is organized, the degree of hierarchy and the degree of instrumentalism embodied in its values. Figure 13 contains a diagram of these relationships.

Figure 13 requires further explanation. The method of analysis involves two systems. The first system, A–A3, involving relationships between modernization, stratification, political subsystems, and values, represents a set of relationships between discontent and ideology. This system is identifiable at the level of the total society. Expression of discontent, which increases with increasing modernization, varies in status, class, and caste systems and is intensified or channeled depending upon the way in which stratification, A1 is organized. As suggested in chapter iv, most modernizing societies have elements of both class and status hierarchies, and some, such as India or South Africa, have all three forms present to some extent. Variations in stratification, then, particularize discontent and provide a mobilizable basis for political organization.

Such political organizations, A2, we have called political subsystems and have, in chapter vi, attempted to point out the relevant variables. Particular forms of leadership-follower relationships, the articulation of grievances, and the organization of discontent in order to direct it toward particular political accomplishments are all found in political subgroups such as factions, coalitions, parties of representation, and parties of solidarity. The efforts of

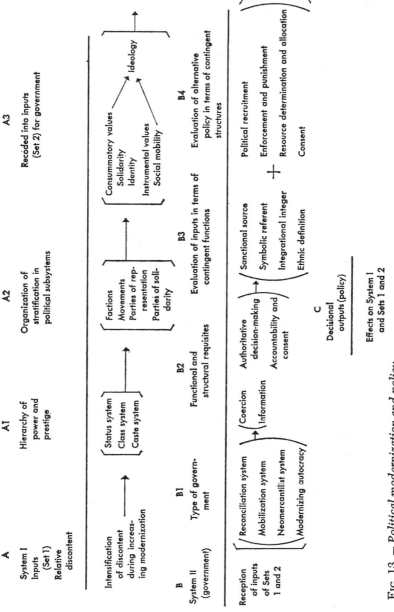

FIG. 13. — *Political modernization and policy.*

these groups to transform grievances into rights and to capture power, help, in fact, to establish authority. In this respect, political parties, for example, are intervening variables between stratification — which embodies norms about the propriety of power and prestige rankings — and values, both consummatory and instrumental, A3, both of which represent the outer limits within which legitimacy is recognized.

Consummatory values are related to stratification and political actions but are cast in a wider pattern of ultimate ends. They are methodologically non-rational, that is, they have consequences for individual and social actions that go beyond purely empirical ends. Technically, we may say that they involve empirical means germane to non-empirical ends. To the degree that these ultimate ends pervade particular acts, we say that the acts are predominantly consummatory.

Instrumental values are methodologically rational in the sense that they are empirical. They are empirical means germane to empirical ends, or as Pareto called them, "intermediate" ends. Most economic objectives are of this nature. When empirical means are employed to achieve instrumental ends, we are able to observe a norm of rationality through its practice. If the ends of a society are instrumental, with consummatory aspects reduced to a minimum, or segregated, we may say that its values are predominantly instrumental.

The ramifications of the relationship between consummatory and instrumental values can be observed in terms of structure and behavior. Structurally, consummatory values provide the basis for solidarity in the community. They are a community-building factor in social life. Behaviorally, they provide identity for individuals. In fact, they create a range of identities that are mutually coherent.

Instrumental values, on the other hand, affect the intermediate range of ends, which may be identified in the widest context as command over resources. Hence, social mobility is the critical consequence of instrumental values in the sense that it is largely a maximizing concept (that is, the individual maximizes his command over resources). To the degree that a society is predominantly consummatory, we may assume that it will not be interested in social mobility and the maximizing process. To the degree that it is predominantly instrumental, it may be assumed to be interested in maximizing its resources and, therefore, concerned with social mobility. The latter type of society is thus the one most directly involved in modernization and development.

Under special circumstances, societies can combine instrumental and consummatory values. Indeed, the special value of a mobilization system is that it elevates certain instrumental objectives (industrialization, raising per capita income) to the level of symbolic and transcendental ends. The result is that intermediate and ultimate ends are the same. My assumption, however, is that *this condition can only be temporary and will produce long-run conditions of conflict in solidarity and identity.*

These differences in values may be given a more unified expression by means of an ideology. Different ideologies represent a ranking or priority of values, consummatory and instrumental, along with a recipe for action or policy. They represent an effort to organize ideas deriving from consummatory and instrumental values into a doctrine affecting solidarity and identity, on the one hand, and to employ values appropriate to stratification, on the other.

The set of relationships embodied in an ideology may be identified as a system in itself. But as a system, it shows certain specific relationships to government, the strategic subsystem for the larger system, B–B4. From this point of view, each of the variables in the first system becomes an input for the second. Inputs thus arise, in the process of modernization, from stratification systems, from political group and subsystem actions, and from the limits placed on government by the mixture of consummatory and instrumental values on which legitimacy is based. These inputs are then screened and coded by governments. Not all governments screen and code in the same manner, however.

Each type, *B1* (reconciliation, mobilization, neomercantilist, and modernizing autocracy), because it represents a different set of relationships between coercion and information and authority and accountability, *B2*, will evaluate the inputs differently. What represents a symbolically significant input in a highly coercive mobilization system may be considered symbolically unimportant in a reconciliation system based on high information. The evaluation of inputs, then, will vary between systems of government, and the significance assigned to each may be observed in terms of the contingent functions and structures of government *B3–4*. On this basis, policy will be made.

This second system — government — because it occupies a strategic place in the larger system, has independent power to affect, through its decisions, the range of inputs of System I. Indeed, policy *C*, is directed toward just that aim. Insofar as the system of government changes the character of modernization and therefore stratification, political groups, and values, it can be treated as the independent variable. Insofar as it merely responds to inputs, it is an intervening variable. It is in industrial societies as distinct from modernizing ones that government as an intervening variable comes to prevail. There the independent power of government to act is drastically curtailed by the complexity of the industrial process itself.

Finally, it will be suggested further that as modernization proceeds and a society moves closer to industrialization the government will find itself in increasing difficulty. The conversion mechanism through which government as the independent variable becomes government as an intervening variable is most complicated and barely understood. *It is one of the central hypotheses of this study that this conversion is most satisfactorily achieved by some form of mobilization system.*

The policy implications of this hypothesis are rather frightening. In Latin America, for example, the implication would be that as modernizing processes become transformed into industrialization processes we may expect to see an increase in the power and number of mobilization systems whether of the right, as might occur in Argentina with a neo-Peronista regime, or of the left, as in Cuba. More explicitly, if the Alliance for Progress is a great success in Latin America, it is likely to result in the creation of more mobilization systems, which are by their very nature offensive to most Americans.

Some of the implications of this set of assumptions will be discussed in the following chapters. We have not followed the arrangements of the diagram, however, in presenting the material. For the moment, we are concerned with the general theory of political modernization rather than its empirical applications. Meanwhile, some illustrations will be of use in clarifying the foregoing remarks.

TWO HYPOTHETICAL CASES

Let us consider the following combinations of the variables. Relative scarcity has begun to decline, and inequality is spaced out among a highly complex set of differentials. Political groups include in their membership parties and coalitions of interest groups organized in parties of representation. Political leadership of the parties is largely institutionalized, with virtually no opportunities for charismatic leadership. Authoritative decision-making is widely dispersed through a highly organized pattern of central and local authorities rather than concentrated in a single body and is counterpoised with a consent mechanism that has, at times, the potentiality of active decision-making. Accountability is regularized and elaborated and, in addition, highly dispersed throughout the organized groups of the system. The contingent structures show that political recruitment is based on elections rather than appointment, and that resource determination and allocation are decentralized, regulated by policy but rarely directed. Enforcement and punishment operate largely through a framework of restitutive law. Legislative bodies act as consent groups.

How might we describe such a unit in general? We might describe it as pluralistic, constitutional, and decentralized, a system having a high degree of information and a low degree of coercion. We would expect to find that the basis of its policy was a system of mutual compromises worked out between competing groups in which the fringe groups of the coalitional parties served to remind government of its responsibilities. We would also expect government under such circumstances to be relatively conservative, at best interested in widening the mobility opportunities of the system without altering the stratification system itself. Relative scarcity would not be the most pressing problem; however, inequality would. By inequality in this situation, I mean the contradictions that arise when the power and prestige hierarchy is based more and more on education; education itself becomes the crucial entry point into the hierarchy, which, in the name of equality, has been transformed into a hierarchy of talent and ability (natural inequality).

Our description would fit the system of the United States. The English system would also fit this description, although with some modifications: There political groups are more clearly parties of representation than coalitions. Authoritative decision-making is more highly centralized and more clearly segregated from consent groups. A customary constitution and the Crown as an embodiment of custom serve as a sanctional source and a symbolic referent as well as a basis for ethnic definition; the prime minister and cabinet serve the integrational function.

Consider another case, a caste or class system in which generational, religious, and ethnic factors generate extreme forms of cultural strain. A political movement arises that attempts to achieve large-scale change by rearranging roles and by creating some new ones. The movement, which embodies widely different elements in the population, is so diverse in membership that it is held together only by a charismatic leader who transforms the movement into a party of solidarity. Successful in occupying positions of significance, the political bureau of the party of solidarity becomes the effective government. Consummatory values are expressed through the charismatic leader, who serves as a sanctional source, symbolic referent, integrational integer, and embodiment of the ethnic definition. Authoritative decision-making inheres in the leader and his close associates. There are few consent groups. Those groups that might have acted in such a capacity are eliminated (for example, army leaders, leading civil servants, or other political parties). Since it is always possible that within the authoritative decision-making body there might develop an implicit consent group, purges become characteristic. Political recruitment is largely appointive. Enforcement and punishment reflect a high degree of repressive law. Resource determination and allocation are controlled by the political leaders. Information is low and coercion high. Choice is difficult, expensive, and dangerous. Consummatory values are imperiled because of political cynicism. The danger to instrumental values arises from excessive costs.

These two hypothetical cases illustrate two modernizing situations that are at opposite ends of a continuum and tend toward the normative ideal types I have called the secular-libertarian and the sacred-collectivity models. They define their political problems differently, and they see different alternative courses of action.

The crucial conditions of political choice are the functional requisites of government. Without information, there is no choice. There is no choice because there is no perception of alternatives or courses of action to be pursued. With only a little information, choice is capricious, and capriciousness creates tension and opposition. With a great deal of information, choice becomes rational.

Without coercion, there are no consequences of choice. Choice without consequence is tantamount to no choice at all. Coercion does not necessarily require physical force or even direct control. It may mean merely the laying down of particular values that define loyalty. It is a system of public discipline.

Choice, the primary activity of all governments, is determined then by the relationship between coercion and information. The choice of a government differs from the choices of all other groups or individuals in that it is binding upon all the members of the unit. The mixture of coercion and information determines the structural arrangements of government, that is, the pattern of decision-making and accountability. The forms of authority and the proportions of consummatory and instrumental values blended in each situation of choice become the basis for the analysis of modernization. Thus the same general categories employed in the analysis of traditional societies may be employed in the analysis of modernizing ones (see Figure 14).

Value Type	Authority Type		
	Hierarchical	Pyramidal	Segmental
Consummatory	A China	C Israel	Soviet bloc
Instrumental	B Morocco	D India	Western alliance

FIG. 14. — *Types of modernizing societies. I know of no modern country that at present has a segmental system of authority. The possibility of its emergence, however, should not be completely discounted.*

AUTHORITY TYPES AND VALUES

So far we have seen the problems of modernizing nations as a set of responses to the inputs of innovation and as a set of dynamic functional categories for analysis. Typically, modernizing nations show the social dislocations produced by ill-digested bits of modernization, and the response to innovation is rarely smooth or pleasant.

Once a period of modernization has occurred and an independent polity seeks to control it, a kind of retraditionalization begins. This retraditionalization involves the stabilization of a pattern of authority. Not just any effort at retraditionalization will do, however. One characteristic pattern involves the use of tradition to validate current practices. This is frequently achieved by sentimentalizing the past and rendering it functional to present authority. Sometimes this is a deliberate policy choice, an explicit manipulation of ideas, as when a political leader incorporates traditional symbols of state or ancient practices that seem to symbolize national pride. In many of the African countries today, for example, we find attempts to show associations with ancient civilizations and to explain the paucity of modern artifacts in indigenous culture in terms of foreign exploitation.[22]

There are, of course, many other ways to assert authority. The charismatic leader may successfully ritualize his personal power. The modernizing monarch may use his traditional position as the legitimization for change, as Hassan II has done in Morocco.[23] Or the framework of law may be contrived so as to encompass change by mediating between rival claimants for improvement, or innovation, or privilege. The systems of authority we have mentioned tend to handle this problem differently. The mobilization system tries to rebuild society in such a way that both the instrumentalities of government and the values associated with change are altered. Countries of this type in Africa, for example, have regimes that incline toward the belief that in order to produce the "new Africa" the structural precedents of African society,

[22] See, for example, Cheikh Anta Diop, *Nations Negres et Culture* (Paris: Présence Africaine, 1955). See also G. K. Osei, *Fifty Unknown Facts about the African* (pamphlet; Accra, 1963), which includes the "unknown facts" that Pushkin had African ancestry, that Africans taught the Greeks geography, and that Hannibal was an African.

[23] See Rom Landau, *Hassan II, King of Morocco* (London: George Allen & Unwin, Ltd., 1962), chapter viii.

especially the stratification structure, must be radically altered
and a new system of loyalties created around the idea that economic progress is the basis of a modern society. For such changes,
the consummatory values of the system must validate hierarchical
authority and invalidate consent groups. Acceptable accountability groups are typically factions within the party in a single-
party system or are small groups within the bureaucracy, trade
unions, or other functionally significant groupings. Enforcement
and punishment are applied to many aspects of social life, since
total allegiance, or at least a monopoly of the individual's loyalties,
is required. Anything short of that may be considered subversive.
There is considerable manipulation of ideologies that are functional to the industrializing process, which in itself asserts the
need for discipline in the society by automatically imposing
greater coherence among roles and by making necessary the
allocation of resources, which in turn involves planning, government control, and/or government ownership of property. Recruitment is based on (1) political power (that is, political leaders
who may have independent followings and therefore constitute
politically significant individuals), (2) party loyalty (that is,
those who have served the party or the state exceptionally well
and expect some post or sinecure on an official level), and (3)
skill and talent (that is, those with the necessary training to be
managers and organizers). The last group is normally enlarged at
the expense of the other two, a difficult process.[24]

[24] One indication of the status of a new government is the particular mixture of the three types of recruitment. In many modernizing nations, the
ministerial system of government is extremely useful because it allows political decisions to be made by those who have been rewarded for party loyalty
with remunerative party posts. They, in turn, rely for their own sustained
tenure on the effectiveness of their civil service staff or other experts who remain subordinate to them. Equally as useful is a host of advisory boards,
committees, and the like, to which people with political power (that is, an
important following) can be appointed. If there are important issues of land
tenure, for example, a land tenure commission may be set up, advisory to
a minister of land tenure or a minister of local government. If the trade
unions are important, some trade union leaders may be given posts on a
labor advisory commission to a minister of trade and labor, or other special

Mobilization systems show an unmistakable tendency toward what I have called omnivorousness.[25] Implicit in the system is direct government control over constantly widening sectors of social life, eventually coming to include family life and kinship, education and training, to the exclusion and obliteration of the idea of privacy. This view of society in its extreme form conceives of the state as a living organism embodying the immortality of a cause and linked with a people through the continuity of the state. Extreme cases of mobilization systems are thus philosophically monistic. With its great stress on loyalty, the organic interrelationship of the community can be described as an effort to combine two competing and contradictory practices, the establishment of the functional requisites of government and the alteration of the hierarchy of power and prestige. The extreme case is almost invariably totalitarian. Most new nations fall far short of that.

Perhaps the most important conflict that the mobilization system entertains is that between the political party and technical bureaucracy. The parties, as one observer put it, have an "itch" to command and periodically assert the primacy of the party of solidarity. This would suggest that the holders of consummatory values in a system are centered in the party of solidarity, whereas those holding instrumental values may be found more often in the technical services. In other words, a conflict over values occurs between what might be called political ideologues and technocrats. The party of solidarity will play a mediating role in modernization until its characteristic of solidarity begins to disappear. At that point, it will assert its command, accompanied by an increase in coercion in government and a decline of infor-

---

assignments such as the preparation of memorandums on labor conditions, housing, and so on. The mobilization system that can effectively blend the three forms of recruitment can promote the mutual interdependence of voluntary associations and semigovernment commissions for the maintenance of an effective pattern of authority.

[25] See David E. Apter, "Nationalism, Government, and Economic Growth," *Economic Development and Cultural Change*, VII (January, 1959).

mation that reduces the significance of tecnical information in decision-making.

The opposite form of authority type, the reconciliation system, with its pyramidal authority, has retrospective and residual consummatory values that encourage compromises between groups expressing prevailing political objectives and views. Since reconciliation systems consist of single political units made up of constituent political units that have not lost their political identity, they can be relatively loose confederations that have a recognized structure or much more highly organized parliamentary regimes. But such systems must demonstrate equity, which may require enormous changes in the social structure and may, in fact, not be forthcoming.

Reconciliation systems take several forms. Their classic problem is that, during modernization, consummatory values give way to instrumental values but the instrumental ones remain unrealized. This is a danger whether the reconciliation system is the Western conciliar model or a single-party system in which a broad coalition of interests and subgroups are represented that mediate their differences in consultation with one another.[26]

The modernizing autocracy is an interesting case, for it is able to use consummatory values to maintain authority even if instrumental values remain unfulfilled. It is not that such a system remains unchanged by innovation but that innovation is somehow rendered into terms that people perceive as traditional. Hence, a change that might be harmful to certain forms of traditional society, or even subversive, such as the spread of education, becomes the opposite. Japan is a case in point, where modern education was seized upon directly and spread throughout the country. Buganda is another example. These modernizing autocracies are usually combinations of the other authority types in the

[26] Political recruitment in the latter type of system is determined by the all-or-nothing list system, that is, the system in which the winning list in an election takes all the seats in the assembly and which is based on considerable autonomy in the subgroup structure of the society. Dahomey, for example, would fall in this category.

following respect: through religious or political beliefs, the monistic quality of the state is confined largely to the political area and the other areas of the society retain a large amount of privacy and pluralism. Such systems tend not to take over property, for example, on the grounds that all property ultimately belongs to the king anyway and private entrepreneurs are helping to develop it. Social life is generally regulated by custom, although too great a departure from custom will politicize the custom in question. The most important feature of the modernizing autocracy is that the hierarchy of roles expands through modernization but does not change its shape. Here is its greatest point of difference from the mobilization system, which modernizes by changing the shape of the stratification system itself.

To mention again an example given in chapter iii, in Uganda, the Buganda kingdom was able to employ new skills, modernize the school system, and expand social welfare activities. A civil service replaced the patrimonial bureaucratic system, meanwhile retaining intact the traditional modes of authority. Hence, despite real change, the modernizing autocracy kept its character and manifested a profound internal solidarity based on ethnic factors or religion, by means of which the political leaders or king, who makes claims on the members of the system and controls them, retained support.

We can see then that the value problems of these types of systems are fundamentally different from one another; this has important implications for the definition of modernization problems and the ways a country deals with them.

THE PACE OF MODERNIZATION

In the mobilization system, the goals of economic growth are not only important but gradually acquire a certain sacred quality. Therefore, it does not matter that many industrialization goals are unattainable. Indeed, many of them must be placed just

beyond the normal capacities of available technology and resources. This reduces the importance of instrumental values for
establishing legitimacy. To attempt to achieve what is in effect
the unachievable provides the basis for legitimacy in government.
Institutions can be created for the purpose of obliterating others
that are identified as restricting the processes of economic development. The social cement that sustains the system of authority
is a new-found puritanism. Some form of socialism is its contemporary expression, with an emphasis on discipline and hard
work. This emphasis makes it possible to restructure society so that
roles and tasks that are functional to a modern economic order
will become dominant and displace traditional ones. This is why
the mobilization system places great stress on militancy and party
organization. Government enterprise becomes the major mechanism for economic growth. Correspondingly, high government investments are made in education and social welfare on grounds
that an efficient labor force is the *sine qua non* of economic development. Such systems need a powerful organizational nucleus to
take the major responsibility for the establishment and achievement of goals.

The reconciliation system, on the other hand, with its pyramidal
authority and a relatively weak emphasis on consummatory
values, cannot raise instrumental values to the level of the sacred.
Indeed, its sacred values are confined to a legal framework that
embodies beliefs about the regulation of group conflict. Reconciliation systems depend for their legitimacy on the efficiency of
their framework, which, if challenged, can easily be transposed
into another type. Instrumentalism in the reconciliation type is
directly related to pyramidal authority, through which power and
belief are distributed in such a way that the entire system is based
on conflict and competition.

Just as political power is more diffuse in the reconciliation
system, so is economic power. Private entrepreneurship is normally
the characteristic means toward further development, and modernization is embodied in the entrepreneurial role, delimited by

a legal framework. It may happen, of course, that the reconciliation system becomes politically stalemated; the framework becomes loosened, and the system then changes to something else. Goals in such systems tend to be moderate and require a high rate of "payoff" in order to keep people reasonably happy. Relative scarcity and inequality are typical. Indeed, the unevenness of modernization is reflected in inequality based largely on economic criteria of stratification and reinforced by differences in educational opportunity, status competition among the powerful, class competition between the rich and the poor, and quite often, elements of caste rank originating in ethnic discrimination.

The modernizing autocracy exhibits certain structural similarities with the mobilization system — a hierarchical structure of authority and consummatory values in the political sphere. However, precisely because the modernizing autocracies modernize not by changing roles but by enlarging the potentialities of roles and the hierarchy, the result is not only greater stability but also more limited economic goals. Hence, economic growth is usually more restricted and less symbolic than in the mobilization system. If the latent consequences of modernization produce political groups that represent a challenge to traditional authority, the challenge is likely to be met by a combination of instrumental values and traditionalism that will appear as militarism.

It will be noted that I have not discussed the military oligarchy, which, possessing characteristics very similar to a modernizing autocracy, often emerges after the achievements of the latter have begun to threaten the legitimacy of the system. In Japan in the 1930's, for example, when the modernizing autocracy was successful in moving toward an industrial revolution, the result was the evolution of political parties, trade unions, and the like, each clamoring for greater democratization of the system. If this had been granted, coercion would have been drastically reduced; consent groups (the Diet, for example) would have become much more powerful; and a change to a reconciliation system would have been very likely. Instead, a military oligarchy took over and, by blending tradition with industrialization, established a very special relationship between consummatory and instrumental values by means of a state religion. Ideologies combining nationalism and socialism are frequently the result in such cases, although the combination is not always found in military oligarchies nor are military oligarchies the only forms of government in which it occurs.

The striking feature of military oligarchies, however, is that they *fail* to modernize society. As Morris Janowitz points out, although military roles are technological, rational, and bureaucratic and in a real sense represent organizational modernity, they lack the ability to modernize a total community. Perhaps one reason for this is that military personnel tend to take the purposes of society as given, and restrict their interest to carrying out limited tasks. Even when military officers take political office, they tend to reduce the importance of their erstwhile comrades and use the army to maintain themselves in power instead of as a modernizing instrument. The most notable example of this is Egypt. Similar instances are Burma, the Sudan, and Pakistan.

Other reasons for this failure may be found in the military role itself. Either it is technical, involving a certain limitation of competence based on expertise, or it is conceived of as romantic, in which case it is highly unrealistic and likely to be unsuccessful except within the military structure. At the non-commissioned officer level, what might be called the "sergeant-major" mentality is committed to the existence of the organization and is the most limited and bureaucratic of all. The "private" mentality is not unlike that of many habitual offenders in prison. They need the system in order to hate it and need the discipline in order to structure their feelings of violence. These are, of course, merely speculations on my part. It may also be true, and I suspect it is very often true in modernizing societies, that privates are better fed in the army than at home, that sergeant-majors are similar to clerks in their outlook, and that officers feel like civil servants but are too poorly trained to engage in civilian trades.[27]

Having sketched in the functional requisites and their contingent structures, the structural requisites and their contingent structures, and the relation of both pairs to values and modernization, I would now like to turn to the functional aspects of government in greater detail and, in particular, their relationship to political behavior.

[27] The differences between the structural variables in the modernizing autocracy and the military oligarchy are, first, that the military oligarchy usually has a *junta* or bureaucratic leadership that draws its authority from its military rather than its political role and, second, that the military as a subsystem is strategic for the rest of the system.

8

THE FORMATION OF POLITICAL VALUES

In the preceding chapter it was suggested that political values, which were divided into two types, consummatory and instrumental, could be studied in terms of legitimacy. The consummatory aspects of legitimacy were specified as solidarity and identity. The instrumental aspects of legitimacy were discussed in terms of the effectiveness of policy-making. The implications of these aspects of legitimacy can be studied by a form of structural analysis involving a set of functional and structural categories, some requisite and others contingent. This approach directs our attention to the various types of modernizing governments that embody somewhat different forms of legitimacy. It is dynamic analysis in the sense that it is based on the examination of a continuous process in which political forms change, with implications both for the process and for the societies under examination.

It will be readily observed that we have taken consummatory values more or less for granted so far (even though they have been given a strategic position in the approach to analysis employed here). Some might be led to the conclusion that this term has some mysterious or inexplicable quality. It might be argued that, though interesting, it is too mystical to be persuasive as a theoretical category. The reason this term has not been further defined is that probing such matters raises methodological problems so complex that it is almost self-defeating to attempt explanation. Certainly, explanation would carry us away from the structural forms of analysis and into the behavioral, to the human aspects of the formation and perception of proprieties. Indeed, it would bring us to a discussion of the relationship between political and religious life.

In terms of our discussion, we intend the proper subject matter of religion to be understood as transcendental ends. By this I mean ultimate commitments that become personal ends for individuals and cultural ends for societies. Such commitments are non-rational in character. "Political religion" will thus refer to those transcendental ends that define the state as a moral entity. In this sense political religion is the basis for the norms of a society,[1] which we have called its consummatory values.

THE BEHAVIORAL ORIGINS OF LEGITIMACY

Extraordinary men have come forward from time to time in politics as well as in the pulpit; and for much the same reasons, they are effective in establishing authority. Moreover, they give rise to artistic symbols, some of which they themselves manipulate — in particular, language. Such leaders are linguistic artists. They express experience through a moral language that itself becomes art. The significance of art in politics is that it communicates the moral experiences of the leaders and serves to support their authority. When this form of communication is generalized to society, it becomes the manifestation of the political religion of the age and the symbolic expression of good and bad. Tolstoy suggests that "in every age, and in every human society, there

[1] In this definition, religious values establish the conditions for the norms of politics. Political religion, then, refers properly to the norms of the polity. For further discussion of this definition of religion, see Émile Durkheim, *The Elementary Forms of Religious Life*; Bronislaw Malinowski, *Magic, Science, and Religion*; and Marion J. Levy, Jr., *The Structure of Society*.

exists a religious sense, common to that whole society, of what is good and what is bad, and it is this religious conception that decides the value of the feelings transmitted by art."[2] I cite this because the suggested relationship between religion, authority, and art is an interesting one. Tolstoy's comment helps us understand why politics is an art in the most significant sense of communicating moral experiences and why the mechanism of politics is devoted in part to finding ways and means of making such communication possible. It also explains why authority systems that rest their claims to moral authority on the promise of the future have to spend so much of their resources on monolithic buildings, statues of leaders, showpiece projects, and the like.

In describing these aspects of political religion, I will try to call attention to some of the wider implications and manifestations of the religious mode in politics. The implications do not stop at art, but go to the roots of individual personalities. There are certain fundamental needs of individuals that can only be met by their acceptance of transcendental beliefs. The needs, as I see them, are three: (1) the necessity of accepting death, (2) the necessity of establishing an individual personality, and (3) the necessity of identifying objectives. The classic puzzle posed by these three needs results from their paradoxical relationship. If we are all doomed, so to speak, as individuals, why the necessity of finding purpose in living? Why the passionate commitment to life? Why the importance of knowing who and what we are?

These are the problems to which religion addresses itself. It is obvious that our commitments to life are not nullified by the inevitability of death. Religion provides us with some form of immortality through a transcendental haven for souls. Political religion accomplishes the same end through demonstrations of the continuity of the present society with the past and promises of a secure political future. Individuals in a political community are made to feel that they are products of lives lived before theirs

[2] Leo Tolstoy, *What Is Art?* trans. Aylmer Maude (London: Walter Scott, Ltd., n.d.), p. 54.

within the context of the nation. This feeling is translated into family and kinship commitments as secured within the state. Family and kinship systems are thus the building blocks of all political systems; but loyalty to the state continues to take precedence over that to the family. The search for immortality, then, is expressed in both church religion and political religion. Each provides a means of triumphing over death in the face of its inevitability.

With respect to our second and third needs, it is a function of religion to provide identity and purpose for individuals. Identity is the means by which individuals relate to one another, and is closely connected with purpose. All religions try to explain why we exist and to establish a standard of right and justice, at the same time scoring inequity and human cupidity. If anguish, hardship, and suffering are all part of life, it is the function of religion to show that justice and meaning are positive corollaries of these.

This is the reason the state is not merely the legal expression of society. It is also the reason the state may require obligations from the community. Meaning is thus political in relation to identity. The society gives purpose to the individual. The individual relates himself to others within the society. The state bases itself on a superior right to express the purpose and exact from its citizens the obligations that are necessary to ensure success. It may do so in a variety of ways, some of which, indeed, appear to obliterate the individual. Identity, then, through citizenship locates the individual in relation to his obligations.

Obligations are related to our third need, that is, purpose. Just as church religion expresses moral purpose through right conduct and worthy objectives — aims that cleanse, purify, and promote in the individual a sense of personal worth — so, too, does political religion. It combines the ultimate and intermediate aims of individuals in a morally acceptable mixture. In a theocracy, for example, this is easily achieved since the ultimate ends of the state and the moral aims of individuals are one and the same. Political religions introduce changes in the normative order and require individuals to change their moral personalities. Thus, in the U.S.S.R., the political religion requires a new type of individual. Motivation must be altered as egoism is excluded. Selflessness and equalitarianism within the society are the moral imperatives. These moral aims are then translated into work and discipline and, through alteration of the individual's motivational structure, into efficiency. A given technological end thus coincides with the moral end to create a new political puritanism. This result of political religion is particularly attractive to leaders in those new nations with mobilization systems. Countries that make use of political religions, although similar to theocracies, are able to progress more quickly. In contrast to mobilization systems, for example, theocratic countries set more modest economic and moral goals for themselves and demand fewer role alterations from the population. The sense of urgency is less.

THE RELIGIOUS BASIS
OF CONSUMMATORY VALUES

The foregoing general behavioral considerations set the outermost limits of choice. When we speak of government as a mechanism of choice, it is obvious that choice involves both individual and social needs. No matter how particular or mundane the decisions and choices, however, the total pattern will come to reflect those values that ultimately form the basis of consummatory legitimacy. This is what I mean by the moral basis of the community (the ideological expression of which is only the most articulate part).[3] Whatever the range of activities of officeholders and elective or appointive officials, the totality of their acts must satisfy two kinds of demands, more or less simultaneously: the particular demands made upon government, and the continuous demands for veneration and vindication of the larger purposes of the society, Hence,

---

[3] Ideology, for our discussion, can be defined as the explicit and derivative articulation of political norms. For a fuller definition and discussion of ideology as a specific case of political religion, see chapter ix.

no matter how much political leaders manipulate material benefits in return for loyalty, the most equitably arranged society may fail to generate support without an articulated moral element. With such a moral element, the most despotic and capricious regime may continue to elicit veneration.

There is something magical or even sacred about the moral aspect of politics. Political ritual and ideological incantations, broadcast by means of the most up-to-date techniques in the mass media, dispense political grace not in the abstract but in terms of modern development. If in the church bingo and salvation exist side by side, so in politics do instrumental and consummatory values. The balance between them determines the form of legitimacy, and fear of its decline is perhaps the single overriding concern of political leaders in new and modernizing nations.[4] The establishment of a new pattern of legitimacy (which takes on characteristics of religion) affects the prescriptive consequences of political acts. Leaders become guidelines of personal and social meaning. Politics becomes prophetic and spiritual as well as mundane and practical.

All societies have sacred aspects, even though we may rarely relate them to what is normally considered religion. In the religious mode of thought, the explicit concern is the problem of morality, both for individuals and for society (morality as a set

[4] This is one reason they cling to so many of the practices employed by colonial regimes, since these practices allow at least a procedural integration of the society to continue while authority is more solidly rooted in the party, the ideology, or some combination of these elements. For a discussion of procedural integration, see my *Ghana in Transition* (New York: Atheneum, 1963).

Ideas about legitimacy in politics differ depending on whether the basic structure of authority is to be taken for granted. In order to legitimize the handing over of authority in colonial territories, for example, it was necessary for local political leaders to accede to parliamentary government and popular elections. Power could thereby be conveyed to the people and their elected representatives. W. J. M. Mackenzie has written that the "only consistent answer offered by the West to the problem of legitimate power is that government must be based on free elections," but free elections must reflect wider and deeper norms or they will fail, as has been shown in many new nations (Mackenzie, *Free Elections* [London: George Allen & Unwin, Ltd., 1958], p. 11).

of rules for conduct as well as a philosophical inquiry into the nature of those rules and principles). Politics in its moral sense can be described as approaching religion, just as churches in their organizational sense can be said to approach politics.

There are, of course, significant, but also quite simple, indicators of this. All societies have their sacred objects. All have their prophetic heroes or ancestral gods. All have books that contain moral prescriptions for behavior (on penalty of exclusion). All societies have a mechanism of excommunication, deprivation of rights or citizenship. This is most sharply revealed in "primitive" societies when violators of custom were often considered guilty of crimes against the society. In biblical times great transgressors could be stoned to death, exiled, mutilated, or sold into slavery. The symbolic awfulness of such penalties was what Durkheim had in mind by repressive law. Repressive law and the consummatory aspects of authority are thus closely linked, with the one serving as an indicator of the other. Another indicator of consummatory values in a given society is the degree to which "religious art" becomes associated with the regime. By religious art I mean works created as visible evidence of the regime and its power, such as public buildings, paintings, statues, and the like. Political religion has produced some very bad art works, whereas church religions have produced some of the most exalted.

THE RELATIONSHIP BETWEEN BEHAVIOR, VALUES, AND AUTHORITY

In considering the relations between changes in social organization and changes in the personalities of individuals, George Herbert Mead once suggested that

the changes that we make in the social order in which we are implicated necessarily involve our also making changes in ourselves. The social conflicts among the individual members of a given organized human society, which, for their removal, necessitate conscious or intelligent reconstructions and modifications of that society by those individuals, also and equally necessitate such reconstructions or modifications by those individuals of their own selves or personalities. Thus the relations between social reconstruction and self or personality reconstruction are reciprocal and internal or organic; social reconstruction by the individual members of any organized human society entails self or personality reconstruction in some degree or other by each of these individuals and vice versa, for since their selves or personalities are constituted by their organized social relations to one another, they cannot reconstruct those selves or personalities without also reconstructing, to some extent, the given social order, which is, of course, likewise constituted by their organized social relations to one another.[5]

Mead then goes on to link this relationship between the self and the society to government and religion by stressing the role of leadership in the development of personality. In discussing monarchy, for example, Mead suggests that it is "through the feeling of relation to the king [that] one can get a feeling for the vast congeries of communities that do in some way hang together." [6] The sense of enlarged being that comes when the individual identifies with a group leads to very complex feelings of solidarity. The encouragement of such feelings makes up an important part of politics. That is why political life consists of so much more than the mere satisfaction of material ends. What Mead suggests, then, is that the working-out of the self, since it can not occur in isolation, is the basis of the non-material ends of the community. These ends have a moral component, that is, what we have called consummatory values, which cluster in different ways, defining both the self and the social basis of a society differently. Let us discuss this last point more fully.

Consider the paradigms discussed by Meyer Fortes in his most interesting study on Oedipus and Job. These two symbolic figures,

[5] *Mind, Self and Society* (Chicago: University of Chicago Press, 1934), p. 309.
[6] *Ibid.*, p. 311.

Fortes suggests, may be distinguished in terms of the different ideas of fate incorporated in each. For the first,

> fate, like witchcraft, is an involuntary force and can, in the last resort, only be known in retrospect. This in itself generates efforts to discover it in advance and so try to control it. Hence the appeal to oracles. But the oracles do not in fact enable men to master their fate. As with witchcraft, they merely help to reconcile men to its ineluctability. It is best of all, really, to accept this and not to seek arrogantly to probe destiny.[7]

Job, on the other hand, is a figure of justice who reflects a conception of social life as a balanced set of rewards and punishments and as dependent on individual responsibility.

> Job confronts us with a wholly different conception of man and of morality. There is no suggestion here of inscrutable influences ruling the course of an individual's life from the moment of his birth. The good and evil that accrue to a man during his lifetime are the rewards and punishments meted out by an omnipotent, personified God. But God does not act arbitrarily or capriciously. He is . . . bound by a covenant with his creature, man. It is almost a contractual relationship in which God is bound to act justly and mercifully, and man is free to choose between righteousness and sin.[8]

These differing conceptions of being imply quite different views of the self in relation to society. Job's perspective implies a commitment to ideas of natural justice, at the center of which is the idea of individual responsibility and individuality itself. At the heart of Oedipus' cosmos lie the notions of kinship and collectivity. If a man inherits the destiny of his fathers, so does the community have its shared fate.

These ideas are related to the systems of government that I described earlier. In modernizing societies, both the self and society are associated with ideologies of rebirth and regeneration.

---

[7] Fortes, *Oedipus and Job in West African Religion* (Cambridge: Cambridge University Press, 1959), p. 15.

[8] *Ibid.*, pp. 15–16.

In some, the individual and society are so closely associated with the community that they form one organism with the capacity to grow and develop. The view of fate is optimistic and progressive rather than destructive and negative. To put a high premium on consummatory values is to identify fate. Such a fate is exciting, potentially prosperous, and modern. In the new nations a Job-like attitude belongs to a previous age, the age of colonialism perhaps, when one could decry the loss of natural equality through the imposition of alien rule. The "Oedipal" attitude toward fate is characteristic of mobilization systems, and the Job-like attitude is characteristic of reconciliation systems. Perhaps in the phenomenon of charisma the two views may be said to be blended, thereby creating a new system of authority centered on a prophetic figure whose gift of grace may come to mean both justice and heroic destiny.[9] The question, of course, is how this can be done, and the answer is necessarily complex. In this chapter our analysis will be concerned with solidarity as a structural principle, identity as a behavioral principle, and ideology as an empirical indicator of political values.

THE SOLIDARITY ASPECT OF AUTHORITY

The solidarity aspect of consummatory legitimacy was first made explicit by Marx. His views can be briefly summarized as follows. Change in the material conditions of life is expressed in two forms: (1) the intensification of the class struggle, resulting

[9] Etzioni has tried to suggest conditions of charisma and its distribution as follows: "(1) Nature of involvement required (moral versus calculative or coercive). (2) The distribution of means-ends decisions among various organizational positions. (3) The distribution of control over instrumental and expressive activities among various organizational positions. (4) The psychological characteristics of actors typically recruited to various organizational positions. (5) The frequency of interaction between elites and lower participants and the closeness of control over lower participants" (Amitai Etzioni, *A Comparative Analysis of Complex Organization* [New York: Free Press of Glencoe, Inc., 1961], p. 214).

in the emergence of different kinds of systems, and (2) the evolution of a higher form of consciousness that coincides with the evolutionary growth pattern of a system.[10]

Less clear is the degree of determinism Marx attributed to productive relations. This vagueness in the Marxian theory has, of course, been the basis for a great deal of debate. For example, if productive relations determine all aspects of social life, it ought to be unnecessary to study ideology. Yet ideology is very much a concern of the Marxians. Indeed, political religions are usually expressed in ideological terms.

Lenin, for example, as an ideologue of Marxism, reinforced polemics with claims to superior wisdom. From the analysis of "material conditions," he believed the ideologue can lay down a "correct" political line for the public to follow. Superior wisdom becomes ideological authority and thus the means by which the public is converted to the political line.[11] Indeed, ideological

---

[10] See George Lichtheim, *Marxism: An Historical and Critical Study* (London: Routledge & Kegan Paul, Ltd., 1961). Lichtheim points out that there is a conflict here that Marxists in their "objectivism" do not like to admit; namely, that although it is "in accordance with Marx's own manner to take a historical view of his work, such an approach presupposes a vantage-point made available by developments beyond the stage reflected in the Marxian system — in other words, it assumes that the Marxian categories are no longer quite applicable to current history. For obvious reasons, this is an admission which orthodox Marxists find it hard to make, while others may wonder why this particular scruple should arise in the first place. Its emergence is due to the fact that Hegel and, following him, Marx took a view of history which is not the familiar positivist one. They saw history as a process whose meaning reveals itself by stages, the succession of the latter reflecting man's growing awareness of his role in creating the historical world. To comprehend its past, mankind must raise itself to a higher level; hence, our ability to understand our predecessors suggests that we have reached a new altitude" (p. xv).

It was this problem that concerned Mannheim. Although Marxism supported the objectivist school of thought, the consequences of his theories produced the neo-Marxian subjectivist school of the sociology of knowledge. Mannheim and his followers, however, cannot avoid the same criticism to which Marx is subject.

[11] This is brought out nicely in the conflict between the "economists" and Lenin. Consider, for example, the criticisms leveled against *Iskra*, Lenin's newspaper, and Lenin's reply. The criticism: "*Iskra's* excessive predilection for controversy is due primarily to its exaggerated idea of the role of

purity becomes the rock against which waves of deviationism must be dashed if they are not to submerge the promontories of revolution.[12]

Lenin was both ideologue and ideologist. In his hands communism became a revolutionary dogma. Not a philosophy, it con-

---

'ideology' (programme, theories . . .) in the movement, and is partly an echo of the internecine squabbles that have flared up among Russian emigrants in Western Europe, of which they have hastened to inform the world in a number of polemical pamphlets and articles. In our opinion, these disagreements exercise almost no influence upon the actual progress of the Russian Social-Democratic movement except perhaps to damage it by introducing an undesirable schism among the comrades working in Russia. For that reason we cannot but express our disapproval of Iskra's polemical zeal, particularly when it exceeds the bounds of decency." Lenin's reply was characteristic. He flayed the "economists" for not staying ahead of the revolutionary consciousness of the people. He charged that the authors of the attack "failed to understand that an 'ideologist' is worthy of that name only when he marches *ahead* of the spontaneous movement, points out the road, and when he is able, ahead of all others, to solve all the theoretical, political, tactical, and organisational questions which the 'material elements' of the movement spontaneously encounter. In order to give 'consideration to the material elements of the movement' it is necessary to be critical of it, to point out its dangers and defects, and aspire to *elevate* spontaneity to consciousness. To say, however, that ideologists (i.e., conscious leaders) cannot divert the movement created by the interaction of environment and elements from its path is to ignore the elementary truth that consciousness *participates* in this interaction and creation."

For Lenin, ideology was more than the simple manipulation of ideas. It was the creation of those having a higher consciousness and a more informed intelligence about social matters. He calls ideological "elements" those "conscious elements which operate according to plan." See Nikolai Lenin, "A Conversation with Defenders of Economism," in Alexander Trachtenberg (ed.), *Collected Works of Lenin* (New York: International Publishers, 1929), Vol. IV, Book II, "The Iskra Period," pp. 66–67.

[12] This aspect of ideology — the building of solidarity within and confusion and vulnerability without — is one of the reasons that Marxism as an ideology is attractive to many youthful leaders of new states. Marx considered ideology to be those ideas that represent a particular mode of social organization. "To consider ideology as a set of ruling ideas which have been separated from the ruling individuals and given an independent force, an element of creativity in social affairs" is nonsense. The real basis of ideology, he pointed out, is the material conditions of life, in particular, social relationships, division of labor, and productive power. Ideology is thus a screen for reality, or a cloak. Karl Marx and Frederick Engels, *The German Ideology* (New York: International Publishers, 1939), pp. 41, 42, 43; see also Karl Mannheim, *Ideology and Utopia* (New York: Harcourt, Brace & Co., 1946), p. 110.

tained one; not an epistemology, it prescribed one; not a system of values, it was a program for achieving one. And yet ideology remained little more than propaganda. It was Georges Sorel, rather than Lenin, who, spinning out the implications of solidarity to the fullest, "completed" Marx, "instead of making commentaries on his text as his unfortunate disciples have done for so long." [13]

The feature of Sorel's work that makes explicit the solidarity function of legitimacy is his definition of the role of myth — more particularly, the myth of the general strike. Myth is the social equivalent of metaphor, or, to put it another way, myth is to solidarity what metaphor is to identity. For such myths to be useful, Sorel argued, they must be in tune with worthier moral tendencies. It is on a moral basis that ideologies must be evaluated rather than on some vague belief in dialectical progress. He taxes Marxians for failing to recognize that old myths can be revived in order to modify historical processes and thus may lead to reactionary revolution.

> Marx does not seem to have asked himself what would happen if the economic system were on the downgrade; he never dreamt of the possibility of a revolution which would take a return to the past, or even social conservation as its ideal.
> . . .
> These are dreams which Marx looked upon as reactionary, and consequently negligible, because it seemed to him that capitalism was embarked on an irresistible progress; but nowadays we see considerable forces grouped together in the endeavour to reform the capitalist economic system by bringing it, with the aid of laws, nearer to the medieval ideal. Parliamentary Socialism would like to combine with the moralists, the Church, and the democracy, with the common aim of impeding the capitalist movement; and, in view of middle-class cowardice, that would not perhaps be impossible.[14]

[13] Georges Sorel, *Reflections on Violence* (Glencoe: Free Press of Glencoe, Ill., 1950), p. 59.
[14] *Ibid.*, p. 107.

Myths and the utopias provide each great event with its moral dimension. Sorel asks, ". . . What remains of the Revolution when we have taken away the epic of the wars against the coalition, and of that of the victories of the populace? What remains is not very savoury: police operations, proscriptions, and sittings of servile courts of law. . . ." [15]

For Sorel, it is the myth of the proletarian general strike that activates the class struggle and carries it forward. In this sense, we can say he carries Marx to an ideological conclusion, because without the ideology of the general strike, regardless of the full weight of material development and regardless of the evolutionary tendency in dialectical materialism, a revolution may fail or become reactionary. Ideology is a necessary ingredient of progress. [16]

What makes Sorel interesting to us is not only his doctrine of the proletarian general strike or his justification of violence. Rather, it is the claim he makes for ideology. Its role is to build solidarity, and solidarity is the moral basis of society. Solidarity is defined by Sorel as a moral system based on class and held together by myths. This system is the foundation of change. Solidarity-producing myths are "good" when they lead to a higher morality. Hence, his claims for solidarity are also claims for a social personality of higher morality and a superior human community.

The connection between solidarity and morality is the essence of authority, a fact well recognized by leaders of new nations. Solidarity and myth as expressed in ideology are commonly manipulated in order to supply a moral dimension to political forms. In this sense, the creation of myth, the moral solidarity of the community, and the authority of leaders are intimately linked.

[15] *Ibid.*, pp. 118–19.
[16] Sorel, although an admirer of Marx, was by no means dazzled by his doctrine. He quotes with relish a "learned exponent of Socialism" who said that "the art of reconciling opposites by means of nonsense is the most obvious result which he had got from the study of the works of Marx" (*ibid.*, p. 138). See also Ernst Cassirer, *The Myth of the State* (New Haven, Conn.: Yale University Press, 1946), Part I.

THE IDENTITY ASPECT OF AUTHORITY

Sorel helped to clarify the role of solidarity in maintaining authority, that is, in providing bonds among the members of a community, social commitment, and historical perspective. The natural outcome of his analysis is to center attention less on the particular polemics of his own ideology than on the diverse but concrete manifestations of solidarity in ideological form. These include the use of historical myths, the rewriting of history, and the search for a golden age — all efforts to promote the ends of a political community. So far, ideology in society has been our point of reference. But ideology, like language and dreams, is related to morphologies of behavior by universal psychobiological variables. Balance, mastery, and control are the desired results of ideological behavior. Ideas help men control and change their environment. They arise from action rather than pure speculation. This was Freud's view: "It must not be assumed that mankind came to create its first world system through a purely speculative thirst for knowledge. The practical need of mastering the world must have contributed to this effort." [17] These views of Freud's would also apply to all forms of belief, including animism, magic, taboos, and presumably, political beliefs.[18]

For Freud, ideology is a form of personal *rationalization*. (In this, Marx might have agreed with him.) Both he and Marx saw ideas as a cloak behind which "reality" hides, although, of course, each had a different idea of that reality. If, as for Freud, ideologies

[17] A. A. Brill (ed.), *The Basic Writings of Sigmund Freud* (New York: Modern Library, 1938), p. 867.

[18] Perhaps most directly concerned with ideology is Freud's analysis of the "chosen people" myth. Freud's transposition of the Moses legend is remarkable for its imaginative skill. More to the point, Freud argues that "the human intellect has not shown itself elsewhere to be endowed with a very good scent for truth, nor has the human mind displayed any special readiness to accept truth. On the contrary, it is the general experience that the human intellect errs very easily without our suspecting it at all, and that nothing is more readily believed than what — regardless of the truth — meets our wishes and illusions half-way" (Sigmund Freud, *Moses and Monotheism* [New York: Alfred A. Knopf, 1939], p. 204).

are elaborate mental fictions that the observer must penetrate in order to understand personality, then ideology is uniquely personal. The scholar who wishes to understand ideology must approach it like a psychotherapist who is unravelling the mental rationalizations of his patients. It is hard to say whether this speculation makes ideology a pathological condition for Freud. Certainly, he would consider political extremists emotionally suspect. He did not have much taste for the bizarre despite the novelty of his views.

Freud used Moses as a figure for psychoanalytic historical research. Erik H. Erikson, who became concerned with similar matters in his study of Luther, carries forward the traditions and the ideas of Freud in his analysis of the forbidding emotional complex that led to greatness. His concern with the conditions that lead to the formation of creative personalities involves him in a study of ideology and its role in the development of personality. In the study of ideology, Erikson holds, more than in any other form of social analysis, the observer must rely on unorthodox sensitivities as he searches for evidence, clues and dates, much of which has barely been touched by previous analysts. He is more on his own in social analysis than the ordinary historian or social scientist. Erikson's point is that the psychotherapist *cum* social scientist, as he observes ideology in the context of personality, can contribute a great deal to the understanding of why individuals are so receptive to ideology. Erikson establishes a theory of personality formation that is based on the aspect of maturation he calls the search for identity. Because identity search coincides with role search, youth (as well as others who have never quite found themselves, as the vernacular has it) are particularly vulnerable to ideologies. This adds another aspect of the study of ideology to the one offered by the Marxians, namely, motivation. None of the Marxians can explain why class interests must exist, and they are confused enough to deny the universality of the proposition by showing that some individuals are able to emancipate themselves from their class interests. This is an im-

portant weakness in Marxian theory; for although Marx would
have liked to deny the independent validity of ideas for action,
he had to leave some loopholes for the gratuitous entry of non-
working class Marxian ideas. Hence, the link between material
conditions and class behavior cannot be axiomatic. The result is
an incomplete and inconclusive treatment of ideology. Erikson
defines ideology as

> an unconscious tendency underlying religious and scientific
> as well as political thought: the tendency at a given time to
> make facts amenable to ideas, and ideas to facts, in order to
> create a world image convincing enough to support the col-
> lective and the individual sense of identity. Far from being
> arbitrary or consciously manageable (although it is as ex-
> ploitable as all of man's unconscious strivings), the total
> perspective created by ideological simplification reveals its
> strength by the dominance it exerts on the seeming logic of
> historical events, and by its influence on the identity forma-
> tion of individuals (and thus on their "ego-strength").[19]

This formulation helps us understand why individuals are receptive to authority by showing that authority satisfies an aspect
of identity. By relating identity to maturation (as a critical problem for youth), Erikson suggests the reason that ideology has
a particular attractiveness to youth. The first point provides some
insight into the conditions of personal conflict that lead to the
acceptance or rejection of ideologies. It also helps explain prophets, charismatic leaders, and manipulators of ideology. The
second point is of particular relevance in newly developing communities where the emphasis on youth raises them to a high level
of prominence just at a time when their search for identity is at
its most critical stage.[20]

[19] Erikson, *Young Man Luther: A Study in Psychoanalysis and History*
(London: Faber & Faber, 1958), p. 20. He goes on to describe his book as
a study of "identity and ideology."
    [20] "Youth stands between the past and the future, both in individual
life and in society. It also stands between alternate ways of life. . . ." Ideologies offer to the members of this age-group overly simplified and yet definite
answers to exactly those vague inner states and those urgent questions that

Having suggested the behavioral needs that underly consummatory values, which are represented by solidarity in the community and identity in the individual, we can examine the ways these needs are satisfied in the various political systems we have been discussing.[21]

ASPECTS OF AUTHORITY IN A THEOCRACY

As an example of a theocracy, let me cite classic Greece. Barker comments that in the Greek *polis*, "the state exists for the moral development and perfection of its individual members." It is "the fulfillment and perfection of the individual which means — and is the only thing which means — the perfection of the state." He points out that "a state which is meant for the moral perfection of its members will be an educational institution. Its laws will serve to make men good." Thus its offices will belong ideally to "the men of virtue who have moral discernment. Its chief activity will be that of training and sustaining the mature in the way of righteousness. That is why we may speak of such a state as really a church: like Calvin's church it exercises a 'holy discipline.' Political philosophy thus becomes a sort of moral theology." [22]

There is much in common between the Greek state as described by Barker and the political systems aspired to by several of the new nations of the world, as well as some of the older, militantly Marxist ones, such as China and the U.S.S.R. Of course,

---

arise in consequence of identity conflict. "Ideologies serve to channel youth's forceful earnestness and sincere asceticism as well as its search for excitement and its eager indignation toward that social frontier where the struggle between conservatism and radicalism is most alive. On that frontier, fanatic ideologists do their busy work and psychopathic leaders their dirty work; but there, also, true leaders create significant solidarities" (*ibid.*, p. 39).

[21] A fuller analysis of these aspects of authority is required for a completely satisfactory treatment, but it would take us too far away from the subject of modernization.

[22] E. Barker, *The Politics of Aristotle* (Oxford: Clarendon Press, 1948), p. li. See also the discussion in Barker, *Social and Political Thought in Byzantium* (Oxford: Clarendon Press, 1957), pp. 6–7.

the specifically religious content that was so much a part of the antique world has been downgraded and is now regarded as pre-scientific. Nevertheless, the state provides images of virtue and purpose. The individual's will is bent to serve the goals that the state decides are important. Nor is this done in a spirit of autocracy. Rather, there is an ideal of moral and material uplift that, having as its apotheosis some visible form of political order, will presumably secure human happiness.

In theocracies, political and religious associations are one. Some specialization of political roles is possible, but roles have their main significance in a religious system of ideas. A king is a spiritual counselor as well as a warrior. He is the classic defender of the faith in addition to being a lawgiver. Justice is tempered with divine guidance. The great difficulty faced by theocracies in the past was the control of despotic and corrupt kings and priests, whose transgressions of law offended both human and natural society.

In earlier theocracies the governmental authority was a part of the wider authority of the gods and was shared with them. Revolutions, changes in regime, tyrannicide, and other instabilities were regarded in the same manner as storms, earthquakes, and other natural catastrophes. There was a blending of the sacred and the secular, but the sacred was not debased by the secular.

Most theocratic societies did not question the larger order within which they found themselves. Suffering was religiously meaningful. Kings or priests were the interpreters and lawgivers, acting in the wider context of religious practice. The ancient Jews, for example, had a clear conception of theocratic politics:

> Israel's monarchy is grounded not in the priesthood, but in apostolic prophecy. Israelite kings had the right to perform altar service and were charged with the maintenance of altars and temples. But they never bore the official title "priest"; their priestly function was but a by-role. The Israelite king succeeded to the task of the prophet-judge, not of the priest; the latter never bore secular authority in Israel. The ideal king of the future is a just judge, God-

fearing and mighty; he has no priestly features. Modeled
after the apostolic prophet-judge, the king is the elect of
God. He does not incorporate any divine essence; he does
not control the destiny of the cosmos through the cult; he is
but the bearer of God's grace, appointed to office by his
messenger-prophet. The king is thus another embodiment
of the idea that it is God's will that rules on earth.[23]

Similar cases are China and Japan. In the Confucian tradition of
government, for example, political order was the creation of the
early kings. "The early kings, by virtue of their high intelligence
and perspicacity, received the mandate of Heaven and ruled over
the world. They were of one mind in making it their duty to bring
peace and contentment to the world." [24]

If the king of a theocracy was the elect of God, human society
was part of His universe, to be governed in accordance with His
laws. This authority did not mean that kings, even despotic ones,
had an easy time of it, however. Their responsibilities, although
including human affairs, often transcended the world of man and
spilled over into the world of nature. In many African kingdoms,
for example, kings were held responsible for food supplies, rain,
and other important natural phenomena. In the early Semitic
kingdoms, there were many cases of rulers' being held responsible
as representatives of the deity for the coming of rains, bad crops,
and other natural disasters. "In Babylonia in some prehistoric
period there existed a belief that the king was responsible for the
state of agricultural land, and for the timely occurrence of seasonal
phenomena, and that belief exists today sporadically over the
East." [25]

In theocracies leadership is shared through a priesthood. Many
forms of leadership are therefore possible, but all share two

[23] Yehezkel Kaufman, *The Religion of Israel* (Chicago: University of
Chicago Press, 1960), p. 266.
[24] Ogyu Sorai, "The Confucian Way as a Way of Government," in *Sources
of Japanese Tradition*, ed. William Theodore de Bary *et al.* (New York: Columbia University Press, 1958), p. 426.
[25] S. H. Hooker, *Myth, Ritual and Kingship* (Oxford: Clarendon Press),
pp. 27–28.

major qualities. First, leaders occupy roles that are both personalized and institutionalized. Second, they are representatives of the deity. Their authority derives from these two qualities even if they are selected by the public at large.[26]

For the members of theocracies there is no sharp distinction between the natural universe and the state, the living and the dead, or the real state and the transcendent state, that is, between the kingdom of man and the kingdom of God.

Laws tend to be linked to custom, ritual, and other religious practices and have their origins in prophecy, whether oracular or personal, or in decrees. Changes come about in the effort to conserve and strengthen the existing system rather than in the attempt to transform it.

An important part of the sacred element in the community is maintained by religious practices and special classes of individuals who cater to ritual and custom. Their function is to maintain the purity of the society and prevent the defilement of the sacred by the secular.

In the ancient world, most societies, including those of Greece and Rome, were theocratic, as, more recently, have been communities in Africa, the Middle East, and Asia. Their revolutions,

[26] Roger Callois makes the point as follows: "Power, like the sacred, seems to be an external sign of grace, of which the individual is the temporary abode. It is obtained through investiture, initiation, or consecration. It is lost through degradation, indignity, or abuse. It benefits from the support of the entire society which constitutes its depository. The king wears the crown, scepter, and purple reserved for the Gods. He has guards to protect him. He executes all types of coercion capable of forcing the rebellious to submit. But it must be pointed out that these means do not explain as much as they demonstrate the efficacy of power. To the degree to which people regard them as powerful, or consider them able to subjugate, or reveal reasons for being afraid, it is unnecessary to explain the motives for complaisance and docility. . . .

"Every king is God, descended from God, or ruler by the grace of God. He is a sacred personage. It is consequently necessary to isolate him and to construct watertight compartments between him and the profane. His person harbors a holy force that creates prosperity and maintains the order of the universe. He assures the regularity of the seasons, the fertility of the soil and women . . ." (Callois, *Man and the Sacred* [Glencoe: Free Press of Glencoe, Ill., 1959], pp. 90–91).

if they had any, involved changes in regime rather than fundamental alterations of the conception of authority and community.
The problems of such societies were considered to be part of
the cosmos and thus were no more disturbing than the larger
mysteries of life and the gods themselves.

Systems with political religion elevate the secular to the level
of the sacred and incorporate theocratic elements in it. They
make the universe subservient to and an extension of man and his
society. In theocracies, the cosmos and nature are not divorced
from the state; they are larger than the state and control it. In
systems with political religion, man is the center of the universe.
The reconciliation system is the obverse of theocracy although it
should not be forgotten that all Western reconciliation systems
began as Christian theocratic polities, from which they obtained
their consummatory values.

POLITICAL RELIGION IN THE RECONCILIATION SYSTEM

The reconciliation system, despite its instrumental values, first
originated as a theocracy. This accounts for its Job-like attitude
toward authority in the sense that its concern is with equity and
justice. Perhaps the most commonly used description of it is "a
government of laws and not of men." By this phrase, which is the
foundation of constitutional democracy, not only is it required
that men obey laws, a characteristic of all communities, but that
law embody a wider wisdom than any individual man. Because
of this status, law is venerated for its own sake. Through laws,
prudently adopted and exercised, man perfects his individuality
and protects others from it. Although Plato does not consider law
in *The Republic*, his concept of truth and harmony is itself an
abstract law to be known through reason — the good. Insofar as
law is a standard as well as a framework, Plato begins the tradition of natural law in the Western world.

Since that time law has been the constant preoccupation of secular theorists. How to shape it to human needs without destroying its insulation from the ordinary whim and fancy of men gave rise to great commentaries on law, which are still part of the cultural tradition of the West — Justinian's and Gaius' institutes, the works of the Glossators and the Commentators, Blackstone, Maine, Maitland, and Vinogradoff. Law as the embodiment of wisdom has been a constant object of study. The effort to resolve some of the paradoxes arising between an objective plane of law, at one with the rest of the universe, and the ordinary, day-to-day laws that govern the minutiae of life is a never ending dialogue over the dividing line between natural law and positive law. It is a dialogue that in the medieval period came to involve another division, that between divine law and canon law. These various kinds of law needed to be sorted out into the spheres where their authority would be particular and useful.

The preoccupation with law in the West was one of the important ingredients in the development of a community that regarded its framework of law as the sole and ultimate commitment by which it lived, breathed, and prospered — the reconciliation system. But it was not the only factor relevant to development. The second was the separation of church and state. I shall try to show that the separation of church and state as well as the notion of law, was essential to the development of such a system. This point cannot be emphasized too strongly since the separation of church and state, unaccompanied by a strong belief in the objective quality of law, appears to me to be one cause of the growth of political religion. In a system based on political religion (rule by men and not by law), the legitimacy of the sovereign is substituted for the legitimacy of the law, with the result that politics becomes endowed with sacred characteristics.

The doctrine of the separation of church and state is a curious one and peculiarly Christian. Whatever the historical reasons, and I am sure there are many, Christianity, which originated in a condition of political subservience, saw that its status would be enhanced by winning tolerance — not that it was content with mere tolerance and would not have transformed the community into a theocracy if it could have done so. But by and large it could be content with tolerance and live in a relatively harmonious relationship with secular authorities. Divine law and natural law were never exactly the same but were regarded as complementary. Revealed truth and rationality were not opposites but rather different sides of the same coin. The great achievement of Thomas Aquinas was in effect the strengthening of the accord between church and state and the provision of an intellectual synthesis for it.

Aquinas gave Christianity a profounder basis for a concept that had already been established in principle. It had been expressed first in the Pauline doctrine of rendering unto Caesar the things that were Caesar's. Pope Gelasius made a fundamental point of this at the end of the fifth century:

> The Emperor . . . is the son of the Church, not its director. In matters of religion it is his to learn and not to teach. He has the privileges of his power which he has obtained by the will of God for the sake of public administration. . . .
>
> Before the time of Christ . . . some did have the offices of both king and priest, and in heathen times the devil copied this and the pagan emperors held the office of Pontifex Maximus. But Christ who was both king and priest never entrusted both powers to the same hands, but separated the two offices and the functions and dignities proper to each, and therefore, as Christian emperors stand in need of priests for eternal life, so the priests for the course of temporal things employ the directions of emperors.
>
> There are two authorities by which principally this world is ruled, the sacred authority of the bishops, and the royal power. . . .[27]

The most important consequences of this doctrine, which was reinforced rather than weakened by the historic battles men fought over it, was the conflict between church and state — the separation of temporal and spiritual jurisdictions. The fortunes of

[27] Quoted in Charles Howard McIlwain, *The Growth of Political Thought in the West* (New York: Macmillan & Co., 1932), pp. 164–65.

the one could, and did, vary independently of the other. No matter how religious a monarch, not even during the height of the doctrine of the divine right of kings, was the principle undermined.

What was significant about this? It allowed a complementary balance between consummatory and instrumental values. It provided a philosophical basis for limiting the power of the executive, for the concept of checks and balances rests on a faith that such a system helps to restore a natural harmony to the governance of men, in which the individual may develop his true nature. Civil society ruled by law also rested on a prior spiritual sanction of individualistic action. Protestantism represented a blend of ideas about right conduct guided by a Christian ethic, which set the bounds within which individual freedom (and eventually representative government) could prosper. A high degree of self-restraint in behavior was the essence of the liberal democratic polity.

Even now, when the influence of religion has declined and the burdens of civil society are immense, the concept of limited government has remained strong in the West. Such is the fear of arbitrary power in government that the ideas of parliament and law, as well as of constitutions and social compacts, become the symbolic instruments of civic rule. What there is of the sacred in Western secular government is in the framework itself. All other ideologies have declined. A constitutional framework of law, although it cannot be heroic, gives men the opportunity to make of their society what they will within that framework. Law through representative government is to an important extent the political content of our civilization. It is the means by which we amend our way of life without abdicating individual rights. It is necessarily undramatic and to a large extent without glamour; and change under such circumstances is slow. The competition of individuals and groups, a pluralistic universe with relativistic values, is its main characteristic. Indeed, all values can change save two. One is the dignity of the individual, which can be preserved only through the dignity of law. The other is the principle of representative government.

What are some of the more practical virtues of such a system? Two are perhaps the most important. A government of laws may enhance the authority of law by amendments that temper and ameliorate the difficulties that its citizens face. In that respect, when it functions well, it has resolved the twin problems of a stable society and succession in public office. In addition it allows for the existence of secular values germane to industrialization. Once established, the framework can persist even though the sacred, as distinct from the secular, "sword" has declined. This has not been accomplished without difficulty, however. The decline of religion has imposed on the Western democratic polity the singular problem of how to provide the alternative sources of meaning, faith, and spiritual sustenance that all men need in some degree.[28] There is, therefore, the possibility of a crisis arising in Western society from unsatisfied moral ambitions. And our political framework faithfully mirrors this weakness. Precisely because our problems lie in the moral sphere, those new nations that have developed a system of political religion now appear to be less morally ambiguous than we are. Even though the political religions in the new nations have not emerged in the classic form of theocracies, but in the form of systems of secular beliefs, they define political and moral aims as one and the same, as the earlier systems did. What has been lost is the idea of individualism. The

---

[28] Indeed, not only does the decline of religion cause a change in our discourse; it affects our awareness of earlier purposes, which become lost or at best sentimentalized. T. S. Eliot once commented on the matter in a particularly telling way as follows: "Much has been said everywhere about the decline of religious belief; not so much notice has been taken of the decline of religious sensibility. The trouble of the modern age is not merely the inability to believe certain things about God and man which our forefathers believed, but the inability to *feel* towards God and man as they did. A belief in which you no longer believe is something which to some extent you can still understand; but when religious feeling disappears, the words in which men have struggled to express it become meaningless" (Eliot, *On Poetry and Poets* [New York: Farrar, Straus & Cudahy, 1957], p. 15). For a broad analysis of transition in Western society, see Reinhard Bendix, *Nation-Building and Citizenship* (New York: John Wiley & Sons, 1964), pp. 55–104.

peculiar genius of Western civilization, that is, the relationship between the individual and the law, is held to be imprisoning, reactionary, and parochial. I shall discuss some of the wider implications of this predicament in the final chapter.

At stake is the survival of democracy itself. Reconciliation systems are undergoing a crisis that is intensified by the secularization of the religious sphere. A logical answer to this argument would be to suggest a return to religious belief as the way out of our difficulty. Whatever the merits and logic of this course of action, it is highly unlikely to be adopted. New solutions need to be found. The ever present internal danger is that reconciliation systems may turn to political religions to reinforce their own position or, in an illusory effort, to eradicate enemies both within and without.

POLITICAL RELIGION IN THE MOBILIZATION SYSTEM

The rise of political religion is itself a response to the loss of faith that characterizes present-day reconciliation systems. What I have been suggesting can be rephrased as follows. The sacred may now be employed to develop a system of political legitimacy and to aid in mobilizing the community for secular ends. This makes constitutional democracy irrelevant. Having made political doctrine into political belief, leaders attempt to formalize that faith as a means by which to achieve major aims.[29] In none of the new nations has this entirely succeeded, although particular efforts have been made in Ghana, Mali, Guinea, Egypt, China, and Indonesia.

[29] But, as has been suggested before, if the aims were achieved, they would lose their significance. So it is that political religions need to have aims not all of which can be achieved. One such aim is the transformation of human beings into some higher order of being. The Soviet argument is that capitalism is in the long run a corrupting element in human society and individuals who show capitalistic vestiges are to that extent corrupt. New nations tend to have similar views with regard to tribal society. The latter, having fallen from grace and having been corrupted by colonialism, remains corrupt.

The nations with political religions regard themselves as being without sin. This feeling stems from the notion of rebirth, that is, of new political units rising out of revolution and/or colonial status, with all the purity of the newborn. Their main objectives are regeneration and emancipation of the citizenry from backwardness and other handicaps such as racial discrimination. Rebirth lends itself to messianic government, which makes a rule of law and not of men virtually impossible. Efforts at regeneration make individualism seem backward and restrictive, with the result that public checks on political authority are extremely difficult. Perhaps the best description of what I have been trying to convey is provided by J. L. Talmon, who points out that "the decline of religious authority implied the liberation of man's conscience, but it also implied something else. Religious ethics had to be speedily replaced by secular, social morality. With the rejection of the Church, and of the transcendental justice, the State remained the sole source and sanction of morality." [30] In his distinction between liberal and totalitarian democracy, Talmon suggests that both traditions

> affirm the supreme value of liberty. But whereas one finds the essence of freedom in spontaneity and the absence of coercion, the other believes it to be realized only in the pursuit and attainment of an absolute collective purpose. It is outside our scope to decide whether liberal democracy has the faith that totalitarian democracy claims to have in final aims. What is beyond dispute is that the final aims of liberal democracy have not the same concrete character. They are conceived in rather negative terms, and the use of force for their realization is considered as an evil. Liberal democrats believe that in the absence of coercion men and society may one day reach through a process of trial and error a state of ideal harmony. In the case of totalitarian democracy, this state is precisely defined, and is treated as a matter of immediate urgency, a challenge for direct action, an imminent event.[31]

[30] Talmon, *The Origin of Totalitarian Democracy* (London: Secker & Warburg, 1955), p. 4.
[31] *Ibid.*, p. 2.

The reasons for the rise of political religions among the new nations are not hard to find. Faith is a source of authority. The first problem faced by the new nations is that of creating over-arching loyalties that will transcend the primordial ones of ethnic membership, religious affiliation, and linguistic identification. That such loyalties are stubborn and not easily replaceable can be demonstrated by experience in such new countries as India, Indonesia, and Nigeria. Where hitherto racially compartmentalized groups have been joined in a new nation, the problem is immeasurably more difficult, as in Zambia, Kenya, or Tanzania.

But such loyalties are not blind and unreasoning. Race, ethnicity, religion, and language are the means whereby people identify themselves, organize their community, find meaning for their sentiments, and express their beliefs. If such affiliations are to become increasingly less significant, individuals must find a common interest in a wider polity through which identity, sentiments, and beliefs can be enlarged and strengthened rather than minimized and destroyed. The point is that political religion seeks to do these things and to render massive change heroic and joyful, infectious and liberating. Since this is by no means simple to do, conflicts are engendered in the development of a political religion that can be as fierce and time-consuming as the religious wars of the past.

A second major problem facing the new nations, in addition to the breakdown of parochial attachments (and closely related to it), is the problem of constituting authority. In order for a system to enjoy a constitutional framework, a certain consensus about primordial loyalties must already have gained acceptance in the wider community. Without such a consensus political authority remains the most sensitive political problem in the modernizing nations. Some industrialized countries as well have never been able to overcome similar difficulties. France, for example, has never institutionalized her constitutional order sufficiently. Political authority has yet to be fully integrated within the framework of the law, with the result that the framework itself is demeaned in spite of the very elaborate modern legal structure.

Political leaders in the new nations have only recently attempted to challenge colonial authority and weaken men's obedience to earlier political rule. When popular enthusiasm and revolutionary ardor begin to wane, these political leaders inherit an instability of regime and authority that is partly of their own making. If they endow their roles with sacred elements, their authority becomes stronger and the regime more secure. Moreover, since everything is known about the leaders — their past, their families, their daily routines — they can hardly be remote and distant. Quite the contrary, they characteristically remain friendly and fraternal. If such familiarity is not to result in disrespect for authority, however, the sacred role must turn it to advantage. The public is encouraged to be grateful for the spreading of the sacred largesse. They are made to feel purified by the divine. They see that the "man of the people" remains with the people, but they never confuse him with ordinary men. In this way authority becomes stabilized in the role of the leader, and his manipulation of power and friendliness are accepted as tokens of majesty.

The third major problem that the leaders of new nations face is the material development of their country. Everyone desires the things of this world, and a political religion can survive in the face of austerity only up to a point. In supplying satisfactions, political religion is always less powerful than church religion because of the different kind of reward the former must promise, that is, material abundance in the political kingdom.

Political religions thus require a more specific ideological component than church religions and have built into them a particular kind of rationality — the rationality of economic life. This is both a handicap and an advantage. It is a handicap in that political religions rarely have the extrarational pull on a long-term basis that church religion does. They lack the same sticking power. It is an advantage inasmuch as it turns men's minds to practical tasks and encourages the rationality necessary to achieve them. To the extent that development occurs as a result, the society may consider replacing political religion with a constitutional order. That is the great hope the West has for the U.S.S.R. It is also our hope for the modernizing nations.

Where the state and the regime take on sacred characteristics, the sacred usually extends to civil laws. As I suggested earlier, this can best be explained in terms of Durkheim's distinction between repressive and restitutive law. Repressive law punishes on a symbolic level. The sacred quality of the community, having been violated, must be revenged. Death for treason is an example of repressive law. In communities with a weak political religion, it is hard to find cases of men's being put to death for theft. In communities with an all-encompassing political religion, death for theft is not uncommon.[32]

The sacred quality of the state and regime is also essential for maintaining solidarity in the community. From it, a regime derives legitimacy, which is reinforced in a variety of ways. One way is

[32] Sekou Touré's comment is illustrative: "If you like, we may say that the Party is the brain of our society, while the State is the executive part of it, the part which works according to the spirit and the intentions of the Party.

"The State settles the great problems of a social, economic, financial, or administrative character, in the light [of] the objectives which the Party has decided to attain.

"It is thus that the Party, which has decided to create a new society for the greatest happiness of man, comes up presently against several difficulties. In the present society there are thieves, murderers through imprudence. The thief and the murderer constitute a social danger. They make the members of the society feel worried and unsafe; they injure the property and the life of other people. Neither of them concerns himself in any way with the properties and the lives around him; they feel no respect for the social surroundings in which they live and operate, they have no sense of a solidarity with all the men who make up society. The role of the State is to protect society from the evil deeds of such men.

"That is why, at the suggestion of the Party, the Government has decided to deal with them with the utmost severity. In future, no pity will be shown to thieves. We shall impose extreme penalties on them. We have said that, if you caught a thief in the act of breaking open your door you could shoot at him. In our eyes, the thief is an evil being. Whether he steals several millions or only a pin, his behaviour comes from a mentality which we intend to destroy. Whoever he may be, whatever the conditions in which his theft has been committed, we shall punish him with the utmost severity. No one will be excepted." *Toward Full Re-Africanization* (Paris: Présence Africaine, 1959), p. 46.

by renewing interest in a semimythical past in order to produce
antecedents for the regime. Another way is a persistent attack on
a particular enemy. The attack on colonialism, for example, may be
enlarged to include neocolonialism, which then becomes a higher
form of villainy against which the new nations must be ever
vigilant.

The mythical past, in addition to stressing continuity with an
earlier period, also serves to demarcate a particular period as a
time of disgrace and misfortune. In new nations this is the period
of colonialism. Both the new era and the golden past serve as
reminders of the suffering and degradation through which the
public passed and magnify the achievement of independence.
The birth of the nation is thus a religious event, forming a fund
of political grace that can be dispensed over the years.

The agent of rebirth is normally an individual — an Nkrumah,
a Touré — who, as the leader of the political movement, might be
said to be the midwife. This is sometimes expressed in songs and
chants and at other times in political prayers.

Sékou Touré	Sékou Touré
Grand-Merci à toi, Touré	O don Divin à la Guinée
La libération de la Guinée	Salut à toi, soit béni
Ne nous surprend guère.	O toi, bienfaiteur de la Guinée
L'affamé ne sent-il pas de loin	Apôtre de la bonne cause
Le fumet du plat salutaire.	O l'enfant prodige.[33]

Political leadership centers in an individual with characteristics
of revealed truth. From leader to party to state is a single progression embodied in the twin notions of personal authority and collective responsibility. The goals of the society are demanding
and laid down from above. By achieving them, men become honorable and moral, reborn and closer to perfection. The influence
of the leader is sometimes considered to extend beyond a country's own borders. The former chairman of the Convention People's Party and minister of presidential affairs in Ghana, in an
officially distributed pamphlet, wrote the following:

[33] From a poem, "Indépendance," by Diely Mamoudou Kande printed in
Présence Africaine (Paris), December, 1959–January, 1960, p. 95.

Today . . . barely three years after the birth of Ghana, to
millions of people living both inside and outside the continent of Africa, Kwame Nkrumah is Africa and Africa is
Kwame Nkrumah. When the question is asked: "What is
going to happen to Africa?" it is to one man that everyone
looks for the answer: Kwame Nkrumah. To the imperialists
and colonialists his name is a curse on their lips; to the
settlers his name is a warning that the good old days at the
expense of the Africans are coming to an end; to Africans
suffering under foreign domination, his name is a breath
of hope and means freedom, brotherhood and racial equality; to us, his people, Kwame Nkrumah is our father,
teacher, our brother, our friend, indeed our very lives, for
without him we would no doubt have existed, but we would
not have lived; there would have been no hope of a cure for
our sick souls, no taste of glorious victory after a life-time of
suffering. What we owe him is greater even than the air we
breathe, for he made us as surely as he made Ghana.[34]

As the leader is the state, so is the party the state. Those who do
not accept this unity are suspect. Nkrumah himself has written:

The Convention People's Party is Ghana and Ghana is the
Convention People's Party. There are some people who not
only choose to forget this, but who go out of their way to
teach others to forget it also. There are some persons, both
staff and students [of the University of Ghana], who mis-
takenly believe that the words "academic freedom" carry
with them a spirit of hostility to our Party and the Government, the same Party of the workers and the farmers,
and the same Government whose money founded the University and maintains it and provides them with their education in the hope that they will one day repay their country-
men by giving loyal and devoted service to the Government
of the People.

The Convention People's Party cannot allow this confusion of academic freedom with disloyalty and anti-Govern-
ment ideas.

In the future we shall attach the greatest importance to

[34] Tawia Adamafio, A Portrait of the Osagyefo Dr. Kwame Nkrumah (Accra: Government Printer, 1960), p. 95.

the ideological education of the youth. The establishment of the Young Pioneers will be a step further in this direction. The Youth Section of the Party will be fully mobilized under the close guidance of the Youth Bureau of the National Secretariat. We shall make our party ideology fully understood in every section of the community. We must regard it as an honor to belong to the Convention People's Party. And I repeat we must work loyally and with singleness of purpose for that is the essence of the true Party spirit, the spirit that routed imperialism from our soil and the spirit which we must recapture for the struggle that lies ahead.[35]

The case of Ghana is similar to many others. The party contains an elect. Control is centralized. There is purification in belonging, comfort in comradeship, democracy in loyalty, brotherhood in membership.[36] In Guinea, for example the structure of the party extends into each village. There is a hierarchy of councils. At the top

[35] Kwame Nkrumah, "What the Party Stands For," *The Party* (C.P.P. monthly journal), I (September, 1960).

[36] The messiah-like qualities of the president of Ghana have been to some extent ritualized and made more permanent, both in ceremony and in thought, than was true in the past. Religion itself has not confronted this development but has more or less found a different level in those interstices between the metaphysics of national philosophy and the transcendental and personal beliefs of individuals. The mixture is called "consciencism."

The case of Mali is very similar, although a very high proportion of the population is Moslem. There is an acceptance of Islam by the government, and traditional religious and social beliefs are modified through deliberate government policy. Recently I attended a wedding in Mali that illustrates this point. The traditional extended clan unit had been recognized by the government although the chief had been removed from office, as had most traditional chiefs who had previously worked with the French. A very old man from a royal lineage had been elected in his place. He carried the ceremonial sword at the wedding, and all groups gave respect to it. The actual leader of the ceremony was an important government official very high in the party, the Union Soudanaise. The various traditional sections of the clan — women, elders, children, and men — danced and participated in the ceremony, not only in their traditional roles, but also as members of the clan women's brigade, the youth organizations, and the party section, as the case might be. Blessings were invoked to fall on the marriage partners and the clan and, simultaneously, on the party and the state. Here, then, is an example of the blending of old and new, church and political religions, within the context of older cultural and social groups.

the party assumes the directing role in the life of the nation and as such controls all the power of the nation: the political power, judicial, administrative, economic, and technical, is in the hands of the Parti Démocratique de Guinée. It is this, then, that designates the chief of state through the voice of direct universal suffrage.[37]

And again, in the words of Sekou Touré:

> We have often said that in our eyes, there are no soldiers, no civil servants, no intellectuals; there are only supporters of the Party. It is among the supporters of the Party that the standards of value, of faithfulness, of courage, of unselfishness are. It will be the supporters who established [sic] make possible the prosperity of Guinea, as they made possible its independence. *If the Party wants the State to run as it desires, it should fortify its basic organization and ensure that democracy remains the essential and permanent principle of its activities.*[38]

Spreading the consummatory values abroad has also been attempted. The effort to establish a mobilization system in the Congo failed, but in that tragedy some of the relationships between fellow political religionists were revealed. In one of his famous "Dear Patrice" letters to Lumumba, Nkrumah wrote,

> In any crisis I will mobilize the Afro-Asian bloc and other friendly nations as in the present attempt to *dethrone* you. Whenever in doubt consult me. Brother, we have been in the game for some time now and we know how to handle the imperialists and the colonialists. The only colonialist or imperialist I trust is a dead one. If you do not want to bring the Congo into ruin, follow the advice I have given.[39]

These illustrations from the experience of Guinea and Ghana show the way in which consummatory values develop into an

---

[37] Sekou Touré, *Cinquieme Congres National du Parti Démocratique de Guinée,* Rapport de Doctrine et de Politique General (Conakry: Imprimerie Nationale, 1959), p. 38 [my translation].

[38] Sekou Touré, *Toward Full Re-Africanization,* p. 89 [my italics].

[39] Quoted in Colin Legum, *Congo Disaster* (Baltimore: Penguin Books, 1961), p. 154 [my italics].

explicit political religion within a totalitarian democracy. There are, of course, many other examples — Indonesia, China, Mali, to mention only a few. China is, of course, an extreme case — as are her problems — since most mobilization systems are not communist. The failure to distinguish between the more general phenomenon of political religion and the particular brand of political religion and structural form of Soviet or Chinese communism often leads to broad errors of judgment about noncommunist mobilization systems.

If political religions are to satisfy the needs of individuals as I have defined them, what are the means open to them? First, prophets are needed to interpret immortality, identity, and purpose through their own personal gifts of grace. They need to be father and teacher as well as founder of the community. They are the present equivalent of ancestral gods in theocracies or those mythological figures associated with the founding of older societies.

Such prophets need to light tinder of hope at the ordinary day-to-day level of human demands.[40] In new nations this can be done by creating something new, a new polity for future generations. Hence, political religions are for the young and are directed toward the future. They provide hope and a belief in progress. To create hope and a belief in progress is to reinforce the immortality gained through family, kinship, and the society itself.

By following the prophet, one joins a select group. Identity and comradeship, human relationships and group functions, are then combined, and each person finds his place in the scheme of development. Purpose and individual dignity, useful roles and satisfying work, are enhanced by the link they provide with the messianic leader. Roles become more than functionally satisfying: they also partake of grace.

[40] Some prophets may become charismatic leaders, but this is the special case. For the most part, prophets articulate prevailing norms and point out discrepancies between norms and their realization. Charismatic leaders create new norms.

To achieve this new polity, however, requires more than a prophet. It requires effective organization. Indeed, a prophet without an organized militant following will be less than without honor — he will be unsuccessful. To organize mobilization systems, the political religion is turned into an ideology and expressed through the mechanism of the single party. We have seen how leader, party, and the state come to represent one and the same authority. The community is organized by a translation of political values, via the leader, into a popular but controlled system of roles.

After the initial stage, political religion comes to concentrate on three main objects: the development of a single system of central authority, the material development of the country, and the institutionalization of instrumental values. All three are intimately connected as processes. All can be aided in important ways by political religion.

More specifically, political religion in mobilization systems fits individual moral purposes and ways of life to technological dynamism. Individual roles are acceptable only insofar as they enlarge that dynamism and share in it. Hence, the roles that an individual plays are both morally and technologically functional. By this definition, individual purpose and national purpose are the same. In mobilization systems older roles are either objectionable, branding their occupants as enemies, or sentimentalized and relegated to a pleasant museum along with old costumes, antique artifacts, and other symbols of the past. Indeed, by becoming sentimental, they may become functionally serviceable.

Immortality, identity, meaning, and purpose are among the profound individual needs that both church religion and political religion satisfy. By satisfying them, sometimes in the same and sometimes in different spheres, they give men a sense of purpose, even in the face of death, and promote solidarity and cooperation.

A SUMMARY OF THE CHARACTERISTICS OF POLITICAL RELIGION

The characteristics of political religion in mobilization systems may be summarized as follows. There are similarities with church religion. There are saints and villains. There are prophets and missionaries. For each individual, the possibility of a political calling replaces the possibility of a religious calling. There is mysticism and authority. Justice is phrased less in terms of equity than in terms of purpose, with purpose directed toward collective ends. The search for meaning and identity results in such concepts as "African personality," Nkrumaism, or Sukarno's five principles. An earnest effort is made to ascribe new meaning to group life.

Ultimate ends are bound up directly with the state. It is the state, not the church, that will fulfil the psychological and social needs that lie behind political religions. The means include modernity and development, industrialization and science, which, becoming identified with human potentiality, are elevated to the status of transcendental beliefs. At this point a difficulty arises because they are not in fact transcendental but concrete and, as such, exert a secularizing influence upon the social body. This influence is ordinarily kept in check by identifying concrete ends with "science." Modernity and technology become the prevailing "laws" of human schemes.[41]

All this, of course, is in sharp contrast to the system built around a constitutional framework. The latter posits universal ends beyond the state, which are largely derivative from an earlier period of church religion. The state is merely an organized means for reconciling the multiplicity of objectives among the members. This kind of state cannot provide identity but only membership.

[41] In many mobilization systems, the leaders are supporters of church religion as well, that is, non-political religious groups and beliefs. They may be hostile to specific churches, however. In other words, political prophets can be religious men in the usual sense of the term.

It cannot provide meaning, for its policy is an amalgam of the purposes of many groups and individuals. Purpose is left to individuals, to seek out as they can. There is a separate role for church religions as such. In reconciliation systems, justice and political morality are more largely a matter of individual and social conscience. Things as they are, are often the measure of things as they should be.

Hence, we may say that modernizing nations may be distinguished less by the formal structure of politics than by whether or not they have a political religion. Those without a political religion have a constitutional framework that provides for the achievement of the objectives of individuals. If these objectives are cheap and demeaning, so will the society appear cheap and demeaned; if the citizenry has some loftier conception of its values, this conception, too, will be mirrored in the society, for a constitutional framework is a mirror held up to the working community. In a very real sense, it is what democracy is all about. Leaders in countries with political religions have a great deal of difficulty understanding this, or if they understand it, accepting it, for it requires seeing and taking into account the needs and desires of one's self and one's fellows.

In the terms laid out above, political religion qualifies as "religion." Although, as I said earlier, I believe church religion to be more ethically powerful than political religion, its decline in reconciliation systems, and the resulting spiritual lacunae, has given political religion a singular opportunity to satisfy the basic needs of individuals to find immortality, define identity, and determine their fate.

As a political community, the mobilization system, with a party of solidarity led by a prophetic leader (who is the repository of final authority), expresses itself by mobilizing the resources of the community to suit the ideological and organizational needs of its newly developing country. By bringing together wide participation in social and material life and militantly disciplined political control, it enhances stability and organization in the name of sacrifice and lofty objectives.

Can mobilization systems with political religions transform themselves into reconciliation systems, whose commitment is to a liberal framework of law? This is a question of great concern to the West. One factor that favors transformation to a reconciliation system is the eventual necessity for a mobilization system that is successful in promoting economic development to confront its own successes. It will need to decentralize authority and increase its economic efficiency. This could have the effect of reducing the prophetic element and, as well, diffusing and spreading authority. (One may be able to see the beginnings of this process in the Soviet Union. Evidence, admittedly slender and subject to less sanguine explanations, can be found in Khrushchev's Twentieth and Twenty-second Congress speeches.) Even if one grants the possibility of this tendency, however, the question remains whether or not political religions themselves possess sufficient flexibility to tolerate structural changes from one type of system to another.

Another factor possibly favorable to the decline of political religions is that they are successful only so long as ultimate ends and material ends are highly integrated. This integration can remain intact only when what might be called the "aspirational gap" between material ends and genuine potentialities is extremely wide. Material ends appear to embody happiness, prosperity, well-being, dignity, and achievement and similar venerated ultimate ends. It is the wisdom of the rich, of course, to know that material ends embody nothing of the sort. It cannot be denied that an industrial society has some pride of achievement and a sense of technological and political superiority that rankles those who are poorer. But evidence in the West shows that, despite a high rate of material achievement, a society in which there has been a decline in church religion leaves its members emotionally starved and dangerously anomic. We might expect, therefore, that an increase in material prosperity would increase secularization and weaken both the organizational and the ideological strengths of a country with political religion.

Another factor that may contribute to the decline of political religion is a generational one. Once a revolution has been consolidated, its revolutionary achievements become remote to the next generation. Only if its prophets are made to appear larger than life size can the religious aspect be institutionalized. If this is not successfully done, the revolutionaries may become less than folk heroes and even comic and absurd. Prophetic statements lose the power of prophecy, and "young pioneers" simply try to get ahead like everyone else. Will political religion lose its creativity through the mere erosion of time and generation? This is one possibility, since political religion is an integral part of the mechanism of government in mobilization systems. Beliefs may themselves become tarnished if the state becomes a center of antagonism. Cynicism is as serious a threat to political religion as iconoclasm is to church religion.

THE RITUALIZATION OF POLITICAL RELIGION

I have suggested that among modernization societies it is the mobilization systems that have strong theocratic elements. Because of this characteristic, however, they also are subject to political cynicism, which may threaten the consummatory legitimacy of the state. A number of interesting possibilities present themselves. One is the transformation of the mobilization system into a reconciliation system. I shall discuss the possibilities of that later on in this book. Another, more immediate possibility is the formation of a modernizing autocracy or military oligarchy. Indeed, the latter development is common in mobilization systems when the transfer of authority from a charismatic leader to his successor has not been successful; the resulting struggle for power between rival claimants elevates the role of the military as a political force.

More important for our purposes than the military oligarchy, however, is the neomercantilist system. If a mobilization system should begin to ritualize its leadership and traditionalize its consummatory values, by making them into a new and effective link between novelty and the past, this important alternative system becomes possible.

The ritualization of political religion within a new form — the neomercantilist society — leads to interesting speculation about some of the probable characteristics.[42] Tendencies may already be identified. Formal monarchies are not likely to be established. More than likely are presidential systems, or, more accurately, "presidential monarchies," with the presidential monarch embodying both non-dynastic aspects of the role and dynastic aspects associated with the ceremonial and ritual functions of kingship. A presidential monarch can play an active political role, by utilizing concentrated power, as well as a ritualized religious role, by representing the symbolic qualities of the entire nation. The ritualization of this role allows a smooth transition from predominantly consummatory to predominantly instrumental values.

In the neomercantilist system the nationalist single party comes to form the new group of guardians and warriors of the state. The members of this group carry on the modern functions of entrepreneurship through state enterprise and leadership. As an elect, they are the purveyors of ritual. Among them are those who interpret and explain matters of dogma and ritual to the public. If not high priests, they are nevertheless appointed keepers of the sacred texts. The formation of this elite helps to retain the system of hierarchical authority inherited from the former mobilization system.

The texts themselves are a blend of ideology and theology. Mixtures of mysticism and pragmatism, they tend to be non-program-

---

[42] For a general discussion, see S. N. Eisenstadt, "Institutionalization and Change," *American Sociological Review*, XXIX (April, 1964).

matic so that innovation will not be offended by any strict doctrine. They provide precise guides to moral conduct, however, and help define individual relationships to the state and to the leader. Beyond ordinary ideology, they strive to enhance individual immortality by linking individuals to the leader as founder of the state, provide purpose by defining it, and picture a hopeful future to be achieved through the political kingdom. One would expect that the norms of egalitarianism, mass participation in social life, opportunity, and abundance (the values expressed in the totalitarian democratic tradition, as described by Talmon) will all be expressed. The language of these texts, some of which already exist and have mainly been written by the leaders themselves, follows the terminology of socialism in an extremely wide and loose sense. We can cite two main examples from Africa. One consists of the writings of the President of Guinea, whose militant socialist version of *négritude* has blended the communal and aesthetic properties of African traditional life with modern socialist values and practices. Another is Nkrumaism in Ghana, an effort to combine in a philosophical system aspects of socialism, with an emphasis on the African personality, and certain traditional customs and social forms. Notably absent are two central concerns of socialist doctrine, property and class.

The enemies, in the view of the leaders of the neomercantilist system, include capitalism (as distinct from investment capital), neocolonialism or neo-imperialism, racial discrimination, traditionalism, and those individuals or groups that show antagonism to the leader, regime, or political religion. The notion of evil is sometimes also extended to include those roles that are not functional to the performance of modernized social and political activities supported by the state. Political religion may help in this task by distinguishing "good" and "bad" roles and tying them to the needs of the modernizing state.

It is, of course, impossible to do more than briefly sketch in some likely characteristics of the neomercantilist system. Not all of the new states will follow this pattern, which should go without saying. Those that do, will show widely differing practices. In some, civil servants may be surrounded by a kind of "positive neutralism" within the state that has the effect of exempting them from ritualized practices and religious observances. Groups representing church religions may be similarly neutralized.[43]

Political ritualization can help to blend the new roles of leader, priests, and elect into an effective system, supported by a ritualized doctrine that is a mixture of modernizing values (as in socialism) and unique traditions (as in *négritude*). This effort stresses change within continuity and forms the basis of authority in the society. The ritualization of values is therefore one way to institutionalize the new roles of the polity and most particularly the role of presidential monarch.[44]

CONCLUSION

The importance of political religion lies precisely in the barriers it places in the way of smooth transition from societies in which politics is sacred to those in which it is not and, correspondingly, the transition from mobilization systems to reconciliation systems. Hence, mobilization systems that attempt to fight secularization, whether it derives from the ultimate incompatibilities resulting from the elevation of material ends to sacred rank or from the growth of disillusionment and cynicism, may nevertheless be transformed into neomercantilist systems.

If these assumptions are correct, the most likely form of stable polity is a neomercantilist system that has evolved from an earlier mobilization period through ritualization — a process that would limit the functional consequences of religion without destroying its relation to authority. Political leadership would still derive

[43] For a fuller discussion of these matters, as illustrated in Indonesia, Japan, Africa, and the Middle East, see David E. Apter (ed.), *Ideology and Discontent* (New York: Free Press of Glencoe, Inc., 1964).
[44] See my *Ghana in Transition* (New York: Atheneum, 1963), chap. xv, for an analysis of the presidential monarchy in Ghana.

from strongly ritualistic roles. The exact specifications of these roles would be impossible to predict, but they would certainly have strong traditionalistic features at least superficially attached to them. We can see a hint of this already in the titles taken by Nkrumah in Ghana, which include a number of traditional forms in addition to "Osagyefo" (military savior). At this point, Tocqueville's words on the French Revolution are relevant.

> They will say that a country governed by an absolute ruler is a *democracy* because he governs by such laws and maintains such institutions as are favorable to the great mass of the people. Such a government, it will be said, is *democratic, a democratic monarchy.*
>
> But *democratic government, democratic monarchy* can mean only one thing in the true sense of these words: a government where the people more or less participate in their government. Its sense is intimately bound to the idea of political liberty. To give the democratic epithet to a government where there is no political liberty is a palpable absurdity, since this departs from the natural meaning of these words.
>
> Such false or obscure expressions are adopted: (a) because of the wish to give the masses illusions, for the expression "democratic government" will always evoke a certain degree of appeal; (b) because of the embarrassing difficulty in finding a single term which would explain the complex system of an absolute government where the people do not at all participate in public affairs but where the upper classes have no privileges either and where legislation aims to provide as much material welfare as possible.[45]

The phenomenon of which Tocqueville speaks is not entirely dissimilar from the situation in the mobilization systems of new states that have become neomercantilist. They are "presidential monarchies." Through corporate discipline the state provides immortality, meaning, and purpose for individuals. But even

---

[45] Alexis de Tocqueville, *The European Revolution; and Correspondence with Gobineau*, ed. and trans. John Lukacs (New York: Doubleday & Co., Inc., 1959), pp. 102–3.

when such political religions are compelling for other reasons, they are less profound than church religions because of the intermingling of the sacred and the secular. Political religions rarely incorporate the spiritual or wider meanings of human life, although they may make explicit and even ennoble the narrower aspects of social life. They cannot contemplate the concept of fate itself, although they, in fact, determine the careers and opportunities of individuals. They cannot give immortality even when they provide for the perpetuation of the race, the protection of the officeholders, and the security of the family and society.

What should be clear is that some form of religion is the general condition for the establishment of a system of authority. Even the deists had their beliefs in the social compact as an embodiment of man's volition and rationality, a view erected on a profoundly religious base. Whether expressed in monistic or pluralistic terms, the belief that underlies all systems of authority in modernizing nations is that the chief, king, president, or other central political leader is the representative of the public (that is, a broader interpretation of populism than popular sovereignty). The individual who represents the public also serves as the symbolic referent. The role may be separate, like that of a constitutional monarch, or it may be combined with other roles, like that of a presidential monarch. This can be determined in the analysis of the contingent functions of government. Does leadership assume the quality of a symbolic referent? Are the roles that form the political constellation around the symbolic referent regulated by the belief that in the uniqueness of the arrangement lies a higher intelligence and a special genius? Is the source of sanctions revealed through a special wisdom that inheres in the leaders, or in some document or person having oracular power?

Political religion is thus one basis for solidarity and identity in government. The mixtures of consummatory and instrumental values may vary, but two things are clear — consummatory values are essential in varying degrees in all societies that are concerned with the establishment of authority, and there will be tension between these values and instrumental values when they work at cross-purposes. Hence, not any political religion will do. Inherent in the modernization process is the need to find a political ideology that is powerful enough to maintain consummatory values in the political sphere while also encouraging instrumental values sufficient to attain material goals.

9

IDEOLOGY IN
MODERNIZING
SOCIETIES

So far our discussion has centered on the general problem of authority. We have discussed some of the normative factors that, by determining legitimacy, set the conditions that governments try to meet. It is our task in this chapter to indicate the relationship between governing, on the one hand, and political religion and ideology, on the other. This relationship will become visible in the analysis of the formulation and effects of government policy.

It has been suggested earlier that government's manipulation of instrumental ends can be observed through a set of decisions that effect the prevailing hierarchy of power and prestige. Actions involving the contingent structures (consent, enforcement and punishment, political recruitment, and resource determination and allocation) can be evaluated in terms of their effect on social stratification.[1]

Government policy affects consummatory rather than instrumental values through the manipulation of ideology. Ideological "policy" is thus related to the contingent functions of government in its symbolic, sanctional, integrational, and definitional aspects.

[1] See chapter iv.

The reason for this has been discussed in chapter viii, in which the
attempt was made to relate the contingent functions to the consummatory values of identity and solidarity. At this point a more
direct discussion of the ideological forms that political religion
may take is required.

TOWARD A DEFINITION OF IDEOLOGY

Ideology involves more than doctrine. It links particular actions
and mundane practices with a wider set of meanings, giving
social conduct a more honorable and dignified complexion. This
is, of course, a generous view. From another viewpoint, ideology
is a cloak for shabby motives and appearances. The more generous version lays emphasis on the behavior of individuals in a
setting of action-in-relation-to-principle.

"Ideology" is a generic term applying to general ideas that are
potent in specific situations of conduct. For example, not *any*
ideals, but political ones; not *any* values, but those establishing
a given set of preferences; not *any* beliefs, but those governing
particular modes of thought. Because it is the link between action
and fundamental belief, ideology helps to make more explicit the
moral basis of action.

Furthermore, ideology is not philosophy. It is in the curious
position of being an abstraction that is less abstract than the
abstractions contained within it. Powerful ideologies and creative
ideologists do much to enlarge the significance of the individual
(as do religious ideas and innovative clerics). This is the reason
the role of ideology is so central to the thinking of revolutionaries.
To them, the working out of an ideology is a way of indicating
the moral superiority of new ideas.

Political ideology is an application of particular moral prescriptions to collectivities. Any ideology can become political. Hegel-
ianism became the ideological justification for the Prussian state.
Marxism-Leninism is the ideology of Communist societies. The

initial claims to superiority of both of these ideologies lay in a presumed relationship between a higher development of human consciousness and more highly evolved forms of productive processes. The ideologist is the one who makes the intellectual and moral leap forward. By virtue of his superior knowledge, his view ought to prevail.[2]

Karl Mannheim argues that the discovery that much thought is ideological challenges the validity of thought itself.

> Man's thought had from time immemorial appeared to him as a segment of his spiritual existence and not simply as a discrete objective fact. Reorientation had in the past frequently meant a change in man himself. In these earlier periods it was mostly a case of slow shifts in values and norms, of a gradual transformation of the frame of reference from which men's actions derived their ultimate orientation. But in modern times it is a much more profoundly disorganizing affair. The resort to the unconscious tended to dig up the soil out of which the varying points of views emerged. The roots from which human thought had hitherto derived its nourishment were exposed. Gradually it becomes clear to all of us that we cannot go on living in the same way once we know about our unconscious motives as we did when we were ignorant of them. What we now experience is more than a new idea, and the questions we raise constitute more than a new problem. What we are concerned with here is the elemental perplexity of our time, which can be epitomized in the symptomatic question, "How is it possible for man to continue to think and live in a time when the problems of ideology and utopia are being radically raised and thought through in all their implications?"[3]

To expose the ideological aspects of human thinking, however, does not make ideological thought impossible. It merely divides it into new forms. One form is dogma, which can easily lead to

[2] See George Lichtheim, *Marxism: An Historical and Critical Study* (London: Routledge & Kegan Paul, Ltd., 1961), Parts I and II.

[3] Mannheim, *Ideology and Utopia* (New York: Harcourt, Brace & Co., 1946), pp. 37–38.

violence and dissension. Those who see the world in stereotypes seek to protect their beliefs from those who would undermine them.[4]

The more hopeful alternative is science. It is in this sense that science can be said to have become an ideology. Science is the ultimate talisman against cynicism. It defines its own purposes through the logic of inquiry. Some years ago, Michael Polanyi pointed this out very clearly; what he said then of science applies equally to *social* science today.

> Professional scientists form a very small minority in the community, perhaps one in ten thousand. The ideas and opinions of so small a group can be of importance only by virtue of the response which they evoke from the general public. This response is indispensable to science, which depends on it for money to pay the costs of research and for recruits to replenish the ranks of the profession. . . . Why do people decide to accept science as valid? Can they not see the limitations of scientific demonstration — in the pre-selected evidence, the pre-conceived theories, the always basically deficient documentation? They may see these shortcomings, or at least they may be made to see them. The fact remains that they must make up their minds about their material surroundings in one way or another. Men must form ideas about the material universe and must embrace definite convictions on the subject. No part of the human race has ever been known to exist without a system of such convictions, and it is clear that their absence would mean intellectual annihilation. The public must choose, therefore, either to believe in science or else in some rival explanation of nature, such as that offered by Aristotle, the Bible, Astrology or Magic. Of all such alternatives, the public of our times has in its majority chosen science.[5]

The "Polanyi choice" is in some ways illusory. The "public" cannot make the choice; only individuals can. In modernizing

[4] See Robert Lane, *Political Ideology* (New York: Free Press of Glencoe, Inc., 1962), *passim*.

[5] Polanyi, *The Logic of Liberty* (Chicago: University of Chicago Press, 1958), pp. 57–58.

nations, few individuals have the opportunity. In industrial countries, those that opt for science leave the rest behind.

We can discuss these matters in the context of four ideological tendencies, three of which will receive special attention. The three are nationalism, socialism, and science (considered as an ideology). The fourth is national socialism, or some new form of fascism, which may emerge as a force to be reckoned with, particularly in neomercantilist societies. It is the relationship between the first three that will concern us here. We will illustrate them briefly with particular cases and indicate some of the uses to which ideology has been put, both by government and by various political groups. An underlying assumption is that socialism and nationalism will fluctuate vis-à-vis each other and that in the process of modernization, and especially industrialization, the ideology of science will increasingly gain influence.

The ideology of science, and the professional roles and norms associated with it, is an important bridge between the modernizing and the industrial nations. Planners, manpower experts, social survey teams, management experts, all embody some elements of the scientific ethic in their professional roles. In modernizing nations, they serve as the main link between their countries and the various technical commissions of the United Nations and their counterparts in the industrial nations. Just as in a previous generation in India the Indian Civil Service represented the core of modernity, so today the technical personnel of modernizing nations as well as the political leaders are identified with it.

What this means is that the uneven pattern of modernization in most countries has created a special group of people whose professional-technical careers are essential to modernization. Associated with the intellectuals, on the one hand, and with the political leaders, on the other, they are a functional grouping that looks to their much more powerful counterparts in the industrial countries for support. For it is in the latter that the role of the scientist and the social scientist is becoming more and more powerful — so powerful, indeed, that technical advice is involved in virtually every major decision. In this sense, science is the ideology of modernity, and by comparison, other ideologies, whether or not they make the claim to be scientific, have become "vulgar."

Although the increasing prominence of science and the scientific ideology in industrial societies exerts a significant stimulus to the education and formation of technical-professionals in modernizing societies, the latter can rarely make the same use of such personnel as the industrial societies. More often, the technical-professionals represent a kind of exhibit; they are formally consulted, but their advice is not followed. Often the reasons for this are very sound. It is sometimes the case, for example, that the expert who trained in the universities of the industrial countries is, in effect, overtrained for the conditions of his own country, with the result that his suggestions lack realism. Isolated from the actual problems to be solved, he feels helpless and annoyed. In the past, this has been the situation in medicine. Today it characterizes planning, fiscal, and management experts who, complete with their Harvard Business School diplomas, are unable to cope with the practical world.

It is not surprising, then, to find that carefully worked-out plans have been shelved when, to the despair of the planner, political decisions have taken priority over technical matters. This is often attributed to the lack of sophistication of the politician when, in fact, the reverse is true. It is the scientist who is unsophisticated.

This brings up the important problem of criteria for modernization and the relationship of criteria to ideology. Despite the fact that the ideologies of modernization quite often profess to be scientific and embody objectives that are similar to those of science, they are not scientific because their objectives are not scientific. They need to serve authority, and they are employed in building a nation. It is enough if the ideology directs the attention of the public toward modernization goals. Such a function, however, is vastly different from the spread of the ideology of science. The reasons are not very hard to find. Ideology in modernizing nations is meaningful to the public less for its specific content than for its symbolic expression of dissatisfaction; and as people withdraw from primordial associations and observe around them a different level of standards, they begin to adopt these as their own.[6]

HOW IDEOLOGIES ARE FORMED

Coherent ideologies, expressed by political leaders, represent the culmination of a process. In this process, individual identities are frequently expressed in metaphor, with some persons describing themselves as worthy cultivators in a new moral system. Modernity, in this sense, is a moral ideology, not a scientific one. Such an ideology needs to create a picture of the roundness and wholeness of society. Ideology and political religion are thus closely related. Ideology is often the expression of political religion.

Ideologies do not spring from a sudden revelation but have first passed through a latent period. This latent period ends when confusion in belief is manifested in anger and bitterness.

To examine the significance of ideology, let us consider the various authority types we have described as constant in relation to three types of ideology. Two of the types are characteristic of modernizing societies — socialism and nationalism — and the third is characteristic of industrializing societies — science. Participants in every society, colonial or postcolonial, old or new, ancient or modern, cloak reality in different ways. The process may be detected in the rise of Middle Eastern nationalism or the Nazi movement, in the peasant revolts in Europe, and in the Jacobin society

[6] See the discussion of ideology and primordial sentiments in Clifford Geertz, "Primordial Sentiments and Civil Policies in the New States," in *Old Societies and New States* (New York: Free Press of Glencoe, Inc., 1963). See also Geertz's article "Ideology as a Cultural System," in David E. Apter (ed.), *Ideology and Discontent* (New York: Free Press of Glencoe, Inc., 1964).

during the French Revolution. These ideological perceptions of reality are linked with authority, on the one hand, through the functional requisites of government, and with political groups, on the other.

The sequence in which ideologies arise is as follows. First, there is the growth of *multiple images* held by elites and counterelites. These multiple images are the ways different groups in society observe different features of the same events, assign different weights to what they observe, and reach different conclusions. At the beginning of such a process, the images are translatable one into the other, so that a common denominator of meaning is shared.[7]

The next step in the cycle of perception is the operation of the principle of *selective recall*. The area of meaningful discourse shrinks because only the salient features of each of the multiple images remain; the contextual meaning is lost. This step emphasizes points of disagreement, and earlier points of agreement begin to drop out of the dialogue altogether. Disagreement becomes the focal point for interrelationship.

After a time, what might be called a *relative threshold* is passed. What has been selectively recalled now becomes the basis of perceived reality, and there is no way of going back to the former stage. The original dialogue between opposing groups in a system is irretrievably lost. Each side sees in the other's point of view only enough to validate a currently held position.

The next stage is the piecing together by key individuals of the meaning of these ideological disputes to see in them an explanation of the antagonist's conduct within a wider theoretical context. Such a search for meaning defines goals, identifies friends, and excoriates enemies. This is the period of *hortatory realism*.[8]

---

[7] To take an example, following Khrushchev's Twentieth Congress speech, there were noticeably different interpretations of the meaning of Marxism-Leninism, especially with respect to what has now come to be known as Stalinism. There was a meaningful dialogue between the holders of these multiple images, however, even though each stressed a different interpretation.

[8] Hence, the Chinese ideological attack on the Soviet Union, for example,

Next comes the period of what can be called *political fantasy.* It is accompanied by ideological rage mixed with simplistic notions of how to solve problems. It is the particular talent of the charismatic leader to manipulate political fantasy, which also serves to create new consummatory values.

The final stage in the formation of ideology is the period of *practical realism,* in which a working consensus on the integration of roles is reflected in a general similarity of views.

The importance of this process — multiple images, selective recall, relative threshold, hortatory realism, political fantasy, and practical realism — is that it relates ideology to consciousness. By that I mean consciousness of grievance and conflict, which is gradually articulated in such a way that issues are polarized and sharpened. These issues come to embody the powerful moral feelings that are associated with the identity of the individual and the solidarity of the community. It is when an ideology can be related to such terms as these that it becomes a factor in the legitimation of authority. Otherwise, an ideology will simply remain a particular set of ideas without much political consequence.

The cycle occurs in connection with other events and describes a period in which old meanings change and people become receptive to the new. Selective recall creates or magnifies grievance. Once the relative threshold is passed, grievance becomes mythologized. It becomes an inheritance with a stubborn degree of persistence, handed down from father to son, from leader to follower. This generalized grievance takes the form of self-hatred in many modernizing nations, of bitterness over failure, which the political leaders direct against an outside object, especially the previous regime or a former metropolitan power. The period of hortatory realism allows a new appraisal of self and promises a release from self-hatred and social doubt. Political leaders, in particular, try to explain conditions of backwardness by blaming outside exploitation or oppression. Indeed, this is one reason that

shows not only that the latter's position is bad Marxism-Leninism but also that the abolition of the leaders who hold the position will achieve a more perfected form of Marxism-Leninism.

socialism has been so powerful as an ideology in developing areas;
it provides a simple explanation of the causes of backwardness,
with the further advantage of placing guilt squarely on a foreign
country.

When a utopian element appears (along with claims to legitimacy), the period of political fantasy begins. At this time, the
political leader puts together idealized programs for progress. A
new society is described. A millennial quality is introduced. Most
political leaders employ hortatory realism and political fantasy in
combination — a reasonable explanation of experience and a
morally uplifting social solution — in claiming the authority to
rule.

Under such circumstances, it is the more "vulgar" ideologies,
the more simplistic ones with stylized programmatic objectives,
that have the most impact. These also show the closest links to
political religion and may comprise the dogma of political religion. The most effective ideologies of modernization, in this
sense, have been the Protestantism of Calvin and Marxism. Both
have integrated consummatory and instrumental values so that
each reinforces the other.

In the process of ideology formation, we can also see a very
delicate and interesting relationship between the type of authority in the system and the uses it makes of ideology. Reconciliation
systems tend to wear away at ideologies so that grievances never
really reach the stage where individuals might pass a relative
threshold. Quite the contrary, inequities in the system may help
to produce the first two stages, multiple images and selective recall, but afterward they are used to distinguish individuals and
groups from one another and to give them identity based on conflict and local solidarity based on competition for influence and
power. If the reconciliation system should not prove responsive
and alienation set in, it is possible that a relative threshold might
be passed, after which grievances would become fundamental
and the basis for a new set of consummatory values. It is at this

stage that political religion is important and charismatic leaders become strategically possible.

Once the relative threshold is passed, the rest of the process occurs quite rapidly. Hortatory realism defines the new moral norms. Political fantasy introduces the millennial quality that we have described as political religion. If a period of practical realism follows, it does so in the form of political cynicism. Ideology then breaks down in a new round of conflict in which multiple images are formed.

This approach to the analysis of ideology leads us directly to a discussion of the manipulators of ideas. Some are ideologues who believe blindly in their own dogmas. Others are ideologists who combine an intellectual skill in analysis with a determined search for formulas of change. Although such leadership takes many forms, three roles, in particular, have the most significant impact: the "Robin Hood" role, the ideologue, and the scientists.

ROLES AND IDEOLOGY

If the network of obligation that forms society becomes ruptured in a period of change, the custodial aspect of human existence — the sense of receiving an inheritance from the past — must be carefully nourished, amplified, and passed to the future; when this inheritance is lost, the result is an intense preoccupation with self and self-assertion. The definition of personality and the acquisition of position and place, skill and competencies, become critical motives.

During a period of modernization, such a breakdown of traditional obligation is, of course, quite common. The corporate grouping in industrializing societies becomes the unit of continuity, with the individual's role being derived from it. These roles are bureaucratic, organized by the particular enterprise and acquiring obligations from the set of rules of that enterprise. If, under such circumstances, personal ties are weakened, obligation itself is not; in fact, it becomes increasingly contractual, regularized, and enforceable. These roles, which we have called careers, are particularized by professionalization. It is the occupant of the career role who becomes the member of the establishment in the modern period, with all the trappings of professionalism: a code of ethics; a set of clubs or associations that embody the code and set standards of behavior; and the power to affect conditions of employment. The career role has power, but it is rarely a power role per se. On the positive side, professionalism produces a modesty and discipline in people that has caused them to be labeled "organization men," with all the negative and positive implications of that expression. Bureaucratic career roles and professional roles are typical of the industrial society. Of the roles important in ideology formation, the role of scientist is a career role but the roles of Robin Hood and ideologue are entrepreneurial roles.

THE ROBIN HOOD ROLE

It is the *Robin Hood role* that is particularly important in modernizing societies. The Robin Hood role arises during the period of political fantasy, which is also a period of role confusion. It is filled by role-testers — individuals who, by defining their roles a bit larger than life, encourage others to follow suit. To do this, the typical "Robin Hood" must act in the name of a public, or some wide and relatively significant grouping that manipulates virtue, defining it in such a way that it derives from an attack on authority. The Robin Hood role lies between the roles of the outlaw and the politician. It has a small set of support-roles, the "band," and it is always in part clandestine.

In the extreme form, the Robin Hood role may lead to charismatic authority. What may have begun in small clublike organizations can blossom into powerful parties of solidarity, as we have called them. Robin Hood roles are created by patterns of relative grievance, particularly in modernizing societies when older patterns of obligation break down, and by the need for the assertion of new-found rights and obligations to be personal and moral.[9]

THE ROLE OF THE IDEOLOGUE

Heroic figures — philosophers, mystics, politicians — may all help to organize a set of ideas into an ideology. When such ideologies have been established, the problems of transferring them into the consciousness of a population becomes a matter of proselytizing and propaganda. Those who exhort, sway, and in various ways attempt to bend and shape the attitudes of people around an ideology we may call ideologues. Ideologues are most common in connection with vulgar ideologies. They are individuals cast in the role of the unquestioning militant, convinced of their own rightness and acting in accordance with simplified remedial doctrine around which the public is to be organized.

At the beginning stage of the formation of ideology (the period of multiple images), little opportunity is present for the ideologue, although he may provide differing images of the same phenomenon. He becomes a bit more important in the second stage (selective recall) by reinforcing certain salient facts while allowing others to lapse. When the relative threshold is passed, however, and the different perceptions of individuals begin to have consequences for self and society — for identity and solidarity — then the ideologue assumes a leadership role in manipulating the differing political values that result. Political fantasy is then possible, and it is in this period that the ideologue is most successful.

Nationalist and socialist ideologies are typical during the periods of hortatory realism and political fantasy. Such periods, common immediately after a revolution or after a new nation has obtained its independence, give exceptional opportunities to political leaders to exert their leadership in the moral sphere. The leaders may draw a picture of a new society in terms of socialism

[9] The most recent "Robin Hood" has been Fidel Castro.

and nationalism, both ideologies being manipulated to prevent the operation of practical realism.

The vulgar ideologies may be based on some meaningful conception of truth, but because they are not experimental in the political sphere, they have little importance at this stage. The ideology of science functions only in a period of practical realism, and is ultimately antagonistic to any other ideology, even though in the short run it may work for it. For this reason, the ideologues of modernizing societies, which for political reasons use ideology to maintain authority, cannot fully accept science.

THE ROLE OF THE SCIENTIST

In a functional and rationalistic universe, scientists (and social scientists) are accorded an increasingly powerful position in political life. This is not because scientists possess a kind of Platonic predisposition to lead. Quite the contrary, most of them share with others the ambiguity that surrounds positions of power. But by gaining a superior insight into the conduct of their fellows, they create a new role and an ideology that follows from it — a hierarchy of power and prestige based on intellectual ability, which, in its extreme form, is what Michael Young has called the "meritocracy." Once the scientist discovered that there was a discrepancy between observed behavior and felt behavior, between the act and the realization, between the conscious and the subconscious, and between virtue and conduct, he fashioned a new role for himself — the theoretically omniscient observer. Human mysteries are for him technical problems. In the modern developing communities, he is asked to apply his knowledge. He displaces the physician as a new symbol of aloofness.

Each of these three roles has special relevance in the process of ideology formation. The Robin Hood role is important during the formation of multiple images; the ideologue, in the periods of hortatory realism and political fantasy; and the scientist, in the period of practical realism. All three affect the formation of consummatory values.

The three roles may become ideologically compatible if the role of the scientist is subordinated to the Robin Hood or ideologue role on the basis of its narrow functional definition. Functional expertise is a claim to significance but not to senior authority. The mechanisms whereby functionally specific roles are made significant but subordinate are career identification and professionalization. The professional almost by definition has a bounded sphere of competence beyond which he is not expected to act.

HOW IDEOLOGIES BECOME EFFECTIVE

During the periods of hortatory realism and political fantasy, there is, ordinarily, a great deal of ideological experimentation. Some ideas are attractive and symbolize a great deal more than their surfaces communicate. Or, to put it another way, ideological language tends to be metaphorical. Indeed, in modernizing societies, few of the ideologies are dogmatic and many represent a blend of ancient and modern ideas, with strongly evangelical overtones, to make them spiritually uplifting. But if they are subject to change and experiment, what makes them significant?

One point that must be made is that most ideologies in modernizing societies are significant for a relatively short period of time. In very few cases has ideology served as a deeply satisfying explanation of, or even a useful programmatic guide to, social and political life. In other words, ideology has not been a very durable basis for building consensus. Ideologies have been particularly useful, however, during periods of hortatory realism and political fantasy. Historically, they are pieced together just prior to and during a revolution or other form of systems change. For example, such periods existed in Guinea from approximately 1957 to 1961 and in Ghana from 1949 until roughly 1960. It is not that ideology disappears. Quite the contrary, it only changes its emphasis, as we shall see. But after these periods it does not have quite the same impact.

What gives an ideology its real force and conviction during its period of maximum effectiveness is its contribution to establishing identity and solidarity. If an ideology can reduce anxiety and increase self-confidence, if it can displace fear to a foreign or outside group, and if it can give individuals a sense of their own worth and significance, then an ideology will be powerful on an individual level. In other words, it must satisfy an identity function.

For the political leader, if an ideology can be sufficiently generalized and if it can be made the basis of shared feelings and a universal language of understanding in the sense of communicating a common condition under which many labor, it will be useful in building solidarity. The powerful ideologies, then, are those that at crucial moments during the cycle of perception give individuals a sense of identity and solidarity with their fellows — all in a political context.

For these purposes, the ideologies of nationalism, socialism, and possibly, national socialism are more satisfactory than the ideology of science.

SOCIALISM AS AN IDEOLOGY

Most of the political leaders in the developing areas profess to be socialist. This ideology enables them to repudiate prevailing hierarchies of power and prestige, which are generally associated with traditionalism or colonialism. Moreover, socialism helps define as temporary (as only a phase in economic growth) the commercial "marketplace" or "bazaar" economy.[10] Although socialism accepts the secularism of the marketplace, it rejects the form; that is, the importance of roles associated with the marketplace is minimized.

[10] For a discussion of the bazaar economy, see David E. Apter, "Political Organization and Ideology," in Wilbert E. Moore and Arnold S. Feldman (eds.), *Labor Commitment and Social Change in Developing Areas* (New York: Social Science Research Council, 1960), p. 337.

In this sense, socialism has a very special meaning for the new nations. It becomes the ethic for a system of political discipline emphasizing science — science for its own sake as a symbol of progress and as a form of political wisdom. In keeping with this aim, socialism offers a set of unified developmental goals that stress roles functional to modernization and the achievement of a workmanlike, rational society in which people lend one another a helping hand because they feel themselves a part of the community effort toward industrialization.

Such forms of socialism have very little to say about religion. They are largely silent on the subject of class antagonism. And they are vague about the role of property, a central factor in Western socialist ideologies. The African variety, for example, prefers at present to delineate core values appropriate to modernization rather than limit itself prematurely to particular economic forms.

In this sense African socialism, like its counterparts in other developing areas, tends to look backward and forward at the same time. Although it may speak in the name of "revolution," in most cases political leaders are forced to make changes slowly by opening up the system to modernized roles. The result, quite often, is that the socialism of Africa is merely another name for nationalism.[11]

The common element of the various forms of socialism, irrespective of their other ingredients, is the emphasis on development goals, for which individuals must make sacrifices. Government is accepted as the main source of development. National citizenship, representing unity, is the critical form of allegiance, with no other loyalties taking precedence over loyalty to the state. Behind unity is the concept of society as a natural, organic body

[11] Nationalism may be a revolutionary ideology vis-à-vis colonialism, but it is not normally so with respect to other aspects of social life. It is largely silent on the forms of economic organization. See the discussion by Charles Andrain, "Democracy and Socialism: Ideologies of African Leaders," in David E. Apter (ed.), *Ideology and Discontent*. See also Pierre Bonnafé, *Nationalismes africaines* (Série D: Textes et Documents, No. 4 [Paris: Fondation Nationale des Sciences Politiques, October, 1962]).

all parts of which have appointed functions, including the parts linked to the development process, which have the most significant functions.

Socialism is held to be more rational than capitalism because of its emphasis on planning: more scientific, more secular, and more suited to the need to fit together and develop functionally modern roles. Socialism, then, has two aspects. As an ideology, it defines modernity. As an application of ideology, it defines social discipline as manifested in solidarity groupings whose *raison d'être* is the functional quality of their roles for development. This functionality, in turn, sets down the terms of individual identity and establishes a new system of motivation that emphasizes achievement.[12]

NATIONALISM AS AN IDEOLOGY — THE JAPANESE ILLUSTRATION

Nationalism either preserves an identity that is carried over from the traditions of the past or creates a new set of attachments centering on the modern state. Sometimes, in new nations, both forms of nationalism exist side by side. They may conflict, but more commonly, the leaders of the new society attempt to blend them. Most ideologies prevalent in modernizing societies try to emphasize continuity with the past at the same time that they provide for innovation in order to promote a social solidarity that will encompass all earlier organizational forms. In Africa this attempt is reflected in the search for an African "personality" as well as in the interpretation of the new concepts of African socialism in terms of traditional values. These mixtures are designed to optimize both identity and solidarity in the midst of change.

[12] See David C. McClelland, "The Achievement Motive in Economic Growth," in Bert F. Hoselitz and Wilbert E. Moore (eds.), *Industrialization and Society* (Paris: UNESCO-Mouton, 1963), p. 74. McClelland points out that achievement motivation becomes linked with identity because it does not represent a desire to do well for the sake of social recognition or prestige but "to attain an inner feeling of personal accomplishment." Ultimately, socialism as an egalitarian system is an effort to induce such achievement motivation.

Such an ideological synthesis is characteristic of many new nations. Since they contain traditional, nationalist, and socialist elements, the emphasis may shift from one to another as the need arises. Moreover, different groups may stress different elements. Ethnic nationalism within a country may persist along with the more generalized nationalism of the nation-state.

The distinctions we have made are more in the nature of differing emphases rather than absolute differences between modernizing ideologies, which are in the main eclectic.

Quite often socialism, no matter how vaguely defined, breaks down into a number of competing dogmas, a process that has the effect of weakening solidarity and confusing identity. When this danger arises, political leaders in developing communities may opt for nationalism as the dominant ideology. Nationalism incorporates primordial loyalties in a readily understandable synthesis, taking up the slack in identity and solidarity left by the failure of socialism. Diffuse enough to encompass all specific forms of loyalty and tradition, it elevates them to a national inheritance. The value of nationalism lies in its functional flexibility.[13]

As M. J. Herskovits has pointed out,

African leaders faced with the challenge of economic growth and the need to establish higher living standards began to re-examine traditional communal patterns with the objective of shaping them to fit the requirements of a new economic order. This re-examination occurred both where patterns of individual effort had become established and where socialistically oriented plans sought to use traditional communalism as an instrument to make the new system function.[14]

[13] See, for example, Janheinz Jahn, *Muntu: An Outline of Neo-African Culture*, trans. Marjorie Grene (New York: Grove Press, Inc., 1961). See also the interesting discussion of the conflict between "traditional" and "Promethean" ideologies in L. V. Thomas, *Les idéologies négro-africaines d'aujourd'hui* ("Publications of the Faculty of Letters and Human Sciences, Philosophy and Social Science," No. 1; Dakar: University of Dakar, 1965), pp. 12–20.

[14] M. J. Herskovits, *The Human Factor in Changing Africa* (New York: Alfred A. Knopf, 1962), p. 467.

In this process, certain older values had to give way, that is, age, hereditary status, kinship, and chieftaincy. The remaining aspects of traditional life could then be translated into more modern circumstances.

In this situation nationalism takes on a more explicitly ideological complexion. Perhaps the best example, and certainly the best studied, is Japan. What makes the Japanese case so interesting is the ability of the country to develop rapidly within the shell of traditional culture. Existing social beliefs, mainly of an instrumental nature, allowed a bending and shaping of well-understood institutions, which, despite their alteration, provided a public sense of continuity. Some of these beliefs were employed in promotion of education for instrumental ends. Robert N. Bellah points out that in Japan learning for its own sake "tends to be despised. The merely erudite man is not worthy of respect. Rather, learning should eventuate in practice. A truly learned man will be a truly loyal and filial man." [15]

The same considerations were applied to Japanese religion. "It was seen almost as a system of training which aided in the self-abnegating performance of actions expressing loyalty to one's lord." [16]

Religion and education, community and family, all found their natural and practical expression in the state, which was therefore able to consider change since it was confident of the loyalties of its members. (We have in mind the massive alterations that occurred when the Tokugawa regime was displaced by Meiji Japan.) The primacy of political values and the emphasis on the polity allowed modification in social institutions, particularly in the economic sphere, without dramatically rupturing the values and social beliefs of the Japanese.

This process is not my concern, nor am I qualified to discuss the

[15] Bellah, *Tokugawa Religion* (Glencoe: Free Press of Glencoe, Ill., and Falcon's Wing Press, 1957), p. 16. See also Ruth Benedict, *The Chrysanthemum and the Sword* (Boston: Houghton-Mifflin Co., 1946).

[16] *Ibid.*, p. 17.

many relevant factors. Certain later developments are significant for our discussion, however. Even in Japan, the accumulated changes could not all be absorbed by the nationalist ideology and political framework. The result was the growth of Japanese militarism from 1900 onward. If the Meiji government represented a "logical fulfillment of a conception of the polity which already existed in the Tokugawa Period," as Bellah indicates, militarism was a natural outgrowth of both, inasmuch as it combined instrumentalism in the economic sphere with nationalism in the political.[17] Militarism was the imperial answer to the rise of trade unions, liberal and left-wing political thought, and those who desired a genuine parliamentary government.

As a result, education, religion, and the polity were brought together in an explicit orthodoxy, perhaps stated most clearly in the Japanese document, *Kokutai No Hongi; or Cardinal Principles of the National Entity of Japan.* This document illustrates the uses of ideology in building and maintaining solidarity and identity in Japan. (It also illustrates how ideology as an instrument of solidarity can be applied through education.) As the editor points out in his introduction, it is "primarily an educational book written for educators." [18] Hardly a pamphlet or tract in the ordinary sense, it is a religious document that links together mythical history ("the great august Will of the Emperor in the administration of the nation is constantly clearly reflected in our history"), the role of the emperor in religious ceremony ("the Emperor, venerating in person the divine spirits of the Imperial Ancestors, increasingly becomes one in essence with Imperial Ancestry"), loyalty ("loyalty means to reverence the Emperor as our pivot and to follow him implicitly"), and familial and national harmony ("in order to bring national harmony to fruition there is no way but for every person in the nation to do his allotted duty and to

[17] *Ibid.,* p. 20.
[18] *Kokutai No Hongi; or Cardinal Principles of the National Entity of Japan,* ed. Robert King Hall (Cambridge, Mass.: Harvard University Press, 1949), p. 30.

exalt it"). The nation, then, is like the family and the emperor like the father, and in the cultivation of both, people venerate themselves and realize higher purposes.[19]

What makes this document so interesting is its explicit rejection of Occidental individualism and liberalism. War is regarded as an expression of development that will lead to great harmony. The martial spirit is sacred. Life and death are basically one. "The monistic truth is found where life and death are transcended. Through this is life, and through this is death. However, to treat life and death as two opposites and to hate death and to seek life is to be taken up with one's own interest, and is a thing of which warriors are ashamed. To fulfill the Way of loyalty, counting life and death as one, is Bushido." [20]

Here we have a striking emphasis on loyalty and filial bonds, which extends the notion of sacrifice and service farther than in any Western ideology. At the same time, the primacy of national solidarity is linked to specific institutions whose lineage may be traced to antiquity. The most immediate effects of modernization and industrialization are thereby deflected without hindering development in the economic sphere. Rather, education, industrial employment, the enlargement of urban life, all help to reinforce rather than destroy the organic conception of society. Individual identity is acquired through service to the state and the emperor. Solidarity is expressed through the network of familial obligations, which include the royal house. What are thus, in other systems, normal sources of tension, dislocation, and cultural strain are in the Japanese case twisted into advantages. An explicitly traditionalist ideology, embodying instrumental ends, was deliberately employed to make the identity and solidarity problems simpler. (Witness, for example, the extraordinary expansion of the educational system in the nineteenth century.) Nationalism in Japan was able to do what socialism in the developing

---

[19] *Ibid.*, p. 94.
[20] *Ibid.*, p. 145.

areas could not do, that is, serve its functional purposes while transmitting a scientific temper.[21]

SOME RELATIONSHIPS BETWEEN NATIONALISM AND SOCIALISM

The process of shaping new principles or changing old ones is not without its tensions. One could almost say that there is a kind of "dialectical" relationship between an ideologically oriented party and reality. The ideological party attempts to change reality and, in this way, is a revolutionary force; the new, changed reality for a while corresponds to the ideology even while gradually changing itself; in time, the ideology may become a conservative force; a new adjustment is eventually forced, and the ideology may then again become a revolutionary force.[22]

In the new, developing communities this "dialectic" is to be found between nationalism and socialism. Each of these ideological forces emphasizes different attachments, meaning, and evaluations of solidarity, identity, and motivation.[23] Socialism tends to be more universalistic and secular; nationalism incorporates specific elements of tradition in order to establish a solidly rooted, meaningful sense of identity and solidarity.

In countries moving from dependent to independent status, the periods of nationalism build up slowly. At first there is emphasis on a common citizenship leading to more effective participation in agencies of rule and greater educational opportunity. Primordial loyalties continue to serve as the basis of the society's uniqueness and to promote pride in identity. The period of nationalism, therefore, accepts the main structure of society as it stands

---

[21] See Robert A. Scalapino, "Ideology and Modernization — The Japanese Case," in David E. Apter (ed.), Ideology and Discontent. See also Reinhard Bendix, Nation-Building and Citizenship (New York: John Wiley & Sons, 1964), pp. 177–213.

[22] A. K. Brzezinski, Ideology and Power in Soviet Politics (New York: Praeger, 1962), p. 115.

[23] For a fuller discussion of this aspect of ideology, see David E. Apter, "Political Religion in the New Nations," in Clifford Geertz (ed.), Old Societies and New States.

while seeking greater opportunities. It is "radical" only in one political context — colonialism.

Quite often nationalist movements take a leftward turn during the last phase of the struggle for independence. The "radicalization of nationalism" results from a changed political emphasis. Independence is no longer the issue. The obvious act of changing authority from outside to inside turns out to be less simple than it appeared. Hence, nationalism finds it necessary to employ socialism as a developmental ideology. A secular system of loyalty replaces the traditional forms. Radicalization adds a sense of community — aspects of which are egalitarianism and a sense of shared purpose in the scientific evolution of the society — to the nationalist emphasis on common membership in the national state.

Radicalization also effects the individual more directly. For those who have been involved in nationalism, identity is bound up with roles of daring innovation often involving personal risk, for example, Robin Hood roles.

A third effect is the transformation of the Robin Hood roles of the independence period into something else. Whether the main thrust of the political ideology is nationalist or socialist (although the one may be employed to reinforce the other), the Robin Hood role becomes fundamentally altered. In the first case the enemy, the colonial government, is no longer close at hand, although it may still be attacked as neocolonialist and as remote from the daily lives of people. The Robin Hoods themselves are no longer the members of a hardy band, striking out of secret places to attack the established government. Quite the contrary, they occupy party or governmental roles and are the basis of the system. Hence, the special heroic quality of the Robin Hood role and the roles contingent on it changes when they have become the authority roles in the system.

To protect at least some aspects of the Robin Hood role, a socialist ideology is more useful than a nationalist one. The former has the advantage of deflecting popular antagonism from the government toward the representatives of foreign firms who bring in external capital, local entrepreneurs, and others in the private sector of the economy, on the basis that they somehow limit the authority of the state and infringe on its sovereignty. The implication of less than full independence and authority creates a situation in which aspects of the Robin Hood role can be retained. By manipulating exchange ratios, taxation, nationalization, and other measures (sometimes exercised capriciously in order to flaunt power as well as incite antagonism), the state itself can play a kind of national Robin Hood game of the poor nations against the rich.

A fourth effect of the relationship between nationalism and socialism is increasingly important over time. As the band of loyal followers, particularly in the party of solidarity, becomes regularized into a party bureaucracy, it becomes important and essential that some of the lesser Robin Hoods be removed from the political scene, to be replaced by nearer life-size roleholders. The movement back and forth between ideologies of nationalism and socialism allows political leaders to eliminate some roles and elevate others. During a period of socialism, for example, it might be important to raise to the level of the civil service planning roles in agriculture, marketing, and the like — positions that had hitherto been given to Robin Hoods as rewards for political service, when as local nationalists, with local followings, it had been necessary for the political movement or party of solidarity to retain their loyalty and support. By transforming their roles into professional or life-size roles, their authority is changed from that of a Robin Hood to that of an expert, from personal loyalty to institutional obligation.

The reverse process may also occur during a change from socialism to nationalism. Roles once held by civil servants may be politicized, particularly if the incumbents are regarded as unsympathetic to the new regime.

Perhaps a diagram will summarize more adequately the relationship between socialism and nationalism (see Figure 15).

At point A in Figure 15 we have the drawing-together of a

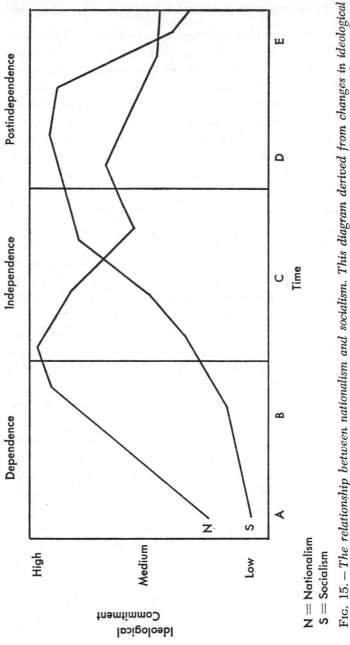

N = Nationalism
S = Socialism

Fig. 15. — *The relationship between nationalism and socialism. This diagram derived from changes in ideological orientation in Indonesia, Egypt, Guinea, and Ghana. Each country shows its own particular pattern. Other combinations would show a different pattern. Ideological commitment is measured by intensity of commitment and span of commitment, that is, number of followers and sympathizers.*

variety of social groups, which become increasingly "politicized" as they seek out a sharper definition of national society in political terms. At point B a socialist "revolutionary" ideology usually coincides with a new group of political entrepreneurs who take power away from the older and perhaps more tradition-bound members of the community. Also at this point, there is an emphasis on corporate community and functionally significant roles. Just after independence, nationalism goes through its apotheosis, and parochial and personal interests pale before the accomplishments of independence. At point C, then, solidarity and identity are linked with achievement. Old institutions become honorable and new ones exciting. At point D, the contradictions in culture, in social groups, and in solidarity and identity have resulted in a sweeping re-evaluation of society in the name of progress. This is the high point of socialism. Point D is the major ideological crisis point in the political life of a country, because it is then that the state may become either militantly socialist or, employing moderately socialist ideas, accommodationist. In the case of Africa, the choice at this point in the ideological dialogue is between a more revolutionary view of socialism and African socialism, which affects not only competition among leaders but policy with respect to education and indoctrination, or what is more broadly known as political socialization, as well. When point E is reached, nationalism and socialism can be blended in a form of national socialism, or both may begin to decline in favor of what we have called the ideology of science. However, to achieve that condition takes a long time and is a very complex process.

Changes among the four main variables we have been discussing form one basis for evaluating the relationship between nationalism and socialism. The conditions of solidarity and identity, for example, change when nationalism is weakened and socialism strengthened. Or, conversely, the need for nationalism or socialism may be recognized as a result of changes in solidarity or identity. Each set of variables, the ideological and the functional, can be, in turn, treated as independent or dependent for research purposes.

Weakness in solidarity and identity, when socialism is the ideology, may cause political leaders to turn toward a greater emphasis on nationalism. This change may have the unwanted effect of creating a provincial identity and a parochial solidarity, which will have to be countered by the more universal appeal of socialism.[24]

Nationalism and socialism are ideologies that, better than most, provide the coherence necessary for retraditionalization during the process of change. Nationalism, for example, helps to center authority on certain aspects of tradition, asserts the continuity of society, and links the present with the past and, by so doing, asserts the immortality of the society, its on-going and life-giving characteristics. The definition of membership in the society, the sanctity of the past, and the symbolism of political forms are made explicit, reinforced, and stipulated as part of a modernizing culture.

IDEOLOGICAL CHANGE AND YOUTH AS A POLITICAL SUBCULTURE

The ideological shifts that take place between nationalism and socialism tend to coincide with claims to power from a new political generation. In modernizing societies, such generations tend to be short — perhaps four or five years. Over time, those in power commonly become more rather than less parochial in their outlook, and youth subcultures are generally antipathetic to them. In a postrevolutionary situation, for example, particularly when political leaders embrace some form of radicalism, whether socialist or nationalist, youth may find it difficult to gain entry into the

[24] Other examples of interesting hypothetical conditions could be given to show the possible dynamic relationships between the ideological and functional factors discussed so far. See, for example, O. Mannoni, *Prospero and Caliban: The Psychology of Colonization* (New York: Frederick A. Praeger, 1964), *passim.*

hierarchy of power and prestige without some particular ideological claim. Hence, if government is predominantly socialist in its ideological orientation, youth will tend to be nationalist; if government is predominantly nationalist in its orientation, youth will press for some form of socialism. Varying vis-à-vis each other, then, are two sets of tendencies – one set embodying universalism and parochialism, the other nationalism and socialism. The combinations that result represent the counterclaims to legitimacy on the part of youth.

The young, however, are not merely driven by ordinary motives of political gain. All societies confront the difficulties of a youth subculture. The reasons ideological matters take such a sharp form among youth in modernizing societies are that their identity problems are exaggerated and their identity choices often lead to culturally discontinuous sequences resulting in inconsistent and often misleading behavior.[25]

Resentful of the anxieties that result from a search for identity, or role, the youth in new nations characteristically seek their identity through revolt against the system. This is why the socialism of youth may result in an attack on nationalism and an urge toward universality, whereas "socialists" who have come to power through nationalism may respond by becoming more nationalist than socialist. The long-term trend is the nationalization of socialism. Sekou Touré, for example, once the exponent of the militant left in Africa, is widely regarded as a right-wing "deviationist" by members of the Federation of African Students in France.[26]

Where development depends a great deal on the training (both political and technical) and commitment of youth, a number of

---

[25] Moreover, this search for identity by youth coincides with a period of relative social freedom – the period of role search – when role-testing and observation are at a maximum. Role search leads to anxiety over premature identity choices, such anxiety being a crucial element in the searching process, that may lead to temporary alienation from society. There have always been angry young men. In new nations that rely heavily on youth as the backbone of the society, however, identity problems undermine solidarity, which leads to serious political difficulties.

[26] See, for example, the study by J. P. N'Diaye, *Enquête sur les étudiants noirs en France* (Paris: Éditions Réalités Africaines, 1962).

alienated counterelites commonly emerges. These subgroups develop their own ideologies and identity, with solidarity based on deviation from society. Indeed, if solidarity and identity are treated as independent variables, the youth group with a high solidarity-potential based on deviation will quite often be revealed as triggering the ideological shift from socialism to nationalism in order to maintain a wider solidarity in the development community.

We have stressed the backward and forward movement between socialism and nationalism for two reasons. The first is that in themselves both are classic embodiments of some major themes of political life that at the same time provide more than purely rational satisfactions from political activity. Emphasis on functional skills in both socialism and nationalism places the technician and the scientist in an important political position, although clearly subordinate to the topmost level of leadership. This last is reserved for those who can represent more than science and can perform all the non-empirical duties that are required of leadership, including the satisfaction of those meanings and identities that are starved in a world in extreme cultural transition. Such are the usual uses of ideology, which have reached their greatest significance today in the developing areas of the world. Indeed, ideologies at times take on the proportions of a political religion.[27]

Some of the ideologies making their appearance in modernizing societies emphasize, by means of anti-Westernism, an antibourgeois attack, a demand for selflessness on the part of the people, a new-found cultural superiority coupled with an expression of deliberate racial renaissance, and a blend of mystical elements, sacred objects, eternal fires, and all the rest. In short, as nationalism and socialism become intertwined, some of the modernizing ideologies may well come to resemble fascism more than any other. This can have an important consequence for spreading modernization if the emphasis on functional groupings results in

[27] This aspect is treated in chapter viii.

their being politically represented on the basis of their contribution to the modern sector of society; this would be not unlike the representation of corporations under classical fascism.

SCIENCE AND IDEOLOGY IN INDUSTRIAL SOCIETIES

The ideologies of nationalism and socialism are linked with the periods of hortatory realism and political fantasy. Nationalism has, almost invariably, a high degree of political fantasy built into it. In contrast, the ideology of science involves high information and practical realism. The logic of fact and verification is the basis of rationality. It would be foolish to claim that in all systems that employ practical realism the ideology of science prevails; however, it is the case that a climate of practical realism is most congenial for the ideology of science.

The ideology of science is not merely a style of thinking about problems, nor is it solely a derivation from the functional significance of science in an industrialized world, although this is clearly the origin of its power. Rather, it is the application of rational methods and experimentalism to social affairs. In this respect, the ideology of science accepts the principle of potentiality as the basis of its ultimate legitimacy. The figures who have been associated with the evolution of the ideology of science, although we might include Marx and, more recently, J. D. Bernal, whose book *The Social Function of Science* is perhaps a key ideological text, comprise a wide-ranging and largely anonymous group. The size of this group in absolute numbers is perhaps less relevant than the fact that "science is doubling every twelve years or thereabouts, so that the subjective impression that things are changing faster and faster is quantitatively confirmed. The exponential acceleration means that each generation's life and problems differ more and more from those of its forebears." [28]

[28] See Maurice Goldsmith and Alan Mackay (eds.), *Society and Science* (New York: Simon & Schuster, 1964), p. 13.

As societies modernize, the ideologies of socialism and nationalism can be expected to give way to the generalized ideology of science, which today includes social science. Science as an ideology takes shape in highly advanced development communities when the following conditions have been achieved: (1) there is general acceptance of common membership in the society, with the result that nationalism has become internalized and implicit; (2) sufficient development has already occurred so that social dislocations require fine adjustments rather than gross "solutions"; (3) a consensus prevails about the roles that are functional to the continuous process of development. Industrial societies are no longer in the process of changing from traditional to modern forms of social life. As a consequence, they look beyond programmatic ideologies with their simplified remedial suggestions. One of their outstanding characteristics is broad agreement on fundamentals and a corresponding magnification of minor issues. The great problem of the industrial society is that its ideology of science cannot be shared by all, as nationalism or socialism can. The latter are all-embracing; the former is necessarily exclusive. This difference is reflected in a division between the scientific elite and the rest of the community.

The characteristics of science as an ideology can be summarized as follows: (1) Science is a well-defined ideology possessing norms of empiricism, predictability, and rationality as guides to conduct. (2) Social science is becoming accepted as scientific, and scientific norms are increasingly accepted as guides to social conduct. (3) There is a universal trend toward planning, calculation, and rationalistic goals concerned with the future in both the developing and the developed areas. (4) In the developing areas, vulgar ideologies adopt the values of science through some form of socialism in association with the national independence movement (for example, African socialism, Egyptian socialism, and Indonesian socialism). (5) In the industrial countries, the new ideology expresses itself in a meritocracy. Recruitment of talent is on the basis of competitive school and university examinations, with increasingly close links between the educational establishment and the bureaucratic establishment.

The ideology of science can do little, however, to promote solidarity and identity. Quite the contrary, science tends to downgrade the beliefs that other ideologies promote. The social discipline imposed by the scientific ideology is professionalism. The key to the scientific "establishment" is its professional status. Authority derives from "superior" knowledge. Science has a code of ethics that enshrines integrity. Moreover, the integrity of the research worker is only slightly less entrenched than the code it derives from, academic freedom, which is, in turn, linked with the concept of free inquiry. And in an area where free inquiry produces a superior range of technological social alternatives for decision-makers, its concrete advantages become manifest.

The body of theory, the set of ideas that contains universals and represents the intellectual inheritance that will be enlarged by the incumbents of professional roles, is set apart from the community. Indeed, even older professional roles come in time to be regarded as functional rather than professional. The reverse movement — into the scientific establishment — does occur, however, whenever a particular group adopts a code of ethics and builds up some theory of its work, some transmittable body of ideas that can be called "scientific." [29]

Professionalization, then, gives identity and solidarity to roles and to the organization but not to the society. It only links the

[29] Public relations experts who run polls and do sample studies for private firms on a contract basis and thus are in between the universities proper and corporate business are examples. The Bureau of Applied Social Research at Columbia, the National Opinion Research Center at the University of Chicago, and the Stanford Research Institute all represent bodies that, although clearly professional, are doing contract work. The next step is for the large-scale private firms to claim the same professional status, followed by the more skilled advertising technicians. By this means — the relation of needed skills to transmittable theory and the theory to some broad ethical consideration, such as the determination of public attitudes and opinion — professionalization occurs. See Caryl P. Haskins, *The Scientific Revolution and World Politics* (New York: Harper and Row, 1964), *passim*.

professional to the establishment, in contrast to the vulgar ideologies, which relate individuals and roles to society as a whole.

Moreover, the professionalization process goes well beyond the creation of "the professions" as we ordinarily conceive them. Professions involve a long training period that leads to a relatively stable position in a calling. A consequence of professionalization, particularly of professional training, is the development of a wide range of careers, which are not confined to a single occupation or to a particular calling but may be a combination of several occupations. Falling between occupation and profession, careers may represent a cluster of roles that administer the rules governing resources, information, or people.

As careers spread, they differentiate. Those with the greatest degree of professionalization tend to embody norms of science as an ideology. Technicians who manipulate resources and manpower represent one such differentiated group. There is, then, some relationship between an increase in the differentiation of career roles in a system and the ideology of science. Indeed, it could well be argued that in a given population the degree to which members can perceive and identify career roles indicates as well the degree of receptivity to an ideology of science.

This new ideology is more sophisticated than the old and it is no less significant. Indeed, it buttresses the authority of politicians with a universal appeal to scientific reason. The advice of those in career roles, the scientists or technicians, is frequently the basis for claiming the legitimacy of political actions, whether the particular occasion is development, civil rights, the Common Market, nuclear disarmament, or any other highly critical issue. The battle of the politicians is in some measure enlarged, taking on the form of charge and refutation by opposing experts employed by novices. In the West, this conflict had a great deal to do with stimulating the ideology of science. It also fits into our traditions, in that the appeal to reason requires the competitive play of ideas in order to maximize complete information, which, in turn, leads to the correct course of action. In the new societies, the professional becomes the symbol of progress. He is the establishment, employed by the politicians. The social scientist, as well, comes to embody a new form of solidarity and identity based on professional status. The appeal to science is an appeal to authority. The scientific establishment is itself based on a natural hierarchy of talent in which equal opportunities result in unequal distribution of roles.

The social scientist, as a part of the establishment, has assumed a new force in modernizing societies. His ideology differs in outward appearance from the other forms. It is not polemical. On the contrary, its practitioners embody the norm of "scientific" modesty. Social scientists are the first to warn of the inadequacies of their disciplines when applied to social problems.

Underneath the modesty, however, is a lively belief in the norms and values associated with science and the useful potentialities of social science in political life. Special studies on every subject imaginable, from race relations to nuclear disarmament, represent the application of social science techniques to problems of everyday life. Training, specialization, and research are the basis of knowledge. This is the reason, as we suggested earlier, the public is increasingly divided into the expert, including the expert social scientist, and the layman. The layman, as a citizen, does not have the facts on which to base important decisions. He may be irritated in the face of such expertise, but it is difficult for him to contradict it. Indeed, one token of the rising significance of the social scientist as a member of the political establishment is the attacks against him, particularly from members of the "old" establishments, namely, law and medicine.[30]

If the ideology of science is to become significant in modernizing societies, its strengths and weaknesses ought first to be assessed in those societies in which it has become significant. For

---

[30] Lawyers are by definition manipulators of custom, that is, laws. A developing community is less constrained by law than more stable systems. It cannot wait for law to catch up with the needs of development. In the case of medicine, the emphasis is now on the medical theorist or scientist rather than the practitioner.

the remainder of this chapter, we shall digress from the subject of modernization and discuss the implications of this new form of ideology for industrialized countries, with particular reference to the United States. We shall return to such matters in the final chapter as well.

In most Western industrialized countries, there is a growing bifurcation between the scientifically literate and the scientifically illiterate. Older claims to power and prestige have often declined, as, for example, in the cases of the small businessman and the doctor.[31]

A functional hierarchy (based on achievement) intensifies the hostility and personal anguish of those at the bottom of the hierarchy. No one can draw satisfaction from lower status roles. The prospect now facing the highly developed communities is the increasing numbers of functionally superfluous people, particularly in unskilled occupations, that is, those who are largely unemployable.

Any major political issue serves to illustrate this situation. Any political conflict quickly turns into a problem of evaluating evidence. Interested bodies employ their own experts to bring in findings in conformity with their own views. Laymen must then decide which expert advice to accept. But the expert has been involved in the decision-making process. What happens to the non-expert? Too often he cannot follow the debate. He withdraws, and the resulting separation is more complete than one might ordinarily imagine. Modern society can thus be said to be composed of a small but powerful group of intellectually participating citizens, trained, educated, and sophisticated, and

[31] This helps explain a peculiar lack of personal constraint in the performance of insecure high status positions. Knowing their status-tenure is temporary, they do not have the sense of obligation or duty to the community that a more permanent high status group might have. When status competition is a motivational system, the result is grave weakness in solidarity and an agonizing search for identity. See Seymour M. Lipset, "The Sources of the 'Radical Right' — 1955," in Daniel Bell (ed.), The Radical Right (New York: Doubleday & Co., 1963), pp. 260–64.

a far larger number who are reduced in stature because they are scientifically illiterate.

In practice, of course, there is no single professional group. It is possible to be scientifically intelligent about some subjects and completely ignorant in others. Hence, there is no sharp dividing line between the establishment and non-professional groups. There is a full-time establishment and a part-time one, and people with very little training may be in the latter. But their participation in political problems and their interest in the community is largely limited to their expertise. The result is, for them, a decline in their civic responsibilities and obligations.

ALIENATION AND THE IDEOLOGY OF SCIENCE

Democracy is a reconciliation system of government requiring a high level of self-restraint. Where such restraint does not prevail, the government rapidly degenerates into a system of plunder, limited only by the mutual check of hostile and antagonistic groups in the society. Social reforms become bargaining points — by-products of political life. Under such circumstances, democratic reform "does not have any unifying appeal, nor does it give a younger generation the outlet for 'self-expression' and 'self-definition' that it wants."[32]

Perhaps such alienation is a permanent feature of democratic society.[33] Even the establishment may feel it, particularly if its members have well-developed sensitivities. Not easily corrupted by power, the new scientific establishment can easily feel com-

[32] Daniel Bell, *The End of Ideology* (Glencoe: Free Press of Glencoe, Ill., 1960), p. 375. See also Reinhard Bendix, "The Age of Ideology: Persistent and Changing," in David E. Apter (ed.), *Ideology and Discontent.*

[33] Is alienation a permanent condition in a democratic society? Marx's concept of alienation emerged from his analysis of nineteenth-century England, at a time when the "British way of life," which appeared to be outdistancing all others in industry and entrepreneurial daring, was resulting in a general smugness.

promised by it. The scientific personality is, on the whole, a modest one, especially at the top levels. It can become alienated by its own successes. It does not like to be a pawn in the politician's game. One illustration of the professional establishment's ambiguity can be found in the distaste for, yet participation in, politics evidenced by scientists all over the world. Soviet scientists, too, are likely to push political matters aside in order to maintain a certain scientific chastity unviolated by political dogma. Despite noticeable lapses, especially in the biological field, they wear their professional status like a caste mark.

The ideology of science has very peculiar and diverse effects. On the one hand, it serves to identify a group of people who are themselves important and significant because they can manipulate the scientific culture. On the other, it casts out of the charmed circle those who are hopelessly incapable of understanding it. But it is not science itself that causes alienation. It is the realization of the limits of one's abilities, with the consequent tempering of boundless hope and bitterness against the system, if only because the alternative to alienation is self-hatred. And modern societies do exhibit a large proportion of people with extraordinary degrees of self-hatred.

SOME CONSEQUENCES OF BIFURCATION

Our own society is subject to an interesting bifurcation within its elite structure that has implications for the entire system of social stratification. This bifurcation occurs between the growing scientific establishment, whose status is based on function, and the previously existing elite, whose status is based on class and property representation. The functional status group finds its way into advisory and appointive posts, whereas the older group acquires status through election. Since expertise is required for much of modern decision-making, the new status group effectively restricts the old.

Moreover, in an interesting reversal of an earlier tradition in which status claims were based on particularistic criteria, the new establishment's status is based on universalistic criteria. High ability and extended programs of education and technical training are needed for entry. The result is an extraordinary situation in which the status hierarchy has more universalistic standards of entry than the class hierarchy but is also considerably harder to enter. This situation is particularly difficult for the "disestablished middle." If it cannot enter the status hierarchy, it is in danger of becoming part of that group which was once called the "working class" but which, as industrialization and automation increase, is now fast becoming a functionally superfluous body. Indeed, the obsolescence of the working class and the rise of the functionally superfluous are ever present pressures on the middle class, whose elected representatives, anxious to preserve their own positions, find their jurisdictions being limited by the dependence on expert advice. Opportunities to move from the bottom of the class hierarchy into the status hierarchy do exist, and efforts are being made to increase them, but they remain rare, as exemplified by the great obstacles overcome by Negro members of the establishment (the extreme case). The middle group tries to restrict mobility from the bottom into the middle and to restrict the growth of the establishment (growth both in proportion and in significance). Squeezed by the new establishment and the functionally superfluous, the disestablished middle fights back either by attacking the social science and science ideologies or by ensuring entry into them for its children. (See Figure 16.)

In industrial societies, the search for talent begins at an early age — witness the eleven-plus examination in England and aptitude tests and intelligence tests in American elementary schools. Parents who want their children to be members of the new "establishment" try to encourage in them the proper desire for study and work. Solidarity, centered in the establishment, causes non-establishment people to become increasingly superfluous, since functional roles are those relevant to planning, policy, and research. The new ideology of science is increasingly rooted in a professional cadre of highly trained men. Solidarity within — alienation without; identity within — lack of identity without. What Robert S. Weiss and David Riesman have suggested in connection with the working class holds true increasingly for the non-professionals in Western society. They point out that one of the things wrong with the working-class job is simply that it is working class. "In a culture where the worth of a man is measured

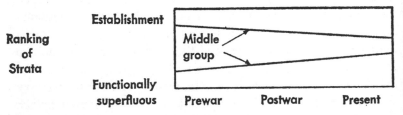

FIG. 16. — *Division in the community.*

by how far he has gotten, the unskilled laborer or service worker, despite the pieties that may be uttered periodically about the dignity of labor, knows that he has not gotten very far."[34]

Technological superfluousness leads to social superfluousness. Nor is this simply a matter of technology. The necessity of alleviating distress and the requirements of planning and calculation involved in modern politics, whether in urban development or overseas aid, have helped create a new role for the scientists. The businessman, once the heroic figure of Western society, has increasingly become an administrator. The old-fashioned ideal of capitalism, particularly in its more rural forms, has become his and other older professional groups' ideological defense against their social displacement.[35]

[34] Weiss and Riesman, "Social Problems and Disorganization in the World of Work," in Robert Merton and Robert Nisbet (eds.), *Contemporary Social Problems* (New York: Harcourt, Brace & World, Inc., 1961), pp. 484–85.

[35] One interesting role that combines a valuation as superfluous with an ambiguous but real functional value is that of salesman. It is recognized that the salesman plays a key role in the success of modern business enter-

In each of the three groups, solidarity and identity are different. Solidarity in the establishment centers on high status *esprit* and a desire for more effective communications between disciplines and between specialists. C. P. Snow's Rede lectures can be understood as an exhortation to solidarity between intellectuals and scientists. His concern over their differences in point of view presumes, on his part, a fundamental unity of outlook.[36] In Snow's terms solidarity would involve greater intellectual breadth and a shared appreciation of values of the modern scientific community. Identity would derive from the widespread understanding of the significance of work engaged in by the individual, whose own personal satisfactions are in some measure a reflection of the acceptance he receives within the establishment.

The disestablished are excluded from this. For them, solidarity and identity have in the past been associated with the business community and have been localized in villages, towns, and cities throughout the country. The establishment is a national elite. The disestablished, until recent times, have formed localized elites, with solidarity centering around churches, voluntary associations, and similar bodies.[37] These local groups have become increasingly parochialized and no longer provide solidarity satisfactions. The result, among some of the disestablished, is an increase in the significance of patriotic organizations associated with the radical right. Such groups try to link the local with the national and thus to embody a new unity by means of which the disestablished would again become powerful. At the same time, the disestablished are losing the identities provided by middle-class business values and, in suffering this loss, are left bewildered and insecure.

prise but also that he is associated with deceit, lack of dignity, and redundancy.
[36] See Snow, *The Two Cultures and the Scientific Revolution* (New York: Cambridge University Press, 1959); see also my article, "New Nations and the Scientific Revolution," *Bulletin of the Atomic Scientists*, XVII (February, 1961); and Caryl P. Haskins, *The Scientific Revolution and World Politics.*
[37] See Bryan R. Wilson, "An Analysis of Sect Development," *American Sociological Review*, XXIV (February, 1959).

The functionally superfluous have virtually no solidarity and are extremely difficult to organize because of their preoccupation not only with basic poverty and all its consequences but, in some measure as well — in an affluent society — with escape. Hence, there are very few permanent identity symbols but only shifting popular ones, with behavior divided between apathy and hysteria. For the superfluous, the situation is critical and utterly devastating.

CONCLUSION

Modernizing societies, as we have already noted, place primary emphasis on the political. Social welfare, development, reform, and revolution all place new responsibilities on governments. In order to live up to these responsibilities, governments seek advice. Authority is enlarged as responsibilities become more complex. The exercise of power is justified by the prospect of endless political reform through technical expertise.

These conditions have the effect of polarizing identities and dividing solidarities. Lacking a heroic dimension and requiring a wide range of intellectual discriminations, they impose the burden of natural inequality upon the members of the community.

So far I have suggested that ideology helps to establish solidarity in a society and identity for individuals within it. We have indicated that, in modernizing societies, socialist ideology is helpful in bringing about some integration of the system and in providing programmatic guides for functional roles, whereas nationalist ideology helps promote solidarity and identity through appeals to primordial attachments. It has also been suggested that the claims of socialism to be scientific provide political leaders in developing areas with a sanction for authority, but that their socialist ideologies do not belong in the same intellectual class as nineteenth-century socialism or, for that matter, Marxism. Claiming the heritage of socialism enables political leaders in developing areas to make a general connection with the philosophical heritage of Marxism without necessarily applying it. Most industrial countries have gone beyond this stage.

Socialism has become an unthought-out assumption, a collection of economic recipes, and a nagging critique, from a distance, of existing institutions. The fresh self-confidence, the wonderful feeling of relevant discovery, the convincing air of ethical righteousness, and the vibrant expectation of a total — and significant — transformation of the entire life of society have nearly disappeared from the socialist movement and from socialist thought since the mid-twenties. The belief that socialist aims enabled one to see reality more realistically and fruitfully, the belief that socialism was a "way of life" and not just a scheme for operating factories and wholesale enterprises has in the main evaporated.[38]

It should be clear, then, that not only are the political consequences of differing ideologies very great but they presuppose very different social conditions. The uses of socialism and nationalism in maintaining authority, insofar as they provide solidarity and identity, are not the same as the uses of science. The former work best during a period of political fantasy and hortatory realism, the latter in a climate of practical realism. Nationalism and socialism may employ science and, indeed, may claim to be scientific, as in the case of Marxism-Leninism in the Soviet Union. But sooner or later the scientist will implicitly ignore this claim and possibly reject it.

What should be clear is that the public in modernizing societies has a great deal in common with the disestablished in industrial societies. As the former develop, however, they will confront much the same bifurcation as presently exists in industrial countries. Meanwhile, those who subscribe to the ideology of science live in an intellectual world vastly different from those who subscribe to ideologies of socialism and nationalism. Indeed, there exist between them multiple images of the same situation. This is

[38] See Edward Shils's introduction to Georges Sorel, *Reflections on Violence* (Glencoe: Free Press of Glencoe, Ill., 1950), p. 14.

one reason that it is so important to create conditions of practical realism in modernizing societies and to build a scientifically literate elite, capable of emphasizing the instrumental values of society. This elite is hardly likely to be powerful enough to control a modernizing society, but it may be important in maintaining at least a few checks on the ideological fantasies of political leaders.

This chapter has been concerned with the ideologies and their particular role in authority. It is now time to turn to the instrumental values of a community and to examine the claims to power and prestige, and the significance of such claims, for the maintenance of authority during modernization.

10

THE MOBILIZATION SYSTEM AS A MODERNIZATION PROTOTYPE

Modernization is, of course, too broad a process to be seen in moral terms except in an abstract way. Not merely a broad or bland or wavelike pattern of evolution, it is punctuated by flash points of conflict and dramatic confrontations. Certain political figures, the social movements they create, and their political organizations serve as promontories both for countries whose condition is similar to theirs and for the wider world as well. This was true of Gandhi in India, especially before World War II, and of the nationalist movement in Ghana after the war. Other examples are Guinea in 1958 after the famous De Gaulle referendum on independence in French West Africa and perhaps Cuba today. Such promontory situations represent a significant moral force. They do not always result in mobilization systems, but they do represent efforts to universalize a revolution – to see it in its widest historical perspective. The most dramatic and disturbing cases are the militant mobilization systems, and what Marx said of bourgeois revolutions applies to them as well.

Bourgeois revolutions, like those of the eighteenth century, storm more swiftly from success to success; their dramatic effects outdo each other; men and things seem set in sparkling brilliants; ecstasy is the everyday spirit; but they are shortlived; soon they have attained their zenith, and a long depression lays hold of society before it learns soberly to assimilate the results of its storm and stress period.[1]

If Marx's description is just, then the modern nationalist revolutions are more like bourgeois revolutions than proletarian. During the "revolutionary" period, or at least during the transition to self-government and independence, excitement may reach the point of ecstasy. The human spirit seems to shine clearly as people free themselves from old bonds and restrictions. But then, as if to prevent the predicted "long depression," a condition of continuous revolution often sets in, which maintains the purity of emotion and single-minded pursuit of ends described by Marx. The struggle continues against real and fancied enemies. As the heroic new country vanquishes one set, another takes its place. These conditions make the politics of many modernizing societies into modern miracle plays — unreal but moral. It is these conditions that are particularly well represented in mobilization systems.

There are, of course, many variations in mobilization systems; they range from monolithic and totalitarian polities, such as China, to more loosely fragmented and comfortable ones. Systems in pursuit of quick and ruthless industrialization will perhaps tend toward the totalitarian form. Systems in pursuit of quick modernization (with industrialization only as a possible long-range objective) will tend rather toward the more liberal and moderate types. Quite often the first turns into the second simply because the polity cannot mobilize for industrialization and lacks "industrial discipline." How monolithic a mobilization system becomes (and how weak or strong) will obviously depend on

[1] Karl Marx, *The Eighteenth Brumaire of Louis Bonaparte*, ed. C. P. Dutt (New York: International Publishers, n.d.), pp. 16–17.

many factors, not the least of which is the morale of its members and their conviction about the need for internal unity.

Political support, as well as creative leadership, will depend in large part on the effectiveness of political organization. The attraction of the most extreme mobilization systems lies in their promise to realize many of the values commonly held today all over the world. Their leaders seek to generate power with which to correct the inequities of the previous system and enlarge the community on moral and material grounds. Emphasis on solidarity is a way of generating power. Equity through equality, a fundamental feature of the revolutionary mystique, promises to each person the opportunity to begin anew with a fresh set of life-chances. Through such a revolution, the leaders claim, a better basis for man's relation to man will be established.

THE MOBILIZATION SYSTEM AND NATION-BUILDING

Let us turn to the conditions of a mobilization system. Here the emphasis is on realizing potentiality. As we have been using this term, it implies a hierarchical system of authority. Instrumental values are elevated to the level of consummatory values, with the result that the goals of the state, particularly those of modernization and industrialization, become sacrosanct. The postponement of immediate gratifications in consumption is identified as social discipline and is a required feature of the individual's orientation to the community. Thrift, saving, and other forms of abstinence are linked to the creation of a future society in which abundance, personal dignity, and natural benevolence will be the conditions of life. Quite apart from the strong utopian element to be found in all mobilization systems, which provides the moral basis of their social discipline, they are oriented toward the future. They are for the youth, not the aged; the future, not the past.

There are other, more concrete characteristics that are typical. They usually contain a party of solidarity that either monopolizes power openly or in other ways makes all other groups dependent on it. The party of solidarity helps to generate political power by acting as a unifying instrument. Such a party is usually divided into three parts: (a) the militant vanguard that is the instrument of the founder or leader; (b) a set of functional auxiliaries such as trade unions, youth organizations, and agricultural communes or co-operatives; and (c) a generalized membership in branches that are geographically organized. This network is, in effect, the structure of the new society. The founders are usually charismatic or have shown strong charismatic qualities. They emphasize the rebirth and regeneration of the community through the combined action of the whole. Claims to leadership are based on political purity. The selflessness and superior wisdom of the leader are embodied in an ideology, in the form of political religion, that, even if it does not bear the leader's name, is inextricably linked with his life and thought.

Possessing an ideology of the future with an emphasis on the urgency of action turns the mobilization system toward direct planning and the drastic restratification of society. The atmosphere of mobilization is one of crisis and attack. Normalcy or passivity can even be regarded as dangerous. Individuals are called upon to declare themselves even in the most humble activities. There is no legitimate sphere of personal privacy, nor is privacy a recognized value. All social life becomes politicized. In the most extreme forms of mobilization system, having children is even endowed with supreme national importance. In the end, the state exerts its primacy over everything.

In these respects, mobilization systems differ from other forms having hierarchical authority, both in kind and degree. Military oligarchies do not politicize all of social life. Quite the contrary, they try to restrict the activities of politics to the practical manipulation of power. Modernizing autocracies are preoccupied with fitting a past tradition to necessary innovations. In neither case is there ordinarily an attempt to restratify society. The modernizing autocracy may have a personalized leader, as in the mobilization system, but he is never charismatic. He embodies, at best, ritualized charisma that inheres in the role, not the man. (In the mobilization system, the charisma originates in the man, not the role.)

These remarks would seem to imply that the mobilization system is little more than an irrational appeal to public emotions by means of a demagogue's view of the universe that has been transposed into a political theory. To some extent this is true. Even if it were entirely true, the significance of the mobilization system would in no way be diminished. It has enormous irrational appeal; but there is more to it than that. At a more practical level, the mobilization system can supply a political framework where other alternatives would be out of the question because of excessive political fragmentation, the absence of civic feeling, and economic stagnation. Indeed, the danger of stagnation reduces the attractiveness of the reconciliation model. Pluralism, privacy, individual ends, and shared power may seem less desirable than a lock-step social order, and the mindlessness and provincialism that the mobilization system tends to produce.

In too many modernizing nations, primordial loyalties to ethnic groups, language groups, and the like, ensure such widespread conflict that, under a reconciliation system, government activity would be virtually at a standstill. Roadways, waterways, electrical plants, towns, dams, and the like, can provide a basis for economic life only if there is sufficient coherence in social conduct to make use of them. Without such coherence, the co-operation necessary to build a state will be lacking. That is the reason, as Rupert Emerson has pointed out, that new nations so often center around heroic leaders.[2] That is also the reason that reconciliation systems are, in any case, rarely democratic.

[2] See Emerson, *From Empire to Nation* (Cambridge, Mass.: Harvard University Press, 1960). "This personalization of loyalties and movements must be attributed in large part to the lack of political experience and sophistication of the mass of the people who require the personal figure of a leader

Groups with a plurality of interests in a community do not necessarily create a pluralistic society. If they fragment the community to any great extent, they may confound people to the point that no society exists in a meaningful sense. What is generated instead is hostility, tension, antagonism, a basic unwillingness to compromise. More particularly, apathy may result. This has happened in the Congo.[3] *Immobilisme* is the consequence — and perhaps the best that can be hoped for, since conflict and civil war are the more likely alternatives. Fear of immobilizing conflict is one reason contemporary political leaders use a party of solidarity to break down the insularity of competing groups by reorganizing them around local party organs.

The actual means that government has at its disposal to optimize the relationship between loyalty and efficiency can be thought of as natural resources — that is, the stock of raw materials and social resources, including the stock of human skills. Together these form the wealth of the community. Whether this wealth will be mobilized for modernization purposes is to a very large extent a question of entrepreneurship. Reconciliation societies rely heavily on private entrepreneurship, which, by bringing together the factors of production, actively engages in what might be called dynamic modernization, or, in other words, the creation of agents that will generate more modernization, for example, the multiplication of industrial firms, co-operatives, and the like. In mobilization societies, the emphasis is upon political entrepreneurs. Government accepts the prime burdens of modernization.

---

to bring political abstractions down to the level of comprehensive reality. Another party may perhaps be linked to the general phenomenon of centralization of power in time of national crisis, as in the growth in stature of the American presidency in wartime. On such grounds, it is not difficult to explain why the role of the leader should have expanded in Asian and African countries as they came to the critical struggles for independence, national consolidation, and economic development" (p. 281).

[3] See the interesting description by Philip Whitaker and Jonathan Silvey in "A Visit to Congo, Rwanda and Burundi," in the *Makerere Journal*, No. 9, 1964.

The economic role of government leads, in turn, to an emphasis on social mobilization to compensate for a lack of wealth in natural resources. Labor is the source of wealth, the basis of savings, and the origin of investment. The rationale for stringency is the need to increase efficiency in order to mobilize social resources effectively.

The two main instruments of the mobilization of social resources are, in most mobilization systems, the administrative machinery and the party of solidarity. The administrative machinery carries out specialized tasks, while the party, providing intermediary or linkage groupings, imposes social discipline upon the whole. There is a heavy emphasis on central planning, with the party playing a "spontaneity-producing" role. Critical careers in the system lie mainly in the party and the civil service.

THE ROLE OF THE PARTY OF SOLIDARITY

Given the status of the party of solidarity in many mobilization systems, it is not surprising that it often becomes the main instrument for carrying out the mobilization objectives of government. As a microcosm of the new society, its discipline becomes the discipline of the nation. The problem posed by this dual role is that although it is also its own instrument of coercion it must not alienate the population. It is supposed to remain close to the people and by this means gather information. The party becomes caught in the same contradiction that affects the system as a whole.

The special role of the party of solidarity is to serve directly as a coercive instrument (to apply social pressures such as ostracism, control over patronage, and the preferential allocation of resources). Its public activities and pronouncements, however, display a devotion to populism. This populism can best be observed in the relationship of the party to stratification. Since the party of solidarity is also a mechanism of social mobility (by means of which it controls the hierarchy of power and prestige), it is the most important single mechanism of government in a mobilization system because, through it, many of the contingent structures of government actually operate.

A unique route to power and prestige, it recruits the alienated, those who have a desire for a more perfect social system, and potential dissidents. Parties of solidarity have their middle ranks filled with individuals who can satisfy their cravings for significance only by changing society as a whole. They are restless people who possess diverse, if partial, skills.[4]

There can also be found in the party of solidarity party technicians — specialists in organization. Usually lacking the training or discipline necessary for the civil service, such organizers are ambitious and manipulative. When the party technicians begin to assume great prominence, the party of solidarity undergoes a subtle transformation. The excitement of it, its novelty, and its use as a route to status and power decline. The political entrepreneurs are pushed aside in favor of the technocrats.

No matter how important the role of the party of solidarity in mobilization systems, the power that it generates is always legiti-

[4] In many African parties, the middle ranks of parties of solidarity have been educated in primary and middle school, have had some technical training or apprenticeship, and have served as electricians, pharmacists, clerks and hospital attendants. A large proportion have taken a teacher education program and have begun teaching. This is the characteristic middle leadership found in virtually all solidarity parties. Their alienation from the status quo is an alienation from their own status, generalized into a desire to elevate everyone, including themselves. This motivation can in turn be mobilized by the more effective senior leaders whom the middle leaders respect. The former are journalists, doctors, lawyers, contractors, and others whose qualifications would have resulted in successful careers, but perhaps not brilliant, not "soul-satisfying" in some manner because of grievances deriving in part from a certain lack of dignity in the society itself. Senior leaders have often been attracted to politics because their alienation has been more individual and at the same time more grand. These are men with the ability to generalize, within historical perspective, a role for themselves. It is only in moments of considerable political confusion and change that this is possible. It is a creative moment in the development of a nation and, as we suggested in chapter i, helps to make modernization in new nations so exciting to study.

mized through government. This is particularly true of systems in which the total range of roles, that is, the stratification hierarchy, is being drastically altered and modified. Once the stratification system is effectively changed, and a new coherence imposed, a new traditionalization of authority results and the party of solidarity begins to lose its significance. Solidarity now inheres in the nation. Heroic leadership begins to change; factionalism emerges again. With modernization, a new set of groups becomes critical — groups with functional rather than political coherence. The party technicians and the civil servants assume greater prominence.

The only way to prevent this evolution is by periodic purges. But such purges are dangerous because the mobilization system and party of solidarity are mutual creations of each other. The party of solidarity helps generate power by intervening as an intermediate social structure between otherwise isolated and mutually antagonistic social groups. By doing so, it becomes the central instrument by which groups are linked together. Government employs the party to strengthen these links by other social transactions, for example, the fitting and adjustment of roles to each other. This is why the party becomes the central instrument of authority. Purges can easily weaken the capacity of the party. Hence, the mobilization system is basically an unstable system, likely to change into another type unless the conditions for continuous transformation are present. This is only likely in the early stages of industrialization.

THE USES OF POLITICAL RELIGION

Among the types of systems that have been presented, the mobilization system has the strongest tendency to develop a political religion. This tendency results from a desire on the part of political leaders to transform the prevailing hierarchy of power and prestige rather than merely reallocate old roles. In order to change the hierarchy itself, they must redefine roles according to explicit moral principles. Political religion is the means used because it translates morality into authority.

Without political religion, older and more established conventions may be able effectively to resist innovation, that is, new roles may fail to replace those old ones associated with the exercise of power and prestige and the authority of the mobilization system will thus be weakened. By proliferating a new set of modernized roles and endowing them with a moral component (defined and ritually explicit), authority will not be weakened but strengthened. With the addition of political religion, the mobilization system becomes a prototype for what ought to obtain in other systems. The state is not only the teacher and guide for its own citizens; it is a religious heartland for the conversion of infidels abroad. The translation of political morals into political religion becomes a practical art. Teaching the new generations (in need of indoctrination) is one important expression; building a body of missionaries and agents is another.

There are thus several uses of political religion. To establish and reinforce values associated with hard work, thrift, and enterprise is one use to which it can be put. It also may be used to emphasize individual creativity through discipline. These values are shaped and bent into the context of the collectivity. Society becomes the instrument through which creativity is expressed. This "collectivity orientation" becomes prescriptive as a consummatory political value, embodying the legitimacy of the society. Another use of political religion is to impose an organization on the political structure of society — that of a secular church in which party cadres carry the primary job of indoctrinating the youth. Finally, the political religion may come to serve as a universal church. Its agents are the missionaries. Opposition to it appears as a new form of imperialism.

THE ROLE OF YOUTH

The most likely candidates for conversion to a political religion are the youth. Future-oriented, they find the perspective of the past unattractive. (Certainly, it does not seem like anything that should arouse nostalgia.) Older people, finding it difficult to dismiss the past so readily (because to do so would mean denying much of their own personal history) feel pushed aside by the prominence of youth. The natural affinity of youth for the mobilization system is repaid by youth's being accorded a very special place in the system. This worship of youth has two effects. It denies respect to the aged and thereby restricts their influence. (The aged become purveyors of an antique culture; the youth are carriers of the new one.) It provides excitement and power. This accounts for the remarkable acquiescence in the "system" by youth.[5] They play a part in it long before they are mature enough.[6]

There are other reasons, however, for this special role of youth.

[5] The role of youth is peculiarly paradoxical. On the one hand, youth is a rebellious subculture, which changes in most developing areas. But at a certain stage during the development of a mobilization system, youth are docile and well-connected with government.

[6] The following statement by Sekou Touré could be echoed by many other leaders, from Sukarno to Nasser. "In view of the huge works of construction which we have undertaken since we reached independence and full sovereignty, youth wants to play a leading role. What matters always, is the absolute necessity for every supporter of the Party, for the young in particular, to approach the specific problem of the young through a clear conception of the major objectives of the Nation. More than ever, the action of the young must necessarily reflect the chief concerns of the country.

"We are led by an essential principle to which the Party has never ceased to grant a tremendous importance. It is the absolute necessity to frame the action of the young, their national action, within the limits of the general action of the Party. Youth must become an active part of the nation; they must realize their responsibilities and be ready to play the dynamic role we want to allot them."

[On the other hand, youth can be hostile, alienated, and dangerous. They must be managed, directed, and unified. Above all, they must be put to work.] "The P.D.G. had managed rightly, then, in unifying youth movements, in realizing concretely the unity of action of all the youth of the country with the J.R.D."

"We want to create a real mystique of work in all districts of the nation, in particular among the young who will be the soul, the most dynamic elements of our national workshops. In fact, the Party has already organized huge collective working areas for works of public interest or for production, within the bounds of a huge programme of development of our economy and society." Touré, *Towards Full Re-Africanization* (Paris: Présence Africaine, 1959), pp. 83–84.

The status of youth exists prior to the acquisition of other statuses. Youth has less to divide it and thus has a great potential for solidarity. Weakness in solidarity is regarded by youth as an adult phenomenon and, almost by definition, as prejudicing the future by opening the door to all sorts of other frailties such as opportunism and diversity. Among African students in France, for example, the most passionate preoccupation is with the purity of emotion expressed by youth and the ways this may be translated into organizational power. This may help to explain the often apparently direct communion of young Africans along a single political plane, socialism, and a single aesthetic-racial plane, blackness.

A denial of differences between individuals is one key to the higher morality of mobilization systems. Differences are seen as petty and demeaning, as disguising egotism and individualism. It is not surprising that, ultimately, it is against individualism that the modern mobilizational ideologies are directed. Individualism and the associated evils of egotism, pettiness, and deracination threaten just those sentiments that bind people together. For the youth in a mobilization system, the central problem is not freedom but how to bring the elite into contact with the mass, the educated with the uneducated. The young conceive of society as a means of preventing individuals from *feeling* their individuality since this tends to result not only in loneliness and isolation but in alienation from the aims of society. Moreover, they have no real sense of time, only a generalized feeling of urgency. For them the mobilization system must abolish time. All history serves one purpose, the making of the present. Patience is exhausted. The desire to grasp the nettles of power becomes also a desire to destroy all those threads of association that represent an objectionable inheritance.

Yet, to destroy time engenders deep-rooted feelings of self-hatred. To live only for the moment implies acceptance of the judgment of past weakness and second-rateness expressed by outsiders. This is supported by a study of African students in France by J. P. N'Diaye. Almost twice as many students held unfavorable views of the characters and personalities of their fellow students as held favorable views.[7] This is not unique among students abroad. A considerable degree of self-hatred, which is often expressed as antagonism against "excessive individualism," characterizes the mobilization man. Individualism, or any lack of a sense of solidarity is regarded as an indication of opportunism.

The young, perhaps in common with many mobilization men, are in effect pleading for release from the prison of their limitations, for the forces that made them to be obliterated, even at the risk of self-immolation. But such self-hatred is the peculiar quality of the statusless, not of the new inheritors of prestige. What happens when the power in the youth movements, the promises, and the like, are real? What is the result when a student returns from abroad or finishes his studies? Is he offered a good post in government? If he is, he is less inclined to be liberated from his own individuality. He then begins to regard the fulfilment of society as depending on the self. With this mild form of pleasure, cynicism begins. Only the humorless and the ones who include in their sense of history an awareness of tragedy can continue as revolutionary personalities.[8]

[7] Among the negative factors that African students specified were the lack of consciousness of responsibilities in political actions, the lack of ideals, and so on. The corresponding virtues were fraternal solidarity, selflessness, and patriotism. These same students ranked the countries they admired most in the following order: U.S.S.R. (25 per cent), China (20 per cent), Israel (12.4 per cent), Cuba (12 per cent), France (8 per cent), Switzerland (6 per cent), and the United States (3.3 per cent). See J. P. N'Diaye, *Enquête sur les étudiants noirs en France* (Paris: Éditions Réalités Africaines, 1962), p. 243. Nor are the French-speaking Africans conspicuously different from others. There is a remarkable similarity between the findings of N'Diaye and those of Conrad Brandt in his analysis of the elite of the Chinese Communist party that had been educated in France. The same identification with the liberal forces of history and the same urgency that history end in the present mark the attitudes of many of the elite of Africa today and of China yesterday. See Brandt, "The French-returned Elite in the Chinese Communist Party" (Reprint No. 13, Center for Chinese Studies, Institute of International Studies, University of California, Berkeley).

[8] Perhaps the best example of this kind of political personality in recent years is Ben Bella in Algeria, whose austerity, drive, and militancy have expressed themselves in the sense of solidarity described by the African stu-

The revolutionary personality needs to be sustained by political religion and its consummatory values. The acts of the day must be identified as moral. The political religionists require prophets, ideologists, party organizers, and the like. Morality is unified with technique. Without these elements of political religion, the basis of the mobilization society disappears like youth itself. Few mobilization systems can withstand middle age.[9]

THE ROLE OF THE MILITARY

The military man is a particularly interesting example of the combination of political moralist and technician. Noted for his practicality and hardheadedness, the army officer is symbolic of the revolutionary tradition. Along with great cement palaces and statues in the heroic cast, the army on parade is a representation of virtue. Just as the local agricultural institute cannot simply teach agronomy or animal husbandry but must teach students that the soil is to be treated as sacred soil and the cow as a sacred cow, so the army must teach its recruits to protect the sacred cows and soil, statues, and cement palaces in addition to their technical duties. To understand its tasks, a revolutionary army needs to possess political consciousness but, at the same time, to avoid political questioning. Modernization provides the larger goals as well as the circumscribed technical competency. The army cannot be a people's army but must be a technically advanced one. As Lucian W. Pye suggests, "The fact that these new armies in preindustrial societies are modeled after industrial-based organizations has many implications for their political roles.

---

dents, driving out all opposition, including those who fought most effectively for Algerian independence while Ben Bella himself languished in a French jail.

[9] What are some of the practical effects of this unity? For one thing, intellectuals are squeezed out. Mobilization systems are hard on their intellectuals; they force them to become pamphleteers for the regime or regard them as useless. The model individual is the fair-minded, high-minded technician whose standards of integrity and skill derive from the objectives of the regime, which objectives he dares not question. Intellectuals are confusing and given to egotism. They produce a kind of political *dégoûtisme*.

One of their characteristics is particularly significant: the specialization that modern armies demand in skills and functions is only distantly related to the command of violence." [10] They must combine a sense of patriotic virtue with technical skill — indeed, the new mode of conduct for all functional groups in the mobilization system. The officer cadres, like the show-piece projects and technical institutes, express solidarity in a collectivity. Massiveness is identified with power. That is the reason the paraphernalia of an army — weapons, services, and parades — all help to inoculate society against a decline in the proper spirit of service. Every training program serves as an indoctrination period.

Such armies do not have independent power to stand alone unless they become divorced from the public. The party of solidarity sees to it that they are surrounded by auxiliary organizations such as a people's militia, sports clubs emphasizing military skills, and paramilitary youth organizations much given to ideological devotions.

The mobilization system turns the military role into a career involving the skills of a techician. (Unlike the officer in a military oligarchy, who is the embodiment of nationalism, the protector of the constitution, and the repository of civic virtue, in the name of which he may intervene in civilian political life, the officer in a mobilization system is clearly a functional subordinate of the party and the state.) The mobilization system treats the military officer much as it does the civil servant.

THE ROLE OF THE CIVIL SERVANT

The role of the civil servant in a mobilization system is determined by two tendencies. The first tendency is for the role to be upgraded in functional significance because of the emphasis on modernization. And the second, a result of this, is the increase in political significance of the civil servant, which causes the party

[10] Pye, "The Process of Political Modernization," in John J. Johnson (ed.), *The Role of the Military in Underdeveloped Countries* (Princeton, N. J.: Princeton University Press, 1962), p. 76.

and government to become dependent on him. For these reasons, the civil servant ordinarily comes into conflict with senior political leaders, who, often less well educated and ignorant about technical matters (other than organization), may feel inferior in his presence. One way for mobilization leaders to limit the power of the civil servant is to define his role within a fairly narrow range of competence. Functionally defined roles reduce an expert's potential authority. The result is a tug of war between party bureaucrats and government officials over the role of the civil service. One characteristic response is growing corruption, as bargains are struck between the two groups. A second response is periodic changes in the organization of the civil service initiated by the party. Ordinarily, mobilization systems must depend on the particular *modus vivendi* worked out between the civil servants and the politicians.

Today we can observe the different stages of the process I have just described in the various mobilization systems. In some of the possible examples, the mobilization system is giving way to a reconciliation system. The leadership enlarges itself. Authoritative decision-making is widened. Accountability groups are made more significant. The area of repressive law is reduced. The use of punishment as a political device declines. Resource determination and allocation take place more often on the local level, with new formulas being accepted. New consent groups emerge. Perhaps the most interesting example is Yugoslavia, where worker participation and the decentralization of decision-making are factors. Along with these structural developments go changes in the symbolic, integrational, ethnically-defining, and sanctional sources of authority. Ghana may be another example. There the President is trying to institutionalize his charismatic authority in the form of a presidential monarchy. The tendency appears to be away from the present mobilization system and toward a neo-mercantilist system, as may also be occurring in Egypt. Increasingly national socialist in ideology, the mobilization system in

Egypt may sustain itself in a new form of fascism — a fascism of development.

It is, of course, very dangerous to generalize from the short histories of most of the modernizing countries, even though these countries may be the most challenging to analyze. Guinea, for example, is evolving slowly along lines that depart from the rhetoric of revolution, although it remains revolutionary in spirit. The ideology of Guinean socialism, we are told, follows the guiding political doctrine of "democratic centralism," about which the President of Guinea has said the following:

Democratic centralism carries the following principles:

(a) All responsible men in the Party are directly and democratically chosen by the supporters who enjoy total liberty of conscience and of expression within the Party.

(b) An affair of the state of Guinea is the affair of all the citizens of Guinea. The programme of the Party is democratically discussed. As long as no decision has been made, each is free to say what he thinks or what he wishes. But when, after extensive discussion in Congress or in Assembly, a decision has been arrived at by a unanimous vote or by a majority, the supporters and the leaders are bound to apply it correctly.

(c) *The responsibility for leadership is not shared. Only the responsibility for a decision is shared. Thus, no distortion of discipline should be permitted.*[11]

This statement by Sekou Touré lays down the foundation for the mobilization system in Guinea. The structure of authoritative decision-making is highly concentrated and hierarchical in form. Accountability is shared between party organs and territorial councils, although none of these can serve as a veto group. The consent mechanism, the National Assembly, is so controlled by the party that its powers are more formal than real. Local party

[11] Sekou Touré, "Address to the P.D.G. Congress, Conakry, September 14, 1959," quoted in Colin Legum, *Pan-Africanism: A Short Political Guide* (London and Dunmow: Pall Mall Press Ltd., 1961), pp. 124–25 [my italics].

units, special courts, and magistrates, all share in administering justice, which has become politicized and involves an area of repressive law, particularly for theft, which is regarded as a crime against the community and therefore punishable by the most severe means. Political recruitment is a dualistic structure, employing appointment as well as a mixture of elections and co-optation in both territorial and party councils.

Resource allocation is determined mainly through state planning, with a heavy emphasis on government ownership in the form of *sociétés nationales*. Government control is extended through elaborate licensing procedures, especially for private traders. Forced savings include *investissement humain*, which are community self-help projects.

The first Guinean Three Year Plan is too thunderingly simple about its hopes for a revolutionary transformation of society.

. . . Let us again fall back on a simple image. In the forest two men are fighting in order to determine which will get the bough of a tree that both of them discovered and that both of them need to reinforce the roofs of their huts. If, instead of quarreling and fighting, they had used the time and energy spent doing this in cutting down another bough, they would have been mutually satisfied.

Thus, the discords that take place within a society, the conflicts of interest, the conflicts arising from irrational elements, the moral mediocrity of a society, are just as many negative forces that act like a brake on the development of production and that, as a result, inhibit the development and the evolution of society.

In assigning to itself specific objectives in the realm of activity, the society that develops into a planned economy transcends the negative social forces and transforms them into productive power.

Such a society creates a new mentality that will increase its productive capacities and its social evolution.[12]

[12] *Plan triennal de développement économique et social de la République de Guinée* (Conakry: Imprimerie Nationale, 1960), Book V, pp. 104-5 [my translation].

Emphasis on the moral and intellectual aspects of planning, for example, may be intended to disguise the fact that the practice of political life falls far short of such grand objectives. Is it not the case, after all, that Guinea, like most other modernizing countries today, is more pragmatic in its socialism than doctrinaire, more disorderly than planned in its social life?[13]

This may be the reason that the ideology of democratic centralism in Guinea is embodied in an African socialist community, the *société communaucratique*, in which modernization and the development organs of government provide the sanctional sources. Links between approved roles are established by Sekou Touré (the symbolic referent) and three organizational secretaries, all of whom are part of the political bureau of the party (the integrational integer). Ethnic definition is provided by the presumed identity of party and nation in a single, undifferentiated community in which divisions by class, tribe, or rural or urban residence are not recognized. The source of sanctions is modernization itself, symbolized by Touré and the party, as indicated above; the new ideology is linked to tradition through an idealized version of the community of the past as a socialist commonwealth. There is, however, conflict between those who would prefer the more universal form of socialism and those who prefer an African version of it (which, of course, indicates disagreement over the source of sanctions — whether it should be the efficiency of modernization or the continuity of the community).

Such a system emphasizes egalitarianism, development, and mobility. It tries to eliminate traders, private entrepreneurs, and the like, as antisocial elements (although in this effort it has been forced to make compromises). Having reduced the significance

[13] What I have suggested about the political life of Guinea is even more applicable to countries like Indonesia, where the differences between the language of revolutionary consciousness and the practice of revolutionary development are very great. In a very real sense, Nigeria and Indonesia, for example, are more similar to each other than China and Indonesia, even though the political language of the latter two may have a closer resemblance.

of the former metropole as the source of modernization roles, it has diversified its dependence on industrial countries, East and West. Guinea is a useful illustration of the mobilization system in action. It has appreciably changed traditional stratification by eliminating its forms of power and prestige (for example, it has rendered chieftaincy powerless). It has raised the status of dock workers, porters, and the like, through the trade union movement. It has tried to eliminate ethnic discrimination through a drastically expanded educational system. Although it has not succeeded in many of its objectives, Guinea gives the general impression of wanting to achieve a revolution, populist in nature, from above.

Guinea's objectives have the advantage of an aura of puritanism, symbolized to some extent by the dramatic rupture with France. The sparing application of the charismatic factor (as compared with the situation in Ghana or Egypt) is itself significant. A certain sharpness of form and explicitness in formulating goals is characteristic of Guinea and contrasts with the policy-making of other African mobilization systems. Grievance is turned into activism, frustration into energy — or so it appears. The aim of Guinea's stratification policy is the organization of roles functional to modernization. Moreover, by the successful manipulation of morality, a moral community has been established around which Guinea expects other African countries to rally.

This brief description of Guinea will perhaps help to indicate why the mobilization system is attractive to many leaders of new nations. It is a dynamic form and provides a new basis for integrating the nation around roles functional to modernization — all in a context of morality, on which the government's authority is based.

The mobilization system is exciting; but even in Guinea, is it very durable? For one thing, the effect of democratic centralism has already caused fear and inaction among key groups in the community, particularly civil servants. It is more and more diffi-

cult, despite the elaborate pattern of advisory councils, to gain
accurate information about the effect of stratification decisions on
loyalties. There are errors in planning and distribution that have
led the people to doubt the efficiency of the regime. Supports
based on efficiency have weakened, while those based on tradition have been so drastically reinterpreted as to have become
sentimental rather than substantive. It is increasingly difficult to
conceive of immortality through kinship or the state (although
it is still possible through religion, which is one explanation of
the existence of religious tolerance in Africa). Purpose is becoming individualized. Such conditions are still, for the most part,
latent; how seriously they will affect Guinea's ability to modernize remains at present a matter of speculation.

The crisis in Guinea is much less deep than in Ghana, where
the transformation of charismatic leadership has turned a reconciliation system into a mobilization system, which may now be
in the process of becoming a neomercantilist system. Although
the president remains the symbolic referent of the system, the
sanctional sources are increasingly confused, accountability has
been drastically reduced, and parliament as a consent group no
longer functions in any but a formal capacity. This formal capacity is important for sanctional purposes but little else, since the
usual activities of a parliamentary body have been curtailed. In
a most interesting passage, J. M. Lee has commented on these
changes in the following terms:

> It is one of the principal ironies of the transplantation of
> the Westminister model from Britain to Ghana that it has
> produced almost a complete reversal of the "decorative"
> and "efficient" institutions of government to which Bagehot
> referred. The President of Ghana has inherited from the
> British a position which corresponds very closely to the pre-
> rogative of the English Crown under common law, and yet
> remains the "efficient" part of the Constitution. The Na-
> tional Assembly of Ghana, in contrast, might well be re-
> garded as the "decorative" part. It would be psychologically
> difficult to replace a parliament of M.P.'s by a congress of

party secretaries in Ghana because such an action would be contrary to the constitutional mythology of the nation's origin. The suggestion would face a storm of moral indignation similar to that meeting any proposal for returning Britain into a Republic. The Ghana M.P. has to be retained for his "decorative" value. The prerogative of the President of Ghana places him under no legal obligation to publish his directives, even his executive instruments, and under no compulsion to seek the approval of Parliament to treaties or other instruments signed on behalf of the state in foreign affairs. Parliament provides a showground of considerable "decorative" value for any item which the president wishes to bring to popular attention . . .[14]

Ghana's system is a particularly interesting illustration because there the mobilization impetus has declined. Factionalism between party wings, auxiliaries, bureaucratic organization, and regional and constituency organizations has begun to emerge as the predominant political characteristic. The result is intrigue, mistrust, and fear. Capriciousness in the exercise of political power is widespread, particularly in the middle leadership. What helps Ghana is the residual set of practices left by the colonial regime (an aid that was denied to Guinea). It is interesting, for example, to contrast the crescendo of propaganda in the daily press in Ghana with the moderate tone used by civil servants and economists in the discussion of the objectives of the Seven Year Plan:

Our socialist policy is based on certain fundamentals, which include the following:

(i) The economy must be developed rapidly and efficiently so that it shall within the shortest time possible, assure a high rate of productivity and a high standard of living for each citizen based on gainful employment.

(ii) The income from our physical assets and from the labor of our people applied to these assets year by year must be

[14] Lee, "Parliament in Republican Ghana," *Parliamentary Affairs,* XVI (Autumn, 1963), 389–90.

utilized for socially purposeful ends. Never must public want and private affluence be allowed to co-exist in Ghana. And among the most important ends that the community must provide for out of its income should be the education and welfare of its children, and the continued expansion of the economy itself.

(iii) The community through its Government must play a major role in the economy, thus enabling it to assure the maintenance of a high level of economic activity, the provision of adequate employment opportunities, the distribution of the nation's output, and the availability of the means of satisfying over-riding social ends. Accordingly, the need for the most rapid growth of the public and co-operative sector in productive enterprise must be kept in the forefront of government policy.[15]

The objectives of the government, as embodied in this plan, read more like a Fabian tract than a revolutionary call to arms.

THE DECLINE OF THE MOBILIZATION SYSTEM

Mobilization systems utilize hierarchical structures of authority, as we have said. Authority derives from the mobilized public, as embodied in some particular instrumentality of the state, such as the single party or the army, within which the functions of government center on a single political leader. If a mobilization system has hierarchical authority and a high degree of consummatory values, each act acquires a sacred significance. More important, the goals of the leaders come to be endowed with these consummatory values. The effects are the stimulation of the population to great efforts, the development of their creativity and sense of excitement, and the liberation and ennoblement of individuals. Militant socialist ideologies are particularly suitable for

[15] See Office of the Planning Commission, *Seven Year Plan for National Reconstruction and Development* (Accra: Government Printing Department, January, 1964), p. 2.

this purpose because, despite their philosophical emphasis on materialism, they are basically antimaterialistic, as indicated by their attacks on the bourgeoisie. How grasping is the free enter-priser who wishes to undermine the new Jerusalem.

With such characteristics, the mobilization systems claim a higher morality than that possessed by reconciliation systems or modernizing autocracies. Cast in a more heroic mold, they hold out the promise of regeneration and self-improvement rather than expediency and compromise, and even when they fail, they remind the world of higher purposes. If they destroy some of their most cherished ends, and their leaders become harassed, perverse, and capricious, at least they have served to identify a political vision. This is perhaps the reason they are important. They represent troublesome moral promontories in political life. Most mobilization systems are closer to reconciliation systems in actual practice than in the way they see their goals during modernization.

Even in the most monolithic mobilization system, government is always Janus-faced in the sense that, as the strategic mecha-nism of choice in the system, it is the instrument for maintaining the boundaries of all other subsystems of choice. Its limits depend on political support; hence, all governments try to approximate public desires to some degree and to relate these desires to long-term objectives of the state (not all public wishes, of course, are accepted as valid). Analysis of the concrete activities of govern-ment reveals the relationship between the mundane and the sacred, the political and the symbolic, the instrumental and the consummatory.

THE DECLINE OF POLITICAL RELIGION

Characteristically, mobilization systems suffer a decline in po-litical religion, with corresponding losses to the individual's sense of identification with the community.

Mingling the sacred and the secular, the consummatory and

the instrumental, has the effect of reducing the consummatory element. That is, the impact of such values is less when the symbols of political religion have become ritualized.

As the impact of consummatory values lessens, the motivational structure of the society begins to change. Instrumental values assume greater prominence, and there is greater emphasis on the mundane. Growing individual opportunism results in less discipline and weakened organization. Corruption increases. When goals are no longer sufficiently endowed with consummatory values to excite support and voluntary effort, a greater degree of coercion has to be applied by the state. Coercion spreads as political religion begins to lose its effectiveness.[16] Disaffection is manifested first among youth.

GENERATIONAL CONFLICT AND AUTHORITY

Political generations in mobilization systems are very short, perhaps four or five years, after which time a new group of intimates appears as a claimant for political power. The "angry young men" of postrevolutionary periods have no particular goal toward which to direct their energies except to oppose their leaders. As mobilization systems mature, there is a longer period of role search, alienation, and irresponsibility. Despite the sense of sharing in a new society, youth does not take long to form alienated counterelite groups. Its solidarity as a subgroup is then based on deviation from the polity. The emergence of such youth groups with a high-deviancy–high-solidarity potential can trigger an ideological shift. If this should occur — and governments in mobilization systems make every effort to prevent it — the relationship between youth and government becomes extremely delicate. As S. N. Eisenstadt has said,

[16] In the ideal mobilization system, consummatory values motivate people so effectively that coercion is almost unnecessary. Repressive law, with all its symbolic severity, is employed against those who violate the political values of the community. In general, however, countries like Indonesia, Ghana, Mali, and Egypt, have instrumental values, which are embodied in rather grandiose ideologies.

Almost all such modern movements have developed a special "youth ideology." The essence of these ideologies (from the point of view of our analysis) is that the changes which they advocate and struggle for are more or less synonymous with rebellion against the "old" order and generation — a rebellion of youth, a manifestation of the *rejuvenation* of national and social spirit.[17]

Only if the regime of a mobilization system continues to make exceptional provision for youth can it prevent their opposition, and even then it may not be successful. In many of the developing areas, each youth group brought under such "control" becomes a new center of local resistance within the party in power or other control group. This has already happened in Guinea and Ghana.[18]

The mobilization party that allows youth to ventilate its idealism in the service of the state may receive dividends in the form of an effective and vital party. But if the party becomes heavily bureaucratized, forcing the young to work their way up an increasingly complicated ladder of party positions, the likelihood of alienating them and making them politically dangerous increases. Even the most militant parties undergo a natural aging process, and try to lengthen the span of the older generation in effective political life. The prospects of youth are best during the modernization period immediately following independence. A mobilization system must constantly restrict its middle cadres in order for the top leadership to remain on good terms with the youth.

THE DECLINE OF THE PARTY OF SOLIDARITY

It was suggested earlier that the party of solidarity most often results from a political movement that brings together in its ranks all those who are caught up in the excitement of rebuilding

[17] Eisenstadt, *From Generation to Generation* (Glencoe: Free Press of Glencoe, Ill., 1956), p. 311.

[18] See William J. Foltz, "The Radical Left in French-Speaking West Africa," in William H. Lewis (ed.), *Emerging Africa* (Washington, D.C.: Public Affairs Press, 1963), p. 36–38.

a society. The organization of the movement into a more stable structure creates managerial roles, a middle leadership, and an increasingly competitive top leadership. As the populist organization in the mobilization system, the party provides links between diverse groupings — business, bureaucratic, military, and youth. The resulting pattern of coalitions provides opportunities for new generations to find followers and to create new positions of leadership. Hence, the conditions that brought about the formation of parties in the first place, that is, faction and coalition, re-emerge. Coalitions compete, causing internal conflicts in the party of solidarity. Factions arise; purges become common. Intrigue extends not only to regions and constituencies but to local government, trade unions, and youth organizations.

Such conditions aid in spreading both cynicism and opportunism. They may also result in paralysis. Contrast the rhetoric of party policy with party actions in virtually any small village in any mobilization system. Indeed, evidence of a country's mobilization system and party of solidarity is less visible the farther away from the capital or main town one gets.

All voluntary organizations, trade unions, the military, and the bureaucracy must constantly demonstrate devotion to the political leaders. The press and other communications media are controlled by the government. In order to compensate for the diversion of funds that would ordinarily have been used for development, the party of solidarity tends to use raw and "volunteer" labor for primary development. Talent accumulates at the center. The processes of administration are closely linked to the political control of economic development. Political leaders of the second rank and administrators are fearful of being posted far from the centers of power and intrigue.

Coalition and faction are important not only because they result in intrigue. Their implications are great for the society as a whole. They cause the party of solidarity to decline as an instrument of linkage and modernization. As it declines, all relationships are affected. But the party of solidarity does not suddenly disappear. Its apparatus remains, becoming the basis for a network of client-patron relationships. Nepotism, kinship, and favoritism result. Government acts as a superpatron.

THE EVALUATION OF EFFICIENCY

One likely consequence of the party's decline is a loss in modernization efficiency.[19] To evaluate efficiency losses requires an analysis of goals, costs, information, and coercion.

First, we need a sample of key decisions made by the government. They may be articulated in public speeches, manifestoes, and other official documents, or they may be embodied in development plans and the like.[20]

Second, we need an assessment of costs, that is, the expenditures required to achieve goals. This is the heart of the analysis of efficiency, since all governments try to maximize goals and minimize costs. If costs are to be compared, however, it will be necessary to standardize them as items. This is a difficult process, since not only actual allocations in the budget but also alternative, or opportunity, costs are involved.[21]

[19] Efficiency can be defined as the achievement of goals through the most rational deployment of resources in the shortest possible time. Goals are of the two main types, instrumental and consummatory. We may exclude consummatory goals from consideration because their satisfactions are largely moral and aesthetic rather than material. Where mobilization systems posit modernization and industrialization as consummatory values, however, we will need to treat these goals, as defined in development plans, party programs, and the like, as if they were instrumental.

[20] Of course, it is necessary to distinguish between the aspirations and visions opened up by metaphorical phrases, such as the "great leap forward" and *investissement humaine*, and the actual targets that are set. This is much more difficult than it sounds.

[21] Complicating matters still further is the evaluation of different goal schedules in terms of their long-run as compared with their short-run efficiency. For example, mobilization systems may establish goals that would be "unreal" in reconciliation systems. But by relying on the discipline inherent in both the consummatory beliefs and the hierarchical structure of authority, they may force higher rates of savings than could be obtained

Third, we need to assess the information open to decision-makers about the consequences of a decision for the maintenance of the system — not technical information, but rather knowledge of loyalty and support. (Technical information about the purely economic efficiency of a particular enterprise is not difficult to obtain. Experimental stations, pilot studies, and the like, all help to provide technical knowledge.) Most difficult to obtain is information about the effect of decisions on public desires and on the opportunities to provide satisfaction. In "non-information" situations, political cynicism and opportunism give rise to rumors and planted stories about individuals; tales of misdemeanors become the daily political fare. Officials disguise actual occurrences through doctored statistics. These optimistic evaluations of accomplishments require collusion of subordinates, who help deceive their superiors by providing them with carefully euphoric misinformation. Officials, when they travel around plants or commercial establishments, may hear occasional complaints, but more likely, they will be informed that everything goes well regardless of the real state of affairs. Gone are the usual indicators of grievance: strikes, memorials, petitions, opposition political groups, and the like. The result is the setting of goals without reference to their political consequence.

Finally, we need to observe displays of coercion in acts of force, such as detention, or the threat of force by government against individuals and groups of individuals, which cause "non-information" situations.

These four factors are critical to an analysis of efficiency in a mobilization system because government is actively engaged in technological change and economic development. Moreover, the organizational characteristics of government become a central feature of political life. Organization qua organization is always

---

by the latter type of system. This in turn may increase the opportunities for training, educate greater numbers of people for modernization roles, and create new enterprises at a faster rate. Hence, what was unreal and perhaps inefficient at one stage may turn out to be more efficient at another.

somewhat autocratic; and the organizational work of the government becomes pervasive, extending over wide ranges of the social and economic life of the new nation. As a result, people are "acted upon" by an "outside" system, that is, government. This, in turn, leads to a strengthening of the hierarchical and ideological aspects of control over society at large. Goals become consummatory, assuming the characteristics of (a) inviolability and (b) indefiniteness of attainment in a future period. Such goals are therefore profoundly evolutionary, symbolic, and unattainable. This type of system also changes instrumental values into consummatory ones. Even goals of economic development become symbolically important. Emphasizing future social benefits, these goals embody the legitimacy of the regime to the degree that they are unrealistic. Yet mobilization systems continue to try to achieve unrealistic goals and so strain the available resources and technology that they must rely on increasingly frequent acts of territorial expansion.

Such a pattern has a number of effects on economic development. The costs of coercion divert revenue, hitherto available for investment, into military and police activities and other punitive institutions. Security, internal and external, requires stronger standing armies and better military technology. As a consequence, the costs of government rise continuously. The difficulties created by spending investment funds for the expansion of government enterprise are met by raising public revenues and by the intensification of the mobilization process. Simultaneously, an increasing proportion of revenue is diverted to non-productive enterprises, that is, to maintaining the system rather than to development. The most obvious result is a waste of resources.

This would seem to suggest that mobilization systems reach their maximum efficiency quite quickly and then decline. If new nations have such a diversity of groups and factions that they are unable to mobilize the efforts of the community to generate wealth, the use of coercion to restrict diversity will only reduce information and increase costs and may not result in development. Hence, the single virtue of the mobilization system is that it may be able to initiate modernization under conditions that a reconciliation system cannot.[22]

It cannot be hoped that political power will be a substitute for wealth (with political power being generated by unity). Poor countries, lacking discipline, unity, and devotion to common purposes, will find that political power, if they succeed in generating it, can rarely be applied successfully to resolve economic problems.

CONCLUSIONS

Mobilization systems expand the modernization sector, alter the relationships of power and prestige between roles, and traditionalize the new through the manipulation of political religions. In order to accomplish these ends, they promote unrealistic industrialization goals and rely heavily on coercion. The problem of efficiency becomes paramount only after the first period of mobilization.

The mobilization system tends to be a higher coercion system than the reconciliation system, with a consequent loss of information. If it can be shown that the loss of information causes uncertainty in decision-making, a limitation on choice will also have been imposed since the government will be ignorant of all possible relevant alternatives. One indication of a lack of information would be an increase in political capriciousness, itself a condition of uncertainty. Even regimes that see the apotheosis of science as placing rationality firmly at the center of the universe may be marked by instability and irrationality. Few politi-

---

[22] It will be recalled that I have suggested that modernizing societies more than others depend on results as well as potentiality for their legitimacy. Efficiency is thus an important factor in maintaining authority. In this respect, modernizing societies are not much different after independence from what they were during the colonial period. Efficiency and moral uplift remain the justification of government.

cal leaders are prepared for such a situation. The more militantly revolutionary and the more Jacobin the definition of freedom, the greater the coercive reaction on the part of the revolutionary government and the less likely it is to conduct its affairs in a climate of practical realism. Rhetoric is confused with reality, tactics with values, meaning with motives. The leaders are erratic, aggressive, and given to creating their own rules of conduct. By claiming the future, they disclaim responsibility for the present. And by manipulating political religion, they endow such conduct with morality.

So far our discussion of the reasons for the decline of a mobilization system has been essentially empirical: political cynicism causes a decline in support to government; increasing complexity harbors opportunism and opposition; lack of information compounds the difficulties of effective decision-making.

Mobilization systems can also move toward greater totalitarianism and toward the pure sacred-collectivity type. They tend not to, partly because those types of control require either a more elaborate technology and managerial staff or a small and very simple society. The first is out of the question in modernizing nations, and the second is precisely what they are repudiating. Hence, there is not much chance that modernizing societies will become rigorously totalitarian.

There is a more fundamental or purely theoretical reason, however, that mobilization systems decline. This reason is related to the original hypotheses suggested in chapter i. It was said there that systems that conformed to the sacred-collectivity model were based on a deterministic universe. Perfect coercion would therefore imply perfect information because conflict would be impossible and everyone would comply with instructions. Such a situation is not empirically possible, of course, but it is the assumption that lies behind totalitarianism.

We suggested that the greater the degree of information in a system and the lower the degree of coercion, the greater the problem of evaluation. In the reconciliation system, for example, interpretation of information is a major problem. This means that political sampling goes on in reconciliation systems, with probabilities constantly being calculated. In mobilization systems, on the other hand, the deterministic principle operates. There is less uncertainty because there is less information. But there is clearly a paradox here. Ignorance cannot lead to information. The paradox may be resolved if we consider that the knowledge possessed by the political leaders of a mobilization system derives from outside the system (from foreign specialists, newly trained technicians, and the like) or was compiled during a previous period and in a different type of system. Political leaders who have helped form a mobilization system, for example, have gained their political information during the period prior to their success. After they succeed in establishing a mobilization system, their information is increasingly dated, and because of coercion, their new information becomes sparse or is faulty.

Planning and other blueprints for the future are based upon generalized skills formed outside the new society. Mobilization systems do not create new knowledge. At best they are emulative, copying other systems and their technologies. Only if an informational area is "reserved," that is, made into a free zone where research can go on, will new information be created.[23]

Hence, in the mobilization system, the deterministic impulse is restricted, on the one hand, because of the need for new information with which to cope with increasing complexity and, on the other, because of the need to know what forms of coercion are necessary. The mobilization system thus turns out to be a pseudo-deterministic system based on outside information but not self-generated knowledge. It, too, must cope with the problem of uncertainty. The result is manifest in capricious acts by government, intimidation, and further coercion.

[23] Even during the Stalinist period in the U.S.S.R., pure mathematics and, to a considerable extent, physics were such reserved areas, even though some distinguished scientists, such as Peter Kapitza, spent time in detention.

This suggests that mobilization systems are most suitable at points of conversion from one system type to another, because at such points key information is so obvious that action, not information, is the major problem and coercion is a self-evident advantage. Examples are the move from dependent to independent status and from the first stages of modernization to major industrialization. One such point is demonstrated in many new nations at an early stage of modernization when a polity needs to be created. At this stage, however, if the basic social and economic infrastructure is very weak, mobilization will prove impossible and the system will change to another form by means of coups d'état, popular uprisings, or the transformation of authority through its ritualization. Another point at which the mobilization system is appropriate is during the conversion from late modernization to early industrialization. At this point the mobilization system can be a stable method of effecting massive economic change by exerting political control to allocate functional roles essential to development. During this period the mobilization system is likely to grow in strength until the point of high industrialization is reached, at which time it will begin to decline as a result of its great need for information. With a decline in coercion and the widening of accountability through decentralization, the system will change to another type.

II

ALTERNATIVES TO THE MOBILIZATION SYSTEM

The analysis of political types requires us to identify the factors that cause a change in the relationship between the two functional requisites of government, coercion and information. It is an underlying assumption of this analysis that changes in the functional requisites produce over-all change in the system. Consequences of such a change may be observed in terms of three sets of analytical categories. The first is the set of contingent functions. Varying the relationship between coercion and information changes the quality of authority as follows: the symbolic meaning changes; the integrational and sanctional aspects take on different properties; and ethnic definition acquires a different content. Empirically, this leads to an analysis of modernization in terms of legitimacy. But legitimacy is too complex, related as it is to personal identity and, ultimately, to the individual's need for immortality, meaning, and purpose. The functional requisites thus lead directly to the study of authority, which is changed by modernization, as are the attitudes and motives of individuals.

The second main analytical category is the structural requisites. Changes in the functional requisites, coercion and information, result in changes in the structural requisites, that is, in the way in which authority and consent operate vis-à-vis one another. Such alteration marks the transition from one type of political system to another because a change in the proportions of coercion and information also alters decision-making and accountability. The different arrangements of these relationships may be called political systems or developmental types. Illustrative extreme cases or ideal types not found empirically are the secular-libertarian and the sacred-collectivity models. Between these models, clustering around different properties, are more realistic approximations of concrete political systems: the reconciliation system, the modernizing autocracy, the military oligarchy, the neomercantilist society, and the mobilization system. Each of these systems handles modernization differently, even though, in practice, their activities may appear similar. The examination of such differences provides an important basis for the empirical study of the ways in which political form affects modernization.

The study of changes in the structural requisites leads to the third analytical category, the four contingent structures: enforcement and punishment, resource determination and allocation, political recruitment, and the structure of consent. The organization of research data in terms of contingent structures is useful for the analysis of the structural requisites.

The point of optimal efficiency for modernization reached in each political system is the point of intersection between coercion and information at which the greatest proportion of goals is achieved at the lowest cost. This point may be reached in a mobilization system more quickly than in a reconciliation system. A reconciliation system, however, may be able to maintain it longer once it is reached. There is less emphasis on *investissement humain* in reconciliation systems and more on *animation rural*, community development, or village community enterprises.

The relationship between coercion and information may be rephrased in the following hypothesis. *If a country is trying to modernize in the most efficient manner possible, it will seek a regime that will provide a relationship between coercion and information*

that will achieve modernization goals at the least possible cost.
In the effort to find the optimal combination of these variables, modernizing societies will change from one political type to another. Sometimes these changes will be clearly demarcated and abrupt, as in Cuba. At other times the changes will occur very slowly, more in substance than in form. Whatever the mode of alteration, however, it should now be clear that the general process of modernization will be accompanied by periodic changes in types of political systems.

Several propositions have been derived from this method of analysis. We have suggested that in societies where political forms are reinforced by political religion and ideologies, consummatory ends are mundane rather than sacred. We would anticipate from this evaluation that such systems would be susceptible to the growth of political cynicism and opportunism. Most governments confronted with such a decline in a source of legitimacy first try to ritualize political religion by turning it into a dogma that can be learned, absorbed, and utilized as a guide to action (without requiring much thought). Political ritualization is thus an attempt to establish a standard of conduct and customary observances about authority. Should such ritualization be unsuccessful, not only are the attempts to indoctrinate the population likely to fail (in the sense that the norms of the political religion are not accepted), but coercion can be expected to increase. At least the appearance of ritualization (if not its substance) must be observed.

Our second underlying assumption has been that major increases in coercion bring about losses in information. Under such conditions, uncertainty results and is manifested in government decisions concerning important instrumental ends. Virtually every aspect of daily life comes to be endowed with a conspiratorial quality; secrecy is common. (In fact, secrecy could be said to be an attempt to control valid information.) Under such circumstances, opportunism, corruption, error, and incompetency grow. Society becomes a bureaucratic conspiracy in which each individual tries to avoid responsibility. Since no one wants to be held accountable for failure, accountability groups are negligible. Consent groups are non-existent. Junior leaders are afraid of making decisions; instead, they defer them or "push them upstairs." Driven toward greater and greater autocracy by a growing lack of information, government becomes capricious in order to maintain authority. Decisions are equivalent to "speculation."[1] Political speculation is based on decisions taken in ignorance.

In Yugoslavia, or even the U.S.S.R., where the mobilization system lost its political religion, then ritualized it and gained at least outward conformity, such speculation has proved very costly. Now a system change is underway. The system of hierarchical authority is being modified. As the hierarchy is decentralized, information comes in from an increasing number of points. The structural requisites reflect this change in the growth of accountability groups, with more people sharing in decision-making.

Two points should be borne in mind. Other systems than the mobilization type apply coercion; and reconciliation systems are

[1] What Eduard Bernstein once argued about capitalist speculation and economic entrepreneurship is appropriate to political speculation in mobilization systems. "Speculation is conditioned by the relation of the knowable to the unknown circumstances. The more the latter predominates, the more will speculation flourish; the more it is restrained by the former, the more the ground is cut from under its feet. Therefore, the maddest outbursts of commercial speculation come to pass at the dawn of the capitalist era, and speculation celebrates its wildest orgies usually in the countries where the capitalistic development is youngest." See Bernstein, *Evolutionary Socialism* (New York: Schoken Books, 1961), p. 83.

In the period in which a modernizing nation comes into being, employing the property and lives of the state in order to build a new social order and to establish a different framework for society — a framework that cannot be perceived but that takes on vague outlines suggesting hope and betterment — one finds an almost frenetic search for new forms through which new solutions, it is hoped, will suggest themselves. In trying to extricate one's nation from existing conditions, it is believed, all sorts of political and economic adventures can be undertaken. In many modernizing nations, political speculation is the reality of politics, with coercion its cause and information its object.

not necessarily democratic in the Western sense of that term. What is significant about the use of coercion in the mobilization system is its application through higher (centralized) power. This kind of coercion implies the adherence of the members of the system to objectives and forms of conduct laid down by government. Reconciliation systems, on the other hand, use coercion in a scattered and decentralized way. The application does not follow set lines of authority. Indeed, government quite often is a mechanism of appeal against local and private coercive actions. An entirely different situation exists in the mobilization system, in which sanctions are applied to insure the conformity of the population to the goals of state. The most coherent statement of this is expressed in Lenin's concepts of democratic centralism and the role of a vanguard party. It is this aspect of ideology that tends to be attractive to the political leaders of modernizing countries seeking radical transformation of their societies.[2]

The information needed by a government is usually of two kinds: First, decision-makers require knowledge of that which will retain or enlarge support for government. With this kind of information they can anticipate the degree of popularity of various political alternatives. Second, they need information about the utility of actions for advancing the modernization goals of the community. Since these two aspects of information do not necessarily coincide, the critical task of government is how best to establish the optimum circumstances, that is, how to advance the modernization goals of the system with the fullest possible support. Here again, there are marked differences between the mobilization and reconciliation systems. The mobilization system will manipulate ideology in order to achieve support for those goals it regards as necessary, although perhaps unpopular, for rapid modernization. In a reconciliation system, government is likely to settle for goals with a greater possibility of realization.

[2] See the discussion of Leninism in Adam B. Ulam's book, *The Unfinished Revolution* (New York: Vintage Books, 1964), pp. 168–95.

In the course of time, these aspects of government will be reflected in changes in the community as well as in the form of government most suitable for the achievement of goals in each developmental type. For many of the new nations, it is too soon to specify precisely what consequences their actions will have for the future. We do have some indication of what may occur, however, in the examples of Mexico, where the mobilization system has become a single-party reconciliation system, and the old Communist states, particularly the U.S.S.R., Poland, and Yugoslavia, which have begun to inject, particularly the last two, a few of the ingredients of the reconciliation model. In these countries political religion is so completely ritualized that it is no longer required to support authority. Slowly, they are incorporating into hierarchical authority some elements of pyramidal authority as well as greater instrumentalism, particularly in the political sphere.

According to the criteria employed so far, it is possible to arrange a sample of present-day nations along a continuum (see Figure 17). Having reviewed briefly the manner in which political changes during modernization can be analyzed, we can now indicate some of the types of systems other than mobilization that are likely to be found during modernization.

In the preceding chapter we described certain characteristics of the mobilization system, in particular its tendency to decline rapidly during the early stages of modernization when restratification possibilities have come to an end and ritualization of authority has begun. The type of system most likely to result is one that shares certain properties of the mobilization model used in this analysis, namely, hierarchical authority and instrumental values. As we have suggested, the mobilization system is likely to end abruptly in a military coup d'état, which transforms it into a military oligarchy, or to change gradually into a neomercantilist system. Both of these systems are in the same general category as the modernizing autocracy, although all three differ in subtype characteristics. A military oligarchy is a state run by the authority of the army; a modernizing autocracy is commonly a traditional system of kingship, with the ability, however, to assimilate innovation; and the neomercantilist system tends to be a presidential monarchy, with ritualized charisma and a stable one-party government. Before discussing these types further, we will comment briefly on the system most clearly the obverse of the mobilization system, the reconciliation system.

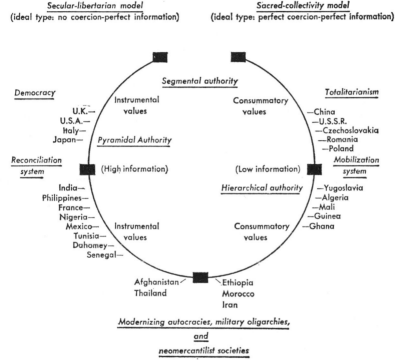

Secular-libertarian model
(ideal type: no coercion-perfect information)

Sacred-collectivity model
(ideal type: perfect coercion-perfect information)

Segmental authority

Democracy

Instrumental values

Consummatory values

Totalitarianism

U.K.—
U.S.A.—
Italy—
Japan—

Pyramidal Authority

—China
—U.S.S.R.
—Czechoslovakia
—Romania
—Poland

Reconciliation system

(High information)

(Low information)

Mobilization system

India—
Philippines—
France—
Nigeria—
Mexico—
Tunisia—
Dahomey—
Senegal—

Hierarchical authority

Instrumental values

Consummatory values

—Yugoslavia
—Algeria
—Mali
—Guinea
—Ghana

Afghanistan
Thailand

Ethiopia
Morocco
Iran

Modernizing autocracies, military oligarchies,
and
neomercantilist societies

FIG. 17. — *Nations according to authority types.*

THE DEVELOPMENT PROCESS IN THE RECONCILIATION SYSTEM

In both the reconciliation system and the modernizing autocracy, leaders are more willing to accommodate goals to public demands than in the mobilization system. In trying to effect economic development, the mobilization system seeks to overhaul society in general through technological change. Precisely because of the ideological needs incurred in that process, the mobilization system attaches great symbolic meaning to general goals, which become the moral basis of coercive politics.

The goals of the reconciliation system are based on information rather than on a vision of the future. They are high information systems. "Inexpensive" information is made available to decision-makers by the variety of interest groups, voluntary associations, and political parties in the society, which express their demands to government. Goals are in closer relation to resources and public desires, and government has less need to rely extensively on coercive techniques. In addition, since reconciliation systems are based upon the restrictions on government power inherent in this authority structure, their governments can rarely gain sufficient political consensus to enact coercive measures. Reconciliation systems can act autocratically only under very extreme circumstances, such as war.

Acting on the basis of information rather than through coercion, the government must evolve flexible strategies that will enable it to win compliance. A high proportion of available resources can be utilized for economic development. There is, however, at least one practical limitation inherent in the situation: a high rate of forced savings is politically impossible. Therefore, the rate of capital investment is likely to be lower than that in the mobilization system, barring unforeseen windfalls. Government's efforts take the form of stimulating non-governmental development or local entrepreneurship. This may be done by providing sources of credit for private entrepreneurs, by expanding the possibilities of joint government and private enterprises, such as industrial development corporations and similar projects, and by encouraging foreign investment.

The role of government in a reconciliation system is not organizational; rather, it works to reconcile diverse interests; it mediates, integrates, and above all, co-ordinates, rather than organizes and mobilizes. In contrast to the mobilization system, which "fights" society, the reconciliation system is often a prisoner of society. Where stagnancy exists, for example, high information may simply show that government cannot achieve goals expected by the public in the absence of forced measures. If the public is unwilling to sacrifice current consumption for the sake of future consumption and otherwise to modify its behavior in order to attain these goals, then the result will be (even if the government is democratic) personal frustration, political corruption, and compromise. Thus, the degree of modernization in a reconciliation system depends on a balance of steadfast motives among the top political leaders and public determination to enforce self-discipline. Only then (along with local participation in economic enterprise) can a high level of development be ensured. When there are lags in the acceptance of economic goals or voluntary means of achieving them (and when, also, great cultural discontinuities persist long after a new government has established itself), governments of the reconciliation type may be condemned to such a slow rate of economic progress that they create their own disaster. This is, in fact, likely to be so, at least in the short run.[3] The long-run prospects may, of course, be vastly different.

The reconciliation system, because it needs to make constant efforts to find local sources of talent and engage them in the development process, uses many semitraditional but commercialized groupings, parochial in outlook but serviceable in the first stages of modernization. The technical elites become separated from these semimodern groups, with the result that the elites cannot be used in a decentralized economy. When the processes of economic growth are dispersed (not only between the private and the public sectors of the economy, but also be-

[3] One need only compare India and China in this regard. See the discussion of economic growth and planning in the *Report of the Commission of Enquiry on Emoluments and Conditions of Service of Central Governmental Employees, 1957–59* (Delhi, 1959), pp. 35–45.

tween the provinces and the center), they are less efficient than they should be precisely because of this separation of the modernizing elites from the semimodern middle groupings. Local decision-making and local capital investment mean a great dependence of the development process on village and local committees. Rapid economic growth is possible, however, in a reconciliation system, but only if there is extensive self-discipline, popular participation, civic devotion, and above all, a planning mechanism. These preconditions occur very rarely in the modernizing nations.[4]

Reconciliation systems are not necessarily democratic. They are close to the Western notion of democracy only to the extent that they accept the normative implications of the secular-libertarian model. Premature reconciliation systems were common among the republics established in Latin America between 1809 and 1825. I say "premature" because most of them were plagued with violence and revolution. More successful examples today are perhaps Nigeria and Senegal. Each shows a high degree of pluralism, and even where, as in Senegal, there is a single dominant party, it has remained essentially a coalition of parties of representation. Each of these countries remains a low coercion and high information system, with accountability in decision-making dispersed over a wide variety of party and governmental groups including provincial and local governments and party units.

But even these examples are moving in the direction of the neomercantilist society. The struggle over whether to establish a presidential monarchy is presently underway in Nigeria. In Senegal, the president has assumed such a role to his constituents (although presenting a bland and "democratic" countenance to his political friends abroad).[5]

---

[4] See the excellent discussion of this problem in Edward Shils's "Political Development in the New States," *Comparative Studies in Society and History*, II (1960), Part II.

[5] Tanganyika had already made the move. See Julius Nyerere's discussion

The reasons are not hard to find. The reconciliation system has few consummatory values to carry it beyond its functional or utilitarian basis. I have pointed out that, in the West, the values of this system, as embedded in law, derived from a general commitment to traditional religiously enshrined values, which in turn derived from an earlier theocratic period. The rise of representative government can be seen as the realization of particular Judeo-Christian religious beliefs. But what can hold a system of pyramidal authority together in the absence of directly religious consummatory values? Only a very high rate of return, that is, a combination of promise and payoff to groups that might serve to check the government and prevent its functioning. Today reconciliation systems need to be rich in order to be successful (and even then they rarely appeal to younger political generations), and in newly modernizing societies they are not likely to be. No doubt there are times when they are more efficient than they appear to be. In the allocation of resources, for example, graft and corruption may turn out to be economically more efficient than the gross errors resulting from overplanning in a mobilization system. But their greatest problem is that stratification easily becomes fixed and hardened. The gap between rich and poor increases, along with economic strangulation. Reconciliation systems in the history of Latin America are particularly to the point. They have paid lip service to democratic ideals, but they have failed to distribute opportunity. Inequality has increased, and access to power and prestige is more and more restricted — whether on the basis of kinship, economic, political, generational, or educational criteria. No wonder such governments are inevitably precarious. For those countries whose sanctional source was a rejection of colonialism, the reconciliation system is also rejected; the symbolism of representative government may even come to be regarded as comic. The integrational function of government may be inundated by a wave of internal conflicts between governmental bodies. In

---

of the principle of one-party democracy in "One-Party System," *Spearhead: The Pan-African Review*, II (January, 1963).

other words, the malfunctioning of the structures may eventually come to weaken the ability of government to perform its functions, with the result that the system will begin to change into something else.[6]

Moreover, reconciliation systems of modernization show only a meager participation of citizens in society. Even though repressive law is limited, equity remains a matter of competitive bargaining between groups, mediated by government and regulated by rules. But since so few participate, the system could be described as taking place in a vacuum.

THE DEVELOPMENT PROCESS IN THE MODERNIZING AUTOCRACY

The modernizing autocracy presents a curious alternative to the mobilization and reconciliation systems. Able to modify its goals more easily than the mobilization system, the modernizing autocracy has open to it certain traditional coercive techniques.[7] These may not immediately result in restrictions on the flow of information.

Likely coercive techniques available to political decision-makers are those that have a long tradition and are thoroughly understood by the public. Alongside these techniques, regularized compensatory means of public expression have grown up over time. Typically, the latter have reinforced traditional or traditionalized limits on the power of decision-makers (by custom and belief). As a result, there are special means for expressing public preferences — and more particularly, elite preferences — concerning government policies. The difficulty facing the modernizing autocracy is the possibility that changes effected in the economic sphere may eventually threaten the

[6] This suggests by implication that democratic forms of government are not likely to be successful as systems for modernization.
[7] That is, traditional pressures from religions, clan, family, and so on.

principle of hierarchical authority in the political sphere, with consequent demands for the substantial alteration of the system. A few words on this type of system may help to clarify these comments.

The typical modernizing autocracy is a monarchical-bureaucratic system of rule with an advisory council. It is traditionally organized, but its traditions are flexible, its values instrumental. The symbolic position of the ruler is heavily emphasized. Opportunities for establishing a patrimony are available to him. Economic development proceeds as larger numbers of educated and technically trained personnel are absorbed into the traditional hierarchy. These new members of the hierarchy may express a desire for greater participation in the decision-making process. The political, therefore, rather than the economic, consequences of technological change and development create the most serious difficulties for the modernizing autocracy. Such systems commonly predate modernization and remain intact while achieving it. The outstanding example is Japan. Present-day examples are Thailand, Afghanistan, and Ethiopia.

Precedent, custom, and traditional behavioral prescriptions, having persisted through time, are central mechanisms of control over both leaders and led in the modernizing autocracy. At the same time, the principle of hierarchical authority and autocracy results in leaders' being relatively less accountable to the public than they are in the reconciliation system. Hence, they play an important role in innovation. Modernizing autocracies emphasize technological change and encourage public acceptance of it because innovations introduced by the government can be validated through traditional patterns of authority. Insofar as the government sets realistic economic goals, considerable compliance and acceptance are assured without increasing costs of coercion and, equally important, without losing information. Modernizing autocracies are common historically, but they rarely endure beyond modernization and into a major period of industrialization without serious internal difficulties. Prussia and Tsarist Russia are two cases in point, with the former terminating in a neomercantilist, corporate system, Naziism, and the latter in an extreme form of the mobilization system, Leninism.

The typical modernizing autocracy is centered on a monarch, who represents hierarchical authority. He embodies complete and awesome power; he is the state personified. He is the personal lord of every citizen — the relationship between king and subject is direct and immediate.[8] His council is a court, not a check on authority. From this relationship, two contrasting forms of behavior ensue. First, the direct use of authority is acceptable. Second, the subject feels that if he has complaints he may personally lay them at the feet of his king and expect remedial action. (Both the mobilization system and the modernizing autocracy have this one attribute in common, that is, a tendency to personal government.)[9]

One consequence of this set of circumstances is that well-institutionalized modernizing autocracies can experiment with goals without paying the penalty of immediate instability. For example, despite the magnitude of the economic changes at the beginning of industrialization (during the mercantilist period), England was able to remain relatively stable — a factor not unrelated to the economy's ability to expand as rapidly as it did. Economic development also helped England to change from a modernizing autocracy to a democratic type of reconciliation system. (Tsarist Russia is a less fortunate example. The excesses of the bureaucracy, corruption, war, and poverty after the emancipation of the serfs in 1861 required more effective and drastic structural reorganization than the government could provide. In this respect, the modernizing autocracies of Russia, Japan, and

---

[8] See the discussion of the modernizing autocracy in my book *The Political Kingdom in Uganda* (Princeton, N.J.: Princeton University Press, 1961), *passim.*

[9] In the former type of system, ideologized justifications cover up capriciousness; in the latter, custom restrains it. See Thomas Hodgkin, *Nationalism in Colonial Africa* (London: Muller, Ltd., 1956), chapter v. See also William Kornhauser, *The Politics of Mass Society* (Glencoe: Free Press of Glencoe, Ill., 1959), chapter iii.

Germany at the turn of the century had many features in common.)

Modernizing autocracies can promote economic development and maintain stability only in the short run, because they are not able to absorb the new elites sufficiently into the traditional hierarchy. The new elites become the spearhead of political reform, which modernizing autocracies can suffer only on a limited scale. (The rare exception, England, transformed the practice of the system while retaining the form.)[10]

In the modernizing autocracy, goals are restricted by their implications for the system of hierarchical authority. Those that seem to entail substantial alterations in the political framework of the society are necessarily abhorred by the government. Those that allow the system to continue while at the same time satisfying the public — particularly with respect to the expansion of material needs and the raising of income levels — are adopted. Successful modernizing autocracies like Ethiopia, Thailand, Afghanistan, and Iran are rare. Few monarchical systems have in fact been able to maintain their authority structure intact while modernizing.

THE MILITARY OLIGARCHY

Perhaps the main significance of the military oligarchy is that it is a potentiality in all systems in which the force of nationalism

[10] The new elites prefer either a reconciliation or a mobilization system. When they begin to express their preferences, economic goals may be restricted by the monarch to prevent change that he cannot control. Opposing groups can then easily charge the system with being feudal and archaic. Political difficulties are inherent in the system. Turkey remains one of the most interesting examples to study. There the shift to Kemalism after the downfall of the Ottoman Empire can be described as a change from a modernizing autocracy of the traditional variety to a mobilization system, with a move toward a reconciliation system in the decades since World War II. This movement has now reversed itself in an abrupt transition to a neomercantilist system. See T. Feyzioglu, "Les partis politiques en Turquie," *Revue Française de science politique*, I (January-March, 1954).

is strong. The military comes to represent sovereignty and independence and, as such, is the ultimate coercive force in the state. In this sense, it is an important subgroup in all societies — the more important the more intimate the relation to coercion as a functional requisite of government.

Military oligarchies come into being in different political systems in a number of ways: (1) In a reconciliation system, a military oligarchy most often takes over by a coup d'état. This has occurred most often in Latin America and parts of Southeast Asia. (2) In a mobilization system this is less likely. The hierarchical structure of administration may create the conditions for militarizing society. In effect, social life becomes militarized. Workers are "soldiers" of the state. Discipline is required of all. Crimes are punished not by jury trials but, in effect, by courts martial. Perhaps, to some extent, this has happened in China as a result of the long march in the thirties — not to speak of the civil war — which created a paramilitary system (although it remains a mobilization system with a revolutionary outlook). (3) In a modernizing autocracy or neomercantilist society, a military oligarchy comes to power through the institutionalization and professionalization of authority, which has come to rely on the military as an organization.

The different ways of coming into being suggest that the military oligarchy itself takes several forms. It may not be overtly military (in the sense that it inheres in an army) in order to result in the "militarization" of political life. For example, China, although clearly a mobilization system in our terms, nevertheless shows some of the characteristics of the military oligarchy. Perhaps all extreme mobilization systems do. Nor does it mean that the military leaders, once they have come to power, need remain military in their outlook. The example of Egypt, where military leaders have become civilianized, is a case in point. The analytical justification for the military oligarchy is that it is a significant tendency within other types of systems, as well as a type of its own. Leadership is hierarchical and bureaucratic rather than personal — a command system without a single heroic leader at the top. To this extent, the military oligarchy is more like the neomercantilist society than any other system, although with a different pattern of leadership.[11]

The *military* aspect is, however, important. Military oligarchies show the effects of professionalization in engineering and administration. The military increasingly operates as a career group with a sense of its own identity. Moreover, especially in Latin America, officers may come to feel that as a group they are the agents of modernity. They represent modernism against virtually all forms of traditionalism, whether of caste, class, or premodern cultural attributes.

In addition, the military, as represented by officers, tends to be one of the best educated groups having access to the means of power. It can support professionalization with superior education. As the military generations become shorter (the result, in part, of changes during modernization in the whole concept of generation), the oligarchs who come to power get younger; whereas in an earlier day, they tended to be older than the politicians they displaced. This has two consequences: first, the military oligarchy can more readily capture the youth and identify with their sense of impatience; and second, the period of participation of the military in policy-making is much longer. Again, in an earlier period, the military officer made a poor administrator if only because his accustomed period of command was very short. Most of his career was spent in taking orders from superiors rather than giving them and in carrying out policy rather than making it. This is less and less the case. In effect, the modern military oligarchy no longer represents the old guard versus the vanguard, as in the classical cases. It may also become even more youthful by getting rid of senior officers. In this respect, the military oligarchy will continue to represent one of the most common modernization responses.

[11] See Fig. 2 in chapter i.

THE NEOMERCANTILIST SOCIETY

So far I have speculated on modernization as a political phenomenon; I have also argued a point of view. I have considered the sacred-collectivity model as a normative standard against which to compare other systems. Obedience, command, and the universalization of political religion in the mundane sphere — indeed, in the name of science — are all characteristics. Since instrumental efficiency is low, achievement comes at great cost and suffering.[12]

Mobilization systems derive from this type. If their use of coercion rarely affects the entire population, it is because political religion has turned into political cynicism (despite indoctrination and efforts at political socialization). They usually attempt to raise mundane goals (modernization and industrialization) to the level of consummatory goals, doing so in the name of socialism. Guinea, Egypt, and Indonesia are examples of such systems. Some mobilization systems are moving away from the sacred-collectivity extreme and toward a form of modernizing autocracy that I call the neomercantilist society. As charismatic leadership declines in Ghana and Guinea, for example, authority is becoming ritualized in the role of presidential monarch. These two countries are modern corporate states that employ ritualized forms of political religion in which considerable pluralism survives. Authority is distributed between powerful functional auxiliaries of the sole political party.

There is a difference between modernizing autocracies and neomercantilist societies; the latter arrive at this particular form as the result of a retraditionalization process in which values and goals proximate to the modernization process are themselves legitimized. In other words, the content of the values of the neomercantilist society is different from the content of those of

---

[12] The extreme case of a sacred-collectivity system is high coercion and low information; the ideal — perfect coercion and, therefore, perfect information — is never achieved. Nevertheless, in the attempt to achieve the ideal political goals become consummatory values.

the modernizing autocracy, and therefore a similar structural form of government may be put to different uses when the commitments of the system are different from earlier ones.[13] As we have suggested, the neomercantilist. society is the optimum structural form after- primary or early-stage modernization. As each of the other forms of political system gets into trouble, it will move in the direction of a neomercantilist system. The reasons are clear enough.

If a modernizing country began as a reconciliation system, it will move, as it modernizes, toward a neomercantilist society by increasing coercion. Conversely, the mobilization system will move toward a neomercantilist society by decreasing coercion. This suggests that the best balance to achieve modernization goals, at minimum cost, is at the intersection of coercion and information typically provided by the neomercantilist society. (The diagram in Figure 18 illustrates these remarks.) If this hypothesis is correct, the neomercantilist society will also provide the discipline necessary to achieve these goals.

Perhaps we should remind ourselves of the characteristics of

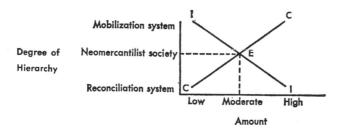

Degree of Hierarchy

Mobilization system

Neomercantilist society

Reconciliation system

Low   Moderate   High

Amount

I = Information
C = Coercion
E = Equilibrium

Fig. 18. — *Information and coercion.*

[13] The fundamental structural similarity is the personalized role of a presidential monarch who is the functional equivalent of a king in the old modernizing autocracy.

this developmental type. It may be monarchical or republican. Consummatory values in the political framework are subordinate to but must support instrumental values. The language of the mobilization system may be employed for this, and some neomercantilist societies may sound like militant Marxian socialist states. But this is largely rhetoric. In practice, innovation is related to well-understood sets of symbols that are both vague and satisfying to those who hear them and that allow multiple interpretations. Goals impossible to achieve are ruled out. In the neomercantilist society, political religion, having given way to the ritualization of authority, creates a new tradition.

How long can a neomercantilist society remain efficient? I would suggest that, by and large, it will be more efficient for a longer period of time than a mobilization system and more stable than a reconciliation system. As I originally suggested, however, each of these systems is vulnerable to the others and none represents a kind of end point. Perhaps the most that can be said is that the long-term tendency for systems that have successfully modernized is for all to become less stable near the end of the modernization process, and prior to the industrialization process, when the political means to integrate roles are less effective. Countries like Argentina and Brazil are examples of what may happen when the modernization process has been achieved without much corresponding growth in the industrial sector.

The neomercantilist society, then, is subject to the same long-term instabilities as the other forms. An attempt may be made to postpone this outcome by the institutionalization of leadership. The neomercantilist societies can become dynastic. A small group of people around a "presidential monarch" may become the equivalent of a royal lineage. They may choose incumbents of political office by very particularistic means. Only if they fragment their authority by conflict between themselves and their supporters will instability result and induce a different form of government. What Ibn Khaldûn long ago suggested probably remains relevant, that a dynasty depends on the number of its supporters for its strength but that it is rarely established when there are many different tribes and groups. He suggested that even the best of dynasties cannot last for much more than three generations. Authority becomes lax; luxury abounds, corrupting the character of those men who are supposed to be towers of strength. As the degree of coercion changes, so will the regime change.[14]

Is there any evidence for the proposition that the neomercantilist society provides considerable stability in the face of modernization? I think there is. For one thing, the presidential monarchy is a fairly stable form of chief executive, at least during the time span of the first presidential monarch. This form coincides with a tendency to stress nationalism as an ideology rather more than socialism (although most of the presidential monarchs profess to be socialist). The effort to universalize the faith abroad disappears. The restratification of society ends. The key to the process is the ritualization of authority. When this occurs along with considerable coercion in connection with the achievement of modernization goals, the neomercantilist society is likely to be an optimal form of politics for modernization.

Although the neomercantilist society is politically closer to the mobilization system in its structure of authority and gains some of its political advantages, it is economically closer to the reconciliation system in terms of instrumental values. It is likely to use private enterprise, controlled in some measure politically but not necessarily owned by the state.[15] Indeed, the economic mode of neomercantilism could be labelled "state capitalism."

[14] Ibn Khaldûn, *The Muqaddimah* (New York: Pantheon Books, 1958), Vol. I, pp. 327–53.
[15] Early examples, which actually were modernizing autocracies, were Prussia and Japan, where state intervention, involving support of private banking and fiscal organizations and various other forms of treasury activity, helped stimulate private capitalization in both commerce and industry. In the mixed public and private enterprise of many of the developing nations, one

What are the critical factors that determine whether or not a system will change to another type? The first of these is the effectiveness with which the society, and the goals identified for it, are realized. The second is the organization of the system for the achievement of its goals.[16] Where both factors exist, the symbolic and sanctional aspects of authority are not easily undermined. But what is the sanctional source of a government that everyone mistrusts? It is unlikely, however, that structural changes designed to bring more information into the system and to reduce coercion will be introduced to prevent the breakdown of the two contingent functions of authority. One ought not expect decentralization of decision-making and the widening of accountability, especially in the first stages of the modernization process. This is why I emphasize the prospects of the neomercantilist society.

PROSPECTS FOR STABILITY IN THE NEOMERCANTILIST SOCIETY

Different from its older, more theocratic form, the modernizing autocracy (but still recognizably similar), the neomercantilist

---

can catch a glimpse of the old charter company pattern, in which, under charter from a king, enterprising gentlemen carried on flourishing trade and manufactures. This is today's neomercantilism, even when the language is that of socialism, with all its emphasis on community responsibility and social thrift, science and industry. In Latin America it is called the Neo-Bismarckian model. In Africa Houphouet-Boigny calls it "state capitalism."

[16] Where there is a high degree of coercion, goals take on a consummatory quality beyond the ordinary criteria of achievement. Indeed, their main purpose is to endow the society with a sense of ultimate purpose rather than a realizable objective. Extreme hierarchy is supported under such a system. Modernization merely refines the organizational techniques, making the system totalitarian, until it has become so complex that it needs to introduce some measure of pluralism. Such systems ordinarily begin with a political movement able to arouse and amalgamate both moral outrage at the pattern of institutionalized hierarchy and anger at relative deprivation. This movement has its own organizational dynamics. Its "system" problem grows with its success, that is, it responds to the need for pluralism by greater monism and to the need for greater information by greater coercion, for, as we have seen, its implicit assumption is that perfect coercion equals perfect information. Since perfect coercion is impossible, however, what is left is a high-cost system with unrealistic goals, depending for its long-run existence on the sus-

society shares some of the characteristics of both the reconciliation and mobilization systems. There is more pluralism than in the modernizing autocracy, but the structure of authority remains predominantly hierarchical. There is a wide range of instrumental values; indeed, the preoccupation of the entire society is the maximization of intermediate goals. The consummatory values proposed are in the form of transitional myths so as to make the new seem familiar and comfortable. The ideologies are characteristically both nationalist and socialist, with a neomercantilist orientation to government enterprise rather than a Marxian one. There is a broadly conceived ideal of transforming the power and prestige hierarchy; but this is mainly realized by widening opportunity while expanding the number of positions connected with the government's economic activities, which remain the largest employer of trained individuals. Such systems have greater information than mobilization systems and require less coercion. Hence, they have more accurate knowledge of the mood and loyalties of their people. Yet they are inclined to use coercion when political cynicism casts doubt on the symbolic and sanctional aspects of authority — hence, the emergence of the presidential monarchy to provide opportunities for the exceptional or heroic leader. In the main, however, such systems rest on technical and commercial roles, and functional claims to authority still count for much. Authority on the basis of expertise is thus part of the pluralism of the system, and the technician and expert are not entirely under the discipline of the state.

The neomercantilist society usually emerges after the decline of political religion in a mobilization system. Changes in political religion are accompanied by all the intense conflict that characterized religious movements in the past. There is an effort to

_____
tained apathy and despair of its people. Because it is a high-cost system, it is very inefficient. Hence, it can not attract support on the basis of its benefits (which are outweighed by its costs) or on the basis of its moral imperatives (because the system is built on deception). The instability of the mobilization system increases, then, as it approaches the extremes of inefficiency and immorality.

obliterate the opponent, or to humiliate him, if only that is possible, and to re-establish orthodoxy or the new ideological variant. Systems that are based on political religion, then, are extremely vulnerable to change in the area of belief, that is, in the sphere of consummatory values; the full weight of hierarchical authority comes down on one side or the other when a conflict develops. In the neomercantilist society, however, political religion rarely goes quite that far. Indeed, it is of some interest that even in those modernizing countries that have gone farthest in the direction of hierarchical authority and the establishment of consummatory values (for example, mobilization systems such as Ghana and Indonesia), church religion has not been restricted. The reasons they have permitted its continued existence are necessarily complex, but in the measure they have done so, their political religions have been somewhat halfhearted. The sacred writings and texts of the leader may lack conviction. If a "cult of personality" remains, however, it is more and more as ritualized authority, embodied in the person of the founder.

In the neomercantilist society, this ritualization process has been completed. Features of this new form of the modernizing autocracy include personalized leadership in government, a high degree of centralization, and a legislature acting largely in a consultative capacity. The position of the legislator is largely one of dispensing patronage, through which perquisites and income are provided to loyal party followers. Politics is organized around the civil service and the party, each with its own bureaucracy and each in competition for the favor of the presidential monarch, who is the leader of both in his dual capacities as head of state and head of party. Functional auxiliaries create a certain amount of discipline in the society and pluralism within the party, with their leaders being utilized to carry out national purposes in local areas.

Emphasis is on expanded education, functional skills, and technical training, and quite often a camaraderie of technicians evolves that includes members of both party and civil service.

Ideological emphases are in two opposite directions: the one toward the past, by means of which traditional life is rendered meaningful in contemporary terms, and the other toward the future and the promise of a better life under the regime and the presidential monarchy. The gap between past and present is bridged by the wisdom and paternalism of the presidential monarch, who, although a representative of tradition, nevertheless speaks in the name of science. Populist and egalitarian but also the highest point of an organizational hierarchy, the presidential monarch is anxious to expand his economic as well as political control over the society and to introduce planning and modern techniques of industry. Hence, a large part of the economic sector either is directly owned by government, which then turns it over to contract technicians from overseas to operate, or remains privately owned but is hedged with restrictions to prevent outside capital from exercising internal political influence. In this situation, the application of the terms neoimperialist and neocolonialist become a kind of litany repeated in an attempt to preserve political autonomy in the face of actual dependency on outsiders.

This is a general description of the way in which neomercantilist societies work. They differ from mobilization systems only to the degree that they are retraditionalized; this process begins when charismatic leadership is ritualized into the more stable role of presidential monarch. When a new range of accustomed behavior becomes firmly established, the process sets in in earnest. The neomercantilist society may even be a stabilized and less politicized form of a mobilization system, in which continuity, the training of new leadership cadres, and most important, the beginnings of practical realism can be observed. But since the hierarchy of power and prestige is selectively amended, rather than transformed, it is also profoundly conservative. Nationalism-socialism is a likely name for the ideology. The neomercantilist society, as a relatively stable system, is a *new form of the corporate state*. It is the modern functional equivalent of the modernizing autocracy, which has become almost obsolete. The prospects of the neomercantilist society as a new form of corporate state are as yet barely discernible but may well result in a rebirth of fascism, stripped of its more atavistic qualities. The neomercantilist society may also be distinguished from the mobilization system by the predominance of instrumental rather than consummatory values. The best indicator of this difference, aside from the ideological context of each system, is the pattern of stratification. The mobilization system changes the ranking of power and prestige roles, and thus the values attached to a change in hierarchy as well. The neomercantilist society accepts a particular pattern of stratification and enlarges the pyramid without changing the values associated with rank.

It would be wrong to conclude from these remarks that the mobilization system is communist and the neomercantilist society is fascist. Such a characterization is a plausible and likely one but not inevitable. A community that has a radical fascist program of total mobilization, including restratification, may also have a high emphasis on consummatory values; and a communist system, having accomplished its main mobilization objectives, may turn into a neomercantilist society. It would be interesting to test a conjecture that in the majority of cases neomercantilist societies are strongly nationalist in ideology and mobilization systems are socialist.

CONCLUSIONS

These general characteristics of change between political systems can now be summarized. The mobilization system must find the optimal balance between the achievement of forward-looking goals and the allocation of real income between coercion and investment. (The degree of coercion is restricted by the influence of its cost on the processes of economic growth.)[17] The hierarchi-

---

[17] If coercion becomes the primary means of assuring compliance, then there may be a change from a mobilization system employing a mild autoc-

cal authority of the mobilization system seeks not only to maintain itself but to intervene in all aspects of social life. Economic development becomes the rationale for demanding total allegiance. Tactical flexibility is essential to assure immediate control over the problems that may emerge in the economic process. Minimum public accountability is the chief characteristic of the mobilization system.

The reconciliation system, on the other hand, must rely heavily on information to define its goals and the means of achieving them. It cannot utilize much coercion — if it does, it will be transformed into a mobilization system. Its distinguishing features are its participation in different aspects of group life and its stimulation of the public to participate more fully in economic processes.[18]

In the reconciliation system collective legitimacy results from the representative principle. This principle, however, because of the danger of economic stagnation, group separatism, and even secession by one or more of the constituent elements, may also weaken legitimacy and impose a real limitation upon the freedom of the political leaders. Since multiple loyalties exist, economic development is by no means seen solely in terms of the state but, instead, in terms of special interests. In India, for example, the political demands of various local interests made it necessary to construct an additional oil refinery in a less advantageous part of the country in order to gain acceptance to build a needed refinery in the most economically desirable location.

Since compromise is innate in a reconciliation system, the pace of development is determined by the willingness of the political

---

racy to a mobilization system employing more totalitarian methods. Should this occur, coercion and information will coincide for all practical purposes and the perfect information system become the perfect coercive system.

[18] An important task for the government is the crystallization of economic goals — to present them to the public in such a way that the people respond enthusiastically to the difficulties inevitable in economic development.

A different but related problem of information is that, if information is to be effective, it must be translated into goals by efficient decision-making. If so much information is available that it cannot be "processed," decision-making suffers and the system becomes inefficient.

leaders and the public to follow the policy of the central government. The pace of growth is never more dramatic than that which the public is prepared to accept, since policy must conform to public desires. Frequently, the result is a greater degree of superficial instability in the system, with much spontaneous conflict and expressions of bitterness among the parts. In spite of this, coercive techniques remain at a minimum; and it can be argued that the strength of the reconciliation system lies, in some measure, in the perpetuation of these conflicts. Each group bases its loyalty to the system on parochial interests and the hope of satisfying such interests. The hypotheses of both Georg Simmel and Max Gluckman concerning the social utility of conflict are relevant here. Conflict is not necessarily destructive of the social fabric.[19] On the contrary, under a reconciliation system, conflict may give people a vested interest in the system as a whole. In this sense, there is little resemblance to the modernizing autocracy. Leaders in modernizing autocracies are suspicious of advanced, dramatic programs for economic development that have political implications. They tend to isolate those aspects of economic reforms that seem capable of being absorbed without introducing new sources of conflict.

Clearly, no system is exclusively appropriate to modernization. Some are very useful for particular contingencies. The mobilization system is a response to the problem of unity, especially during the formation of a national political system. Neomercantilist societies appear to have better long-run potentialities for stability. Mobilization systems are perhaps most suitable as conversion systems, that is, during the transition from modernization to industrialization. Reconciliation systems are characteristic responses to conditions of pluralism in which groups resist amalgamation. They also are able to handle the problem of complexity by decentralizing decision-making. Moreover, the reconciliation

---

[19] See Simmel, *Conflict* (Glencoe: Free Press of Glencoe, Ill., 1955); and Gluckman, *Custom and Conflict in Africa* (Glencoe: Free Press of Glencoe, Ill., 1955).

system has one long-term advantage over the others. Because it is based on relatively high information and relatively low coercion (although not the absence of it), it can cope with the institutional complexity that is associated with the modernization revolution, or what might be called the communications and information revolution, in industrial societies. The reconciliation system provides exceptional opportunities for a scientific and communicating elite to fashion an appropriate polity in such societies. But it is not easily adopted by modernizing societies. As was the case in industrializing countries like Germany in the late nineteenth century, Japan in the early twentieth century, and the Soviet Union during the thirties, modernizing nations today represent a blend of government and private enterprise in polities that balance co-operation and coercion, ideology and information. In a real sense, what they have in common, aside from their aspirations, is their tendency to become neomercantilist states.[20]

If my assumptions about changes in systems are correct, then some mobilization systems may become neomercantilist societies — not the old form of modernizing autocracy, which was a traditional kingship system, but the new form of presidential monarchy. (One the other hand, some of the old modernizing autocracies such as Iran or Morocco, may well change into mobilization systems, just as reconciliation systems, such as Nigeria, may easily become mobilization systems.) The potentialities of change during modernization are roughly delineated in Figure 19.

The long-term tendency toward a neomercantilist society exists only during the modernizing period. And it should be

[20] See Bert F. Hoselitz et al., *Theories of Economic Growth* (Glencoe: Free Press of Glencoe, Ill., 1960); in particular, the recapitulation of mercantilist theories of growth by J. J. Spengler is relevant here. See also Eli F. Heckscher, *Mercantilism* (London: George Allen & Unwin, Ltd., 1955). The term is particularly appropriate in Heckscher's definition because he suggests that its primary political significance was *unification*. See the discussion on pp. 21–28.

clear that it is no more than a tendency. The prospect today in
Latin America, for example, is for those countries on the verge
of industrialization to move toward mobilization systems.
It is possible to indicate leads and lags in the relationship
between a stage of development and a political system. To take
the example of Latin America again, in the early nineteenth
century, reconciliation systems, embodied in formal structures

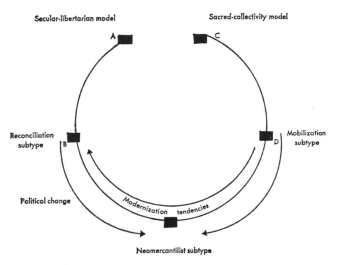

FIG. 19. — *Tendencies in modernization.*

of representative government, proved, in most cases, clearly un-
suitable for the prevailing level of social and economic development. Such structures might be appropriate to present-day
conditions (because of the differentiation and specialization in
social and economic life that has occurred), but it is more likely
that mobilization systems will be better able to provide a sufficient political focus to establish goals, to organize a ramified
system of coercion, and to create institutions that can provide
information and a framework that can assess costs.
If this analysis is correct, then the following inferences may

be drawn.[21] (1) Neomercantilist societies are the optimal form of political system for consolidation in countries in the early stages of modernization. (2) Mobilization systems are optimal systems for countries that are reaching the end of a period of modernization and are about to industrialize. (3) Reconciliation systems are optimal systems for well-established and highly complex industrial states, as Figure 19 suggests. Each system is likely to be stable for a given type of development. Within each major period (modernization or industrialization), however, other variables that we have discussed, which promote more immediate changes, are at work. Hence, a country may well move from a mobilization to a reconciliation system during modernization, although, in my view, the reconciliation system will be less efficient (other things being equal) than the neomercantilist society.

Mobilization systems, because they rely on coercion, create uncertainty, which makes co-ordination of the modernization process difficult. In the long run, the mobilization system will become increasingly inefficient because it loses sources of information.

[21] So far I have been speculating about modernization and system change. Let me now return to the original distinction I made between industrialization and modernization. If it is true to say that the tendency for systems undergoing modernization is toward neomercantilism, the situation is quite different with respect to industrialization.

12

THE FUTURE OF
DEMOCRATIC SOCIETY

In comparative studies, general theory remains more separate and distinct from the practice of research than is healthy for a satisfactory job of analysis. Imagination leaps ahead of the sober limits of operations. Categories that seem to make sense at first glance may, on reflection, become so divorced from data or be so inclusive that they hinder rather than help understanding. Everyone who has worked in this field is familiar with the frustrations produced by the current state of theory, and attempts to pass beyond the limitations imposed by data or by concepts may merely compound the problems. As new theoretical jumps are made, attempts to operationalize concepts become more difficult rather than less. If anyone has a picture in his mind of the development of theory by means of experimental techniques and the accumulation of proved and tested knowledge, one short look at the field should indicate to him how wrong this is, especially in the social sciences. Our theorists, like grasshoppers, jump about the terrain. It is quite impossible to determine in which direction they will jump next.

All of these problems are as much a part of science as they are an embarrassment to its proponents. If there should be a hue and cry raised against science, it might properly be directed against those who conceive of scholarship as the accumulation of vast amounts of information by drones and intellectual pack rats whose interest and capability ends there. The danger of excessive professionalization in the social sciences, especially in the absence of good experimental techniques, is that our universities will produce large numbers of such dutiful research workers, who believe that patience and precision can disguise dullness and ignorance.

One seeks a point somewhere between the grasshoppers and the drones. In a real sense the problem of making concepts and theories operational is the search for that point. In the analysis that has been undertaken in this book, the problem is particularly acute. Take, for example, the use of the two functional requisites, coercion and information. High information systems may overload the interpretive devices of the system. In addition, information may exist within strategic and functional subsystems but not between them. Indeed, one consequence of the use of coercion may be to help develop a unified "information culture." Certain kinds of coercion may produce information, in particular, information concerning the limits within which coercion can be usefully applied. These are only a few of the points to consider as we try to use these functional categories. But the difficulties do not end here. We have sought, for example, precise or at least logically clearer distinctions between terms like consummatory and instrumental values, particularly since these distinctions are crucial to the delineation of the models employed. But logical clarity is not enough. To define consummatory values as empirical-means-germane-to-non-empirical ends still leaves the content of non-empirical ends ambiguous. And to define instrumental values as empirical-means-germane-to-empirical-ends, although it is logically useful, fails to establish a point of division between empirical and non-empirical ends. The same problem plagues the use of all highly general dichotomized variables. Valid complaints about them are almost as common as their use.

This produces some quaint results. Functional studies have the appearance of being more precise than they really are and leave a great deal to be desired at the empirical level. There is a gap between the identification of an item of information and the criteria by which it is placed in one category or another. There are gaps in the procedures and operations by which the functional categories themselves are derived. Indeed, functional theories are grasshopper jumps, with logic employed afterward to tidy up the categories. Even though this may be a legitimate method, the accompanying formidable terminology is easily resented by those whose modesty is offended by jargon. And this is by no means the only sin that functionalists commit when making a claim to method.

Whatever the faults, the practice of research is ultimately the sobering element. In comparative studies, in particular, one's categories may become lunar capsules — so confining that they obscure the understanding of familiar things. And, as we have said, the resulting frustration and efforts to comprehend the surrounding landscape may merely compound error. There is a danger in obscuring the familiar just as there is a danger that appearance and reality may be falsely identified in the common-sense world in which we all prefer to live.

All of these problems are dangers in the present approach, particularly in some of the main categories that still require empirical clarification. More precise meanings must be attached to dichotomous variables like consummatory and instrumental values. The functions and structures of government and the functions of careers must be examined in great detail. We need to be able to distinguish conditions under which instrumental and consummatory values are highly integrated and reinforce each other from those under which they are contradictory and produce internal conflict. We need also to examine the functional and structural requisites of government empirically. It can readily be seen that future research should be directed toward the study of processes under which career roles and political roles conflict (in terms of the functions of careers), the relationships of coercion and information that arise in government (in terms of the structural requisites and contingent structures of government), and the relationship of authority to decision-making (in terms of the functional requisites and contingent functions of government). Particularly important, therefore, are the following research emphases: (1) the examination of modernization roles as careers, (2) the study of ideology in relation to the functional requisites of government, and (3) the study of policy (decision-making) in relation to the structural requisites of government.

In an empirical study (as distinct from the present attempt to develop sets of theoretical relationships on the basis of previous work), many of the categories that have remained almost obscure here will emerge as central. This is particularly the case with the structural variables, which can only be realistically examined empirically.

Leaving these large matters aside, what kind of summing up can we make? Perhaps the most that can be said is that by raising the problem of modernization to practical prominence we have at least recognized its seriousness. The theories are important only because the problems are so great. The willingness to attempt this elaborate formulation is a result of the complexity of the modernization process itself. By recognizing its complexity and trying to disentangle some of its elements, we may familiarize ourselves with the unfamiliar. That at least is a beginning. Moreover, posing alternative concepts to those that currently prevail helps to sensitize us to patterns of change. It raises questions about the utility of our concepts and the sensitivities to various themes that each implies.

Moreover, if some of the assumptions we have been making about the long-term tendencies of change in systems are correct, certain very important problems can be identified. One of these concerns our own society. Just as the integrated relationship between Protestantism and capitalism once created a powerful moral-practical synthesis, as pointed out by Weber, so the present remoteness of consummatory values from life in the United States is a serious source of vulnerability. We have become completely preoccupied with instrumental ends. Our society has become so devoted to the pursuit of individual gain that our original and larger meanings have been lost. (Only those few in the information-producing elite effectively create consummatory values, and they do it rather badly.) Our society is morally vulnerable.

What does vulnerability mean in such a case? Those who recognize the political dangers inherent in the loss of consummatory values and who would like to revive them or create new ones may turn to hierarchical forms of authority as a desirable means of achieving this result. Weakness in consummatory values, that is, is likely to produce a desire for change in the form of authority — in our terms, a change away from the pyramidal structure associated with democracy toward a more militant hierarchical form. (Figure 20a contains a diagram of this tendency.) This is the object of the radical left and the radical right. To restore consummatory values, they argue, stringent means are required.

Value Type	Authority Type	
	Hierarchical	Pyramidal
Consummatory	↖	United States (1800)
Instrumental		United States (today)

FIG. 20a. — *Long-term tendencies of change in the United States.*

Having lost its religious basis, our society is in danger of becoming a system of organized plunder in which meaning derives only from personal gain, orderliness becomes mere containment of anarchy, and the concept of humanness has no wider dimension than an individual's functional value. This is the ultimate and disastrous consequence of the utilitarianism omnipresent in our schools and colleges and in daily life. How to restore identity and solidarity is the key problem of our society. Either we solve that problem or our system will change to another type, perhaps along the path indicated in Figure 20a or perhaps to an entirely different kind of unit, so that it is no longer the United States (which is the meaningful reconciliation system) but a larger state system, such as western Europe. Unfortunately, a discussion of this latter prospect would take us too far afield.

The U.S.S.R. is faced with a similar set of problems. Figure 20b contains a diagram of its situation. One might argue that the

Value Type	Authority Type	
	Hierarchical	Pyramidal
Consummatory	U.S.S.R. (1940) ↓	
Instrumental	U.S.S.R. (today) – – – – –+– – – →	

FIG. 20b. – Long-term tendencies of change in the U.S.S.R.

U.S.S.R., as a mobilization system, intensified its commitment to consummatory values and hierarchical authority under Stalinism. The maximum point of its mobilization system was in fact reached during the purges of the old Bolsheviks, which was one of the reasons for the highly symbolic quality of the trials and the inversions of meaning that were achieved there. (Nathan Leites and Elsa Bernaut discuss these aspects of the trials in *Ritual of Liquidation* [Glencoe: Free Press of Glencoe, Ill., 1954].) As the system has become industrialized, however, and as new generations have emerged that are less committed to Marxism as a consummatory value, instrumentalism and the measurement of achievement as material output rather than moral expression have become more and more evident. Moreover, there are signs today that the shift to instrumental values, although by no means complete, is accompanied by the need to decentralize the system and to create a pyramidal system of authority. By 1964 the importance of Libermanism (which introduced elements of the market into the Soviet economic system) was emphasized by Trapeznikov,

the director of the Soviet Institute of Automation and Teleme-
chanics, who argued for a flexible pricing system so that adequate
computer techniques could be applied in industry. Without an
adequate pricing system, the computer would merely maximize
errors. Hence, the emphasis on instrumental values, productivity
and output, requires a change in authority, from the hierarchical
to the pyramidal type, if this kind of values is to be achieved.
Marxism and the older ideologies of socialism remain, but they
are less and less a source of moral inspiration and more and more
a ritualized expression of antecedent values. This tendency will
make the Soviet Union vulnerable in much the same way as the
United States.

One might conclude then that the long-term problem of highly
industrialized countries is how to cope with weakness in the
sphere of consummatory values that accompanies a utilitarian
emphasis on instrumental values. This is what modern alienation
means. Individuals may not necessarily recognize their alienation.
Indeed, the Marxian use of the term is hardly appropriate (although it may have a certain sentimental resonance). But alienation in the sense of a loss of individual identity and a lack of
solidarity within the system is a common phenomenon in modern
industrial societies. The roles of psychiatrist and social therapist
are a token of this.

The tendency in countries that are still in the early stages of
the modernization process and that have only recently established
the political framework for modernization is toward a system of
hierarchical authority and instrumental values. These instrumental values may be reinforced by a ritualized form of authority,
such as a presidential monarchy, or by a sentimentalized history
and a manipulated tradition that comes to include events of the
recent past, such as the struggle against colonialism. If the new
polity is a mobilization system, its ideology will change meaning
in the society more quickly than form. If the new polity is a reconciliation system, some particular grouping, military, ethnic, or
class, that dominates the polity will drive out organized and regu-

larized forms of competitive political activity, thus changing form more quickly than meaning. In order to sustain a mobilization system during early-stage modernization, a condition of permanent revolution is required; but permanent revolution is likely to make modernization more difficult to achieve rather than less. If a reconciliation system in an early stage of modernization succeeds in sustaining itself, the result is likely to be stagnation, accompanied by conditions of mass alienation within the system. (See Figure 20c.) Indeed, a reconciliation system that has under-

Value Type	Authority Type	
	Hierarchical	Pyramidal
Consummatory	Mobilization ↑	
Instrumental	Neomercantilism ←	Reconciliation

FIG. 20c. — *Long-term tendencies of change in early-stage modernizing societies.*

gone modernization for a long period of time and has resisted repeated attempts to transform it either into a mobilization system or some other type is likely to be ready for the mobilization system as a conversion mechanism. Such "readiness" is manifested when the system becomes increasingly ideologized, with its ideology containing programmatic ends that make possible group solidarity and individual identity and thereby end the moral isolation of the individual. By this means a pattern of counterlegitimacy is set up that provides the moral basis for a change in system. Immortality, meaning, and purpose are now centered about a revolutionary polity, and total transformation of the hierarchy of power and prestige becomes the new goal, to be accompanied by new patterns of allocation of power and responsibility, decision-making, and accountability.

It is the systems that have undergone a long period of modernization preceded by a long period of stagnation that are most interesting and dangerous. Countries like Argentina, Mexico, and Chile are particularly significant for our analysis because they have alternated, at various stages, between non-democratic and democratic forms of the reconciliation system without any retrospective consummatory values associated with politics. What consummatory values existed in the past were associated with Spain and the Roman Catholic church, and the rebellions and revolutions that established independence in Latin America were antagonistic to both these forces. Moreover, when the reconciliation systems failed to produce a satisfactory system of internal development, the consummatory values of the revolutions, as well, became slightly absurd. The result has been a constant movement between different types of authority, between hierarchical and pyramidal forms, but without changes in consummatory values. This pattern is precisely what makes the revolution in Cuba so different and potentially so important. It represents the application of consummatory values to hierarchical authority. That constitutes its genuinely revolutionary character.

The tendencies discussed above, however, ought not to be mistaken for more than that. There is nothing inevitable about any of the processes we have described. Empirical deviations from a particular tendency are more likely than conformity (depending upon the way the other systems variables and subsystems variables perform). Indeed, the identification of a tendency is designed to direct attention to the deviant cases so that a better set of strategic variables or a more powerful generalized set can be derived.

These, then, are some of the points that can be highlighted for further study. In a book concerned with problems of this nature, it would be premature to seek one central theme or overriding principle. Scientific explanation remains a goal, but it is the moral problems of society to which such explanations should be directed and in the light of which they must be evaluated. The present approach makes possible the application of normative, structural, and behavioral aspects of theory to the analysis of how political systems change. We are now at the beginning of that task. But no simplified schemes can handle the multiple planes of meaning, the overlapping sets of symbols. Nor can theories alone raise us from the level of exploring man's humanity to the level of helping that humanity survive; and that, in the long run, is the issue at stake in all of our studies. In today's world, many have been attracted by the simplicity of developing countries, which seem to demonstrate, at least at the beginning of their political lives, a terrifying purity, a vision that baffles and frustrates observers from highly complex systems. But this is a false impression. Corruption and virtue confound each other in new nations as well as in old ones. It is our own society that may well demonstrate the most serious problems that modernization creates, the problems, that is, that arise in a highly complex industrial system. Durkheim pointed out one of the most serious long ago, namely, the fragmentation of social life along a single plane of functional significance. If the evaluation of a man's worth is made in terms of what he does, then modern society will remain ethically muted, a universe of compromise and a confusion of choices. Perhaps the main conclusion of this book remains its point of departure. We have learned how to achieve modernization; we have not yet learned how to live modern lives.

These are some of the wider implications of the normative dimension of modernization. They make it clear why I suggested in chapter i that the political types employed here are to be viewed first as moral tendencies reflecting the perpetual tension between two fundamentally different conceptions of man in society, the secular-libertarian and the sacred-collectivity. Such moral tension gives meaning to the choices we make both in terms of political type, our structural category, and in terms of the act of choosing, our behavioral starting point.

In the context of modernization, this moral tension takes on various aspects. During early-stage modernization, it is clearest in the conflict between career and entrepreneurial roles. In industrialized societies, it occurs between the scientific elites and the ideologues and represents a polarization of ideologies between the scientific and the non-scientific. Indeed, industrial societies have one common characteristic, namely, the formation of an information-creating and information-utilizing elite, embodying a revolution in knowledge independent of the particular political form. The need for information thus presupposes a group of people, in addition to politicians, who can receive information and make it useful for political purposes, including modernization purposes. This information elite interposes itself between the politician and the public regardless of the type of political system. How well it functions depends upon the amount of coercion in each system. The relationship between coercion and information is particularly sensitive vis-à-vis the information elite. Hence the position of the elite depends upon the competitive control over careers, as suggested in chapter v, and the efficiency of the elite as well depends upon the degree of coercion in the system.

The information elite is a scientific elite. It may employ a large non-scientific but literate corps of intellectuals to translate the technical languages of the scientist and social scientist into statements of comprehensible policy and ideology. The scientific elite may extend into the universities and training colleges, on the one hand, and into bureaucratic and civil service positions, on the other. In societies where modernization has been extensively achieved, this elite tends not only to displace the older elites (lawyers, for example) but, in addition, to make the old-fashioned politicians obsolete. The information elite therefore creates great political tension. The need for information requires an increasing diversity of types of information and techniques for gathering information. In addition to *translators* of expertise, it requires *technicians* of expertise. In this respect the scientific elite becomes a complex group with a universalized political function. This is one of the long-term tendencies, or consequences, of the modernization process.

The scientific elite is now being recognized in a large and growing literature. It is not an ordinary elite — the kind that makes itself exclusive or "inaccessible," to use Kornhauser's description, by virtue of political barriers carefully interposed between itself and the public. Rather, its inaccessibility derives from its degree of specialization and the linkages of careers in a circle of communication. This should not imply, however, that the scientific elite is a single homogenous body, sealed off from the public by a mysterious language and exotic practices. As a set of interlocking careers, it is not ordinarily subject to the control of public understanding or of responsible public action. It can be controlled by political leaders; but if they apply excessive coercion, they minimize the production of information.

In industrialized countries, as the subtypes and subspecialties within the information elite grow, the group that began as an elite grows into a class. It becomes possible for the class to create its own ideology. This ideology includes the belief that human knowledge must be utilized in the improvement of human affairs. The application of knowledge by political means — and not the responsiveness of government to private wants — becomes the test of good government. What might be called the rise of the scientific elite is thus a result of industrialization, affecting the degree of modernization and the course of development through the instrumentalities of government. In this respect, the problem of modernization becomes a constant struggle over two conflicting principles of rule, namely, the public interest as seen by the public and the public interest as seen by the scientific elite. The politicians are likely to be caught in the middle.

One underlying theme in this book has been the political problem of integration. Another theme has been the specification of role conflict, which becomes intense during modernization and reaches its peak just prior to the jump to industrialization. The paradox of political modernization is clear enough. Modernization itself helps to create those conflicts that political leaders must solve in order to pursue modernization.

Precisely because of this tendency, we have considered different forms of political systems as alternative ways of containing the conflicts produced by modernization. No one political system may be expected to endure throughout such a long and complex process (unless it operates under exceptionally favorable conditions).

In addition to changes in political systems, the process of modernization encourages certain secular tendencies. These include the broadening of certain techniques through their application in modernization projects, the expansion of career roles, and the professionalization of certain modernizing elites. Indeed, the most direct impact of highly industrial societies on modernizing ones is the extrasystemic pull that establishes certain relationships between roles that have a universal impact. It is the universalization of certain careers, their elite status, and their peculiar relationship to information that will concern us here. This discussion will end with a consideration of the significance of the new scientific ideology, not only for modernizing nations, but for our own society as well. My assumption is that highly industrialized societies are about to undergo a major transformation — an informational revolution. I assume further that this informational revolution will have great force and impact in ways only dimly understood at present. These remarks will conclude, therefore, on a speculative note — the informational revolution and its implications for democratic society.

THE ROLE OF THE NEW SCIENTIFIC ELITE

Until recently the norms of science have supplied its ideology. Such norms have an honorable tradition, associated as they are with such names as Diderot and d'Alembert, Holbach and Helvetius, Condillac and Voltaire, Rousseau and Hume. What all these thinkers shared was a belief in the natural goodness of men, who, under the proper conditions of knowledge and understanding of the natural causes of their behavior, would be able to change their situation and improve it. Such notions relied on principles of natural reason, which was assumed to form the basis of our understanding of the laws of nature — laws, one might add, which were common to man as well as to things.

The norms of science suffered somewhat during the nineteenth century when they became mixed with metaphysics. Science was suffused with mysterious implications even by those who, like Comte, argued loudest in its defense. When science became romantic, it moved away from the practical workman's universe of the earlier period. Thus, science, and also philosophy, lacked a sufficiently clear and unambiguous basis to be useful during the sudden rise to political importance of a scientific establishment. In particular what was lacking was a theory and a doctrine with which to establish an appropriate relationship between the scientist and his society. It is therefore not surprising that the one explicitly antimetaphysical yet powerful nineteenth-century theory, Marxism, which successfully combined a moral aim, a universal explanation of social change, and a hortatory doctrine, attracted the attention of scientists concerned with their new role in society. When applied to science, Marxism illuminated what had become obscured, namely, the common basis of the natural and the social sciences. Moreover, it prophesied a more powerful political and social framework than capitalism, more rational and scientific. This is the reason so many socially aware and responsible scientists have been (and still are) Marxists, particularly in England and France. In the United States, in contrast, but for the same reason, scientists have tended to participate in new trends in behavioral science. These new approaches, however, lack the characteristic that remains fresh in Marxism, a particularized moral center and a universalized goal. These allow the scientist power together with morality.

With the increasing pace of scientific innovation in both industrialized and modernizing countries, it would merely compound our problems to rely on theories formulated in the nineteenth century as the basis of a contemporary relationship between science and society. Required is a more elaborate set of theories, more comprehensive and less innocent. For this purpose, Marxism is too narrow because of its teleological and economic orientation. Today a scientific theory must include an adequate explanation of choice and the conditions of choice, both within political systems and between them. A new synthesis must take into account the more recent developments in the social sciences.

What becomes of the "moral center" when teleology is removed? One answer, inevitably partial, is that it is then to be found in succeeding situations of choice rather than in a single universalized situation. This view emphasizes change rather than permanence and also particular problems requiring political and scientific attention. In the United States, for example, such problems include residual poverty and the rights of Negroes. In the world at large the moral center is modernization. Indeed, the reason I began this book with Camus's commentary on Sisyphus was to emphasize my belief that modernization has become the moral center of our time, creating consummatory values and a new role for the scientific elite.

The scientific ethic is based on the need for free exchange of knowledge and information. This is particularly necessary in modernizing societies, where, although their numbers are small, scientists, social scientists, and technicians are the modernizers. They occupy a set of elite career roles. They train manpower, educating it to occupy modern functional roles. They are responsible for new towns, dams, highways, fiscal reform, and the like. Of course, by being dispersed through the system, they may be controlled and manipulated by the political authorities, as occurs, for example, in totalitarian societies. One method of control in totalitarian regimes is to create pockets of freedom in which scientists have access to necessary materials that are sealed off from the rest of the community; but this is costly. The more often scientific bodies are directly linked to the political life of the country through technical agencies in government, the more dependent the latter become on the skills of the scientists. As a result, the scientific career occupies an exceptional place in a modernizing society. Not likely to be taken in by propaganda, the scientist takes for granted the existence of a variety of political forms. Scientists today want to know where their societies are going.[1]

Moreover, as has been suggested before, the community of science is world wide. The universities of the world are linked together by special bonds. People read each other's works and conduct research on each other's problems. The academic world is moving closer together all the time, and exchanges of teaching and research personnel are increasing. In addition to conducting research and providing for communications, universities serve to screen the community and select those best qualified for scientific work and the scientific role. This function is most significant in modernizing countries where universities are almost the only instrument for selecting and recruiting scientists.

Nor is the scientific spirit limited to scientists. By subscribing to norms of modernization, the professionals, lawyers, journalists, and indeed, all those who are educated, accept the scientific ethic, which includes an emphasis on rationality and the importance of empirical research, an awareness of what constitutes valid evidence, and a feeling that what is known must be susceptible of verification. The scientific spirit is the basis of an ideology that provides a measure of identity for those who subscribe to it and a measure of solidarity for the members of a society in the midst of change.

Today the ideology of science includes social science. The application of scientific techniques to social problems first became possible in economics, coinciding with the enormous growth in

---

[1] See Don K. Price, "The Scientific Establishment," in Robert Gilpin and Christopher Wright (eds.), *Scientists and National Policy Making* (New York: Columbia University Press, 1964), p. 19. See also Jacques Ellul, *The Technological Society* (New York: Alfred A. Knopf, 1964), *passim*.

productive capacity that had been made possible by new technological developments.[2]

The evolving position of social science provides exceptional opportunities for social scientists who occupy roles half-way between research and policy. These roles are increasingly played by those in universities and related research bodies. Indeed, the emphasis on research in the modern university has itself done much to extend the norms of science to the social sciences and has, as well, attracted government support for policy research on a very large scale.

In the United States the framework for policy research and the home of the scientific establishment are the major universities. This is increasingly the case in England as well, especially now that the university system is being expanded. In fact, the prototype of the policy-research role originated in England around the turn of the century — the Fabian Society. Three elements were important in the development of this role: the homogeneity in outlook among a considerable number of middle-class intellectuals, the close relationship between the administrative class of the civil service and the universities, and the accessibility of parliamentarians and county councilors to the particular blend of amateur and expert advice that the British had developed to a high art and that was so characteristic of the Fabians. The Fabian Society was the prototype of the new establishment. Fabians conducted research and wrote tracts on virtually every subject of significance. They were reformist and scientific. They remained detached from particular party affiliations despite their close ties with the Labour party. They had a very great effect on policy in Britain, particularly with respect to finance, education, housing,

[2] Durkheim remarked about the pioneering role of economics: "For two centuries economic life has taken on an expansion it never knew before. From being a secondary function, despised and left to inferior classes, it passed on to one of first rank. We see the military, governmental and religious functions falling back more and more in face of it. The scientific functions alone are in a position to dispute its ground . . ." (Émile Durkheim, *Professional Ethics and Civic Morals* [Glencoe: Free Press of Glencoe, Ill., 1958], p. 11).

and welfare, which are, of course, the subjects that the social science branch of the scientific establishment is preoccupied with.[3]

The Fabians foreshadowed the modern scientific establishment, which draws its strength from many different sources. In France, for example, the scientific establishment may include both Marxists and Christian Socialists. Perhaps the most research-minded group in the social sciences is concentrated around François Perroux and the journal *Économie appliquée*. Père Lebret and his associates (who are directly concerned with planning for economic development in Africa and Latin America) and such anonymous bodies as the Société d'Études pour le Développement Économique et Social and the Institut Pédagogique National, which have undertaken special studies on education in African countries, are typical of those groups engaged in developmental work abroad. It appears that the scientific establishment that plays such an increasingly important role at home is also perfectly capable of discovering and supplying the research needs of modernizing societies and is, in fact, becoming an instrument of foreign policy. Through the scientific establishment, links are maintained between the industrial nations and those just beginning to industrialize.

In industrialized societies, governments are the greatest single consumers of all forms of science. They not only stimulate policy research but also consume the product.[4] This is particularly true

[3] Perhaps the most enlightening description of the role of the Fabian Society is by Margaret Cole, *The Story of Fabian Socialism* (Stanford, Calif.: Stanford University Press, 1961). See also the commentary by George Lichtheim in *Encounter*, March, 1956. Lichtheim says, "The Fabians were a body of professional men and women drawn from the middle class; they were thus able to reformulate socialism in terms which appealed to the rising managerial stratum, and to the educated class in general. Moreover, their ideology was anti-liberal as well as anti-Marxist. It thus made contact with the authoritarian temper prevalent among civil servants and others disgusted with *laissez-faire* and vaguely sympathetic to 'planning.' . . . The Fabians, in short, could turn themselves into the nucleus of a new governing elite, while their Marxist rivals could not (at any rate not in Britain). In our present technological age this is a considerable advantage" (p. 72).

[4] One finds evidence for this in the mounting financial support for social

in the economic sphere. Raul Prebish has pointed out that economic planning and development require state intervention: "(*a*) The State must intervene because the pointers afforded by the market do not always lead to action that will promote the most economic use of the available resources, and (*b*) it must do so because the indications provided by market forces have a bearing only on some of the decisions of the individual, not on all of them, and in particular not on those that are of considerable importance in development. State intervention is essential to guide private activity, and to induce it, without coercion of any kind, to fulfill certain development aims." [5] But the problem is wider than economics and may be expressed in general terms as the need to reduce the significance of intermediate semimodern roles. To do this without coercion is one of the most difficult tasks of our time.

To discover which roles are critical we must examine the career roles of the modernizing elites. (The exceptional characteristic of the modernizing role is that it is not confined to a particular modernizing or industrial society but participates in a common dialogue with its counterparts in other societies regardless of their stage of development.) Indeed, the common aims of industrial and modernizing societies are a reflection of the values and objectives held in common by such elites (particularly the "scientific" and political elites). The world-wide scientific community subscribes to the same general ideology of science. If the elites in the modernizing nations are to maintain their expertise, they need to keep abreast of the new developments occurring in their specialties. Today's careers are part of a world-wide intellectual community, no matter how provincial their immediate locale.

science research given to universities and to other bodies. This support is also indirect evidence of the degree to which social science is recognized as having become scientific. For an indication of the criteria of science, see Thomas S. Kuhn, *The Structure of Scientific Revolutions* (Chicago: University of Chicago Press, 1962), pp. 52–65.

[5] Prebish, *Towards a Dynamic Development Policy for Latin America* (New York: United Nations Publication, Document E/CN.12/680/Rev. 1, 1963), p. 61.

In order to resist provincialism, these elites must increase their functional expertise as agronomists, mathematicians, engineers, and teachers but must also become aware of the interrelationships of careers. In addition, they need to raise their sights to the political level in order to generate power and attain their goals. If successful, the modernizing elites could constitute a crucial link between modernizing and industrializing countries.[6]

The result of the efforts of the modernizing elites is the universalization of a new type of scientific establishment, which, having made its appearance in the most highly developed industrial systems, has now become critical in modernizing systems. This new establishment is composed of a set of interlocking career roles that screen relevant information received from the society and at the same time create new information for government. The establishment may be subject to checks in systems with a high degree of accountability, or it may remain relatively autonomous. In either case its significance goes well beyond the technical skills it commands. The real significance of the scientific establishment derives from its ability to remain outside, to some extent, the relationship between information and coercion that we have discussed at length above. It can avoid some of the pitfalls of high coercion systems since it is able to draw on information outside the system. It has a fund of professional knowledge at its disposal that does not vary inversely with the amount of coercion in the society.

This characteristic puts the new establishment, as it emerges in modernizing countries, in a peculiarly sensitive position. Insofar as it is an information-creating elite, it needs freedom; however,

[6] Davidson Nicol has put the matter with characteristic clarity. "If the intellectual community is not encouraged or has not got its roots in institutes or universities which have links and connections with the outside world, it is likely to be crushed between politicians and a rising nationalistic middle class. It is also unlikely that without encouragement creative productivity will flourish in those writers, thinkers, and artists who form the majority of the intellectual community" (Nicol, "The Formation of a West African Intellectual Community," in *The West African Intellectual Community*, Proceedings of the Congress for Cultural Freedom [Ibadan: Ibadan University Press, 1962], p. 14).

the information it obtains as a consequence of its freedom may be used by government for coercive purposes.

LEGITIMACY AND THE SCIENTIFIC IDEOLOGY

The consequence of rationalistic planning, with its stress on the role of the technician, is to create a new basis for political legitimacy. A new *Stand* — that of planners — slowly emerges as a result of modernization. Not always subordinate to the political leaders, the new technological positions define an entire sector of modern life. Such positions are powerful and attractive, and those who aspire to them must possess exceptional technical understanding and training. Linked to the educational system, they represent a hierarchy of talent based on egalitarian access. In addition, they exert a strong influence on the more parochial political ideologies (Nkrumaism, Manipol, and so on) because of their direct or indirect support of the scientific ideology. Some modern development communities have accorded the social engineer almost a monitor role in political life. This is not because he possesses a kind of Platonic predisposition for the role of leader; quite the contrary, he usually shares with his fellow citizens a feeling of ambiguity about his role. But he often gains a superior insight into the conduct of his fellows that gives him the power to create a new role, an ideology that follows from it, and a hierarchy of power and prestige based on intellectual ability — what, in its extreme form, Michael Young has called a "meritocracy." Indeed, once the social-scientist discovered that there was a discrepancy between observed behavior and felt behavior, between the act and the rationalization, between the conscious and the subconscious, and between virtue and conduct, he fashioned a new role for himself — the theoretically omniscient observer. He came to believe that human mysteries were technical problems.

Such a position is dangerous for many reasons. The most immediate reason, however, is that it causes a running battle between scientists and ideologues, which is the more intense because of the interdependence of politicians and scientists. Political leaders need to tread lightly in the region between the alienated ideologues and those who desire to apply science to human affairs.

If, as has already been suggested, the dialogue in the modernizing societies is between nationalism and socialism, the conflict in societies moving toward industrialization will be between science and the other ideologies. The ideologue will manipulate slogans. The scientist will ignore him. In such a situation political leaders will have to learn how to rely on the latter without unduly arousing the former.

The tendency of the scientific role is to undermine even the most extreme mobilization system — even when the scientists have been persuaded by the ideologues, at least for a time, to accept a political religion along with their scientific ideology. How many scientists among Poles, Czechs, Russians, and Chinese would secretly agree with Milovan Djilas when he writes:

> The internal monolithic cohesion which was created in the struggle with the oppositionists and with the half-Communist groups is transformed into a unity of obedient counselors and robot-bureaucrats inside the movement. During the climb to power, intolerance, servility, incomplete thinking, control of personal life — which once was comradely aid but is now a form of oligarchic management — hierarchical rigidity and introversion, the nominal and neglected role of women, opportunism, self-centeredness, and outrage, repress the once-existent high principles. The wonderful human characteristics of an isolated movement are slowly transformed into the intolerant and Pharisaical morals of a privileged caste. Thus, politicking and servility replace the former straightforwardness of the revolution. Where the former heroes who were ready to sacrifice everything, including life, for others and for an idea, for the good of the people, have not been killed, or pushed aside, they become self-centered cowards without ideas or comrades, willing to renounce everything — honor, name,

truth, and morals — in order to keep their place in the ruling class and the hierarchical circle.[7]

But the matter does not end there. Djilas himself is an illustration of that. The long-run need of the scientific elite is to reduce coercion and to increase information in order to take advantage of the modern advances in science and social science. To reduce coercion, there must be decentralization in economic controls, wider opportunities for local entrepreneurship, and greater social mobility. An important characteristic of the scientific role is the occupant's concern with achievement and with the exploration of his identity through the making of choices. When these concerns predominate, choices are no longer between systems but within the system. The legitimacy of the system depends on the way the opportunities for choice are optimized. And this optimization depends in turn on knowledge. That is the reason the dynamic factor in industrial societies is information. But even more important is the relationship between information and performance. Information leads to achievement, and there is a high correlation between achievement and continued economic growth. D. C. McClelland has shown that people work hard when the results of their labors are given public recognition and esteem. Only then will they prefer risk and adventure to safety, traditionality, and bureaucracy.[8]

The scientific elite has revolutionary potentialities during modernization. Its role is critical even in the kind of situation found in present-day China, for example, where modernization and industrialization proceed side by side, and the government exercises complete control over press, education, art, and literature. As one observer commented recently, "It must be realized that while persuasive and coercive communications are powerful tools of political development and social control, they are subject to definite limitation." One of the limitations he suggests is "doubletalk." "One therefore wonders," the observer concludes, "whether

[7] Djilas, *The New Class* (New York: Frederick A. Praeger, 1957), p. 155.
[8] McClelland, *The Achieving Society* (Princeton, N.J.: D. Van Nostrand Co., Inc., 1961), *passim*.

the tremendous power unleashed by the Communists and the new forces now set in motion by the Peking regime may not eventually prove too great for the manipulators to handle." [9] When China succeeds in industrializing, the conflicts between these forces ought to become much sharper and the role of the scientist more influential. Already the fields of pure science and atomic research appear to be relatively free of coercion.

The need for information and some relaxation of coercion is not merely a need attached to the role of scientist. The political implications go deeper and rest on the unavoidable contradiction between the exercise of coercion and the maintenance of a high degree of economic efficiency, regardless whether the economic system is socialist or capitalist. The more a society modernizes, the greater need it has for information to spot lags and weaknesses in growth. All modernizing elites, not only scientists and technicians, need knowledge. Moreover, what is necessary in modernizing societies is even more necessary in industrial ones. One of the best indicators of the effects of coercion in industrial societies is the condition of agriculture.

In successful industrial countries, agricultural productivity is very high. But in countries where coercion is high, productivity is low. China, the U.S.S.R., and Czechoslovakia, for example, are high coercion systems, and they all have experienced lags in agriculture. Contrast the tremendous agricultural output of the United States in 1950, with only 12 per cent of the population engaged in agriculture, with that of the Soviet Union in the same year, with 50 per cent so engaged.[10] Such inefficiency extends into virtually all activities, with the exception, perhaps, of those in which the scientific elite has freedom, that is, pure science, mathe-

[9] Frederick T. C. Yu, "Communications and Politics in Communist China," in Lucian Pye (ed.), *Communications and Political Development* (Princeton; N.J.: Princeton University Press, 1963), pp. 296–97. See also Franz Schurmann, "China's 'New Economic Policy' — Transition or Beginning," *China Quarterly*, XVI (January–March, 1964).

[10] Harbison and Myers, *Education, Manpower, and Economic Growth: Strategies of Human Resource Development* (New York: McGraw-Hill Book Co., Inc., 1964), p. 133.

matics, medicine, and other purely technical subjects. (In these areas the efficiency of the U.S.S.R. is formidable indeed.)

In advanced industrial societies the labor force consists mainly of persons employed in trade, finance, education, and the public service. In such societies the labor force thus "has a large number of diverse employing units in contrast to the underdeveloped country in which government dominates the modern sector." [11] The existence of the large number of employers eventually propels the country in the direction of a reconciliation system. As Frederick Harbison and Charles A. Myers have pointed out in an extremely important passage in their book on human resource development, this produces a trend — a trend toward democracy.

> Basically the *trend* in countries at this level is democratic, with a high degree of participation in the political process by the adult population. In part this is a consequence of widespread public education, education for citizenship in a democracy. But these countries have differed with respect to the nature of their leadership groups, particularly in their earlier political development. For example, some countries have had middle-class industrializing elites, with broad democratic and egalitarian philosophies during much of their economic development. Others have had a more rigid class structure inherited from a pre-industrial period, and some have begun their march toward industrialization under what might be called dynastic elites. Finally the Communists or revolutionary intellectuals have provided an ideology which prescribes strategies and policies different from those of the other industrializing elites. [12]

The point is that if the scientific elite joins forces with other modernizing elites it immediately acquires critical political importance. This has already begun to occur within the industrialized countries of the eastern European bloc. A wide variety of systems has developed that could be placed along a continuum between the reconciliation and mobilization extremes. Peter Wiles has gone so far as to suggest that Yugoslavia represents a

[11] *Ibid.*
[12] *Ibid.*, pp. 133–34.

system in which a regulated market determines resource allocation — a regulated market, but a market, nevertheless, and not a command economy.[13] Already, the Yugoslav pattern is being repeated in selected sectors of the command economy in the Soviet Union, particularly in education. Wiles points out that the U.S.S.R. is shaping the educational system according to functional needs, with these needs thus representing an educational "market." He calls this a "Communist secret weapon." [14] Not only is this change an opening wedge for the market principle of allocation, but it also indicates that educated and trained manpower — in other words, a scientific elite — is the principal byproduct of industrialization. It is only a matter of time before the Communists come to recognize that what Wiles suggests is true, that their allocation policy, education policy excepted, is "irrational and therefore a brake on growth. . . ." [15]

Therefore, it may be suggested that four more or less inevitable consequences follow from the growing complexity of industrial societies: First, there is a need for more and more information. Second, there is the growth of an elite that uses and manufactures information and that is critically functional to the continual development of the society. Third, there is the formation of pluralist groups almost in classical Durkheimian terms.[16] Fourth, there is the assumption of leadership by the scientific elite over other modernizing groups. These developments, taken together,

[13] Wiles, *The Political Economy of Communism* (Cambridge, Mass.: Harvard University Press, 1962), p. 71.

[14] *Ibid.*, p. 329.

[15] *Ibid.*, p. 329. See also the discussion of education and professional employment in the U.S.S.R. by Alexander King, "Higher Education, Professional Manpower and the State," *Minerva*, I (Winter, 1962), 182. King points out that "the two aims of Soviet higher education — the inculcation of a political and social ideology and the training of personnel for an advanced society and economy undergoing rapid industrialization in a time of exceptional technological innovation — are not always in harmony. While the former always has some influence on the latter, the strongly functional trends of education demanded by economic realities are often not acknowledged or legitimated by ideological dogma."

[16] See Émile Durkheim, *The Division of Labor* (Glencoe: Free Press, of Glencoe, Ill., 1949), *passim*.

form the basis of the long-term trend in political development toward the reconciliation system, as Harbison and Myers have suggested. Already the second development, the information-using elite, is rapidly becoming a *Stand* in virtually all industrial countries, including the Soviet Union. As Alex Inkeles has remarked,

> Although the vital decisions remain the monopoly of the party leaders, the growing importance of technical problems in the governing of the state has forced an informal sharing of power with the many important scientists, engineers, managers, and other crucial technically skilled personnel. Certainly the recent reorganization of administration on a more decentralized basis represents a diffusion of decision-making power, however much the central elite may take precautions not to lose the decisive initiative and control. The full extent of such sharing has by no means been reached.[17]

And a Yugoslav economist has suggested that with a

> centralized system of management and administrative intervention of the state apparatus, the problem of initiative in economic enterprises had to become increasingly acute. Lines and tasks laid down by central authority do not leave much room for free choice in making decisions within an enterprise. The maximum energy could be used only for the purpose of fulfilling to the utmost possible degree the tasks of the plan, while leaving no great possibilities for correcting eventual discrepancies, or — which is even more important — for an effective utilization of the possibilities and advantages which a centralized plan could not foresee. In an underdeveloped economy, where the whole development is concentrated on a few basic tasks, this problem does not acquire its acute form at the beginning. However, if the economy develops, and if development proves to be an increasingly complex process, then strictly centralized plan-

[17] Inkeles, "Summary and Review: Social Stratification in the Modernization of Russia," in Cyril E. Black (ed.), *The Transformation of Russian Society* (Cambridge, Mass.: Harvard University Press, 1960), p. 246. See also George Fisher, *Science and Politics: The New Sociology in the Soviet Union* (Ithaca, N.Y.: Cornell University, Center for International Studies, 1964); this is a very important study of the new role of social science in the U.S.S.R.

ning and administrative management become less and less capable of making effective use of the numerous possibilities offered by the complex life of a modern economy. To the same extent the problem of insufficient initiative becomes increasingly painful and acute.[18]

These comments are, from my viewpoint, particularly appropriate for industrializing countries. If my assumptions are correct, we may view mobilization systems as the "best" political forms for converting poor but modernized countries into steadily growing economies, since they will also create their own "contradictions," to use the Marxian term, and as a result tend to move in the direction of a reconciliation system. If socialism and nationalism, or their modern combinations, are understood in this light, the mobilization system becomes a temporary form of politics, initiating activity but subject to change because of its success; it will lose the loyalty of its people by becoming inefficient.

If the evidence supports the hypothesis that increasing complexity results in greater pluralism within a society, we will need to explore in particular the question whether or not the scientific elites are the focal points of the development of such pluralism by virtue of their leadership of groups functional to the industrialization process. The further question whether or not they become functionally more and more significant and thereby enlarge the area of their power is one that may be empirically answered. Does their ideology become more explicit within the context of the scientific ethic? Indeed, does this ethic place a high value on knowledge and the free exchange of ideas? If the answers are yes, the pluralistic interplay of groups, under the general influence of scientists, will create a structural basis for a liberal society; pyramidal rather than hierarchical authority will slowly spread by means of the decentralization of decision-making, reinforced by the need to maximize efficiency. If this theory is correct, the

[18] Borivoje Jelic, "Characteristics of the Yugoslav Economic Planning System," *Socialist Thought and Practice* (June, 1961), p. 63. See also Michel Crozier, *The Bureaucratic Phenomenon* (Chicago: University of Chicago Press, 1964), *passim*.

long-run outlook for representative government under such conditions is that it will be a progressive rather than a conservative
force, revolutionary in its implications and attractive to youth
who are otherwise cynical. Of course, not all reconciliation systems will become democracies. The obstacles are better known,
it would seem, than the general tendency[19]

SOME OBSTACLES TO DEMOCRACY

As I have said, even if these theories are correct, it is not inevitable that all industrializing communities will eventually develop
representative governments. The emergence of the scientific elite
only suggests a long-term tendency in industrial countries toward the reconciliation system. Moreover, an industrial country
that achieves a reconciliation system may still be prevented from
becoming democratic by the intrusion of other types of political
system. Thus it appears that any system is vulnerable to its subsystems and that efficiency is not the sole factor in determining
the strength of a regime. If a subsystem of a larger system — the
military, for example, or a party of solidarity, or a bureaucratic
group — takes over, it can transform a highly industrialized reconciliation society into a relatively high coercion system. Any
powerful subsystem can become dominant, seize power, and
attempt to universalize its organization throughout the society as
a whole.[20]

[19] See the excellent discussion of these matters in Carl G. Rosberg, "Democracy of the New African States," in Kenneth Kirkwood (ed.), *African Affairs* ("St. Antony's Papers," Vol. 15, No. 2 [London: Chatto & Windus, Ltd.,
1963]).

[20] The military is a particularly important obstacle to democracy and is
prone to this kind of action. If the military becomes increasingly a center
of modernism, occupying administrative and engineering roles and at the
same time representing sovereignty and independence, the same tendencies
that favor the new scientific elites will work against it. The new scientific
elites do not rely on coercion but rather on information, and they can adapt to
differentiation and complexity — the results of modernization — much more
easily than the military oligarchs.

The causes of vulnerability in reconciliation systems would be an interesting subject for inquiry, but lack of space prevents us from pursuing it here. The matter has been examined recently in the works of Lipset, Selznick, Kornhauser, and others concerned with the problems of the mass society.[21] Kornhauser identifies a cause of vulnerability in his comment that mass politics in democratic society is in effect antidemocratic, "since it contravenes the constitutional order."[22]

Pluralistic subgroups can obstruct the development of democracy in other ways. If several of them achieve a relatively high degree of autonomy, as they often do, the result is immobility and political paralysis, as I have suggested before. Efforts to reduce their autonomy cause problems in the opposite direction — what Michels called "the iron law of oligarchy."

Bureaucratization, the exercise of coercion by means of excessive rules and regulations applied in a discriminating manner, is another form of obstruction. If the functionally significant subgroups of the system — engineers, civil servants, educators, and the like — contrive opportunities for the arbitrary exercise of power, the system as a whole will contain the conditions of a mass society. This is the reason the work of Lipset and others who are concerned with the implications of subsystem organization for the total society is so important.[23] Nothing could be more significant than the discovery of the conditions in industrial societies under which the structure of democratic institutions may be perfected. Indeed, it is precisely this subject that has been the main concern of modern political science.[24]

There are, of course, many other obstacles in the way of democ-

[21] See Philip Selznick, The Organizational Weapon (Glencoe: Free Press of Glencoe, Ill., 1960), chapter vii; William Kornhauser, The Politics of Mass Society (Glencoe: Free Press of Glencoe, Ill., 1959), passim.
[22] Kornhauser, The Politics of Mass Society, p. 227.
[23] See Seymour M. Lipset, Martin Trow, and James Coleman, Union Democracy (Glencoe: Free Press of Glencoe, Ill., 1956), passim.
[24] See Carl J. Friedrich, Constitutional Government and Politics (New York: Harper & Bros., 1937), passim; Robert A. Dahl, A Preface to Democratic Theory (Chicago: University of Chicago Press, 1956), passim.

racy. But I have tried to show that there are some powerful points in its favor. Even though the experience of the modernizing nations indicates that democracy, as we understand it, is not appropriate to their stage of development, we should not ignore the role of democratic sentiments in conjunction with pluralism and the ideology of science. It makes a difference if people *feel* democratic and show strong sentiments of solidarity, equality, and populism.

I would like to suggest that democracy is latent in reconciliation systems but that certain conditions need to be met before it can be realized. Required first is a constitutional framework as the basis for authority. The accountability mechanism must be impervious to the whims of presidents and monarchs. Such ideals are often more obscured by events than they need be. Even a cursory glance at modern constitutions shows that most embody a libertarian ideal. The liberal emphasis has not disappeared from the modernizing nations. Whether in the Burmese constitution, or in the Turkish, Ghanaian, or Tanganyikan, liberal individual rights and values are expressed, whether as aspirations or as immediate conditions. (That they are most often observed in the breach is not really to the point here; they still have an element of sanctity about them.) There remains a *potentiality* for constitutional government in the classic sense of this term. Constitutions are potential warrants of legitimacy. As such, they specify some of the virtues they seek to establish. If these virtues eventually provide a basis for new groups to claim the right to represent the people, the constitutions embodying them will come to be regarded as moral documents.

That the libertarian tradition is not dead in modernizing nations is revealed by the fact that departures from the spirit and letter of the law are almost always justified on grounds of expediency rather than doctrine. Grave crises are cited as the reasons for coercion, for example, terrorist bombs, a military plot, and so on. Another common explanation of official violations of libertarian values is that they are required by political evolution. ("When the conditions necessary to the maintenance of authority have been stabilized, it will be possible to loosen the reins of government.") If the libertarian tradition had no significance, why should the governments of these countries publicly suspend rights already dormant in practice? In the modern world, political expediency at the expense of liberty is almost always accompanied by embarrassment and the search for acceptable explanations.

It is, therefore, not surprising that the democratic constitutions of modernizing states are more likely to remain in the realm of ideals than to be realized in practice. But this is not cause for despair. Libertarian statements of intention embodied in constitutions are extremely important. In order for intention to become reality these ideals must be fought for by individuals who will thereby recreate the libertarian ideology in personal terms.

Hence, in the evolution of democracy, constitutionalism is dependent on the assertion of individuality in the modern world. This in turn is dependent on a refinement of human sensibilities by means of which the worth of individuals will be established on grounds other than economics or politics. Creativity, social commitment, individual expression — these are the needs of the times rather than the intense and frenetic urge to confound society while accepting its standards.

THE TRANSITION TO POLITICAL DEMOCRACY

What other conditions are necessary to ensure the formation of a democratic polity? Clearly the primary emphasis is in the discussion so far has been on information, with coercion treated as a negative and residual factor. This is logical because of the nature of the relationship between the two. All systems employ coercion. If coercion occurs throughout a network of roles in a system as a natural result of the integration of those roles, it will not necessarily reduce information. The best illustration of this is the modernizing autocracy, where coercion is exercised by

454 The Future of Democratic Society

traditional means and does not necessarily reduce information because it has not been initiated by deliberate government policy.

The two most useful general indicators of coercion (when we wish to evaluate it in connection with government) are as follows: (1) the amount of privacy in the system; and (2) the amount of centralized governmental application of coercive measures. The second indicator can be examined empirically through the contingent structures of government. The question of privacy requires further comment.[25]

Where much of social life is politicized, as in most modernizing nations, privacy is regarded as virtually subversive. As an idea, it runs counter to the view of politics in which the collectivity takes precedence over the individual and the individual's personality is regarded as dependent upon the state. Privacy could be said to begin when a man shields his views, feelings, or activities from his fellow man. This shielding process occurs as the result of many developments. Growing urbanization is a stimulus. The anonymity of the city makes possible a kind of privacy impossible in the close rural and kinship environments of earlier times. Bureaucratization, which is often seen as a depersonalizing force in the West, may in fact provide an opportunity for privacy in the modernizing countries. Men may use their professional roles for social discourse and draw on their inner resources to build a private world, as they learn how to avoid trouble. In the process they will convey to their children something of their attitudes. Industrialization helps to create conditions under which privacy becomes possible even in highly politicized states. When the desire for privacy is reinforced by the practical needs of political leaders for accurate information, the opportunity for constitutional government may present itself.

In order to protect privacy, there must be a check on the arbitrary use of state power against the individual. That is, there must be private rights that the state is not empowered to modify. The

[25] I have discussed the conditions of a democratic society in "Some Reflections on the Role of a Political Opposition," *Journal of Comparative History and Society*, January, 1961.

only way to guarantee private rights is to place checks on the executive. These checks may take many forms, but whatever the form, one cannot speak of liberty without a regularized and legitimate form of opposition, a parliament or its equivalent, a multiparty system, and so on. It is no longer Western provincialism to say that a democratic society, as distinct from a reconciliation system, requires freedom, elections, representative institutions, and all the rest.[26]

What are the conditions under which the transition to democracy is possible, and what are the criteria for a functioning democratic society? In terms of the analysis presented in this book, the following general conditions need to prevail for a democratic society to emerge.

1. Privacy must be a consummatory value. "Privacy" is not merely a new name for individualism, although individualism is the consequence of the desire for privacy. This precondition requires that individuals see their identity in private rather than public terms, that they preserve some sense of wholeness and unity. The desire for privacy in modernizing and industrializing societies may be understood as a reaction to the growing visibility of life in the schools, factories, and public places in general; individuals begin to feel the need to be able to withdraw from certain aspects of the modernizing process. Privacy as a consummatory value implies a protected area of life, free from political intervention.

2. Authority problems must be transformed into equity problems. In a modernizing polity, where the paramount emphasis is potentiality, democratic institutions cannot be expected to work very well. When modernization and industrialization have proceeded to the point where inequality and other problems of distributive justice are threats to continued authority, a mechanism

[26] The basis of representation may vary, however. In the West representation is determined largely on the basis of roughly equal geographical areas. It is by no means out of the question, however, that functional roles — that is, students, farmers, workers, engineers, and so on — be the basis of representation instead (as was once suggested in the ill-fated proposals of the guild socialists in England).

for establishing equity, as well as equity itself, should become the new basis for solidarity in the society. Equity as a basis for solidarity implies that (a) a well-defined sense of equity is shared by the public, and (b) regularized political procedures exist for periodically revising the definition of equity.

3. Information must be available from a variety of sources including free public communication media, opposition parties, and the like. This precondition of democracy rests on the faith that coercion will be limited, bounded, and therefore constitutional. In terms of ideology, a climate of practical realism must prevail, with a high degree of accountability registered through parliamentary and legislative bodies.

4. The means of maintaining equity, accountability, and practical realism (and therefore, identity and solidarity) are (a) the constant translation of value conflict into interest conflict, (b) conciliar control over the executive, (c) legal and formalized opposition secured by a representative principle, and (d) a meaningful definition of public sovereignty expressed in universal suffrage and periodic elections.

These are well-worn universals in democratic theory. Modern expressions of them are common enough.[27]

Normatively, what is required for the functioning of a democratic society is that the individual be regarded as autonomous and his privacy as sacrosanct. Behaviorally, what is implied is that individuals are so complex, their levels of comprehension so interwoven, and their motives so diverse that the idea of an individual, rational self-interest, which is inherent in the classical view of what we have called the "secular-libertarian" universe, must give way to an acceptance of wavering and often inconsistent behavior. Privacy as a norm thus reflects the complexity of the individual as a personality. Structurally, the functioning of the democratic society requires far more elaborate forms of representation than exist at present in order to provide adequate information. If individuals are so complex and if this complexity is

[27] See, for example, the writings of Harold Laski and Herman Finer.

the source of the basic information that decision-makers are looking for, our notions of geographical representation or even interest group representation are clearly too limited. What appears to be necessary is a sweeping re-evaluation of the structural practices that modern democracies presently employ. Moreover, we should not mistake some of the underlying tendencies toward democracy such as pluralism, factionalism, or even a multiparty system as the substance of democratic society. In order to make the distinction between the tendencies and their realization, we have defined the reconciliation system as the most general case of pluralism. But in addition to pluralism, democracy as a political condition is associated with very powerful political checks on public power, which, in turn, are reviewed and scrutinized by the people. It rests on norms that are expressed in the secular-libertarian polity. To what extent political democracy is compatible with the norms of the sacred-collectivity, the opposite extreme, remains to be seen. My own feeling is that the latter can be acceptable to those who desire a democratic polity only if it seems to be a temporary system adopted to further the goals of modernization or early industrialization. Otherwise, the norms of the sacred-collectivity are the antithesis of political democracy.

There are no final conclusions to be drawn from this discussion. In normative terms, the antithesis between the secular-libertarian system and the sacred-collectivity reflects the perpetual conflict and changing balance in human affairs between potentiality, equity, and authority. One point, however, should be made. If democracy is to remain a significant force, it must reaffirm those moral dimensions that give it lasting meaning in contrast to other forms based on faith that have gradually lost their significance. The current disrepute, or lack of knowledge, of such philosophers as Dewey, Peirce, and even James and, more generally, our failure to see in a pragmatic philosophy the foundation for a political and social ethic are testimonials not only to the decline of philosophy into an esoteric discipline but to our inability to understand the full implications of the libertarian ideal. The sacred-collectivity is a ready alternative because, as no one has shown more clearly than Plato, it begins precisely where the secular-libertarian system is weakest — that is, its moral basis — one solution to which is the derived personality whose commitments to an ethic are part of the discipline of the state.

To call for a revival of a pragmatic philosophy for all, however, would be a rather pointless exercise. Calls to reason are scarcely likely to be more successful than calls to faith. In structural terms, the democratic society must begin to realize equality in other areas than equal access and equal treatment based on function. The worth of a man must come to include more than his usefulness. This can be achieved by policy, by the widening of the opportunities of choice to include matters other than productivity and efficiency. The human society is not the efficient society. The business enterprise is not the prototype organization for modern life. If we act as if it is, our notions of hierarchy, efficiency, and value will become so concentrated on the market as a mechanism of choice that our humanity will disappear. That, in the last analysis, is what is implied by the notion of the mass society.

We must recognize that just as there are different layers of comprehension and meaning, so are there different forms of perception and desire. Narrow notions of interest and self-interest produce political cynicism because they telescope reality into a single plane, that of direct action. The level of direct action is political, all right, but only in the most mechanistic sense. A mechanistic view of behavior, a structural view of utility, and a normative view of competitive interplay can produce an ideal concept of the world that is crabbed, bitter, and unrewarding.

CONCLUSION

When decision-making in a mobilization system becomes complex enough to require reform of the basic structure of government, several choices are possible. One is to create a more narrow and more centralized system of authoritative decision-making, less accountable and more remote from day-to-day concerns. This choice leads in the direction of totalitarianism, increasing coercion, and inefficiency. An alternative is to decentralize decision-making, thereby increasing accountability. Decentralization may take the form of a proliferation of decison-making subunits, so that the central pattern of government is extended through a number of local governments and becomes more effective on a regional or territorial level. Decisional subunits based on region make it possible for the public to participate in problems that are central to their interests and to develop a tradition of civic responsibility.

Even though it does not seem likely that most of the modernizing countries can move directly in a democratic direction, important subgroups already exist within these societies that are the long-run carriers of democratic values and that will be important in the future for democratic society. I have discussed these subgroups in terms of their need for information and have referred, of course, to those that appear to be non-political, that is, the scientists and social scientists, engineers and technologists.

These are the roles whose functional significance increases as modernization moves into industrialization, and as industrialization intensifies. In order to deal with increasingly complex technical matters, the occupants of these roles require greater and greater amounts of information. Government, too, requires increasing amounts of information in order to operate efficiently and carry out the recommendations of the scientists and technicians. These needs result, as I have said before, in a decline in coercion, a sharing of decision-making, and a widening of accountability. Hence, the scientific elites are fundamentally revolutionary.[28]

[28] Indeed, Michael Polanyi has hailed this new development as the basis of what he calls a "Republic of Science," which, in his view, is dynamic, a "society of explorers," and which, because it is based on self-improvement and excellence, will create a free society. See his fascinating discussion, in "The Republic of Science, Its Political and Economic Theory," *Minerva*, I (Au-

They are revolutionary because of their economic importance. Clearly, scientists and technicians are unlikely, in the long run, to become effective participants in the political sphere, if only because technical expertise generally inheres in functionally subordinate roles. But in the economic sphere, their activities have great importance for basic productivity, the organization of resources, and the utilization of the new technology in the employment of human and physical resources. This, of course, would not in itself make them revolutionary, except for the fact that *in industrializing societies it is the economic variable that is independent.* The political system is the dependent variable — dependent, that is, on the needs of the economic system and the changes in the industrial sphere. The new scientific elite — as a result of the economic changes it can bring about and as a result of its need for information with which to make these changes successfully — must therefore be viewed as a revolutionary force. If this analysis of the role of the scientific elite is correct, it follows that the long-term tendency of industrializing countries is toward reconciliation systems.

How can the reconciliation system be transformed into a democracy, the conditions of which have been outlined above? Obviously, something more is needed than the distribution of information among functionally significant elites. At this point, we must return to the moral sphere. The ideals of liberty and privacy can move a reconciliation system toward democracy in an industrial setting. The scientists and the social scientists, the writers and the intellectuals, the teachers and the students — all will have to fight for these ideals. They cannot be won all at once.

How important, then, are the world-wide associations of scientists and technicians, the links between universities, and the free exchanges of information and knowledge! Modern societies need freedom to continue to evolve even if some of them cannot yet afford it. The ultimate aim of the West ought to be clear from

---

tumn, 1962). Somewhat the same point of view is expressed in the Robbins Report in England.

the foregoing analysis. Not only must we more fully realize freedom in our own society, but must not deny the eventual possibility of freedom to modernizing and industrializing nations. If democratic institutions, as we know them, suffer under hammer blows during the period of modernization, it should come as no surprise. The total modernization process will take a very long time. The fantastic changes required will often run contrary to political convenience. Our objective should be fixed and unchanging, to keep the libertarian option open, since, as we have seen, systems change according to the political needs of modernization and the economic needs of industrialization. We should expect false starts, backward steps, new fashions in political systems, and the explicit downgrading of libertarian values. If we can take a long (and this means a realistic) view of the total process of development from modernization to industrialization, we will find ourselves supporting countries whose policies, in the short run, go counter to everything that we consider important to a democratic way of life. We need to accept countries like Ghana and Mali as changing polities and not mistake stability in form for an incapacity to change. We must consider Yugoslavia and Poland, and perhaps China as well, as prototypes of an early stage of industrialization. Nor should we be surprised if the conversion from late modernization to early industrialization in Latin America is accompanied by the spread of mobilization systems. This is precisely why Cuba is so attractive to many of the more romantic young socialists in these countries.

Clearly, we are going to need to learn to live in a world in which the ethic of science has become the ethic of man. Indeed, the scientific Philistines may already have become a greater danger to democracy than the ideologues. How urgent it becomes to civilize the civilizers, that is, to give those who know something about science and the public welfare a sensitivity to human rights and values. Without such sensitivity, the new technocrats will have little attachment to democracy.

For us in the West, the task is to know what we are about — to know what is important. Questions of property and ownership, for example, are less and less significant. Managerial control (whether the proprietor is the state, a public board, a body of citizens who are joint owners and managers, or an individual) is not an issue any more. Indeed, practical distinctions between private and public enterprise are disappearing almost as quickly as distinctions between private and public university educations. What is important is the problem of inequality, the relationship between equity and freedom. Will this relationship be determined by natural talent rather than particularistic ties, traditional impediments to mobility, or wealth? And will talent produce its own hierarchy? Can democracy come to grips with problems such as these? The answer is important for our own society, as well as for all the others.

Is an information-creating and knowledge-using elite the critical instrumentality for producing the conditions of a reconciliation system? Can the scientific elite be brought into a democratic pattern? These are critical questions.

How well we answer these questions, and others similar to them, will effect our ability to make sensible choices about the future. Nor are such matters purely academic. The continued existence of our way of life hangs in the balance. Political forms do change. If it is true that there is a perpetual dialogue between the two main forms we have discussed, the mobilization system and the reconciliation system, it is also true that they are perpetually vulnerable to each other. By means of empirical comparative studies, we should be able to discover the ways in which this mutual vulnerability is made manifest. Specific queries are in order. For example, if political change in the context of modernization is not an inevitable progressive evolution from predemocratic forms of government, what conditions do favor such a long-term development? What conditions are prerequisite to a successful transition from a modernizing to an industrial society in the direction of democracy? When conditions in a society point to the economic system rather than the political as the independent variable, how are we to evaluate the forms of industrialization and their impact upon the polity? Is it correct to say that, under the conditions of modern industrialization, the need for information is so great that decentralization, the emergence of pyramidal instead of hierarchical authority, and the preoccupation with instrumental rather than consummatory ends are greatly facilitated? Is it meaningful to speak of a political system with a long-term tendency toward a reconciliation system as the form most appropriate for highly industrialized societies? Will our Western definition of democracy continue to be appropriate?

These questions cannot be answered here. I think that in the long run the most revolutionary force in political affairs will be a new form of the secular-libertarian ideal and, more specifically, a democratic system of government. Modernization is a critical step by means of which this ideal will be universalized. A fresh appraisal of our own institutions, however, is required. Democracy cannot be meaningful unless it realizes its libertarian beliefs more completely. It needs to blend its instrumental and consummatory values more effectively. How can the West serve as the model for a highly industrialized society if it fails to utilize the information it so freely creates and ignores many of its obligations in the fields of civil rights, poverty, education, and foreign affairs? If reconciliation systems fail, it will be because of the blindness or inability of the people to comprehend the knowledge they have at their disposal. This is why the need for new methods and theories for organizing and comprehending facts is so urgent. The ability to find wider meanings in information already available and to create new forms of knowledge is the greatest strength our society has. But only if we use it well can choice and freedom give added strength to our democracy. The future of democratic society will depend on its ability to find new and effective ways to secure personal identity through liberty and solidarity through knowledge. This has always been the basis of the democratic ideal. These are the ultimate standards by which we evaluate both ourselves and others.

INDEX

Art: religious, and consummatory values, 272; significance of, in politics, 267–68

Asantehene ("king"), 103, 104, 106, 109; *see also* Ashanti

Ashanti, 92; and CPP, 109, 116; nationalists in, 106; political organization in, 103–4; response of, to innovation, 102, 115–16; in war, 105 n.; *see also* Ghana

Authority, 16, 42, 257; and belief, 311; and contingent functions, 242, 412; and democracy, 452, 455–56; and efficiency, 387 n.; and identity, 282; and ideology, 354–56; in mobilization system, 365; in modernizing autocracy, 37, 404; of modernizing elite, 219; and moral solidarity, 278–79; in neomercantilist system, 37, 413; and party of representation, 222; of political leaders in new nations, 294–95; and political religion, 293–94; and political subgroups, 250; in reconciliation system, 36; ritualization of, 408; and Robin Hood roles, 336–37; in sacred-collectivity model, 34, 35, 226, 227; in secular-libertarian model, 35–36; and structural and functional requisites, 391–92; and support, 21; in theocracy, 283–87

Authority systems, 24–25, 83, 224–25; in early modernization, 428; and functional requisites, 240; in military oligarchy, 37; in mobilization system, 359; in modernizing autocracy, 263; in neomercantilist system, 37, 411–13; in normative models, 34–36; in reconciliation system, 260; in system change, 396; in traditional societies, 83–106; in U.S.S.R., 427–28; and uses of ideology, 322; as variables, 247

Autocracy, as result of low information, 394; *see also* Modernizing autocracy

Babylonia, 285
Back, Kurt W., 46 n.

Baganda, 95, 96 n.; *see also* Buganda
Banfield, Edward, 47, 61
Banfield, L. F., 47, 61
Baran, Paul A., 53 n.
Barber, Bernard, 124 n., 128–29, 138 n.
Barbour, Nevill, 180
Barker, E., 283
Behanzin (king), 99
Behavorial approach, 20–22, 24; and careers, 163; criteria of, 25; to democracy, 456; and government types, 236; and normative models, 28, 31; and sacred-secular distinction, 84
Bell, Daniel, 349
Bellah, Robert N., 332, 333
Ben Bella, A., 369–70 n.
Bendix, Reinhard, 50 n., 291 n., 349 n.
Berger, Morroe, 47 n.
Bernal, J. D., 343
Bernaut, Elsa, 427
Bernstein, Eduard, 394 n.
Binder, Leonard, 86 n., 154
Boyon, J., 107 n.
Brandt, Conrad, 369 n.
Brazil, 157, 235
Brzezinski, A. K., 335
Buganda, 86, 100, 121–22, 261; consequences of clan system in, 105; European treatment of, 110–11; innovation in, 103, 104, 105–6, 111–16; religious factions in, 101
Burckhardt, Jacob, 238 n.
Bureaucracy, 43, 152–53; and careers, 162; under colonialism, 50; military, 143; in modernizing autocracy, 135; as political leadership role, 221; as political party, 218; technical, 259
Bureaucratization, 451; and privacy, 454
Burma, 37, 184, 452; military in, 193 n., 218, 221 n., 264
Burns, Sir Alan, 48

Callois, Roger, 286
Calvinism, 74 n., 322
Camus, Albert, 1

PHOENIX BOOKS
in Political Science

PHOENIX BOOKS
in Law